RCAHMS

NORTH-EAST
PERTH
an archaeological landscape

NORTH-EAST PERTH
an archaeological landscape

ROYAL COMMISSION
ON THE ANCIENT
AND HISTORICAL
MONUMENTS
OF SCOTLAND
1990

Printed in the UK for HMSO. Dd. 287187/HF4782 C13 7/90 (3808)

189 Alyth, Pictish symbol stone

CONTENTS

The Royal Commission on the Ancient and Historical Monuments of Scotland

PREFACE

The issue of this volume, the first of the new series of archaeological surveys to appear in print, represents a significant departure from the practices established by the Commission in the management of survey and the publication of its results. For more than eighty years topographical survey has been concerned with the identification and recording of both archaeological and architectural material, the ultimate objective being to complete an assessment of the entire national heritage at the same level of detailed appraisal. As originally conceived, the completed record was to consist of a series of published *Inventories*, whose contents would chart the gradual county-by-county progress towards a finite goal.

It is now widely realised that, without an impracticably large injection of resources, to cover the entire country in similar detail would take far too long; countless monuments and buildings would have succumbed to the pressures of development or decay before their significance, or perhaps even their existence, could be recognised. Moreover, it is also plain that the finiteness of the record is an outmoded concept; advances in recording technology, the deepening of academic insights, and changing social values will constantly combine to widen the field of reference for those assessing the built environment of Scotland's past.

Accordingly, it has been decided that the 'Inventory of Ancient and Historical Monuments and Constructions' which the Commissioners are charged by Royal Warrant to compile, should be construed as the archives of the National Monuments Record of Scotland, where full details of all Commission survey programmes are publicly accessible; new survey publications, such as this, will therefore present a distillation of the information recorded in separate archaeological and architectural programmes, whose primary purpose will be to record areas or categories of monument not adequately represented in the national archive. In addition, each individual programme will be of smaller compass, seeking to reduce the interval between the collection of data in the field and the publication of the results, whether in book-form or as a series of Record-entries. The overall concern, however, will remain the same as in the past, to help contemporary society to learn more about the culture, civilisation and conditions of life experienced by the people of Scotland in earlier times.

In respect of archaeological survey, attention must also be drawn to other factors which have given rise to changes in the presentation of the published evidence. Foremost among these is the perception that it is no longer satisfactory to survey isolated 'unitary' monuments without regard to the landscape of which they once formed part; nor is it possible to ignore the fact that the modern landscape is a patchwork, often incorporating the complex visible remains of several patterns of past land-use. To record this complexity has called for improved techniques of survey, using computer-based measuring- and draughting-equipment, as well as the greater employment of mapping-scales (which also facilitates the transfer of archaeological information to the Ordnance Survey for use in published maps).

The advantages of this approach are particularly well displayed by the subject of the present volume, which deals with the north-east portion of Perth and Kinross District, Tayside Region. Extending over some 46,600 ha, the area embraces considerable tracts of upland terrain exploited by man at various periods in the past, but now lying beyond the limits of cultivation. In these areas lie extensive stretches of old settlement- and cultivation-remains, many of which, although exceptionally well-preserved, have not previously been recorded. Their publication here represents a significant advance in our ability to understand the successive phases of upland settlement, especially that of the pre-improvement period, evidence for which has rarely been so completely assembled.

The items included in this survey, which is mainly concerned with the archaeological evidence, cover a wide timespan, ranging in period from neolithic funerary sites to deserted farmsteads of nineteenth-century date. All sites and monuments up to 1600 are described (medieval buildings in summary form), but thereafter attention is focused on the pre-Improvement rural landscape, and sites shown as occupied on the first edition of the OS 6-inch map (1860s) are omitted. The following categories are also omitted: buildings in towns; roads, railways and canals; most structures of nineteenth-century and later date. A list of monuments within the survey area that are considered to be worthy of preservation will be included in the forthcoming 25th Report of the Commission.

The text has been written by M M Brown, BA, DipArch, P Corser, BEd, DipArch, S P Halliday, BSc, J N G Ritchie, MA, PhD, FSA, J R Sherriff, BA, AIFA, I M Smith, BA, J B Stevenson, BA, FSA, MIFA, and edited by G S Maxwell, MA, FSA, FRSA and J B Stevenson. The drawings and other illustrative work have been undertaken by J Borland, BA, D R Boyd, A J Leith, I G Parker, and S Scott. The photographs were taken by J D Keggie. The layout has been designed by I G Scott, DA, MAAIS and J N Stevenson, NDD.

The project has greatly benefited from the advice given by the Commission's Archaeological Programme Committee, and particular thanks are owed to Professor L Alcock (Chairman) and Professor G Jobey.

The Commission wishes to acknowledge the assistance given by the owners of the archaeological monuments, who have allowed access for study and survey, and to the field staff of the former OS Archaeology Division, on whose work the present survey was based. Thanks are due to the following for assistance and information: J Anderson, the Duke of Atholl, W Bains, Professor J Caird, Captain A A C Farquharson of Invercauld, L Frazer, D Grant, S Halliday, J Harris, R Hepburn, Dr A Lavery, Sir William and Lady McPherson, the National Library of Scotland, D P Petrie, A Reid (Perth Museum), A G Reid, J Rideout, L M Thoms, S Winton; and to the following for assistance in the field: A Ferguson, M Harman, D Low, N Murray, and J Page.

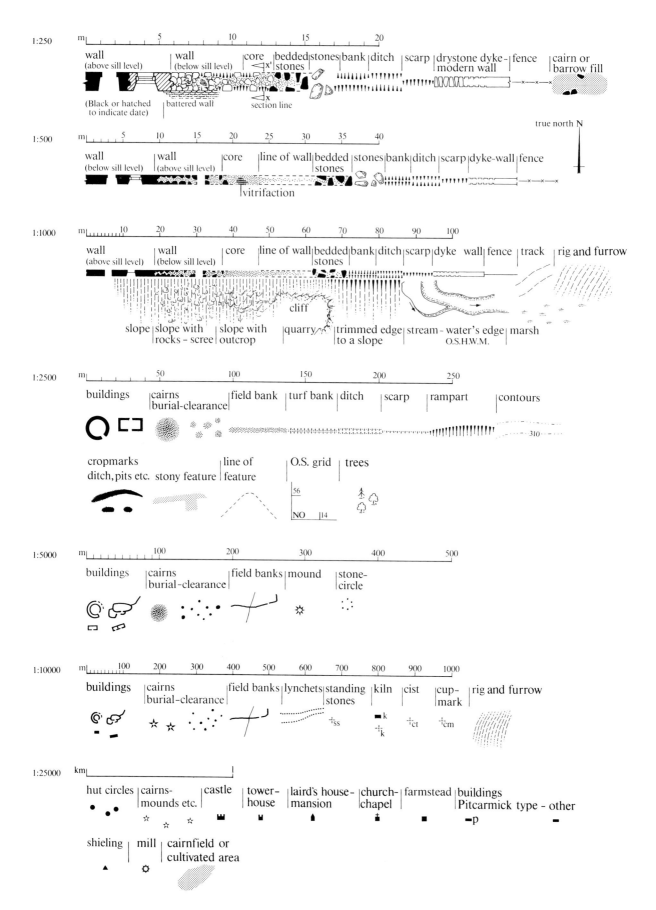

1:250

wall (above sill level) — (Black or hatched to indicate date) | wall (below sill level) — battered wall | core | x' section line x | bedded stones | stones | bank | ditch | scarp | drystone dyke - modern wall | fence | cairn or barrow fill

1:500

wall (below sill level) | wall (above sill level) | core | vitrifaction | line of wall | bedded stones | stones | bank | ditch | scarp | dyke-wall | fence

true north N

1:1000

wall (above sill level) | wall (below sill level) | core | line of wall | bedded stones | bank | ditch | scarp | dyke | wall | fence | track | rig and furrow

cliff

slope | slope with rocks - scree | slope with outcrop | quarry | trimmed edge to a slope | stream - water's edge O.S.H.W.M. | marsh

1:2500

buildings | cairns burial-clearance | field bank | turf bank | ditch | scarp | rampart | contours — 310

cropmarks ditch, pits etc. | stony feature | line of feature | O.S. grid — 56, NO, 14 | trees

1:5000

buildings | cairns burial-clearance | field banks | mound | stone-circle

1:10000

buildings | cairns burial-clearance | field banks | lynchets | standing stones | kiln — k, k | cist — ct | cup-mark — cm | rig and furrow

1:25000

hut circles | cairns-mounds etc. | castle | tower-house | laird's house-mansion | church-chapel | farmstead | buildings — p | Pitcarmick type - other

shieling | mill | cairnfield or cultivated area

Conventional Representation on Plans

EDITORIAL NOTES

The site descriptions published in this volume represent a synthesis of the material gathered in the field, and more detailed accounts of many of the monuments may be consulted in the National Monuments Record of Scotland.

Grid References
At the beginning of each article or sub-article will be found the article number and the appropriate National Grid reference followed by the National Monuments Record of Scotland record card number.

Bibliographical References
Harvard style short titles, which are located within the text or at the end of the appropriate article or sub-article, are expanded in the full bibliography at the end of the volume.

Dates of Visit
Unless stated otherwise all monuments have been visited during the course of the survey (October 1986–November 1988).

Illustrations
All illustrations are treated as Figures and are referred to in the margin. Individual Figures in the Inventory are distinguished by article number and in the Introduction by page number, with a letter suffix where appropriate for further identification.

Scales
Scale of reproduction of an illustration is quoted in the caption as a representative fraction.

Radiocarbon Dates
Radiocarbon dates are quoted in uncorrected bp (before present = before 1950) form.

Copyright
Unless otherwise specified, the contents of this volume are Crown Copyright; copies of the photographs and drawings can be purchased, on application to:

> The Secretary
> The Royal Commission on the Ancient and
>   Historical Monuments of Scotland
> 54 Melville Street
> Edinburgh EH3 7HF

Hill of Drimmie, braided trackways, NO 191 494, from NE

INTRODUCTION

This volume covers the north-east portion of Perth and Kinross District, Tayside Region, and extends from the moorlands of the Forests of Alyth and Clunie in the south, up the River Ericht, to include the valleys of the Ardle and Shee. The north and east boundaries follow the District border, while to the west and south the area of survey is defined by the OS National Grid reference easting NO 05 and northing NO 45 respectively, and to the east of Blairgowrie the Kirriemuir road (A926) has been selected as the south-east boundary.

In the south the area straddles the Highland Boundary Fault which runs along the north side of Strathmore from Dunkeld to Alyth (Walker 1961). Lying to the south of the fault, there are eroded Old Red Sandstones covered with glacial and alluvial deposits. A narrow band of lavas and conglomerates of the Old Red Sandstone Series, which outcrop along the fault, has been eroded into a series of low hills (e.g. Hill of Alyth). To the north there are the more resistant Dalradian rocks (mainly schists, grits and limestone) and intrusive granite, which have given rise to a broken landscape ranging from the rolling moorland of the Forest of Clunie in the south to the Grampian Mountains in the north.

The northern part of the area is drained by the River Ardle and the Shee Water, which combine at Bridge of Cally to form the River Ericht. Strathardle and Glen Shee are both heavily glaciated, with extensively cultivated glacial and alluvial deposits. Flanking the main glens there is a series of side valleys and corries which also contain fluvio-glacial deposits that are suitable for settlement, and the occurrence of these deposits may in part account for the dense prehistoric and later settlement pattern.

Both sides of Strathardle and Glen Shee (south of Dalrulzian) are defined by prominent shoulders (between 250m and 350m OD). At the south end of Glen Shee the east shoulder marks the west edge of the Forest of Alyth, a large expanse of moorland which extends east to Glen Isla and south to the Highland Boundary Fault. On the west side of Strathardle the shoulder defines the east edge of an extensive area of hilly moorland and forest from Bridge of Cally to Kirkmichael. To the north of Kirkmichael the area between Strathardle and Glen Shee is crossed by a network of minor stream valleys which break up the landscape into a series of isolated hills and ridges; in these valleys there are numerous small drift deposits.

Historically, Glen Shee has always been an important route through the Eastern Highlands, and this may well have been the case in prehistoric times. This was the route adopted in the 18th century for the Military Road connecting the Lowlands with Upper Deeside (cf. Graham 1966) and is that followed by the modern road. Towards the head of the glen several other thoroughfares converge. One, which connects with a road between upper Glen Tilt, Gleann Fearnach and Strathardle, was used to effect in the 16th and 17th centuries by the caterans or cattle-thieves ranging from Lochaber and western Scotland. It connects with another hill-track which traversed Coire Shith, a side-glen opening off Gleann Taitneach to the north of Dalmunzie, crossed Gleann Beag and descended into Glen Isla via Glas Maol (the Monega Pass). These roads, together with others, were traditional drove-routes. After the Union of the Parliaments in 1707 they were of increased importance to the economic development of the glen, which was sustained by cattle sales and fairs held regularly at both Spittal of Glenshee and Kirkmichael.

MONUMENT SURVIVAL

The distribution of the archaeological remains reflects the impact of successive phases of agricultural exploitation, each preserving, modifying or destroying the remains of its predecessors. The interplay between survival and destruction began at least as early as the neolithic and continues to the present day, with large-scale afforestation and upland pasture improvement as the latest phase.

Three zones of preservation can be identified. The first is that under cultivation today (about 90 sq km), where only a few standing stones and the occasional pre-improvement farmstead are still visible. It is in this zone that cropmarks occur and where burial cists and prehistoric artefacts are more likely to be discovered (Stevenson 1975). It includes the slopes facing south over Strathmore, but is then restricted by topography to the floors of the main glens.

The second zone is defined in part by the areas of rig-and-furrow which lie beyond the limits of modern cultivation. Little rig-and-furrow survives in the south of the area, but further north it appears, often in company with farmsteads or fermtouns, in a band between the improved fields and the steep, rocky valley sides. At the head of the main glens, particularly Glen Shee where the improved fields do not form a continuous feature, the numbers of surviving farmsteads and fermtouns increase dramatically, and beyond Spittal of Glenshee the pre-Improvement landscape is substantially intact, if restricted by the mountainous terrain to the valley floors and side glens. The occurrence of earlier monuments in this zone is even more restricted than in the first zone; occasional cairns and standing stones survive, but there is little opportunity here for the recognition of either cropmarks or prehistoric burial cists.

The third zone, the heather moorlands, is that in which the majority of the round prehistoric houses (hut-circles) and their attendant field-systems and groups of small cairns are to be found. Here some later ploughing has taken place, but throughout the medieval period much of this zone was given over to cattle and sheep grazing, either as predominantly pastoral farms or shielings. Other areas were taken into the royal forests of Alyth and Clunie, and this may have led to the unwitting preservation of parts of the prehistoric landscape that might otherwise have been under intensive cultivation.

PREHISTORIC ARCHAEOLOGY

The earliest evidence of settlement in the area is provided by the pollen diagrams from Heatheryhaugh (NO 183 519) and Loch Mharaich (NO 117 568; Caseldine 1979). Although no radiocarbon dates are available for either diagram, the decline in the values for elm, and the succeeding woodland clearances, are usually associated with the arrival of farming communities in the neolithic period. Structural traces of these communities, however, are less easy to identify. Unlike Strath Tay to the west

(Stewart 1961, 72–6; Coles and Simpson 1965), no neolithic round barrows or chambered long cairns have been recognised in either Strathardle or Glen Shee. At the beginning of the 19th century a passage is supposed to have been found in the large round cairn at Balnabroich (no. 9), and it is possible that some of the larger round cairns are also of early date. Perhaps of late neolithic date, however, are the five ring-cairns that have been recorded in the course of the survey (nos. 1–4). The dating of these cairns is far from clear, but, together with the three or four known in Angus (RCAHMS 1983, 14, nos. 96–7; *DES 1985*, 60), they form a compact geographical group. With the exception of Lair (no. 2), which is 15 m in overall diameter, the Perthshire examples are small, ranging from 4 m to 7·5 m in maximum diameter. The inner courts, which are their distinctive features, vary from 1·8 m to 4 m across, and at least two (nos. 1·2; 3) appear to have been roughly square. Several of the surrounding kerbs appear to be graded, with the largest stones occurring on the S arc. This feature is also seen at a number of other cairns, where there is no evidence of an inner court (nos. 12; 31·4–·5). Excavation of one of the ring-cairns at Balnabroich (no. 1·1) produced 'great quantities' of white quartz, but again this is a feature common to a wide range of prehistoric cairns and stone settings (Burl 1973, 46–7; 1976, 164, 171).

As might be expected from the patterns of survival and destruction in the glens, the ring-cairns are all marginal to the areas of medieval and later cultivation, and indeed, all are adjacent to groups of hut-circles. A similar pattern can be detected amongst the cupmarked stones (some of which may also be of neolithic date; RCAHMS 1988, 7–10) and the Early Bronze Age burial cairns, as well as the standing stones and stone circles. The implications of this distribution for the extent of neolithic and Early Bronze Age exploitation of the landscape are considerable. It is not unreasonable to suggest that much of the area now occupied by the groups of hut-circles had not only been cleared of trees, but was being farmed or managed by the Early Bronze Age (see below).

There are, however, subtle differences in the relationships of the various types of funerary and ritual monuments to the distribution of the hut-circle groups. There is, for instance, a remarkable assemblage of such monuments amongst the hut-circles at Balnabroich, where no fewer than two ring-cairns (no. 1), four burial cairns (no. 9), and a small stone circle (no. 59) have been recorded. The presence of burial cairns amongst groups of small cairns and hut-circles is not uncommon (e.g. nos. 147; 152), but the juxtaposition of a stone circle is most unusual. Three of the other stone circles are situated outside the zone of medieval and later cultivation, and at least two of them (nos. 74, 78) appear to be peripheral to areas of prehistoric settlement. In contrast, all the single standing stones and paired stones are set on terraces close to the valley floor, and are now in the zone of modern cultivation. The stone circles and standing stones occupy a broad chronological span, and it is unfortunate that so little unambiguous dating evidence for them is available (Stewart 1967). Four-posters (stone circles comprising four stones), which constitute seven of the eight classifiable circles, are attributed to the 2nd millennium BC (Burl 1988, 31–5), but they show considerable . variation in size and shape, and may equally vary in date. One of the newly discovered examples (no. 72) is only 1·3 m square, and the tallest stone stood to a height of no more than 0·8 m; another (no. 74), now reduced to only two stones, is set on a low cairn with a well-defined boulder kerb.

The hut-circle groups of North-east Perth form one of the densest concentrations of prehistoric settlement remains known in Scotland. The pattern of survival of the 845 hut-circles that have now been recorded in the area is largely defined by the extent of the third preservation zone. Prehistoric settlement appears to have been particularly extensive, and some of the hut-circles are set at altitudes not normally associated with this form of prehistoric settlement. In the lower reaches of Glen Shee and Strathardle they attain heights of 300 m to 400 m OD, but in the hills to the north they are often found at up to 450 m OD, and in one instance at almost 500 m OD. A similar pattern can be observed amongst the hut-circles recorded by the OS above Pitlochry to the west, and in Glen Isla to the east.

The richness and variety to be found amongst the hut-circles and groups of small cairns have been known for many years. A detailed account of the groups at Balnabroich (no. 108) and Dalrulzion (no. 120), for instance, was published in 1795 (*Stat. Acct.* 15, 516–20), and a total of forty-seven hut-circles was subsequently depicted on the first edition of the OS 6-inch map (1867). The first attempt to classify the hut-circles, however, was carried out by Thorneycroft (1933, 187–91), based on his observation of sixty-one examples in Glen Shee and Glen Isla. He identified three types: simple single-walled hut-circles; double-walled hut-circles; and tangential pairs. More recently this classification has been refined by Harris (1985). The results of the present survey suggest that the structural remains are even more varied, but little purpose would be served by any attempt to subdivide them further into a plethora of sub-types defined only by minor variations in the character of the remains. As Harris recognised, there are two basic types of hut-circle, those with single walls and those with double walls, and with one exception, the remainder are all variations on those two themes. The exception is the group of structures that incorporate a ring-ditch.

Although there is considerable variation in size and in the details of construction, single-walled structures form by far the majority of the hut-circles (some 78%). They range from 3 m to 15 m in internal diameter, most of them falling between 7 m and 11 m; where visible, their entrances generally lie in the south-east quadrant. Few have escaped stone-robbing and in most examples the walls have been reduced to low stony banks. Some may never have been any more than featureless ring-banks set around timber buildings (e.g. no. 128·5). Elsewhere, facing-stones are visible and these include large upright slabs, which generally belong to the inner face and protrude above the wall-core, while in a few instances impressive circuits of inner face survive. The presence of medial wall-faces and arcs of double-walls (nos. 2–3 on fig.) suggest that at least a few of the hut-circles are of multi-period construction. The original superstructures of the walls are unknown, but the presence of the facing-stones rising above the wall-core suggests that some may have been carried upwards in turf; evidence of a turf component in the walls is provided by the low banks that still survive where hut-circles have been entirely robbed or have been under cultivation (nos. 128·7; 134·5). The interiors of many of the hut-circles have been levelled into the slope, and robbed examples have often been reduced to low platforms which are virtually indistinguishable from platforms for timber buildings. In some instances the whole interior has been dug into the slope, but in others the front of the hut-circle rested on a substantial artificial platform. The back scarps of a small number of these hut-circles divide into two steps, the inner face of the wall extending round the lower step, and the outer facing becoming the inner face of the upper step (nos. 110·1; 121·8; 127·1; 130·5). These particular hut-circles may well be variants of the double-walled hut-circles discussed

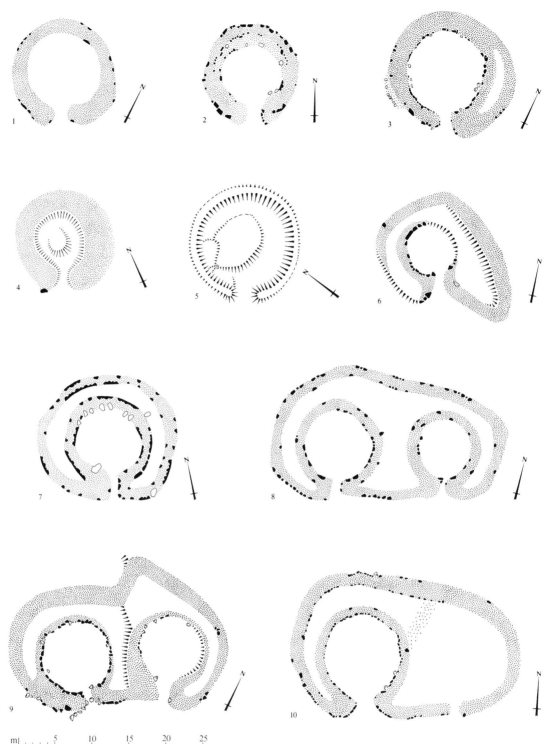

Comparative plans of hut-circles
1 Balnabroich, no. 108(B)
2 Muir of Gormack, no. 149·5(C)
3 Drumderg, no. 122·3(East)
4 Dirnanean, no. 121·3
5 Hill of Alyth, no. 129·2
6 Drumturn Burn, no. 124·10(B)
7 Alyth Burn, no. 103·7
8 Alyth Burn, no. 103·6(A)
9 Drumturn Burn, no. 124·10(A)
10 Pitcarmick (North), no. 154·4(A)

below, as may a series of large hut-circles with inturned entrance-terminals but no evidence of an inner wall (nos. 129·1; 147·1).

Although in the minority, double-walled hut-circles are the most distinctive element of the Perthshire hut-circle groups, representing a form of elaboration rarely seen elsewhere (but see Ogston 1931; Feachem 1965, 105). They range from 6 m to 12 m in internal diameter, the majority lying between 7 m and 10 m, and their entrances are generally in the south-east quadrant. Like the single-walled hut-circles, they have been extensively robbed for stone (some probably in antiquity), but a high proportion have had impressive slab-facing around their interiors and their entrances. Outer facing is usually of lesser stature, and only rarely are facing stones visible on the outer face of the inner wall or the inner face of the outer wall (no. 7 on fig.). In many the two walls are eccentric and the gap between them is wider to one side of the entrance than the other; the eccentricity can become extreme (no. 6 on fig.) and in one case the outer wall is roughly square (no. 121·1). Perhaps more striking than the individual double-walled hut-circles are the groups of two or three enclosed by a single outer wall (no. 8 on fig.; nos. 103·4;

p.3

p.3

3

130·1; 133·6). In a few cases the outer wall loops outwards to form an enclosure with an independent
p.3 entrance (no. 9 on fig.; no. 121·3), and there is one example of an enclosure of the appropriate size and bilobate shape but with no trace of a hut-circle within either half of the interior (no. 105·2). In a few instances individual double-walled hut-circles appear to have been modified to form a pair (nos. 132·1; 133). The function of the space between the two walls of such houses and the extent of the roofed area have been subjects of some debate. It has been suggested that the gap was filled with an ephemeral insulating material (Feachem 1965, 105; RCAHMS 1967, 23) and this may well be the case where the gap is poorly defined, consisting of little more than a shallow groove. In the eccentric examples, however, the gap can be as much as 4 m and is likely to have served as a small yard. The existence of the eccentric examples, particularly the square one, also suggests that the roofs of these buildings rested on the inner wall. Similarly, there can be little doubt that the roofs of the enclosed pairs rested on the inner walls, and the outer walls were no more than enclosures. The single-walled hut-circles with inturned entrance-terminals (*infra*) may best be regarded as composite structures where the stone-built outer wall enclosed a free-standing timber building.

At least forty ring-ditches have now been identified in North-east Perth, most of them as features of other types of hut-circle. Six have been found in double-walled hut-circles, two in enclosed pairs, and most of the rest are enclosed by single-walled hut-circles. Two other groups can be distinguished: the first consists of ring-ditches with overall diameters of between 6·5 m and 9·7 m, enclosed by
p.3 low banks up to 3 m in thickness (no. 4 on fig.; nos. 121·2; 142·7); the second group (nos. 103·2; 147·3; 150·2) comprises four ring-ditches that are more typical of the structures found in the Border hills (Hill 1982, 12–21, 33–9). Their diameters range from 9·5 m to 14·5 m and
p.3 there are only slight traces of any enclosing bank (no. 5 on fig.). Another ring-ditch discovered by the OS in the valley of the Drumturn Burn (no. 124·3) is unlikely to be the remains of a building and may even be a funerary monument. The distribution of ring-ditches in relation to altitude is uneven, and there is a marked concentration above 400 m OD (see below).

Little evidence is available to date any of the types of hut-circle described above. Excavations have taken place at four sites (nos. 103; 119–20; 159), but radiocarbon dates are available only for two hut-circles within the area of the survey, both of them at Tulloch Field. These suggest that at least one of the Tulloch Field hut-circles was occupied at the end of the 2nd millennium BC, but a pit in the other produced a sample dated to the middle of the 1st millennium BC. The assemblages of pottery recovered from Dalnaglar and double-walled hut-circle F at Dalrulzion, while differing in character, are probably of late 2nd or early 1st millennium BC date. The structural diversity visible amongst the ring-ditched hut-circles suggests that the ring-ditches are unlikely to be of chronological significance. Nevertheless, the frequency with which they occur in high locations may indicate that they are a relatively early feature of hut-circle architecture which has been obscured on the lower slopes by later occupation. The ring-ditch houses of East Lothian and Angus, which are superficially comparable with the larger ring-ditches discussed above, have provided radiocarbon dates spanning the middle centuries of the 1st millennium BC.

Despite the problems of dating individual types of hut-circle, the hut-circle groups themselves and the surrounding groups of small cairns and field-systems appear to represent a broad span of prehistory. Although none of the hut-circles can be shown to date from before the late 2nd millennium BC, work elsewhere in Scotland would suggest that many of the groups of small cairns are probably of considerably earlier date. Indeed, in North-east Perth, as elsewhere, the incidence of burial cairns and ring-cairns amongst the groups of small cairns and hut-circles shows that these areas were being exploited, and probably farmed, by the late 3rd or early 2nd millennium BC. The hut-circles themselves almost certainly represent a series of periods of occupation, possibly separated by intervals of abandonment, starting in the late 2nd millennium BC, and it would be unwise to regard any of the hut-circle groups, necessarily, as settlements of contemporary buildings. To some extent this is borne out by the preliminary series of radiocarbon dates from Carn Dubh, a hut-circle group above Pitlochry, which extends from the end of the 2nd millennium BC to the middle centuries of the 1st millennium AD (info. J Rideout). In itself, the development of more elaborate forms of hut-circles in this part of Perth suggests a much wider chronological span than might be anticipated from the dating evidence for hut-circles in western Scotland. It is notable, furthermore, that the altitudinal range of the hut-circles in Glen Shee and Strathardle is comparable to that of settlements spanning the entire 1st millennium BC in the Border counties. To this end, it is unfortunate that the possible beehive quernstone (not earlier than the late first millennium BC) noted by OS surveyors embedded in the
153 wall of a hut-circle at Pitcarmick (no. 153·6) can no longer be located. The final period of occupation at a number of
124·4A, I the hut-circle sites (e.g. nos. 124·4; 151·8) is represented by the Pitcarmick-type buildings (see below).

Numerous instances of sequential construction are present amongst the hut-circle groups, but the evidence is not sufficient to indicate a recurring pattern of succession of different hut-circle types. Inspection of the tangential pairs of hut-circles, which were classified as a group by Thorneycroft (1933), suggests that one of the buildings is often earlier than the other (e.g. no. 124·4). Likewise,
124·4A(F. rows of three or more hut-circles often show evidence of multiperiod construction (e.g. nos. 133; 140·18). A further
133, 140· instance of chronological depth can be seen at Drumturn Burn (no. 124·10), where an enclosed and tangential pair
124·10(C– (the latter both probably of one building phase) overlie and block a trackway leading to a severely robbed double-walled hut-circle. Nevertheless, the existence of rows of hut-circles, particularly those where the field-banks define a courtyard in front of their entrances (e.g. nos. 103·6;
103·6, 13 133), implies the existence of a small number of nucleated settlements; the composition of these rows is variable, including single-walled, double-walled and enclosed pairs of hut-circles, and in two instances the latest structures on the site appear to be hut-circles with unusually small diameters (nos. 133; 140·18). The overall picture of the
133, 140· pattern of prehistoric settlement, however, is one of dispersed individual farmsteads clustered around areas of cultivable land.

The agricultural remains around the hut-circles normally consist of little more than irregular scatters of small cairns and stony banks. Such remains are difficult to date, and their juxtaposition with the hut-circles need not reflect more than the coincidence of land-use over several millennia. Nevertheless, there are field-systems where the arrangement of field-banks appears to be integral to a group of hut-circles. The most spectacular of these is at Drumturn Burn (no. 124·10), where trackways lead
124·10 between the fields to specific hut-circles. At other sites there are large enclosures with broad access ways leading into a courtyard in front of a row of hut-circles (nos. 122·9; 133); one of these, Drumderg, has an unparalleled
122·9, 13 series of lynchets and strip-fields within the enclosure. Another recurring pattern of field-banks consists of a

133, 140·18

large enclosure around a group of hut-circles with its lower edge apparently opening on to boggy ground at the foot of the slope (nos. 133; 140·18; 147·10); the nature of the relationship between these enclosures and the hut-circles is uncertain. On Middleton Muir there are banks both blocking movement along the ridges and forming funnels leading to hut-circles, but wherever the banks and the hut-circle walls come into contact, the banks appear to be secondary (see no. 147·3, ·11).

The identification of five patches of cord rig in North-east Perth is an important discovery (nos. 122·7; 151·9, 18–19, 26). The difficulties of locating this form of ridged cultivation are highlighted by the fact that the four patches recorded in the valley of the Pitcarmick Burn would have been invisible but for an intense moorland fire, which burnt off the thin peaty covering. Doubtless many more patches exist in the area but they are unlikely to be recovered by conventional survey techniques. Elsewhere in Scotland, similar cultivation ridges, which are seldom more than 1·2m broad, can sometimes be shown to be of prehistoric date. Many of the groups of small cairns adjoin traces of broader ridging of much later date.

Other evidence of prehistoric activity in the zone occupied by the hut-circles and groups of small cairns is provided by the twenty-eight burnt mounds that have been identified. Burnt mounds have, hitherto, not been recognised in Perth, and they represent an important addition to the evidence of prehistoric settlement. The mounds themselves are unremarkable; most are relatively small and are crescentic on plan. They have proved difficult to locate, however, and are almost certainly under-represented in this survey. Some occur in groups (no. 180), a pattern familiar elsewhere in Scotland, but others have been found in isolation at heights up to 500m OD (no. 179). No evidence of their date has been recovered in North-east Perth, but there is mounting evidence from elsewhere to suggest that many burnt mounds are Bronze Age in date, and the majority of them are probably cooking places (O'Drisceoil 1988).

With the evidence of intense prehistoric settlement, it is surprising that no forts have been located in either Glen Shee or Strathardle. The only fort recorded is on Barry Hill (no. 102), at the eastern extremity of the area surveyed, one of a number of heavily-defended forts known along the sides of Strathmore. The evidence from Finavon, the only one of these forts for which radiocarbon dates are available (MacKie 1969, 16–18), suggests a long period of occupation, and it is equally likely that Barry Hill, whose defences were extensively remodelled on at least two occasions, also has a long and complex history.

MEDIEVAL AND LATER LANDSCAPE

The first edition of the OS six-inch map presents a very detailed and complete picture of the mid-19th century landscape as it had emerged from the agricultural improvements, and for this reason those features which appear still to have been in use at that date have been omitted from this volume. A number of late 18th- and early 19th-century maps preceded the first edition (e.g. Ainslie 1794; Thomson 1825), the most useful being that by James Stobie, published in 1783 at a scale of one inch to one mile.

Stobie's map depicts settlement at what was probably its maximum extent, and many of the farms shown have remained in use up to the present day, although the 18th-century buildings may have been replaced. A

considerable number, however, were abandoned before the middle of the 19th century, many probably as a direct result of reorganisation during the Improvements. Many of the abandoned farmsteads have been destroyed by later agriculture, but the remains of others have survived, their buildings largely reduced to little more than stone wall-footings.

Whilst settlement patterns display some individual differences, three broad areas of medieval and later settlement activity can be identified: firstly, there are the areas of primary settlement in the main valleys, where the farmsteads and touns are often situated at the break of slope low down on the valley sides; in the tributary valleys and on the lower hills and moorland there is a second area where permanent settlement and shieling activity overlap, and beyond this there is a third area, given over entirely to shielings.

STRATHARDLE

The pattern of settlement is well seen at the northern end of Strathardle, on the modern estates of Ashintully, Balvarran and Dirnanean (a small estate may also have accompanied the tower-house of Whitefield (no. 212)). Apart from their holdings in Strathardle itself, the estates take in the broad valleys of the Allt Doire nan Eun and the Allt Menach, which are flanked by a series of isolated hills and fed by streams flowing from the southern slopes of the high hills overlooking Spittal of Glenshee. In the primary settlement area (i.e. within Strathardle itself or at the mouths of the tributary valleys) Stobie depicts the estate centres of Dirnanean and Balvarran (then called 'Inverchroskie') by mansion symbols, and the tower-houses of Ashintully (no. 199) and Whitefield (no. 212) as ruins, together with numerous settlement symbols, some named, others not. Roy's map shows several of these names and adds others, and still more can be recovered from documentary sources at least as early as the beginning of the 16th century.

Most of these settlements have now vanished without physical trace, although some, probably only a small proportion of the original total, survive around the fringes of arable or improved pasture fields. It is not always possible, however, to associate these with specific names known from documentary sources, and it is unfortunate that the cultivation remains which accompanied them have frequently been destroyed, a process clearly demonstrated at Ashintully (no. 223). Farmsteads no. 223·9 and ·11 and fermtoun no. 223·12 occupy a classic settlement location at the head-dyke, the long established division between the enclosed ground and the hill pastures, but whereas rig-and-furrow is still visible downslope from the two farmsteads, only stone-walled fields of the Improvement period lie downslope from the fermtoun.

In the zone where permanent settlements and shielings overlap, sheep grazing has usually followed desertion and has permitted the survival of both settlement and cultivation remains. Adjacent to the farmstead of Ruigh a' Chaorainn (no. 229·10) for example, there is a well-preserved system of turf-banked fields. That settlement had advanced into former shieling grounds, or had evolved from shielings, is attested not only by the presence of the shieling-huts themselves, but also by the fact that two of the farmsteads preserve the shieling prefix *ruigh* in their names, namely Ruigh a' Chaorainn ('Rechurle' on Stobie) and Ruich Chonnuill ('Rinnaconer' on Stobie). Whether established by advance or evolution, little evidence exists to date the change to permanent settlement. The earliest documentary reference is to the pendicle of 'Menach' in

147·3, 147
122, 151
170
121
255
223·9, ·11–·12

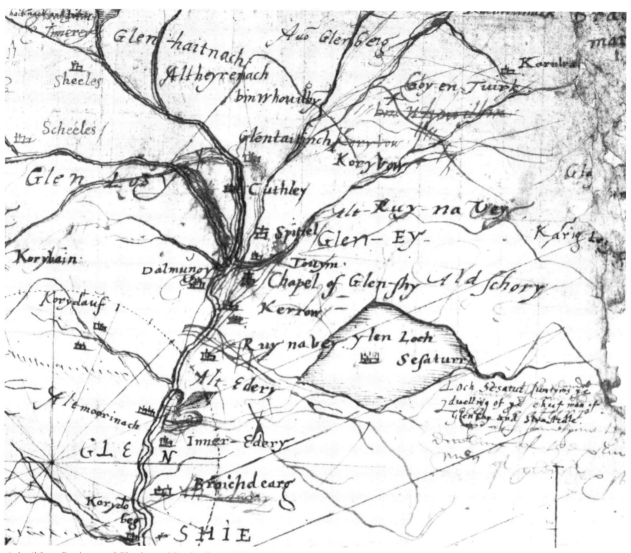

A detail from Pont's map of Glenshee and Strathardle (c.1600)
Reproduced by courtesy of the Trustees of the National
Library of Scotland

1642 (*Retours*, Perth, No. 520), although the same
document refers also to the shielings of Coire Bhuraich.
The granting of grazing rights at 'Richirrell' to Spalding of
Ashintully in 1710 (Spalding 1914, 221) could be
interpreted either way. Evidence for comparable
advances elsewhere in Scotland generally shows them to
have taken place before 1600 (e.g. RCAHMS 1983,
nos. 223, 235, 237, 246), and work in southern Scotland
suggests that there the high-water mark of medieval
settlement and cultivation was often reached in the 12th
century (Parry 1978, 113–16).

ROYAL FORESTS

In North-east Perth better dating evidence of the
expansion of settlement into the overlap zone exists for
the Forest of Clunie (NO 08 50), one of three royal
forests in the area, the others being Drimmie (NO *c*. 17
52) and Alyth (NO 18 55). Clunie and Drimmie are on
record by 1161 (Gilbert 1979, 338), and Alyth was
probably established at about the same time. Drimmie
was probably granted to Coupar Angus Abbey before
1224, but Clunie and Alyth remained in royal hands until
the 15th century, Alyth being alienated before 1463 and
Clunie in 1481 (*Exch. Rolls*, xii, 42). Forest status was not
invariably a barrier to economic exploitation. The

management of forests in Scotland appears to have been
more pragmatic than in England, and from the 13th
century onwards the forests came under increasing
pressure (Gilbert 1979, 248–67). Consequently, in the
14th century there was a trend towards the creation of
parks, which were smaller and more manageable than the
forests and from which it was easier to exclude other
economic activities. Two parks were established on the
fringes of the Forest of Clunie: Buzzart Dikes (no. 216) *216–17*
and Laighwood (no. 217). The date of the Buzzart Dikes
is unknown, but Laighwood was created from lands
granted by Robert II (1371–90) to the Earl of Moray.
These parks may be symptomatic of external pressures
upon the forest, possibly even the encroachment of
settlement, which appears to have taken place by 1459,
when the fermes of the forest come on record.

A number of abandoned settlement sites, described
under Ranageig (no. 310), lie within the forest and were in *310*
existence by about 1600. These are the farmsteads of
Buckinhill, Roughsheal and Dulater, together with the
fermtoun of Sheriffmuir and the Bog Mill. Another small
fermtoun, Craigsheal, where the remains include the
ruins of a laird's or tacksman's house, is on record in *245A*
1635. The names Craigsheal and Roughsheal imply that
they originated as shielings, which were permitted in
some forests, but shieling groups comparable to those
further north in Strathardle and Glen Shee are absent

6

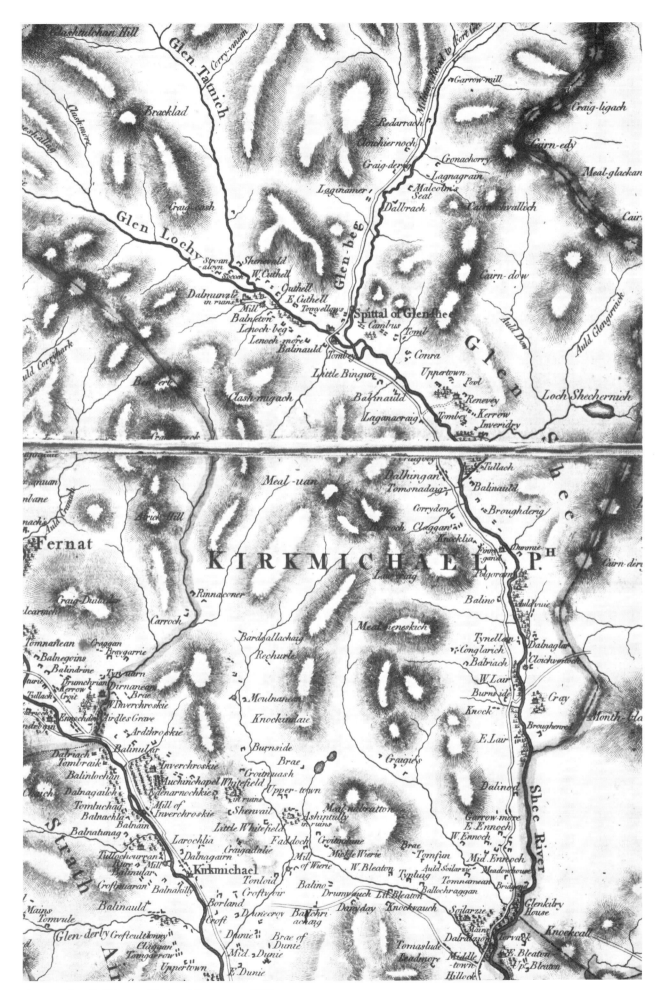

An extract from Stobie's map of Perth and Clackmannan (1783)

7

B

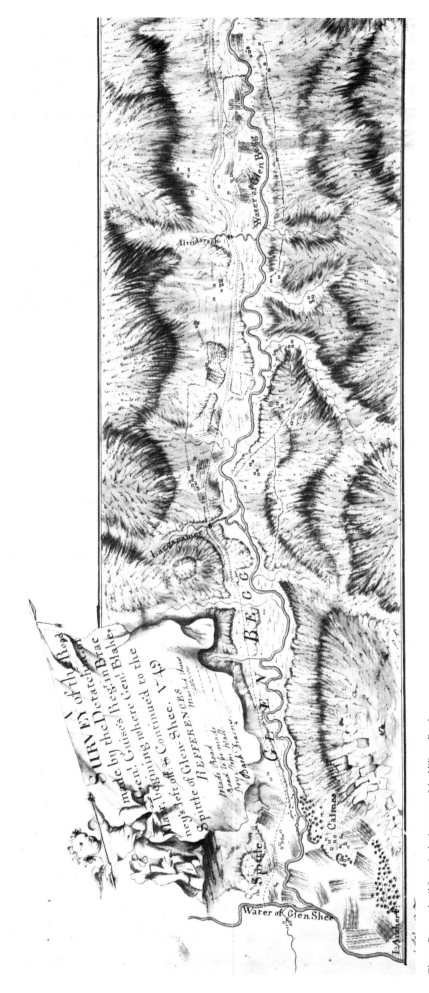

*Gleann Beag, a detail from Archer's survey of the Military Road
from Braemar to Spittal of Glenshee (1749)*
Reproduced by courtesy of the Trustees of the National
Library of Scotland

from both the Forests of Clunie and Alyth, where many of the scattered huts may have been no more than herdsmen's bothies.

GLEN SHEE

Although the topography of Glen Shee differs from that at the north end of Strathardle, similar processes appear to have acted upon the pattern of settlement. The areas of primary settlement can be recognised in the main glen, but it is more difficult to identify the areas of overlap between permanent settlement and shielings. At least one such area exists in Gleann Beag, however, and the pattern is completed by the major shieling groups that are scattered through the higher glens. The levels of preservation and survival in these areas are remarkable; the settlements in both Gleann Beag (no. 265) and Glen Shee west of the Spittal of Glenshee (no. 278) have been mapped in detail at a scale of 1:10,000, while the distribution of surviving farmsteads and shielings in Gleann Taitneach (no. 274) and at Invereddrie (no. 286) are illustrated at 1:25,000.

A charter of 1510, which enumerates the lands of the barony of Dunie, includes Finegand (on record in the 13th century), Binzeanmore, Binzeanbeg, Runavey, Kerrow, Cuthel, Dalmunzie and the toun and mill of Invereddrie (*Reg. Mag. Sig.*, ii, no. 3450). In 1615 the lands of Spittal with the mill, 'Chappell Crofts', Gleann Beag, Cambs, 'Tomyacharrow' and 'Dathnagare' formed part of the newly erected barony of Ashintully (Spalding 1914, 4–5), to which was added in 1674 Cray, Broughdearg and Corrydon, lands formerly lying in the barony of Balmachreuchie (Spalding 1914, 75). Most of these places are identifiable as modern farms or sites, although little evidence of buildings of this date survives.

At Dalmunzie, however, there are the remains of what may have been a laird's house (no. 278·12), though possibly not the earliest on this site. Dalmunzie is on record in 1510 and was for many years the seat of the MacIntoshes, who in the 17th century were stewards of the Earl of Atholl, then the superior of Glen Shee. Pont (*c*.1600) depicts an island-dwelling on Loch Beanie ('Shechernich' on Stobie) and annotates it 'Loch Sesatur, sumtyms ye dwelling of ye chief man of Glenshy and Strathardle'. The identity of the individual is unknown, but the site is still recognisable (no. 210). In addition, there are two inscribed lintels: one, bearing the date 1658, which is re-used in the keeper's cottage at Leanoch Mhor (no. 278·21), may have come from a laird's house at Dalmunzie; the other dated 1668 may have come from a building at Tomb, traces of which survive to the rear of the 19th-century farmhouse (no. 324). From Finegand there is a datestone of 1658 (no. 263), but evidence for a laird's house at Broughdearg, by the mid-16th century the property of the Farquharsons, is lacking. The remains at Dalmunzie and Tomb are noteworthy as both are associated with small fermtouns, but the significance of the Loch Beanie island-dwelling is more difficult to assess.

Stobie's map (1783) again shows the pattern of settlement in Glen Shee at its maximum extent. The farms, most of them still identifiable as extant remains, extend along both sides of the glen and up the tributaries of Gleann Taitneach and Gleann Beag. The distribution of settlement is heavily influenced by the topography. To the south of Spittal of Glenshee, the land suitable for cultivation on the west side of the valley is constricted by the terrain to the haughland of the Shee Water. As a result the farmsteads are strung out in a ribbon and are few in number; some, however, are clearly aligned with the Military Road (1748–9) and may be contemporary with it. By contrast, on the east side of the valley, where the scope for cultivation is greater, there is a series of farmsteads extending south from the fermtoun at Cambs (no. 234). To the west of Spittal of Glenshee as far as Dalmunzie and Sheanval, the pattern is roughly symmetrical on both sides of the valley. This pattern is essentially repeated in Gleann Beag (no. 265), where it is likely that many of the farms themselves developed upon earlier shieling grounds. This seems to be confirmed by the prevalence of the shieling place-name elements *ruigh* and *airigh*, as in Rhiedorrach and Cro na h-Airighe. In Gleann Beag the intake of land for cultivation probably took place towards the close of the 16th century. Prior to this, the glen provided the summer grazings for, amongst others, the farms of Finegand, which had shielings here in the 13th century, Dalrulzion, and the town of Runavey (*Reg. Mag. Sig.*, iii, no. 1841). The principal effect of bringing a greater part of the glen under cultivation was that it may have displaced the shielings to even more marginal positions. In the 19th century, increasing encroachment on traditional shieling grounds, particularly in Gleann Taitneach, involved the Invercauld estate in a lengthy litigation (cf. Michie 1901, 339–40). (For an account of the shielings and the character of the rural economy, see Robertson 1799, 334–40; and for the folk-life, customs and traditions of Glen Shee, see Miller 1929).

Archer's survey of the Military Road, prepared for the Board of Ordnance in 1749, provides an invaluable insight into the pre-Improvement landscape in Gleann Beag. The road is shown only partially constructed but all the principal settlements are in place, together with the head-dykes and the extent of rig-and-furrow. The detail seems to be reasonably accurate; at Gormel (no. 266), for instance, the depiction shows all the buildings (including a kiln) visible today. Cultivation appears to be almost entirely restricted to the west side of the valley, which is perhaps surprising as the farmsteads of Cro na h-Airighe, Lag nan Cnaimhean, Sidh Chaluim and Dail Bhreac, are all on the east side. Alexander Ramsay, tenant in Cro na h-Airighe in 1640, however, is described as 'Grazier' on a headstone in the Spittal of Glenshee burial-ground.

In 1812 preparations were set in train to consolidate the grazings in Gleann Beag, and it is worth comparing Archer's survey with Brown's, the latter prepared for the Invercauld estate in 1808, which catches the glen immediately before transition. The farmsteads are illustrated in detail, together with their relative proportions of arable, meadow, hill-pasture and muir. What is surprising is that the process of depopulation was quite so drawn out, although in Glen Shee this was achieved more quickly than in Gleann Beag. In both valleys the process had been completed by 1862, and it would suggest that there was little forcible eviction but simply that when the tacks expired they were not renewed. The tenant at Cro na h-Airighe transferred to the farm of Rochallie (NO 1513 5111) about 1816.

Accompanying the farmsteads in Glen Shee there is a series of larger touns, and two, which occupy the east side of the valley between Runavey and Invereddrie (nos. 313; 285), are of considerable extent. These bear some resemblance to the fermtoun at Easter Bleaton (no. 258) and probably owe their origin to the presence of an ample valley-basin and shieling grounds close by. Both Invereddrie and Runavey, together with many of the smaller fermtouns, can be broken down into a number of distinct units. Some of these may have functioned as farmsteads in their own right with a single tenant, but more generally the pattern is probably one of joint or multiple tenure with adjoining lands cultivated on a runrig basis. The tail-end of this system of land allotment is probably to be seen on the slopes to the south of Spittal of Glenshee, and north of Sheanval in Gleann Taitneach,

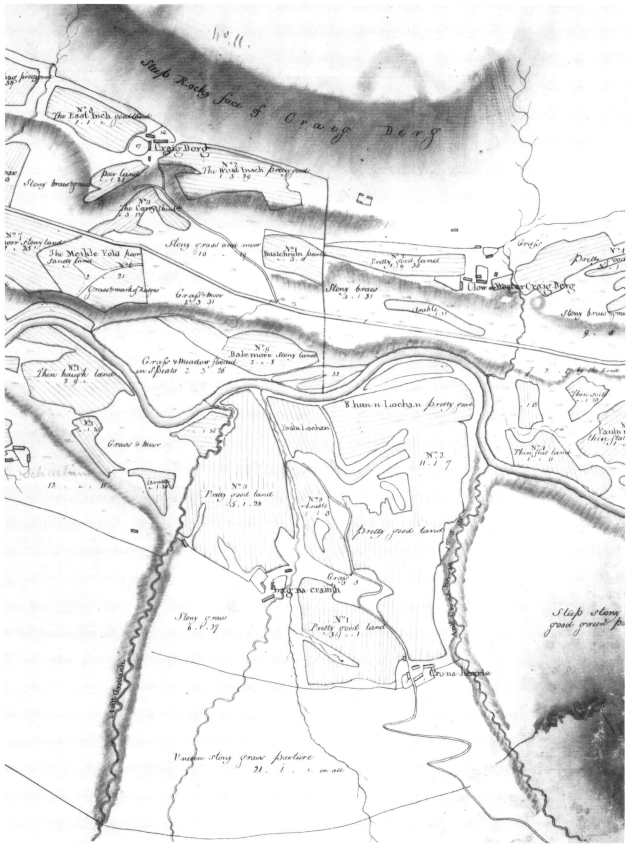

Gleann Beag, a detail from Brown's survey of the Invercauld estate (1808)
Reproduced by permission of Captain A A C Farquharson of Invercauld

where rigs are systematically grouped in lots defined by earth-and-stone banks; in Gleann Taitneach these take the form of broad strip-fields of a type also found in Gleann Fearnach (no. 272·17).

278
In Glen Shee some chronological depth is apparent amongst the cultivation remains, and cultivation ridges of a variety of types are well represented (Graham 1939). Between the church at Spittal of Glenshee and the farmstead of Cuthel (no. 278·4), there is a well-defined lynchet system. Here and elsewhere in the area the lynchets can be shown to have evolved from broad rigs set across slopes. Although the lynchets may have continued in use in the Improvement landscape (Robertson 1799, 123–32), they are emphatically pre-Improvement in character. Those in Glen Shee, which are cut obliquely by later rig-and-furrow, may well be medieval and, the
278·1
presence of an otherwise unattested fermtoun (no. 278·1) at the head of the terraces, taken with its position in relation to the church and mill of Spittal (no. 278·22), is thus of considerable interest.

THE ABBEY OF COUPAR ANGUS

A major influence on the medieval landscape in the south part of the area was the Cistercian abbey of Coupar Angus, founded in 1164 by Malcolm IV (Cowan and Easson 1976, 73–4), who granted to it the royal manor of Coupar. Its lands ultimately included Drimmie (NO 174 504), where there was a grange and a mill, Tullyfergus (NO 218 491), where there was a grange, Balmyle (NO 100 555) and Cally (NO 116 522), where there were mills, and Persie (NO 133 548); at Tullochcurran (NO 070 606) the abbey rented 400 acres from the Bishop of Moray to create a sheep farm (Franklin 1952, 35–7). At the outset it was the practice of the Cistercians to farm the lands themselves, using lay brothers to oversee the work of the granges, but in the 14th century the numbers of lay brothers dwindled and the lands were leased to secular tenants. The last reference to lay brothers in the Coupar Angus records is in 1305 (Easson 1947, xlix), and when the abbey's surviving rental books begin in 1443 (Rogers 1879) the system of leasing is firmly established. The agricultural practices employed on the granges differed from contemporary secular practices in that the lands were not divided in runrig, and when the granges were leased the abbey stipulated that the already fenced arable fields were not to be divided, but were to be cultivated jointly. The fenced meadow and pasture, however, were to be re-fenced to give each tenant his own holding.

From the Rental Book of Coupar Angus (Rogers 1879; 1880) it is possible to estimate the approximate sizes of some of the fermtouns on the estate. For example, at Balmyle in 1460 there were seven tenants, and in 1473 there were eight (Rogers 1879, 142, 181–2). Assuming settlement to be nucleated, their houses together with the ancillary buildings and the houses of the cottars may have created a fermtoun equivalent in size to that at Easter
258A
Bleaton (no. 258), where at least eight units or farmsteads can be tentatively identified. Similarly at Persie in 1443 there were six tenants, and at the former grange of Tullyfergus in 1508 there were seven (Rogers 1879, 120, 268–9). However, whilst life-rents were granted quite frequently, Coupar Angus leases were more usually of five- to seven-year duration, and tenant numbers fluctuated; at Balmyle in the 1440s and at Persie in 1463 there were four tenants (Rogers 1879, 121, 136). Yet equal numbers of people were still required to work the land, and when Persie was set to only two tenants in life-rent in 1473 they had the right to introduce or remove tenants as they thought most expedient (Rogers 1879, 201–2); in a subsequent lease in 1508 Persie was set to

seven tenants on a five-year tack (Rogers 1879, 269).

The Rental Book also provides good illustrations of the process of toun splitting (Dodgshon 1981, 195–204). At Drimmie it had taken place by the middle of the 15th century, when Easter, Wester and Middle Drimmie appear (Rogers 1879, 122, 141), whilst at Persie it may have happened a century later, Easter and Wester Persie coming on record in 1545 and 1550 respectively (Rogers 1880, 72–3, 227), and Over and Nether Persie probably at about the same time (Rogers 1880, 194).

THE ANATOMY OF SETTLEMENT

In the narrower glens the farmsteads of the pre-Improvement landscape are almost invariably set on, or
278
close to, the old head-dykes at the margin between the infield and the rough hill-grazing (cf. Robertson 1799, 108). Generally these fall into two classes which vary only in scale. The first consists of buildings which seem to be more-or-less randomly disposed; the second represents a more ordered layout with buildings ranged around a yard. Due to the varying levels of preservation few distinguishing traits remain and evidence of function is often elusive. Occasionally one building stands out by virtue of size, and in these cases it is a reasonable assumption that it served as the principal dwelling. Often these are of two or more compartments, stone-built and have an entrance central to a side-wall; the presence of a
265·16
window adjacent to the door is evident on three sites. The addition to an end-wall of one or more units, or an outshot, is quite common. Buildings on slopes are generally terraced parallel to the contour into the slope and are frequently provided with a drainage-gully, or bank, upslope.

Few of the buildings display any level of structural refinement, but among the details that have been recorded are cruck-slots, porches, aumbries and an end-wall fireplace. Of note is a building in the Green Glen, probably an illicit still, which has been divided into three
286·2
cruck-bays (no. 286). The only recorded example of a building in Glen Shee with its crucks still in place is a barn at Blacklunans (NO 1513 6055); close by there is also a building with a composite turf-and-stone gable. Byres are often revealed by the presence of transverse or lateral drains issuing either from a doorway or end-wall. In some
285B
cases a terrace is provided in front of the house, and this served to set it apart from the midden, which is often recognisable as a dished depression either to the fore or within the adjoining yard. Buildings with opposed lateral entrances may be threshing-barns. Stack-stands, however, are rare, though stands, which may be for peats, are more common.

In proximity to many of the farmsteads there are corn-drying kilns and these are of several types, including simple bowl-kilns and those with stoking chambers. Only a handful of kiln-barns have been identified, and that at Craigies (no. 277·14) is the best preserved. Amongst the
277
many pens and enclosures are some of a type that may have fulfilled a more specialised function. They are characterised by their elongated and narrow plan and by the fact that they are open at one end. As at Cro na h-Airighe (no. 265·4), pens of this type usually abut an enclosure close to the steading.

A few of the farmsteads are distinguished by the presence of a more substantial building. At Craigsheal
245A–B,
(no. 245), and possibly at Dalmunzie (no. 278·12) and
278·12
Dulater (no. 310·6), there are the remains of lairds' or
310·6
tacksmen's houses, whilst elsewhere, notably in Gleann Beag, there are buildings which may be likened to the lofted farmhouses of open-hall plan which first appeared in Scotland in the first half of the 18th century (Walker

1988). The three examples in Gleann Beag (no. 265) have a mean span of 5·2 m and employ the use of well-built clay-bonded walls. They also have unusually thick end-walls, that at Sidh Chaluim (no. 265·17) preserving a first-floor scarcement.

Nearly all the shielings comprise groups of huts, pens and enclosures with a tract of reasonably good hill-pasture (often improved by successive re-use, cf. Robertson 1799, 336), close to a source of water (Smith 1987, 449). Larger buildings are present at many of the shieling sites, and are probably accounted for by Robertson who asserts that the 'huts ... were in proportion to the affluence and rank of the different possessors' and goes on to describe huts 'consisting of two or three apartments, besides a proper place for the milk' (1799, 336).

Commonly the huts are insubstantial, single-compartment structures, some built entirely of turf, or turf-and-stone, some of drystone masonry. Most are roughly rectangular, though examples of oval and even circular huts are known (e.g. nos. 270; 286·21). At Invereddrie the remains of some of the huts amount to little more than cleared spaces in the scree (no. 286). Occasionally there is evidence for a slightly sunken interior; this is perhaps no more than an attempt to achieve greater headroom. The keeping of livestock within some huts is suggested by the provision of a lintelled creep on one site (no. 274·6) and by drains issuing from end- or side-walls on others (no. 274·7). On a number of sites there are turf-built huts which now appear as mounds, usually incorporating a stone-lined chamber and a funnel-shaped entrance. In some cases the chamber may be an original feature, but it is often eccentric to the mound and has probably been set into it at a later date. Further evidence that the occupation of shielings extended over a wide chronological span is apparent on a number of sites (e.g. nos. 274·4; 307·7).

Generally the buildings in the shieling groups are larger than the huts and of more regular construction. Some have rounded outer angles and battered end-walls, and many are of more than one compartment. As a rule a distinction can be drawn between the overall size of huts and buildings on shieling sites and those elsewhere; many have a narrower span and this probably reflects the use of roof timbers of lighter scantling. Of note are two *274·11* buildings on a shieling in Gleann Taitneach (no. 274), where each is divided into two compartments by a cross-wall; this may have functioned as the support for the roof, which was probably hipped. The use of a gable is attested at only one site (no. 267·3).

Despite the difficulties of dating buildings reduced to their wall-footings, it may be deduced that many probably belong to the immediately pre-Improvement period; others, however, may be much earlier and there is no reason why some at least should not be medieval. In North-east Perth, a series of buildings of a kind hitherto unrecognised has now been identified, at least forty-eight of which have enough characteristics in common for them to be usefully designated as a separate category within medieval and later settlement. They are referred to as Pitcarmick-type buildings, as all of their defining characteristics are seen amongst the group that has been recorded at Pitcarmick.

None of these buildings is conventionally rectangular *p.13* (see fig.). Most have rounded ends or angles, their side-walls are often slightly curved, some appearing as bow-sided, and they are usually broader at one end than the other. They range in length from 10 m to 30 m over stone wall-footings or low spread banks; the majority are from 15 m to 25 m long, and almost invariably they measure between 7 m and 8·5 m in maximum width. The floors of about half of the buildings are partially sunken, usually at the narrow end, a feature possibly deriving from the use of that end of the building as a byre, or perhaps to provide storage beneath a wooden floor. There is normally a single entrance at either the mid-point of one of the long sides or slightly off-centre towards the wider end. The entrance is frequently screened by a porch, and there are the remains of paving outside at least two, Knockali (no. 10 on fig.) and Pitcarmick (no. 7 on fig.); in *p.13* the last instance the paving forms part of a path leading to an adjacent enclosure. At the same Pitcarmick site, as at *227·1A* Balnabroich (no. 227) and Welton of Creuchies (no. 9 on fig.), there are successive Pitcarmick-type buildings, the *p.13* later overlying or impinging upon the earlier, and at Lair (no. 290) there is a sequence of three. Characteristic of *290·3* many of them is the attachment of one or more small enclosures or annexes.

With the exception of the northern glens, Pitcarmick-type buildings are lightly distributed across the whole of North-east Perth, although there are four principal groupings, at Balnabroich (no. 227), Knockali (no. 288), *108A, 124·4* Lair (no. 290) and Pitcarmick (nos. 302–3), which account *151.8* for well over half of the final total. They are seldom found in the vicinity of farmsteads and fermtouns, but with remarkable regularity share the locations of hut-circle groups, and at Balnabroich, Knockali and Pitcarmick they lie within extensive and well-preserved prehistoric landscapes. Unfortunately, there is as yet little conclusive evidence as to their date, and whilst two can be seen to overlie hut-circles (nos. 244; 309) it would be unwise to proceed from this to a general statement that Pitcarmick-type buildings post-date hut-circles. Nevertheless, the patterns of expansion and contraction evident throughout the settlement record suggest that these buildings are likely to reflect an undocumented period of expansion some time after the abandonment of hut-circles. This expansion may follow closely on from the hut-circles, but may equally belong firmly in the medieval period.

Apart from the Pitcarmick-type buildings, there are others that do not lend themselves so easily to classification. Consistently they are found around the fringes of areas of pre-Improvement settlements, or amongst the hut-circle groups. Some may be close relatives of the Pitcarmick types, the pair at Glenkilrie (no. 277·11) for example, but others are clearly buildings *277·11A–B* of a different kind. At Lair there is a marked contrast between the group of three Pitcarmick-type buildings (no. 290), which have left quite substantial remains, and the two buildings (no. 291·13) downslope from the ring-cairn, whose remains are very slight. These buildings are seldom accompanied by the enclosures which would identify them as 'farmsteads', Lair no. 291·9 being perhaps *291·9* the only one which could be fitted into this category, whilst at Pitcarmick no. 305·4, where the two parallel- *305·4* sided, round-ended buildings are accompanied by seven smaller ones, some form of shieling activity might be inferred. Yet other buildings have been found adjacent to small systems of narrow strip-fields. Perhaps the best examples are situated at the northern end of Loch Benachally (no. 310·15–·16), but similar fields have been *310·15–·16* identified in Glen Derby (no. 322) and on the Hill of Cally (no. 283). Comparable field-systems have been recognised elsewhere in Scotland (RCAHMS 1983, no. 224; 1984, no. 117), but not in association with rectangular buildings; the buildings themselves, which survive only in a somewhat wasted condition, are clearly different from those normally found on pre-Improvement settlement sites and shielings. The presence of all these different types of buildings hints at the possibility that the Pitcarmick-type buildings reflect only one of a number of undocumented attempts at permanent settlement in the margins.

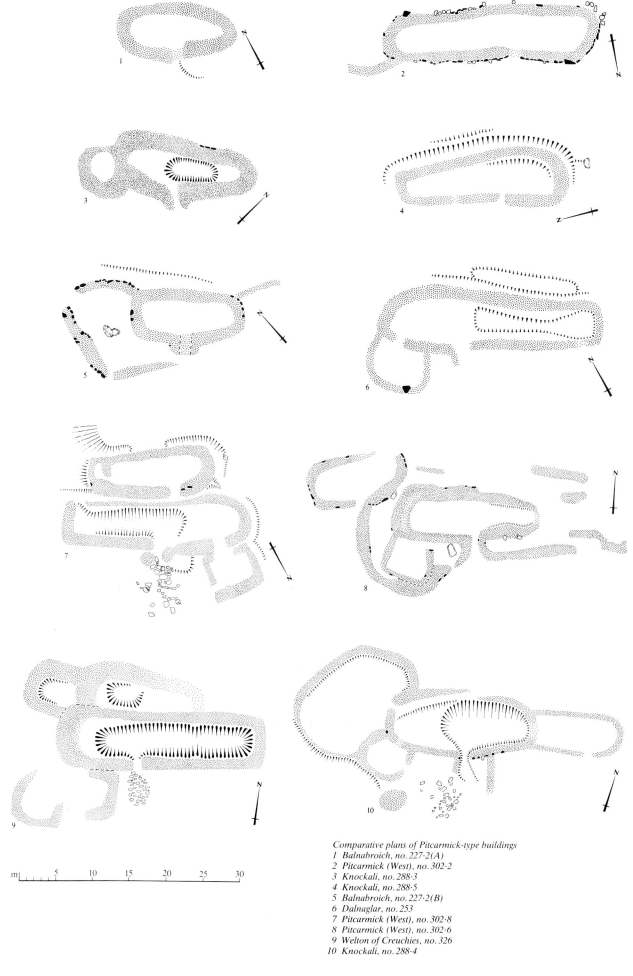

Comparative plans of Pitcarmick-type buildings
1 Balnabroich, no. 227·2(A)
2 Pitcarmick (West), no. 302·2
3 Knockali, no. 288·3
4 Knockali, no. 288·5
5 Balnabroich, no. 227·2(B)
6 Dalnaglar, no. 253
7 Pitcarmick (West), no. 302·8
8 Pitcarmick (West), no. 302·6
9 Welton of Creuchies, no. 326
10 Knockali, no. 288·4

m 5 10 15 20 25 30

13

INVENTORY

RING-CAIRNS

1 Balnabroich, ring-cairns

There are two ring-cairns among the hut-circles, field-systems and small cairns (no. 108) that extend across the moorland to the NE of Balnabroich. The first lies 90 m NE of the Grey Cairn (no. 9·1) and the second is situated immediately beyond the scatter of small cairns some 300 m to the SE.

·1   NO 1013 5707   NO 15 NW 15

The smaller of the two, this ring-cairn is roughly circular on plan and measures about 6·5 m in overall diameter by 0·3 m in height. The most prominent features are four large stones (one displaced), which form the SW arc of

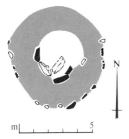

1·1 Balnabroich, ring-cairn, 1:250

the inner kerb, and a series of small outer kerbstones around the S half of the cairn. The function of a small upright slab visible on the E is unclear; while this stone may have formed part of the inner kerb, it may be no more than a supporting slab, possibly for the kerbstone that has been dragged into the centre of the court. The present condition of the ring-cairn is probably the result of Stuart's excavations of 1865, when a 'trench from the NE towards the centre showed a rude pavement, several large flattish flags, and great quantities of white quartz pebbles' (Stuart 1868, 407).

·2   NO 1034 5684   NO 15 NW 57

Roughly oval on plan but with a roughly square central court, this ring-cairn measures 7·5 m by 6·8 m in diameter over a boulder kerb which survives for most of its circuit.

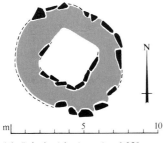

1·2 Balnabroich, ring-cairn, 1:250

The kerbstones appear to be graded in size with the largest (0·4 m high) in the S arc. The court, which may originally have been about 3 m square, is bounded by the remains of a kerb, the stones of which have been laid lengthwise with the tops flush with the crest of the bank. A trench has been driven across the centre of court, but

no mention is made of this site in Stuart's (1868) account of excavations at Balnabroich.

2 Lair, ring-cairn

NO 1387 6376   NO 16 SW 49

This ring-cairn is situated on a low knoll 510 m NW of Lair farmhouse; it overlooks low-lying ground to the S and W but is itself overlooked from the N and E (see also

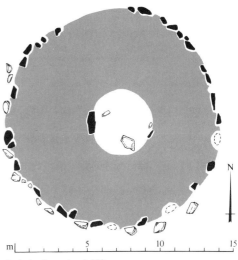

2 Lair, ring-cairn, 1:250

no. 139·3). The cairn is almost perfectly circular on plan and measures 15 m in diameter by 0·3 m in height. The outer edge is defined by a boulder kerb which has been robbed on the NNW (probably during the construction of the adjacent building, no. 291·13); the inner kerb, however, is poorly preserved with only two boulders (the larger measuring 1·4 m in length by 0·7 m in height) remaining *in situ*. The court probably measured about 4 m in diameter and was eccentric to the outer kerb. The interior of the court has been disturbed.

3 Middleton Muir, ring-cairn

NO 1181 4819   NO 14 NW 69

Situated on gently-sloping moorland about 70 m S of the hut-circles no. 147·3, there are the remains of a small ring-cairn. It measures 4 m in diameter over a bank which is

3 Middleton Muir, ring-cairn, 1:250

1·1 m in average thickness and is revetted by a graded boulder kerb up to 0·25 m high on the SW. The court is irregular on plan, but the SW, SE and NE sides are roughly rectilinear, and the inner facing-stones are graded with the largest slabs on the SW.

4 Smyrna, ring-cairn

NO 1842 5281   NO 15 SE 57

A possible ring-cairn is situated on the crest of a low rise on the N side of the Olies Burn about 500 m SSW of the shepherd's cottage at Smyrna. It measures about 5·2 m in diameter overall by 0·3 m in height. At least six stones of

15

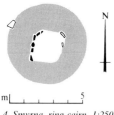

4 Smyrna, ring-cairn, 1:250

an inner kerb protrude through the top of the cairn, but, with the exception of a large earthfast block on the WNW, there is little evidence of an outer kerb.

BARROWS AND CAIRNS

5 Alyth Golf Course, cairns
Nothing is visible of two possible cairns depicted on the first edition of the OS 6-inch map (Perthshire, 1867, sheet 53) close to the E side of what is now Alyth Golf Course.

·1 NO 2669 4848   NO 24 NE 22
Known as Cows Cairn, this cairn is probably situated beneath the 17th tee, where large quantities of stones have been found. In 1867 it was described as a 'circular bank of earth and stone about 2 ft (0·6 m) high and 57 ft (17·4 m) in diameter' (Name Book, Perth, No. 5, p. 85).

·2 NO 2677 4838   NO 24 NE 23
The second cairn stood on the shoulder of a low rise 130 m to the SE of (·1).

Although depicted by the OS as cairns, the Name Book noted that the Cows Cairn was 'supposed to be a burial place or a Pict House' (Perth, No. 5, p. 85), and Meikle (1925, 74) considered it to be a hut-circle, two or three of which survived on the golf course at that time (Meikle 1933, 6). A double-walled hut-circle (no. 104) can still be seen in a clump of trees 80 m to the ENE of the 17th tee, and one or both of the 'cairns' may well have been hut-circles.

6 Baden Burn, cairns
In addition to the groups of small cairns (no. 106·5–·6) and shieling-huts (no. 225) that are scattered across the knolls in the floor of the valley of the Baden Burn, there are two probable burial cairns.

·1 NO 0836 5239   NO 05 SE 43
This kerb cairn occupies the summit of the northernmost knoll, and measures 5·7 m in diameter by 0·5 m in height. Two kerbstones, 0·5 m and 0·4 m high respectively, have been exposed to their full height on the N and W, and the tops of five others can be seen around the edge of the cairn.

·2 NO 0829 5247   NO 05 SE 55
The second cairn lies some 100 m to the NNW on a low spur of the same knoll and measures 7·5 m in diameter by 0·5 m in height.

7 Balchrochan, cairn
NO 0814 5872   NO 05 NE 98
Situated within an arable field and on the edge of a low terrace 410 m SSE of Balchrochan farmhouse, there is a large grass-covered cairn, which measures 15·5 m in

diameter and about 3 m in height. The partially tree-covered mound is composed of a mass of small boulders and slabs; it appears not to have been significantly added to with field-clearance, but its height may have been accentuated by ploughing around its base.

7 Balchrochan, cairn from NE

8 Balloch, cairn
NO 2738 4885   NO 24 NE 21
Several cists containing 'human bones', including one with a Food Vessel (RMS, EE 17), were found in this cairn before it was destroyed about 1863. Its position may be indicated by a low swelling in a field 560 m SSE of Balloch Mill, which would place it about 30 m SSE of the position indicated on the 1st edition of the OS 6-inch map (1867, Perthshire, sheet 53).
— Name Book, Perthshire, No. 5, p. 82; *Proc Soc Antiq Scot*, 6 (1864–6), 11–12 (Accessions); Abercromby 1912, 161, pl. 52, fig. 373.

9 Balnabroich, cairns
There are at least four burial cairns amongst the hut-circles and small cairns that extend across an area of rough pasture and heather moorland to the NE of Balnabroich (see no. 108). All four were partially excavated by John Stuart in 1865.

·1 NO 1006 5700   NO 15 NW 1
Known as the Grey Cairn, this conspicuous heap of stones stands between two shelter belts and measures about 29 m in diameter by 1 m in height. Formerly the cairn was over 7 m high (*Stat. Acct.*, 15 (1795), 516), but it was dug into on two occasions in the 19th century (Stuart 1868, 405–6), which probably accounts for its present disturbed condition. On the first occasion a passage leading towards the centre was discovered, but there was no trace of a chamber. In 1865 digging extended over the entire cairn and an area of burning was revealed at the centre beneath a basal layer of large boulders; the only finds were a perforated stone disc and a small boulder bearing a cupmark. A saddle quern projects from the cairn material on the SE side of the cairn.

·2 NO 1008 5695   NO 15 NW 44
This cairn lies 50 m to the SSE of the Grey Cairn, and the trenches dug into it in 1865 are still clearly visible. It now measures about 10·5 m in diameter by 0·5 m in height, but in 1865 it was 'about 9 yards across, defined by large boulders, with a raised ridge around, and a cup at the centre' (Stuart 1868, 406–7), the latter probably indicating that it had been dug into before. Numerous fragments of white quartz were found at the centre of the cairn, where there was a deposit of burnt bone and charcoal.

·3 NO 1049 5707   NO 15 NW 45
This cairn is situated on a low ridge 400 m E of the Grey Cairn. It measures about 12 m in diameter over a rough kerb of boulders and, where undisturbed, is no more than 0·3 m high. Again the 1865 excavation trenches are clearly

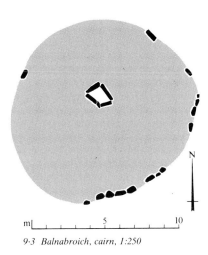

9·3 Balnabroich, cairn, 1:250

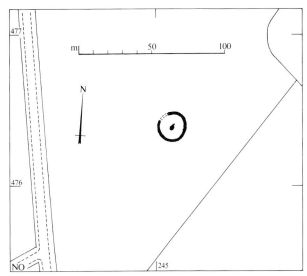

10 Blackbird Inn, barrow, 1:2500

visible and a large cist is exposed at the centre. The cist
measures up to 1·15 m from NW to SE by 0·8 m
transversely and was probably about 0·55 m deep; it had
been emptied prior to 1865 (Stuart 1868, 407) and the
notch in the top of the broken W side-slab probably
shows where a crowbar was inserted beneath the
coverstone.

·4   NO 1021 5712   NO 15 NW 63
A small burial cairn with its centre dug out lies on the
crest of a knoll 180 m NE of the Grey Cairn and
immediately N of the more westerly of a pair of hut-
circles (G on plan). It measures 6·5 m in diameter by 0·4 m
in height, and appears to overlie the outer bank of the
hut-circle (see plan); this relationship, however, may be
the result of upcast from the excavation of its centre,
where a pit containing 'calcined bones and charred wood'
was discovered (Stuart 1868, 407).

In addition to these four cairns, there are two ring-cairns
(no. 1) and a stone-circle (no. 59) at Balnabroich, making
this one of the most remarkable collections of funerary
and ritual monuments in NE Perthshire. The discovery of
a probable cremation beneath one of the comparatively
small cairns is of considerable interest, and it is possible
that several of the other small cairns may have served a
funerary as well as an agricultural function, e.g. two
cairns, 7 m and 6 m in diameter respectively, that lie on the
ridge to the NW of (·3) and which appear on the skyline
when viewed from the Grey Cairn. The majority of the
small cairns, however, are probably no more than
clearance heaps, and none of those dug into around the
stone circle (no. 59) provided any evidence of burials
(Stuart 1868, 407).

10   Blackbird Inn, barrow
      NO 2450 4763   NO 24 NW 45
The cropmark of a ring-ditch, which may once have
enclosed a barrow, has been revealed by aerial survey on
the summit of a low rise 200 m NW of Blackbird Inn. The
internal diameter is about 16·5 m, and there is an irregular
marking near the centre of the interior, possibly
indicating the position of a pit or grave. Significantly,
perhaps, the farm situated 400 m to the SW is known as
East Cairns of Aberbothrie.

11   Bruceton, cairn
      NO 2938 5035   NO 25 SE 24
What may be the remains of a cairn are situated in a thorn
thicket on the NW bank of the River Isla 400 m E of the

Bruceton Pictish symbol stone (no. 191). It survives as a
mound measuring about 20 m in diameter by 0·5 m in
height and is composed of earth and small stones. Traces
of a surrounding ditch were noted in the 19th century
(Name Book, Perthshire, No. 5, p. 60), but all that is now
visible is the hollow of an old trackway which cuts
through the edge of the river terrace immediately to the
SW of the cairn. In the 19th century some 'hand mills'
were found in the cairn.

12   Cairn Gleamnach, cairn
      NO 1585 5544   NO 15 NE 7
The remains of this cairn stand on a low knoll in the
saddle between Hill of Kingseat and Saebeg. It is roughly
circular and measures 19·5 m in maximum diameter over a
boulder kerb and 1 m in height; the two largest kerbstones
are on the S and SW respectively.
— Name Book, Perth, No. 5, p. 7.

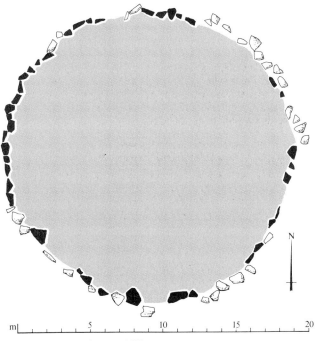

12 Cairn Gleamnach, cairn, 1:250

13   Chapelton, cairn
NO 2137 4691   NO 24 NW 10–11
Nothing remains of a cairn that stood to the N of
Chapelton farmhouse in which 'urns containing ashes'
were found before 1865. This was probably the same cairn
that produced two inverted cinerary urns in the late 18th
century.
— *Stat. Acct.*, 19 (1797), 359; Name Book, Perthshire, No. 9, p. 8;
    McPherson 1885, 70–1.

14   Corra-lairig, cairn
NO 1335 6422   NO 16 SW 44
A probable burial cairn is situated on a gentle SE-facing
slope 200 m SE of the farmstead known as Corra-lairig
(no. 291·16); it measures 10·2 m in diameter by 0·5 m in
maximum height. An arc of seven kerbstones, two of
which have slipped out of position, survives on the SE;
the largest of the kerbstones lies on the S and is 0·8 m
high.

15   Craigies, cairn
NO 1235 6214   NO 16 SW 122
Situated about 20 m S of farmstead no. 277·12, there are
the remains of a cairn measuring 6·3 m in diameter and
0·8 m in height. The N edge of the cairn has been slightly
truncated, but on the S arc there are at least six
kerbstones measuring up to 1 m in length and 0·3 m in
height. The remains of what may be a second cairn
(measuring 6·7 m by 5·2 m and 1 m in height) lie some 50 m
to the SSE; erosion of the turf and heather-covered
mound has revealed a mass of waterworn boulders and
stones.

16   Dalnabreck, barrow
NO 0906 5552   NO 05 NE 123
A large grass-grown mound, which is situated on the edge
153 of a terrace 150 m SE of Dalnabreck farmhouse, may be a
prehistoric barrow. It measures 29 m in diameter by 3·5 m
in height and is composed of gravel and stone.

17   Dalnaglar, cairn
NO 1491 6443   NO 16 SW 75
A cairn, measuring 6·5 m in diameter and 0·2 m in height
over an intermittent boulder kerb, is situated on the
summit of a knoll 410 m SE of Dalnaglar Castle.

18   Drumderg, cairn
NO 1756 5469   NO 15 SE 86
A turf and heather-covered cairn, measuring 6·5 m in
122 diameter and up to 0·6 m in height, is situated on a low
rise on the SW flank of Drumderg, about 980 m N of
Rannagulzion farmhouse.

19   Drumore, cairn
NO c.163 610   NO 16 SE 4
A polished stone axe (RMS, AF 80) was found about
1850 in a cairn near Drumore.
— Neish 1873; *Proc Soc Antiq Scot*, 9 (1870–2), 154, 174–5; NMAS 1892,
    24.

20   Gleann Beag, cairn
NO 1270 7329   NO 17 SW 22
Situated on the edge of a low rise on the E side of Gleann
Beag 750 m S of Rhiedorrach, there are the remains of a
severely robbed burial cairn measuring up to 13·3 m in

diameter over a boulder kerb which is visible only on the
SW and NE. A little to the N of the centre of the cairn,
the NW and NE sides of a cist (about 0·75 m by 0·5 m and
up to 0·3 m in depth) are visible; two further slabs may be
robbed side-slabs or displaced capstones. The W side of
the cairn is partially overlain by a small rectangular
structure.

21   Glenkilrie, cairn
NO 1349 6127   NO 16 SW 87
A probable burial cairn is situated on a low knoll on the
spur about 250 m N of the N corner of Glenkilrie Wood.
The shape and size of the cairn have been distorted by

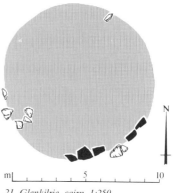

21 Glenkilrie, cairn, 1:250

robbing and the construction of a field-bank, but it
probably measured about 8·5 m in diameter. At least
seven kerbstones, two of them displaced, are visible
around the SE quadrant of the cairn. The field-bank,
which crosses over the cairn from E to W, is probably
associated with the small cairns that are scattered amongst
the knolls on the crest of the hill (see no. 128·4–·5).

22   Glenkilrie Farm, cairn
NO 1429 6056   NO 16 SW 129
A turf-covered cairn, the top of which has been disturbed,
is situated about 170 m SE of Glenkilrie farm steading. It
measures about 24 m in diameter by at least 3 m in height,
and has probably been built on a natural knoll.

23   Haer Cairn, Middle Mause, cairn
NO 1649 4887   NO 14 NE 22
Nothing remains of the Haer Cairn or 'Great Cairn of
Maws', which stood on a low rise 500 m NNW of Middle
Mause. It measured about 24 m in diameter by 1·2 m in
height, and was the largest of the cairns that once existed
in the fields around Middle Mause (see no. 146). In the
late 18th century the Reverend James Playfair, minister of
Bendochy, dug into its centre and found 'a great quantity'
of burnt bones mixed with charcoal. When the cairn was
finally removed, sometime before 1843, more bones were
discovered, as well as two cists 'containing skulls and a
quantity of burnt ashes'. Playfair also found 'burned
bones' in another 'tumulus' nearby.
— *Stat. Acct.*, 19 (1797), 369–70; *NSA*, 10 (Perth), 913; Name Book,
    Perth, No. 11, pp. 52–3.

24   Happy Hillock, Tullymurdoch, cairn
NO 1998 5222   NO 15 SE 1
The Happy Hillock is a heavily robbed cairn situated on a
natural knoll at the W end of a low ridge 280 m SSE of
Tullymurdoch farmhouse; it measures about 21 m in
diameter over a low rim of cairn material which is visible

on the W, S and E. About 7 m from the W edge there is a
large slab (1·5 m by 0·3 m and 0·8 m high) which is set on
edge and may indicate the position of one of the several
cists that were found about 1790 and said to contain
'human remains'.
— Name Book, Perthshire, No. 5, p. 25; Meikle 1925, 100-1; Coutts 1970,
15.

25 Heatheryhaugh, cairn
NO 1891 5115   NO 15 SE 52

A cairn, which survives as a turf-covered mound of
waterworn boulders measuring 6·7 m in diameter and
0·4 m in height, is situated on the top of a low rise 1·2 km
SE of Heatheryhaugh farmhouse.

26 Hill of Alyth, cairn
NO 2255 5014   NO 25 SW 25

This cairn is situated on a terrace at the foot of a knoll on
the W flank of the Hill of Alyth about 300 m NNW of
Whiteside steading. Although severely robbed, it still
forms a stony mound 18·5 m in maximum diameter by

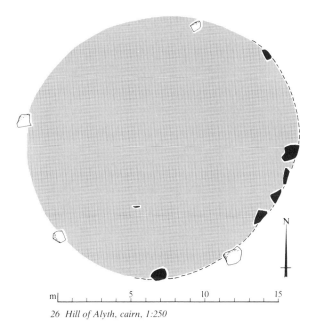

26 Hill of Alyth, cairn, 1:250

0·8 m in height, with ten stones of a substantial boulder
kerb, four of them displaced, surviving around its edge.
In the S quadrant, a small conglomerate slab, set on edge,
protrudes through the turf.

27 Hill of Cally, cairn
NO 1329 5210   NO 15 SW 5

This robbed cairn is situated at the junction of four fields
to the SE of the summit of the Hill of Cally. It stands to a
height of 0·7 m, and measures 20 m in diameter over a
kerb of forty-five boulders; the largest of these (up to
1·4 m long and 0·6 m high) are situated on the SE arc.
When the cairn was robbed to build dykes, a quern was
found (now lost). Immediately to the NW of the centre of
the cairn there is a broken slab which is set on edge,
possibly indicating the position of a cist.
— Name Book, Perthshire, No. 11, p. 25.

28 Hilton Hill, Bamff, cairn
NO 2175 5267   NO 25 SW 23

A robbed cairn, measuring about 6 m in diameter by no
more than 0·2 m in height, is situated at the SE end of the
gently sloping crest of Hilton Hill.

29 Loch Benachally, cairn
NO 0779 5017   NO 05 SE 8

Situated on the summit of one of the ridges that run
parallel to the E side of Loch Benachally, there are the
remains of a cairn measuring 5·6 m in diameter and 0·4 m
in height. At least ten kerbstones are visible, the largest
(on the WSW) measuring 0·7 m in length by 0·4 m in
height; immediately S of the centre the top of a slab
(0·9 m long), which protrudes through the cairn material,
may indicate the position of a cist.

30 Mains of Persie, cairn
NO 1350 5531   NO 15 NW 31

Situated on the edge of a knoll in poorly-drained pasture
200 m NW of Persie Loch, and within an area of small
cairns (no. 135·3), there is a cairn measuring 13 m in
diameter over a rim of turf-covered boulders 0·5 m high.
The edge of the cairn is best preserved on the S and E,
where several large boulders may indicate the line of a
kerb.

31 Middleton Muir, cairns

At least four burial cairns are situated amongst the hut-
circle groups and field-systems that are scattered across
Middleton Muir (no. 147). Most of the cairns lie on the
crests of the ridges that traverse the muir and command
fine views over Strathmore to the SE; many of the smaller
cairns that surround the hut-circle groups occupy similar
positions and some of these may also cover burials. The
four cairns, together with another mound and a destroyed
site noted in the 19th century, are described from N to S.

·1   NO 1293 4909   NO 14 NW 47

This large stony mound is situated amongst the small
cairns and banks to the S of the hut-circles no. 147·11. It
measures 10·7 m by 9·5 m and 0·6 m in height, and its
centre has been dug into. Unlike the other large cairns,
this mound lies on sloping ground, and it may be no more
than a large clearance heap.

·2   NO 1274 4882   NO 14 NW 46

This cairn stands on the summit of a low knoll within the
field-system around the hut-circles no. 147·10. It measures
9·8 m in diameter over a boulder kerb by up to 0·3 m in
height. A thin slab (0·75 m long) visible at the centre of
the cairn may form part of a cist.

·3   NO 1253 4892   NO 14 NW 48

This cairn overlooks the hut-circles no. 147·10 from the
WNW, some 240 m WNW of (·2). It has been reduced to
little more than a low stony platform with a slight lip
around its edge, and measures 11 m in diameter by 0·3 m
to 0·5 m in height.

·4   NO 1294 4837   NO 14 NW 45

This cairn lies within the group of small cairns that
extends WNW from the hut-circles no. 147·7. It measures
12·5 m in diameter over a boulder kerb but has been
reduced to a height of 0·4 m. Thirty-two boulders of the
kerb remain *in situ*; although they are not uniformly
graded in size, the largest (0·8 m in length by 0·3 m in
height) appear to be disposed around the SW arc.

·5   NO 1289 4837   NO 14 NW 45

This cairn, which lies 35 m to the W of (·4), measures
10·5 m by 9·6 m over a boulder kerb and stands to a

maximum height of 0·6m. Thirty-two boulders of its kerb also remain *in situ* and the largest appear to be on the SW.

·6   NO 1257 4769   NO 14 NW 15
Nothing remains of this cairn, which was removed before 1867. Its site lies on one of the ridges within the improved ground to the SE of Middleton Muir, where there are now a series of modern dumps of field-gathered stones.

32   Milton of Drumlochy, barrow
NO 1583 4662   NO 14 NE 25
Nothing remains of what was probably a barrow, which stood on a natural rise 300m WNW of Milton of Drumlochy. An urn and 'a number of human bones' were found when it was trenched in the early 19th century (Name Book, Perth, No. 11, p. 67).

33   Muir of Gormack, cairn
NO 1237 4736   NO 14 NW 63
149   This cairn is situated amongst the small cairns of the field-system around the hut-circles no. 149·5. Lying on the crest of the Muir of Gormack, it measures 8m in diameter by 0·5m in height. There is a large hollow in its centre, which resembles the court of a ring-cairn, but the inner area does not appear to be defined by facing stones.

34   Pictfield, cairns
NO 2152 4604   NO 24 NW 13
Nothing remains of the 'sepulchral cairns' that were removed from the gentle S-facing slope of the field immediately SW of Pictfield steading before 1865.
— *NSA*, 10 (Perthshire), 1188; Name Book, Perthshire, No. 9, p. 12.

35   Pitcarmick, cairns
NO 0614 5811   NO 05 NE 102
153   The remains of two probable burial cairns are situated at the E end of a low rise within the field-system surrounding the hut-circles no. 154·4. The W cairn measures about 9·5m in diameter and 0·7m in height over a boulder kerb; a large depression on the NW is probably the result of robbing. The E cairn (3·5m from the first) measures about 10m in diameter and 1m in height over a kerb of boulders. On the E the edge of the cairn is

overlain by field-clearance, and a shallow depression in the centre probably marks an earlier disturbance.

36   Pitcarmick Burn, cairns
Three cairns are situated in the valley of the Pitcarmick Burn to the E of Pitcarmick Loch. The first lies in a group *151* of small cairns (no. 151·4) on a terrace to the N of the burn, and the other two sit on prominent rounded knolls within a group of small cairns (no. 151·22) to the S of the burn.

·1   NO 0656 5664   NO 05 NE 26
Situated towards the SW corner of a terrace this cairn measures 9·3m in diameter and 1m in height. The edge of the cairn is defined by a kerb of boulders (up to 1·2m long and 0·55m high), and the centre has been disturbed.

·2   NO 0631 5637   NO 05 NE 25
This cairn measures 5·6m in diameter over a boulder kerb by 0·5m in height, and it contains a central cist measuring 1·1m by 0·8m and 0·3m in depth.

·3   NO 0637 5636   NO 05 NE 25
This cairn, which lies 50m to the E of (·2), measures 6·4m in diameter over a boulder kerb by up to 0·6m in height, and it contains a central cist measuring 1·1m by up to 0·55m and 0·4m in depth.

37   Ranageig, cairns
Two burial cairns are situated on either side of a track along the crest of an E-W ridge about 900m E of Ranageig farmhouse.

·1   NO 1129 4917   NO 14 NW 22
This robbed cairn sits on a low rise immediately N of the track and measures 11·8m in diameter over a kerb of boulders by 0·7m in height. At the centre there are the N and W slabs of a cist which originally measured at least 1·2m by 0·6m and 0·5m in depth.

·2   NO 1133 4913   NO 14 NW 13
About 40m SE of (·1) and clipped by the S side of the trackway, there is a second robbed cairn. It measures 18m in diameter by up to 1m in height, and at least fifteen probable kerbstones are visible. At its centre a cist (0·9m by 0·65m and 0·35m deep) has been exposed; its floor-

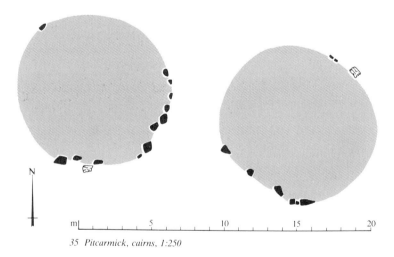

35 Pitcarmick, cairns, 1:250

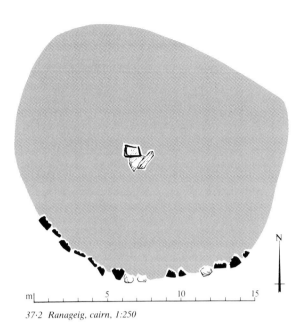

37·2 *Ranageig, cairn,* 1:250

slab is still *in situ*, and the broken capstone lies immediately to the S of the cist.

38 Sheriffmuir, cairn
NO 0924 4949   NO 04 NE 5

140
310·7A
Situated 20 m N of the modern track and 360 m NW of the farmstead of Sheriffmuir (no. 310·7) there is a cairn measuring 7·2 m by 8 m in diameter and 0·6 m in height. On the S there are five kerbstones (the largest measuring 1·5 m by 0·65 m in height), and the centre of the cairn has been disturbed.

39 Spittal of Glenshee, cairn
NO 1053 7045   NO 17 SW 33

278
A robbed cairn, measuring about 17 m in diameter by about 0·3 m in height, is situated on the edge of a terrace 430 m NW of Spittal of Glenshee Church.

40 Tulloch, cairns
·1 NO 0544 6382   NO 06 SE 9

121
This mound stands on the edge of a terrace 480 m NNW of Tulloch cottage. It measures about 27 m in diameter by at least 4 m in height, and it has a flat top 10·5 m in diameter. Although first identified as a motte (Talbot 1974, 56), the mound, which appears to be largely artificial, does not make the best defensive use of the ground, and it is more likely to be a burial cairn.

·2 NO 0531 6409   NO 06 SE 121

121
Situated on a terrace 240 m NNW of (·1) there is a cairn measuring 9 m in diameter and 0·6 m in height. The perimeter of the cairn has been trimmed by the plough but traces of a boulder kerb are visible around the cairn.

BURIALS AND CISTS

41 Achalader, burial
NO 12 45   NO 14 NW 5

A Food Vessel, which was found on the Achalader estate before 1862, is preserved in the Royal Museum of Scotland (EE 153).
— *Proc Soc Antiq Scot*, 96 (1962–3), 364–5, no. 14, fig. 1.

42 Ashintully, cist
NO 10 61   NO 16 SW 1

Some time before 1851 a cist was discovered in a peat moss at Ashintully.
— *Proc Soc Antiq Scot*, 1 (1851–4), 101.

43 Ashmore Home Farm, burial
NO *c*.150 528   NO 15 SE 15

What may have been the remains of a burial were found about 1896, when charred bones, cupmarked stones (now lost) and an artificially-shaped and polished stone point (PMAG 84) were found during drainage operations.

44 Blackhills, cist
NO 2010 4706   NO 24 NW 19

About 1830 a cist, which contained the remains of an inhumation, was discovered when a small mound was levelled; the site is now occupied by farm buildings.
— Name Book, Perthshire, No. 69, p. 24.

45 Blairgowrie, cist
NO 17 45   NO 14 NE 65

A cist, which was found near Blairgowrie before 1879, contained a Food Vessel (British Museum 79, 12–9, 1934).
— Kinnes and Longworth 1985, 153.

46 Bruceton, burials
NO 2905 5083   NO 25 SE 43

In 1908 a grave, aligned N and S, was found in a knoll about 160 m E of Bruceton farmhouse. Another had been found at an earlier date, but there are no further details available for either of the graves.
— Meikle 1925, 146–7.

47 Bruceton, cists and burials
·1 NO *c*.287 502   NO 25 SE 19

In 1924 a cist containing the remains of an adult male inhumation was discovered in a low knoll between 500 m and 600 m SSW of Bruceton steading. It was aligned E and W, and measured 0·96 m by 0·68 m and 0·45 m in depth; the capstone measured 1·32 m by 0·86 m and up to 0·18 m in thickness (Callander 1925, 26–8).

·2 NO 2900 5038   NO 25 SE 15

About 1840 'several coffins' (Stuart 1856, 34) containing 'human bones' (Name Book, Perthshire, No. 5, p. 55) were discovered in the vicinity of the Pictish Symbol Stone no. 191.

·3 NO 28 50   NO 25 SE 38

In the 18th century 'human bones' were found at Brucehaugh, an area of low-lying ground S of Bruceton steading and immediately N of the River Isla (Macfarlane 1906–8, 114).

48 Cochrage Moss, burial
NO 14 49   NO 14 NW 1

Early in the 18th century a 'Roman soldier in full armour' was reputed to have been found in a moss in the vicinity of Mause, probably Cochrage Moss (Name Book, Perth, No. 11, p. 49). There are no contemporary accounts of the discovery, and the author of the *New Statistical Account* entry for Blairgowrie, who had a 'Roman Spearhead' from Cochrage Moss (10, Perth, 914), makes no mention of the burial. It is therefore possible that the report is an embellished account of the discovery of the spearhead.

49   Craighall, cist
        NO c.179 480   NO 14 NE 61
About the turn of the century, a cist was discovered 'below Strageith wood', and on opening was found to contain a 'small quantity of peculiar dust'. Subsequently, the cist was removed and rebuilt in the garden of Craighall House (NO 1750 4817) where it was re-excavated in 1981.
— Unpub. MS, NMRS; *DES (1981)*, 49.

50   Cult, cist
        NO 2772 5030   NO 25 SE 25
About 1825 a cist containing human bones was found immediately E of Cult cottage.
— Name Book, Perthshire, No. 5, p. 51.

51   Easter Bleaton, cist
        NO c.139 586   NO 15 NW 6
In 1882 a possible cist, described as a 'cavity' containing 'black mould', was found in a mound below Easter Bleaton farmhouse; the capstone (now lost) bore up to twenty-one cupmarks (four of which were ringed or partially ringed) as well as grooving.
— MacMillan 1884, 123–5.

52   Glenshee, cist
                        NO 16 NW 91
A cist found 'at Glenshee' sometime before 1880 contained a whetstone (RMS, AL 16).
— NMAS 1892, 51.

53   Loyalbank, cist
        NO 2549 4913   NO 24 NE 19
About 1850 a cist containing an inhumation was discovered in a gravel ridge 470 m SE of Loyalbank steading.
— Name Book, Perthshire, No. 5, p. 81.

54   Mains of Mause, burial
        NO 1663 4889   NO 14 NE 1
In 1950 an inverted cinerary urn, which broke on excavation and is now lost, was found 970 m SSW of Mains of Mause farmhouse.
— Wainwright 1952, 123.

55   Meet Hillock, Blairgowrie, burials
        NO 1774 4501   NO 14 NE 16
About 1823 two cinerary urns containing bones were discovered when a large, probably natural, mound of gravel was removed from an area now occupied by housing; the pottery was discarded by the workmen.
— *NSA*, 10 (Perthshire), 914; Name Book, Perthshire, No. 11, p. 95.

56   Middle Mause, burials
        NO 1675 4883   NO 14 NE 20
Before 1865 two 'urns' were found in a gravel hillock 350 m N of Middle Mause.
— Name Book, Perthshire, No. 11, p. 52.

57   Morn Street, Alyth, cists
        NO 2490 4838   NO 24 NW 7
An unspecified number of cists containing 'portions of human remains' were found before 1865 at the E end of Morn Street, Alyth.
— Name Book, Perthshire, No. 5, p. 77.

58   Woodhill, cist
        NO c.09 54   NO 05 SE 1
A cist, aligned NW to SE and measuring 1·02 m by 0·64 m and 0·58 m in depth, was found in 1857. It contained a crouched inhumation accompanied by a Food Vessel (now lost); a photograph of the pottery and stereoscopic photographs of the cist are in the Department of Archaeology, the Royal Museum of Scotland.
— *Proc Soc Antiq Scot*, 3 (1857–60), 364.

STANDING STONES AND STONE CIRCLES

59   Balnabroich, stone circle
        NO 1021 5698   NO 15 NW 16
This stone circle is situated amongst the small cairns at Balnabroich (see no. 108) 140 m ESE of the Grey Cairn (no. 9·1). It measures about 7 m in diameter, and comprises nine stones, all of which have fallen or are semi-prostrate. The largest of the stones, which measures 1·2 m in length by 1 m in breadth, lies on the WSW. What

108A

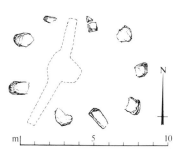

59 Balnabroich, stone circle, 1:250

is probably an outlying standing stone is situated 10 m to the NNW. An excavation trench dug in 1865 is still visible and some 'burned bones' were found on the S (Stuart 1868, 407).

60   Balnabroich, standing stones
        NO 0918 5658   NO 05 NE 2
Situated on a slight rise at the NE end of a plantation and 50 m NE of the steading at Balnabroich, there is pair of standing stones. The N stone is 1·35 m high, rises with straight sides to a flat top, and leans slightly to the S; the S stone is irregular in shape and leans so far to the S that

153

its original height cannot be accurately estimated.
— Coles 1908, 96–8, no. 1.

60 Balnabroich, standing stones, 1:250

61 Balnabroich, standing stone
    NO 0917 5675   NO 05 NE 79
153 This standing stone is situated in level ground in an arable
    field. It rises to a height of 1·7 m and measures up to 1·5 m
    by 1·5 m at the base.
    — Coles 1908, 98–9, no. 2.

62 The Borland Stone, standing stone
    NO 1535 6067   NO 16 SE 6
This stone, which stands on the summit of a prominent
knoll 300 m SE of Borland farmhouse, measures 0·7 m by
0·3 m at the base and 1 m in height.

63 Broad Moss, stone circles and standing stones
The remains of what have been described as two stone
circles and a pair of standing stones, which stood close to
Broad Moss, were destroyed in the early 1950s as a result
of agricultural improvements.

·1 NO 1980 4762   NO 14 NE 13
Two 'stone circles' were depicted on the 1st edition OS 6-
inch map and noted by Coles (1909, 107–9), but it is
possible that they were the poorly preserved remains of
two hut-circles or of natural origin.

·2 NO 1984 4771   NO 14 NE 14
Although these two large prostrate boulders have been
described as fallen standing stones, they were probably no
more than glacial erratics.
— OS 6-inch map, Perthshire, 1st ed. (1867), sheet 52.

64 Broughdearg, standing stones
    NO 1374 6704   NO 16 NW 1
This pair of standing stones is situated immediately SE of
the barn in the steading at Broughdearg. The stones (W

64 Broughdearg, standing stones, 1:250

and E) are 1·6 m and 1·5 m in height respectively, and
both have flat tops.

65 Burnside, standing stone
    NO 2554 4886   NO 24 NE 20
This standing stone is situated on a gentle S-facing slope
300 m NW of Burnside cottage. It rises with sloping sides
to a pointed top at a height of 2·1 m, and measures up to
2 m in breadth by 1 m in thickness.
— Coles 1909, 112, no. 15.

66 Craighall, stone circle
    NO 1842 4807   NO 14 NE 12
Situated on the edge of a terrace immediately E of the
public road and about 100 m NE of the former saw-mill at
Craighall, there are the remains of a four-poster stone
circle. All four stones have fallen, and the S stone has

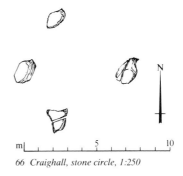

66 Craighall, stone circle, 1:250

broken into two pieces. Quantities of field-gathered
stones have recently been piled in and around the circle.
— Coles 1909, 104–6, no. 10.

67 Craighall, standing stone
    NO 1852 4826   NO 14 NE 11
This massive standing stone is situated on the forward
edge of a terrace 310 m NE of the former saw-mill at
Craighall. Aligned roughly N-S, it measures 2·6 m by
1·7 m at the base, and rises with sloping sides to a flat top
at a height of 2·5 m. On the E face of the stone, near its
base, there are at least nine plain cupmarks measuring up
to 80 mm by 30 mm.
— Coles 1909, 102–3, no. 9.

68 Croft House, standing stone
    NO 0565 6332   NO 06 SE 4
This standing stone is situated immediately E of the
public road (A924) and at the edge of a plantation. It is a   *121*
triangular-based pillar measuring 1 m by 1 m by 1 m at
ground level and rises to a height of 1·5 m.
— Coles 1908, 101–2, no. 5.

69 Drumderrach, standing stone
    NO 2800 5067   NO 25 SE 22
This standing stone, which may once have formed part of
a more complex monument comprising up to five stones
(Panton 1772–3), is situated on a terrace on the S side of
Drumderrach 440 m NNE of Shanzie farmhouse. Aligned
NNE-SSW, it measures 1·4 m by 0·4 m and stands to a
height of 1·4 m; a second boulder, which stands in the
dyke 12 m to the E, has been set up in recent times.
— OS 6-inch map, Perthshire, 1st ed. (1867), sheet 53; Coles 1909,
    110–12, no. 14; Meikle 1925, 102–3.

70 Drumend, standing stone
    NO 2018 4582   NO 24 NW 18
This standing stone is situated on a low knoll 300 m SE of
Drumend steading; it measures 0·9 m by 0·6 m and 1·6 m in
height.
— Coles 1909, 113, no. 16.

71 East Drimmie, standing stone
    NO 1822 4951   NO 14 NE 9
This standing stone, which was removed before 1864, was
situated 410 m SE of East Drimmie farmhouse.
— Name Book, Perthshire, No. 69, p. 15; Coles 1909, 101, no. 7.

C

75A Grave of Diarmid, stone circle from N

72 Faire na Paitig, stone circle
NO 0745 6609   NO 06 NE 22
A four-poster stone circle stands on the crest of a low
121 knoll at a height of 450 m OD on the SW flank of Faire na

72 Faire na Paitig, stone circle, 1:250

Paitig. The N and E stones are still upright, measuring
0·55 m and 0·4 m in height respectively, but the S and W
stones lean towards the NW (see also no. 93).

73 Gleann Beag, standing stones
NO 1212 7318   NO 17 SW 56
Situated on a terrace on the W side of Gleann Beag and
incorporated into a later farmstead (no. 265·8), there are
the remains of a probable prehistoric stone setting, which

comprises either a pair of standing stones or a four-poster
stone circle. Two narrow slabs, 3 m apart and aligned
ENE-WSW, remain erect; the E stone measures 0·8 m by
0·45 m and 1·1 m in height, and forms part of the NW
corner of a later building, whilst the W stone is free-
standing and measures 1 m by 0·3 m and 1 m in height.
Situated 3·9 m and 3·6 m to the N of the E and W stones
respectively, there are two recumbent boulders (1·6 m and
1·4 m in length), which now form the SE angle of a later
building, but originally they may have stood erect and
completed the setting.

74 Glenkilrie, stone circle
NO 1234 6246   NO 16 SW 73
This probable four-poster stone circle is situated in
moorland on the top of a low knoll overlooking the W
bank of the Allt a' Choire Liathaich. Only the two stones
on the SE of the setting survive; the NE stone is 0·6 m
high, and the SW slab, which now leans to the S,
originally rose to a height of about 0·8 m. The setting is
placed at the centre of a roughly circular platform, up to
0·3 m high, which is revetted by a boulder kerb. To the
NW of the stones there is a depression in the mound
which probably marks the site of an excavation.

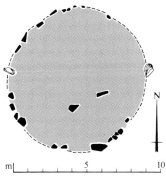

74 Glenkilrie, stone circle, 1:250

75   Grave of Diarmid, stone circle
NO 1171 7017   NO 17 SW 1

The remains of this four-poster stone circle, which commands extensive views down Glenshee, are situated on the top of a glacial moraine 550 m ESE of Old Spittal farmhouse. In 1894 the morainic mound on which the stones are placed was excavated to a depth of 6·71 m

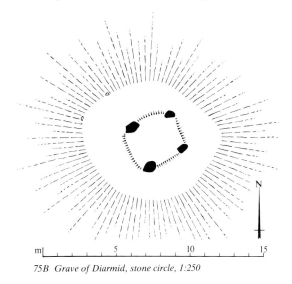

75B   Grave of Diarmid, stone circle, 1:250

(Smith 1895), and it is unclear if the stones of the circle now remain in their original positions. They lie at the corners of a trapezium, with the two largest on the W, and rise to heights of 0·75 m, 0·7 m, 0·3 m and 0·8 m from NW to SW respectively. No finds or structural features were recorded during the excavations, and a slight mound at the centre of the circle probably marks the site of the excavation.

76   Horse Stone, standing stone
NO 1853 5007   NO 15 SE 55

What may be a fallen standing stone lies in a forestry plantation about 50 m ENE of Woodside stone circle (no. 84); the stone measures 3 m by 1 m by 1 m.

77   Kynballoch, stone circle
NO 18 49   NO 14 NE 10

Nothing can now be seen of what may have been a stone circle, or a cairn, that once lay 'not many score yards to the west' (Coles 1909, 102) of the standing stone no. 71. In the 19th century an Enlarged Food Vessel Urn (RMS, EA 2) was discovered in the stone circle; it 'was full of bones, and was protected by stones built round it in a beehive form' (Allen 1881, 89).
— Cowie 1978, 132.

78   Muir of Gormack, stone circle
NO 1173 4751   NO 14 NW 29

This small four-poster stone circle is situated on the top of a low knoll at the W end of the hut-circles and field-system no. 149. The stones are set at the corners of a trapezium with the inner faces of the NW pair originally opposing those of the SE pair. Only the W and E stones

149

78   Muir of Gormack, stone circle, 1:250

are *in situ* (0·5 m and 0·4 m in height respectively); the other two stones have fallen but remain close to their original positions.

79   Parkneuk, stone circle
NO 1953 5145   NO 15 SE 5–6

This four-poster stone circle lies on gently sloping rough pasture on the SW shoulder of an unnamed hill. Three stones remain upright, while the fourth has fallen. The W and S stones are the largest, measuring 1·38 m and 1·2 m in height respectively, and the N stone is 0·9 m high.

Coles (1909, 97–9) refers to a second stone circle on the crest of the spur (NO 1948 5138), but there is no evidence to suggest that the boulders visible at this location formed part of a prehistoric monument.
— Coles 1909, 95–7, no. 3.

79B   Parkneuk, stone circle from SW

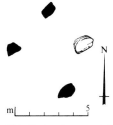

*79A   Parkneuk, stone circle,
1:250*

80   Shanzie, standing stone
    NO 2817 5009   NO 25 SE 21
Early in the 19th century this standing stone was pulled
down and buried.
— Name Book, Perthshire, No. 5, p. 56; Coles 1909, 110, no. 13.

81   Shealwalls, stone circle
    NO 2396 5149   NO 25 SW 26
A small four-poster stone circle is situated in an area of
rough pasture and gorse bushes at the E end of a low
ridge. It measures about 1·3 m square and the fallen stone

81 Shealwalls, stone circle, 1:250

on the SE was probably the tallest. The SW, NW and NE
stones are 0·1 m, 0·4 m and 0·3 m in height respectively,
while the fallen SE stone measures 1 m in length by 0·4 m
in breadth. The circle commands fine views to the NE
over the mouth of Glen Isla, where at least two other
comparable monuments have been recorded (*DES*
(1985), 60; *DES (1986)*, 42).

82   Spittal of Glenshee, standing stone
    NO 1087 7019   NO 17 SW 2
Situated on top of a knoll immediately W of Spittal of
278 Glenshee Church, there is a standing stone; aligned NNE-
SSW, it measures 0·72 m by 0·28 m at the base and 1·8 m in
height.
— Smith 1895, 98–9.

83   Woodend, standing stone
    NO 0600 6299   NO 06 SE 3
This standing stone is situated at the edge of a forestry
plantation on the NE side of the public road about 154 m
SE of Woodend cottage. It measures 1 m by 0·7 m at the
base and rises to a flat top at a height of 1·4 m.

84   Woodside, stone circle
    NO 1848 5005   NO 15 SE 9
The remains of this probable stone circle lie in a dip
between two low ridges, and the greater part of the site is
now within a forestry plantation. Seven prostrate stones

84 Woodside, stone circle, 1:250

are visible, but there is no evidence to support the
suggestion (Burl 1971) that they represent the remains of
a four-poster.
— Coles 1909, 99–102, no. 8.

CUP-AND-RING MARKINGS

(See also nos. 43, 51, 67, 155·3)

85   Arlick, cup-markings
    NO 0833 4668   NO 04 NE 36
A rock outcrop, bearing up to nine cupmarks (each about
50 mm by 10 mm) on its flat upper surface, is situated on
the SE flank of Arlick 490 m N of Cothole cottage.

86   Balvarran, cup-markings
    NO 0744 6218   NO 06 SE 6
This cupmarked boulder is situated at the apex of a small
triangular field 70 m NE of the keeper's cottage at
Balvarran. The boulder measures 2·9 m in length and
0·5 m in height, and four large cupmarks have been cut
into its upper surface. Three of them are set in a line and
measure about 250 mm in diameter by 140 mm in depth;
the fourth is about 200 mm in diameter by 100 mm in
depth.
— Dixon 1921, 95–7.

87   Barry Hill, cup-markings
    NO 262 503   NO 25 SE 23·1
A small cupmarked stone, which was found 'near the top
on the SW side of Barry Hill Fort' (no. 102), can no longer
be located.
— DES (1962), 1.

88   Carnashach Wood, cup-markings
    NO 1449 4819   NO 14 NW 43
This cupmarked boulder (1·9 m by 1·4 m and at least 0·4 m
thick), which lies in woodland 560 m NNE of Middleton
farmhouse, bears about eleven cupmarks (up to 60 mm in
diameter) on its upper surface.

89   Craigend, cup-markings
    NO 0778 4802   NO 04 NE 8
This group of markings could not be found on the date of
visit, and the OS description suggests that they were
unusually small for prehistoric cup-markings.

90   Craighead, cup-markings
    NO 1956 5498   NO 15 SE 23
On a rock outcrop, which lies immediately W of a forestry
track and on the line of the courtyard bank at the hut-   *122*
circle group no. 103·6, there are four badly weathered
plain cupmarks.

91   Craigton, cup-markings
    NO 1237 5863   NO 15 NW 30
On the NE flank of an unnamed hill 660 m SSW of Mains
of Soilzarie farmhouse, there is a rock outcrop on which
there are at least ten cupmarks. The outcrop measures 6 m
by 2·5 m and 0·9 m high, and the cupmarks (up to 70 mm
by 30 mm) are on the flattish upper surface at the SE end.

92   Drumderg, cup-and-ring markings
    ·1 NO 1852 5497   NO 15 SE 27
This heavily-weathered cup-and-ring marked boulder lies
150 m S of the hut-circles no. 122·9. The carvings are on   *122*

the SW face of the boulder and comprise: at least four cups surrounded by single rings; two cups surrounded by triple rings; an oval cup measuring 100 mm by 70 mm surrounded by four rings; and twenty-two plain cupmarks, the largest 60 mm in diameter.

·2   NO 1839 5451   NO 15 SE 14

On the SE flank of Drumderg, about 70 m S of the hut-circle no. 122·8, there is a rock outcrop bearing at least twenty-nine plain cupmarks (measuring up to 80 mm in diameter and 30 mm in depth) and eight double cupmarks (measuring up to 140 mm in length by 70 mm in width and 22 mm in depth).

122

93   Faire na Paitig, cup-markings
NO 0765 6612   NO 06 NE 15

There are traces of at least two cupmarks on the upper face of a large slab lying on the outer edge of a terrace on the SW flank of Faire na Paitig (see also no. 72).

121

94   Glenballoch, cup-markings
NO c. 186 480   NO 14 NE 82

What may have been a cupmarked slab was found about 1861. It was subsequently broken up and built into the steading at Glenballoch (now Kynballoch), but the fragments could not be located on the date of visit.
— *Proc Soc Antiq Scot*, 15 (1880–81), 89–91.

95   Laighwood, cup-markings
NO 07 45   NO 04 NE 4

A cupmarked boulder found before 1882 (Allen 1882, 124) cannot now be located.

96   Loch Beannie, cup-markings
NO 1686 6914   NO 16 NE 7

A large granite boulder bearing six cupmarks (up to 90 mm in diameter and 25 mm in depth) and a pear-shaped hollow on its flat, upper surface, is situated on steep, rocky ground 670 m NE of Loch Beannie.

97   Loch Benachally, cup-and-ring markings
·1   NO 0751 5036   NO 05 SE 10

Situated on the W face of a low ridge 160 m E of Loch Benachally, there is a triangular-shaped boulder, the upper face of which is flush with the turf. It bears two cups with single rings (120 mm and 190 mm in diameter overall respectively) and fourteen plain cups (up to 100 mm by 20 mm).

140

·2   NO 0764 5035   NO 05 SE 9

A rock outcrop, bearing up to fourteen cupmarks (30 mm to 60 mm in diameter and 14 mm deep) on its sloping S face, is situated on the summit of a ridge 290 m E of Loch Benachally.

140

98   Mains of Creuchies, cup-and-ring markings
·1   NO 1965 5114   NO 15 SE 28

Situated in the SE corner of an arable field, there is a boulder (3 m by 3 m and 1·2 m high) which bears on its sloping W face at least fifteen weathered cupmarks, two cups with single rings, and one cup with a possible ring; the cups average 50 mm in diameter by 15 mm in depth.

·2   NO 1975 5156   NO 15 SE 56

On the upper face of a granite boulder (1·3 m by 1·2 m by 0·6 m), which lies in moorland about 430 m NNE of (·1),

there is a single plain cupmark measuring 40 mm in diameter by 15 mm in depth.

99   Muir of Gormack, cup-and-ring markings
·1   NO 1253 4721   NO 14 NW 28

Situated on the S fringe of the settlement and field-system no. 149·4, there is a cup-and-ring marked boulder (1·6 m by 1·4 m by 0·5 m). On its upper surface there are the worn remains of three cups with single rings, one cup and double rings, and five plain cupmarks. The largest of the cups measures 50 mm by 15 mm.

149

·2   NO 1285 4728   NO 14 NW 66

A small boulder, bearing at least one cupmark, lies on the S side of a trackway hollow about 40 m E of the fence that divides the Muir of Gormack into two. Seven other shallow depressions visible on the upper surface of the stone may be heavily weathered cupmarks.

149

100   Pitcarmick Burn, cup-markings
NO 0617 5621   NO 05 NE 24

A large kite-shaped boulder, bearing up to forty cupmarks (up to 90 mm by 15 mm) on its upper surface, is situated on the crest of a ridge at the N end of the settlement and field-system no. 151·20 and 780 m E of Pitcarmick Loch.

151

101   Tulloch, cup-markings
NO 0532 6344   NO 06 SE 92

A large boulder (2·75 m by 0·9 m, and 0·6 m thick), which is situated amongst field-cleared stones some 280 m WNW of Tulloch cottage, bears at least forty cupmarks (up to 70 mm in diameter) on its upper surface. Most are circular, others are oval, and one group has been arranged to form a roughly cruciform pattern.

FORT

102   Barry Hill, fort
NO 262 503   NO 25 SE 23

This fort, which crowns the summit of Barry Hill, overlooks the mouth of Glen Isla and commands an extensive view across Strathmore. Like many of the other forts that fringe Strathmore, Barry Hill is impressive for the sheer scale of the defences. These defences are both complex and multi-period, and, although it is not possible to unravel the full sequence of their construction without excavation, two principal periods can be identified.

The later structural period is probably represented by the massive bank of rubble that forms the innermost defence (A) and the substantial outwork (C) that blocks the S and E approaches. The inner wall (A), presumably the partly vitrified remains of a timber-laced wall, encloses an area measuring 80 m by 25 m and is more than 10 m in thickness, rising 2 m to 2·5 m above the level of the interior. Externally the rubble forms a scree which, on the S, rises as much as 6·8 m from the bottom of an external ditch (B). Relatively small fragments of vitrified stone can be found amongst the scree, but the only earthfast vitrification now visible lies on the ESE beside an entrance causeway through the ditch (D). The floor of the ditch appears to have been dug in segments, and was probably recut along the line of an earlier ditch. The outwork (C) is an earthen rampart built on the same massive scale as the inner wall; for much of its course it is up to 15 m in thickness and it varies from 3·5 m in height on the S to 1·2 m on the E. Like the ditch it partly

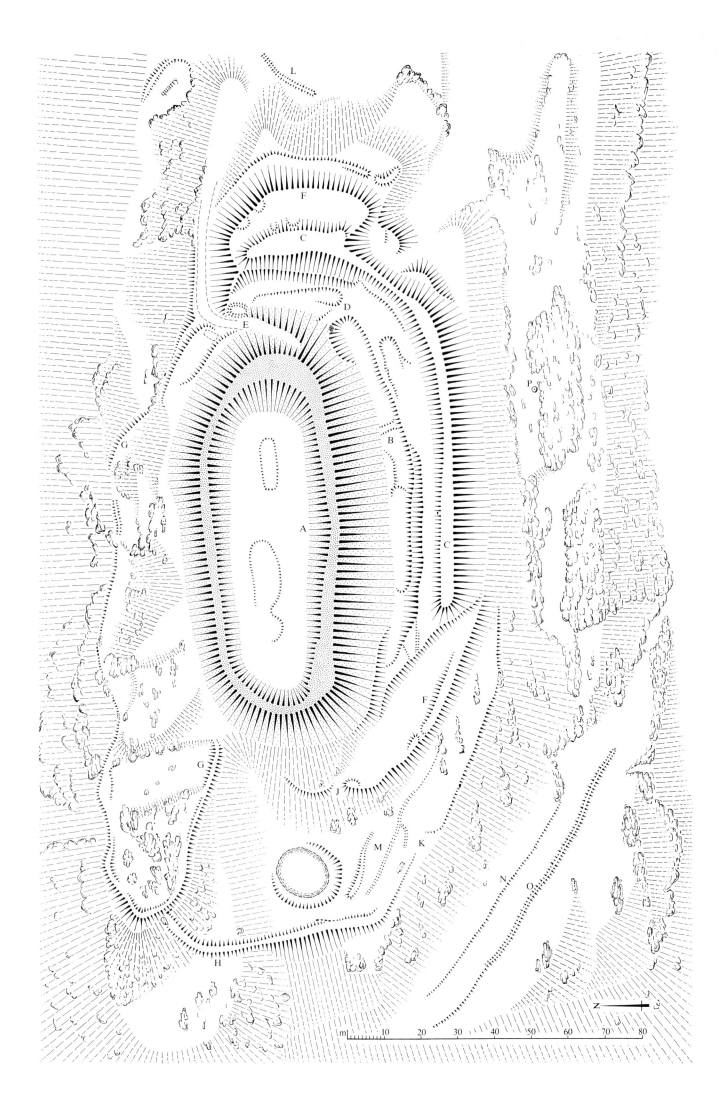

quarry

L

F

C

D

E

G

P

B

A

C

G

F

J

M

K

N

O

H

z

m| 10 20 30 40 50 60 70 80

coincides with an earlier line of defence and masks rampart F on the S side of the fort. On the SE, opposite the causeway across ditch B, the outwork blocks an entrance through an earlier rampart (F); at this point, however, the outwork is of considerably reduced proportions. In its original form it is likely that the outwork was designed to strengthen the defences of this entrance and that the blocking material was inserted at a later date, probably when the entrance (E) on the NE was constructed. The trackway leading from the latter turns through the outer defences and gently rises towards the top of the ruined inner wall.

The two outer ramparts (G and H) on the N and W sides of the hill, together with the rampart beneath the outwork (F), probably belong to an earlier defensive scheme, whose nucleus was a fort hidden beneath the massive inner wall (A). For the most part, rampart F forms little more than a scarp (on the E accompanied by an external ditch with a counterscarp bank), and its relationship to rampart G is not known. The latter can be traced intermittently along the N side of the fort and on the NW, where it encloses a rocky spur. Rampart H buts on to rampart G to form an annexe enclosing a pond (at least in part artificial), at the W end of the fort. At the junction of G and H two outer-facing stones of rampart G survive *in situ*. Apart from the blocked entrance through the earlier defences on the SE, there is a second entrance (J) through rampart F on the W, and possibly a third (K) leading into the annexe from the SW.

No contemporary domestic structures can be identified within the fort or the annexe. A shallow subrectangular depression at the E end of the interior may mark the position of a building of some later period, but the remaining structures within the interior (not shown on plan) have been constructed in recent years and none of them appears on Christison's (1900, 93–6) plan of the fort. A small hut of relatively recent date has been constructed on the E side of the entrance on the NE; a depression on the opposite side of the entrance is a possible excavation trench. Four banks have been recorded around the fort (L—O); one is probably agricultural (L), and the rest are unlikely to be defensive. In later times the conglomerate of the hill has been quarried for millstones, a discarded example of which (P) lies amongst the outcrops below the outwork on the S. For a cupmarked stone found at the fort and a nearby enclosure see nos. 87 and 185.
— *Stat. Acct.*, 1 (1791), 508–9; 6 (1793), 405–6; Mackenzie 1831; RCAHMS Survey of Marginal Lands.

OPEN SETTLEMENT

103 Alyth Burn, hut-circles, field-systems and small cairns

To the N of Tullymurdoch farmsteading there are seven groups of hut-circles in the valley of the Alyth Burn; three lie to the W of the burn (·1–·3) and the remainder to the E, and they are here described from S to N.

·1 NO 201 527 NO 25 SW 5
The remains of three hut-circles are situated at the W end of a low ridge about 380 m NE of Tullymurdoch farmhouse. The W hut-circle (NO 2014 5271) is double-walled and measures about 8·5 m in diameter internally and 16·3 m by 14·7 m overall; both walls are poorly preserved, and the entrance is situated on the S. The S half (including the entrance) of a probable second hut-circle lies immediately to the SE; it measures about 8 m in diameter. The third hut-circle (NO 2017 5270) is situated

to the SE of the second and measures 20·5 m in diameter over a low wall. The large diameter of the house suggests that it may originally have been double-walled, but no trace of an inner wall is visible. The hut-circles are surrounded by a group of small cairns.

·2 NO 1984 5287 NO 15 SE 22
The remains of a well-preserved hut-circle are situated on a terrace about 370 m N of Tullymurdoch farmhouse. It measures 9·8 m in diameter within the turf-covered wall (up to 3 m thick and 0·5 m high) and the entrance (2·1 m wide) is on the SE. About 30 m to the NW there may be the remains of a second house; on the W it has been destroyed by a sunken trackway but on the S and SE it survives as a turf-covered bank measuring up to 3 m in thickness.

·3 NO 199 531 NO 15 SE 21
A group of thirteen hut-circles is situated on either side of the track from Tullymurdoch to Craighead, and lies partly in improved pasture and partly in a forestry plantation. There are six large hut-circles (up to 8·5 m in internal diameter), four small hut-circles (one of which is cut by a later hut-circle and has an enclosure attached, and another overlies an earlier hut-circle), a double-walled house, two probable multi-period hut-circles set on a mound which may be the remains of an earlier hut-circle, and a few stretches of field-bank and at least fifteen small cairns.

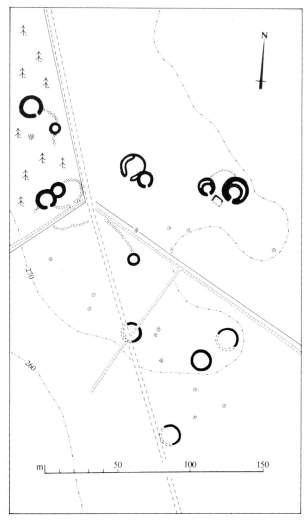

103·3 Alyth Burn, hut-circles, 1:2500

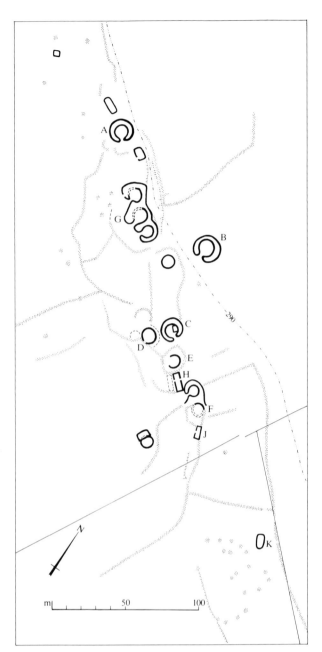

103·4 Alyth Burn, hut-circles and field-system, 1:2500

·4   NO 201 534   NO 25 SW 6

The remains of at least twelve hut-circles, set amidst a field-system, are disposed along the edge of a terrace about 950 m NNE of Tullymurdoch farmhouse (Harris 1985, 210). Overlying the prehistoric remains there are a number of later buildings (one of Pitcarmick type, K on plan) and enclosures, which render interpretation of some of the hut-circles particularly difficult. Nevertheless, at least three of the hut-circles (A-C), and possibly as many as five (D-E), are double walled; their internal diameters range from 7 m to 10 m, and A has an almost complete ring of inner facing-stones around its inner wall. Another two hut-circles belong to a severely robbed enclosed pair (F), while three others are enclosed by a single outer wall (G); the latter range from 6 m to 9·3 m in internal diameter and the smallest has an impressive ring of inner facing-stones. Part of the surrounding field-system has been removed by recent improvements, but a number of banks still survive. Some are probably contemporary with the hut-circles but others are of later date; the small enclosures attached to the NW ends of buildings (H and J), for instance, overlie hut-circles, while another bank blocks the entrance to hut-circle D and overlies a possible platform immediately to the SW.

·5   NO 193 544   NO 15 SE 26

The remains of three hut-circles are situated on the S flank of the Hill of Craighead about 400 m NW of Craighead steading. They lie within a field-system of small cairns and banks which, on the N and E, have been overlain by later cultivation remains.

The W hut-circle (NO 1930 5444) measures 6·5 m in diameter within a bank up to 2·1 m thick and 0·4 m high, and the entrance is on the SSW. The interior has been levelled into the slope, and on the SW and SE stony banks spring from the hut-circle wall. The SE extends to the E and abuts the SW side of a double-walled house (NO 1933 5445), which measures 7·3 m in diameter internally by 14·5 m overall. The interior has been levelled into the slope, and on the N the inner and outer walls are represented by slight scarps. The outwardly-splayed entrance is on the S, and from the E a bank runs downhill to the SE and abuts the SW side of another double-walled house (NO 1938 5440), which has been severely robbed and is marked only by inner and outer robber trenches measuring 9·5 m and 17·2 m in diameter respectively. About 10 m to the WSW there are the wasted remains of what may be a hut-platform, which measures about 8·5 m in diameter.

103·6A Alyth Burn, hut-circles (south tier), 1:500

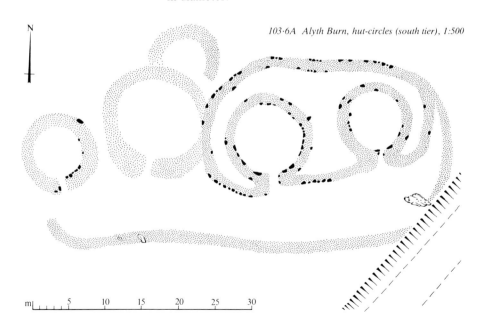

103·6B Alyth Burn, hut-circles, aerial view from SW

·6   NO 195 549   NO 15 SE 23
This group of hut-circles lies in a clearing in a recent forestry plantation on the E flank of the Hill of Craighead. The houses are arranged in two tiers, and they are cut by a forestry road which has clipped the enclosure around the S tier and removed half of one of the houses in the N tier.

The S tier comprises five hut-circles (a twin double-walled pair, and three single-walled houses) around the S side of which there is a embanked courtyard. The double-walled houses cut the wall of the adjacent single-walled house, which in turn lies on top of the smaller hut-circle on the N. Immediately W of the track there is a cupmarked boulder (no. 90) which projects from beneath the courtyard bank.

The N tier is bisected by the forest track and comprises: to the E of the track, a double-walled house; to the W, a large hut-circle or enclosure, and a smaller hut-circle which was partially destroyed by the construction of the track. Excavation of the remaining half of the latter hut-circle revealed a single post-hole and

a pit in the interior, as well as traces of ard cultivation; the finds included a few fragments of pottery (Rideout, forthcoming).

Three stretches of field-bank radiate from the houses; one small cairn survives to the E of the N tier, while another has been destroyed in the afforested area to the S of the S tier. There are four huts, probably shielings, close to the N houses.

·7   NO 185 562   NO 15 NE 17
In a forestry clearing there are four hut-circles, arranged in two pairs. The NW pair comprises a double-walled house (8 m in internal diameter by 19 m overall with an entrance on the S) and what is probably a multiperiod single-walled house. The latter measures 8 m in diameter within a wall 2·5 m thick on the SW; on the N there is a gully in the core of the wall, which probably indicates that the wall is of more than one period of construction. The entrance is on the S. Immediately to the SW of the entrance there is a hut which measures 3 m in internal diameter.

103·7

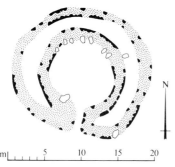

103·7 Alyth Burn, hut-circle, 1:500

Between the two houses there are the remains of what may be two rectilinear buildings measuring 15·2 m and 11·7 m in length respectively.

The second pair lies 120 m to the SE; the larger house is double walled (7·8 m internal diameter by 18 m overall, with an entrance on the SSE), and the smaller is single walled (6·5 m in internal diameter, with an entrance on the SSE). Around the hut-circles there are fragments of a field-system comprising three banks: one extends from the larger of the SE houses around the rear of a knoll to the NW; the second flanks the front of the NW pair of houses; and the third drops from the NW end of the second towards the Thief's Burn.

104 Alyth Golf Course, hut-circle
NO 2677 4850   NO 24 NE 57

The remains of a double-walled hut-circle are situated in a clump of pine trees on the E side of Alyth Golf Course. It measures 9 m internally by up to 20·5 m overall, and it may be one of the hut-circles noted by Meikle (1933, 6). See also no. 5.

105 Ashintully, hut-circles, field-systems and small cairns

These hut-circles and groups of small cairns are, for the most part, situated in the glen that forms the N part of the Ashintully estate. Although it is now approached by a track through a saddle in the hills to the SW, the glen is drained by the headwaters of the Ennoch Burn, which flows SE through the neighbouring estate of Glenkilrie, where numerous other hut-circles have also been recorded (nos. 127–8). To the NW of the march dyke the glen opens out, and the hut-circles are scattered amongst the surrounding hills. The first to be described, however, are situated in the saddle to the NW of the track leading into the glen from Ashintully.

·1   NO 102 622   NO 16 SW 11

Five hut-circles are situated towards the leading edge of a broad terrace above the fermtoun (no. 223·12) that lies immediately beyond the improved fields due N of Ashintully Castle. Of the five, two belong to an enclosed pair, and another is double-walled. The enclosed pair lie at the edge of the terrace, and measure 8·8 m and 9·4 m in internal diameter respectively; within the larger (on the E) there is a possible ring-ditch. The remainder of the hut-circles lie to the N and NW; the double-walled example measures 7 m in internal diameter (16 m overall) and the two single-walled houses 6 m and 12 m respectively. A burnt mound (no. 163) lies to the E, on the slope below the hut-circles.

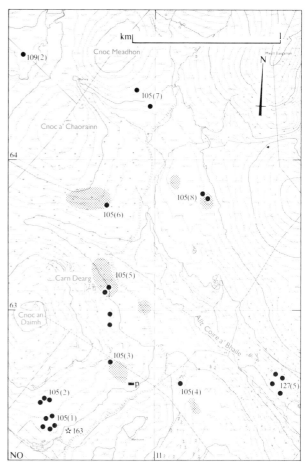

105 Ashintully, 1:25 000

·2   NO 1023 6238   NO 16 SW 62

At the rear of the terrace to the NW of (1) there are a double-walled hut-circle and an enclosure. The double-walled hut-circle measures 8·3 m in internal diameter by 15·8 m overall, and there is a well-defined ring-ditch within its interior. The enclosure (23·3 m by 12 m) is situated on a low rise immediately to the ENE. It may be the remains of an enclosed pair of hut-circles, but there are no traces of any internal walls within the enclosure, and any buildings must have been built entirely of timber.

·3   NO 1070 6265   NO 16 SW 16

Lying at the foot of the SE flank of Cnoc an Daimh 20 m SE of a stone dyke, there is a house platform measuring about 10·6 m in diameter. At least four small cairns are visible on the terrace to the SE, a fifth lies adjacent to the dyke to the NE, and four more can be seen on a terrace lower down the slope. The latter, which are 50 m WNW of a Pitcarmick-type building (no. 222), are enclosed by field-banks of relatively recent date and the cairns may also be of recent date.

·4   NO 1117 6251   NO 16 SW 12–13

What are probably the remains of a hut-circle are situated on a terrace overlooking Coire a' Bhaile. On a higher terrace to the S there are about eight small cairns; one, which is set in a prominent position at the leading edge of the terrace, is significantly larger than the rest and measures 5·8 m in diameter by 0·5 m in height.

·5   NO 106 630   NO 16 SW 18–20

Two hut-circles, two platforms and a scatter of small cairns are visible in the vicinity of the ruins of Carn

Dearg. One of the hut-circles lies on sloping ground 80 m E of the ruins, and one of the platforms is set at the foot of a knoll 25 m to the SSW; the hut-circle measures 10·4 m in internal diameter, and the platform 9·2 m. Most of the small cairns lie to the N of this hut-circle, but there is a group of at least four adjacent to a track about 250 m to the SE. The second hut-circle, which measures 9·4 m by 8·8 m internally, is situated on the summit of a prominent hillock 200 m SSE of Carn Dearg, and the second platform (10 m in diameter) lies at the bottom of a gully a further 60 m to the S.

·6   NO 1067 6368   NO 16 SW 27
This hut-circle, which is situated on the leading edge of a terrace on the SE flank of Cnoc a' Chaorainn, has an internal diameter of about 8 m. A field-bank cuts across the terrace to the N of the hut-circle, and about twenty small cairns are scattered along the hillside to the W. Amongst them there are faint traces of cultivation rigs and at least two rectangular buildings (see no. 277·29).

·7   NO 108 643   NO 16 SW 28
There are two hut-circles on the SE flank of Cnoc Meadhon. The lower lies on a slight rise 160 m N of the lunch-hut in the bottom of the valley; it is one of the best preserved of the hut-circles incorporating an internal ring-ditch that has been recorded in the course of the survey. Slightly oval on plan, it measures 9·9 m by 8·6 m within a wall about 1·6 m in thickness by 0·4 m in height. Despite its mantle of deep heather, several facing-stones can be identified, including two tall inner-stones flanking the entrance on the SE. The ring-ditch is set immediately within the wall and is about 2·4 m in breadth.

The second hut-circle is on a terrace higher up the slope some 150 m to the NW; it measures 10·8 m in internal diameter, and it is notable for its almost complete ring of large inner facing-stones (up to 1·6 m by 0·6 m). Outside the wall on the uphill side of the hut-circle, there is a concentric scarp about 0·3 m high. A field-bank runs across the slope to the SW of the upper hut-circle, and at least three rectangular huts (no. 277·26) are visible on the hillside, as well as traces of a long building (no. 277·27) immediately SE of the lower hut-circle.

·8   NO 113 637   NO 16 SW 25–6
Two hut-circles (6·8 m and 9·8 m in internal diameter respectively) are situated on a terrace at the foot of the W flank of Lamh Dhearg. About eight small cairns are scattered around the hut-circles, and a further eight are visible on a knoll in the bottom of the glen 150 m to the WNW.

106   Baden Burn, hut-circles and small cairns
The valley of the Baden Burn extends northwards for a distance of about 5 km from its junction with the Lornty Burn at Ranageig before reaching its watershed above Loch Charles. At the mouth of the valley there are the extensive remains of medieval or later farmsteads and field-systems, which spread as far as the ruins of Roughsheal and Buckinhill on the E and W sides of the valley respectively (see no. 310·10, ·13). Beyond these two farmsteads there are a series of hut-circles and groups of small cairns, situated at heights of between 320 m and 400 m OD on the knolls, low ridges and terraces that form the floor and W side of the valley. The hut-circles and small cairns in the valley are described from S to N.

·1   NO 0899 5112   NO 05 SE 5
This hut-circle measures 8·9 m in internal diameter, and its entrance is on the SSW. Around the hut-circle, but particularly on a lower terrace to the W, there is a scatter of small cairns.

·2   NO 0845 5099   NO 05 SE 56
A group of five small cairns lies in an area of rig-and-furrow cultivation that extends across a terrace on the W side of the Baden Burn some 300 m SE of Buckinhill.

·3   NO 080 510   NO 05 SE 6
A group of at least seven hut-circles, together with field-banks and small cairns, extends across three parallel ridges that lie to the S and W of Buckinhill. Three of the hut-circles (6 m, 8 m and 6·7 m in internal diameter respectively) are set along the middle ridge, and there are traces of a possible fourth immediately to the E; all are poorly preserved, but the more easterly houses appear to have been linked by low banks. On the ridge below them there is a double-walled hut-circle, and a second lies immediately E of the enclosures to the S of Buckinhill. They measure 7 m and 7·3 m respectively internally by 16·4 m and 15 m overall, but the latter has been severely robbed. On the S side of the lowest ridge there is a pair of hut-circles set side by side. The more westerly is the larger, measuring about 9·7 m in internal diameter; on the E its bank develops two crests, with a thickness of 4 m overall, suggesting at least two periods of construction. The E hut-circle measures 9 m in diameter internally. Several field-banks are visible around the hut-circles on the lowest ridge, and there is a scatter of small cairns across the uppermost ridge. The banks, however, may be of more recent date, given the proximity of the later farmstead.

·4   NO 0813 5155   NO 05 SE 26
A group of four small cairns is situated on the SE flank of a knoll 400 m N of Buckinhill.

·5   NO 084 520   NO 05 SE 57
A group of about twenty small cairns lies on the SW flank of the southernmost of the knolls on the E side of the Baden Burn.

·6   NO 0834 5229   NO 05 SE 44
Four small cairns lie on a W-facing slope about 300 m NW of (·5). To the N there are two burial cairns (no. 6) and a group of shieling-huts (no. 225·1–·2).

·7   NO 0742 5336, 0738 5339   NO 05 SE 32
These two hut-circles are situated at the head of the valley and lie on a low ridge between two burns. They measure 8·2 m and 7·1 m in diameter respectively within low stony walls up to 0·2 m in height.

·8   NO 0756 5354   NO 05 SE 47
About 250 m to the NE of (·7) a double-walled hut-circle is visible on the W end of a rocky ridge which rises abruptly from the foot of the SE flank of Meall Dubh. It measures 8 m in diameter internally and 14·9 m by 13·3 m overall. In addition to a deeply splayed entrance on the SE, there is what appears to be a deliberate gap in the outer wall-face on the E; it is flanked by upright boulders and measures about 2·2 m in width.

·9   NO 078 536   NO 05 SE 54
There is a group of five hut-circles on a rocky ridge which rises from the foot of Meall Dubh to the E of (·8). Four of them are double-walled, ranging from 6·9 m to 8·3 m in diameter internally and from 14·2 m to 15·9 m overall. The fifth hut-circle, which lies on the N side of the group, measures about 6·6 m in internal diameter, and there is an enclosure (13 m by 5·5 m internally) immediately to the E.

108A Balnabroich, hut-circles and field-system, and Pitcarmick-type buildings, 1:5000

A thin scatter of small cairns extends across the SE flank of the ridge below the hut-circles. There is also a series of shieling-huts in the vicinity (no. 225·5).

·10 NO 0785 5383   NO 05 SE 46
The northernmost of the hut-circles in the valley lies on the SE flank of Meall Dubh and overlooks (·9) from the N. Its interior, which has been levelled into the slope on the NW, measures 8 m in diameter. Around the hut-circle there is a group of small cairns, most of which are enclosed by a stony bank.

107   Ballinloan, hut-circles, small cairns and enclosure
·1 NO 0974 5913   NO 05 NE 143
A row of three hut-circles, measuring 8 m to 10·5 m in internal diameter, is situated on the SE corner of a pasture field about 270 m SE of Ballinloan cottage. All have been levelled into the NW-facing slope, and an arc of a ring-ditch is visible in the S half of the central house.

·2 NO 0998 5914   NO 05 NE 142
A line of three hut-circles is situated on a NW-facing slope about 480 m ESE of Ballinloan cottage. The houses, up to 30 m apart, measure from 6·5 m to 8 m in internal diameter, and all three have been levelled into the slope; the two easterly houses are linked by a stony bank.

·3 NO 1006 5899   NO 15 NW 67
Situated on the W face of an area of heather moorland about 160 m SSE of (·2), there are the remains of a probable hut-circle. It measures about 9 m in diameter internally, and the entrance is on the SSW.

·4 NO 103 589   NO 15 NW 66
The remains of two hut-circles are situated on the highest point of the moorland about 260 m E of (·3). The SW house (NO 1031 5893) measures about 8·5 m in diameter within a heather-covered bank (2 m thick) and has an entrance on the S. The NE house (NO 1035 5898) measures 7·5 m in diameter within a wall (1·8 m thick), and what may be an entrance gap is situated on the ESE.

·5 NO 1017 5844   NO 15 NW 12
About ten small cairns are scattered along the SW flank of a low ridge about 200 m N of the march dyke between Mains of Dounie and Balnabroich and 500 m S of (·4). At the NW end of the scatter of cairns there is a roughly circular enclosure measuring 16·5 m in maximum diameter within a low bank 2·5 m in thickness; a large upright slab 0·6 m high flanks the W side of the entrance, which is on the S. Although not a hut-circle in itself, the enclosure is likely to be of prehistoric date, perhaps marking the position of a timber house.

108   Balnabroich, hut-circles, field-systems and small cairns
NO 098 576 to 108 568   NO 15 NW 14
This remarkable group of remains extends across about 1 sq km of rolling moorland and rough pasture. Most of the lower slopes on the E side of Strathardle have been improved, but to the N of Stylemouth the ground is poorly drained and clothed in scrub. The spread of settlement remains occupies the drier ground beyond the woodland, which rises in a series of broad terraces and low ridges to a height of 330 m OD. In addition to the hut-circles, numerous other structures occur amongst the prehistoric settlement remains: these include two ring-cairns (A, see no. 1); a stone circle with an outlying standing stone (B, see no. 59); three burial cairns (C, see no. 9); at least six Pitcarmick-type buildings (D, see

no. 227); two farmsteads (E, see no. 250·1–·2); and a series of rectangular buildings (not lettered).

At least twenty hut-circles have been recorded, but only sixteen of them are still visible. They range from 9 m to 13 m in internal diameter, and in some cases their interiors have been levelled into the slope. One of the hut-circles (F) is an exceptionally large double-walled example (10 m in internal diameter), and a possible saddle quern lies at its centre. Two of the others (G) are probably of multi-period construction; the E hut-circle partially overlies the W hut-circle which itself is of at least two periods. Apart from the probable threefold sequence

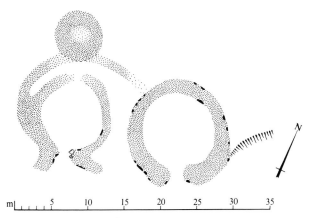

108B   Balnabroich, hut-circles (G), 1:500

of hut-circle construction, the earlier wall of the W hut-circle appears to be overlain by a small cairn with its centre dug out. In 1865 Stuart (1868) found a probable burial in a pit beneath this cairn, and the cairn material apparently overlying the hut-circle wall may in fact be upcast from his excavation.

Two hut-circles (H), which lie at the NW extremity of the scatter of cairns, were probably also built successively, while one of the others (J), remarkable for the two massive boulders that flank its entrance, is also of multi-period construction. Apart from digging into many of the cairns Stuart (1868, 406–8) also trenched at least six of the hut-circles, but it is not possible to match his descriptions to the present plan. The only artefact recovered was a 'fragment of bronze like the pin of a brooch'.

The chronology of the site is far from clear, but the presence of the ring-cairns, the stone-circle and the large burial-cairns, suggests that the area was being exploited as early as the Late Neolithic or Early Bronze Age. The hut-circles are likely to be of later date, but probably reflect a long period of use; although only one is double walled, Stuart refers to what may have been an enclosed pair (1868, 406), now lost beneath the plantation. At least two subsequent periods of occupation are represented by the Pitcarmick-type buildings and the two farmsteads, the latter abandoned by the middle of the 19th century. The traces of cultivation rigs visible between the cairns on the lower slopes are probably of late 18th- or early 19th-century date, but it is not possible to relate the cairns and field-banks to any one phase of occupation. Some of the cairns, such as K (7 m in diameter and 0·7 m in height), which is false-crested on the low ridge forming the NE side of the site, may be burial cairns. The majority, however, are probably the result of clearance for agriculture. As such, they are undatable and likely to arise from any prolonged cultivation of a hillside, but it is probable that their use at least spans the chronological range of the other structures found amongst them. In this instance, many, if not most, probably belong to the Late Neolithic or Early Bronze Age; whether any of the banks

are of comparable antiquity is unknown.
— *Stat. Acct.*, 15 (1795), 516–17; Maclagan 1875, 78–80; Harris 1985, 212.

109   Balvarran, Allt a' Bhuirich, hut-circles
These two hut-circles are situated in the hills at the NE end of the Balvarran estate.

·1   NO 0950 6433   NO 06 SE 49
This hut-circle lies on a terrace overlooking the track from Balvarran about 80 m NW of the point where the Allt a' Bhuirich debouches from a steep-sided gully into the broad valley of the Allt Menach. It measures about 11·2 m in internal diameter but has been severely robbed and is partly obscured by an old field-bank.

·2   NO 1009 6470   NO 16 SW 89
This hut-circle is set on the crest of a low rise on the W side of the Allt a' Bhuirich; it measures about 6·5 m in internal diameter and its entrance is probably on the SSW. What is either a shieling-hut or a small ancillary structure, measuring 2·8 m across its interior, lies immediately to the SE.

110   Balvarran/Ashintully, Cnoc an Daimh, hut-circles, platform and small cairns
Two hut-circles, a platform, and two groups of small cairns are situated on the W flank of Cnoc an Daimh.

·1   NO 095 629   NO 06 SE 66
One of the hut-circles and a circular platform lie below the march dyke between Balvarran and Ashintully. The

wall of the hut-circle only survives on the SE, and its interior (15·5 m by 13·5 m) has been levelled into the slope on the E. Unlike simple platforms, the back scarp descends in two steps, with a total height of 1 m. The platform lies 10 m to the SE and measures about 8·5 m in diameter.

·2   NO 0959 6297   NO 06 SE 67
What may be a hut-circle, with an internal diameter of 6·2 m, is situated on a terrace above the march dyke some 80 m E of (·1). At least three small cairns are scattered along the terrace to the S.

·3   NO 098 628   NO 06 SE 68
A group of at least nine small cairns lies 250 m SE of (·2) on a broad terrace overlooking the shelter belt on the SW flank of the hill.

111   Black Briggs, hut-circles
There are at least two hut-circles close to the public road on the crest of a ridge to the N of Black Briggs; another two hut-circles lie on a terrace 500 m to the SE.

·1   NO 1853 5168   NO 15 SE 4
This double-walled hut-circle is situated immediately S of the public road, the S embankment of which partially overlies the hut-circle wall. It measures 10 m in diameter within a wall up to 2 m thick and 0·3 m high. The outer wall is 19·4 m in diameter over a bank 1·6 m in average thickness and 0·2 m in height; the entrance lies on the SSE, and in the interior there is a ring-ditch (2·8 m wide by 0·1 m deep). Nothing is now visible of a probable hut-

112 Bleaton Hill, hut-circles and field-system, 1:2500

circle which lay immediately to the E. Coles (1909, 94–5) described it and the former as single-walled houses, but as the former is double walled, the precise form of this example must remain uncertain.

·2 NO 1842 5173   NO 15 SE 4
About 120 m WNW of (·1) and immediately N of the road, there is the N arc of a partially destroyed hut-circle measuring about 7·2 m in diameter within a wall 2 m thick and 0·4 m high. About 10 m to the W there is an oval structure; it is severely reduced on the E and W, where it is crossed by a track, and measures 8·8 m by 7·7 m within a bank 1·9 m thick.

·3 NO 1891 5140   NO 15 SE 12
The larger of the two hut-circles on this terrace is double walled and measures 9 m in internal diameter. The other, which lies immediately to the NNE, measures 6·5 m in internal diameter. Although the walls of both hut-circles have been severely robbed, numerous facing stones are visible.

112   Bleaton Hill, hut-circles and field-system
NO 128 605   NO 16 SW 57
Two hut-circles are situated within a small field-system on the E flank of Bleaton Hill. Both buildings measure 9·2 m in internal diameter, and the interior of the W hut-circle has been levelled into the slope on the W. The field-system comprises a series of enclosures defined by stony banks and scarps. There are also three shieling-huts in the vicinity (no. 318·10).

113   Burn of Drimmie, hut-circles and small cairns
Single hut-circles, groups of small cairns and a burnt mound (no. 164) are scattered over the gently sloping ground drained by the Burn of Drimmie. Much of the area was taken into cultivation in the early 19th century (see no. 237) but has now reverted to pasture, and the surviving remains are situated around the perimeter and in the gaps between the improved fields.

·1 NO 1734 5194   NO 15 SE 43
A shallow platform in a field of rough pasture 400 m NW of Burnside of Drimmie may be the remains of a hut-circle. It measures 8·5 m in diameter and has been levelled into the slope on the SW.

·2 NO 166 524 to 171 523   NO 15 SE 10
About ten small cairns are scattered along the crest of a low ridge which drops gently from the WNW to the SW bank of the Burn of Drimmie. On the highest point of the ridge, about 200 m beyond the westernmost of the cairns, there is a severely robbed double-walled hut-circle; it measures 10·5 m in internal diameter by 20·6 m overall (Coles, 1909, 94).

·3 NO 1604 5225   NO 15 SE 44
This hut-circle, which measures 10·6 m in diameter within its stony bank, is situated in an exposed position on the crest of a ridge 200 m ENE of Braes of Cloquhat. The ridge forms the NE side of Glen Ericht, and on the SE the hut-circle commands a spectacular view over the mouth of the glen into Strathmore.

·4 NO 160 529   NO 15 SE 11, 80
A group of at least six small cairns is situated on a low ridge 300 m W of the derelict farmhouse of Gabert of Cloquhat. Four more stony mounds, probably cairns, are visible on the adjacent ridge to the N, and there are two others some 300 m to the WSW (NO 157 528).

·5 NO 168 533   NO 15 SE 79
About fifteen small cairns are scattered across a low knoll 250 m NE of the Burn of Drimmie; the largest are about 5 m in diameter and 0·6 m in height. A stony bank can be traced around the foot of the slope on the N and E. A further twenty-five irregularly-shaped mounds are scattered along a low ridge to the NW; single large boulders protrude from some of them and they may all be natural features. A rectangular building is visible amongst the cairns on the S flank of the knoll (no. 237·5).

114   Craigend, hut-circles, field-systems and small cairns
Several groups of hut-circles and field-systems are situated on the ridge that extends ESE from Craigend to Seefar, a distance of 2·5 km, and on a second ridge that extends S from Craigend to Arlick, a distance of 1·5 km. Much of the area is open moorland, and there is little evidence of later agriculture; only on the summit of Arlick are there extensive remains of rig-and-furrow cultivation, but the presence of a small group of cairns in woodland at Leduckie (·11) suggests that the evidence for prehistoric land-clearance on the lower slopes of the ridges was probably once more extensive.

·1 NO 076 484   NO 04 NE 6
There are four closely-spaced hut-circles immediately N of a cattle-grid about 350 m ENE of Craigend; three lie to the W of the road and the fourth is on the E. They range from 11 m to 7·5 m in diameter within walls from 2·2 m to 3·8 m in thickness, and all have upright slabs forming the inner wall-face. Three have entrances on the ESE, while the fourth is on the E. The two hut-circles closest to the cattle-grid are linked by a pair of banks to form an enclosure between the buildings. To the S of the houses there are at least twenty-five small cairns (measuring up to 5 m by 0·5 m) and faint traces of rig-and-furrow cultivation.

·2 NO 07 48, 08 48   NO 04 NE 6
This group comprises clusters of three and two hut-circles respectively, two isolated houses, and field-banks and small cairns.
The W cluster (NO 079 482) lies at the foot of a scarp and includes three hut-circles, which are disposed in a NNE-SSW line, and two huts. The NNE hut-circle is levelled into the foot of the scarp, measures 8·4 m in diameter within a wall 1·3 m thick and 0·25 m high, and has an entrance on the SSE. The central house measures 12·3 m in diameter within a wall 2·1 m thick and 0·3 m high and has an entrance 2 m wide on the SSE. The large diameter suggests that it may be of double-wall type, but any trace of the inner wall was obscured on the date of visit by deep heather. The SSW hut-circle is small, measuring only 3·5 m in diameter within a wall 1·9 m thick and 0·3 m high; the entrance is on the SSW. What may be either an unusually small hut-circle or a more recent hut (2·5 m in diameter) lies 20 m to the WNW of the central hut-circle, and between the upper two hut-circles there is a later rectangular hut (5·2 m by 2·2 m within a wall 1 m thick with an entrance at the centre of the S side).
The E cluster is situated on the crest of the scarp (NO 080 483). It comprises a single hut-circle (7·8 m in diameter within a wall 2 m thick, with an entrance on the SSE) with a stretch of field-bank springing from its W side. To the SE there is an unusual hut-circle which resembles a twin double-walled house, but it lacks the inner wall of the E portion. To the SSE there are several stretches of field-bank, and on the slopes below the W cluster there is an extensive spread of small cairns which measure up to 7 m in diameter by 0·5 m in height (several show signs of disturbance).

The outlying houses are situated about 90 m to the NNE and 260 m to the WNW of the E cluster respectively. The nearer is a massively built hut-circle (9·75 m in diameter with prominent outer facing-stones), and the other measures 10·9 m in diameter with several stretches of inner facing-stones visible.

·3   NO 076 481   NO 04 NE 6
This group of hut-circles straddles an old trackway and comprises a tangential pair (5·17 m and 4·8 m in diameter respectively) with entrances on the SE and SSE respectively, and a single hut-circle 7·9 m in diameter, with an entrance on the SSE and what are probably field-banks springing from the NW and SW. To the SW of the pair of houses there are two possible turf huts and traces of rig-and-furrow cultivation.

·4   NO 07 47   NO 04 NE 7
Situated on a SE-facing stretch of moorland about 1 km SSE of Craigend, there are nine hut-circles; seven are disposed amongst the braided course of a trackway that crosses the slope from NE to SW, while the remaining two lie upslope, closer to the summit of the hill.

All but one of the group of seven hut-circles (NO 075 474) lie to the S of the northernmost strand of the trackway, and they range from 6·4 m to 12·3 m in diameter within walls up to 2·5 m in thickness and 0·4 m in height. Six have entrances on the SSE and the seventh is on the SE. The westernmost hut-circle (NO 0760 4747) lies within the W half of an oval enclosure, and it may be the W element of a twin double-walled house, the inner E wall of which is no longer visible. A single (probably clearance) cairn can be seen at NO 0761 4744, and there is an area of rig-and-furrow cultivation around the lower hut-circles.

The remaining two hut-circles lie about 50 m SW of the high tension power lines that cross the hill. The larger of the two is a double-walled house measuring 8·2 m internally by 17·3 m overall with a splayed entrance on the SE. Immediately to the SW, and partly overlain by the larger hut-circle, there are the remains of a small hut-circle, which measures 6·9 m in diameter. It appears to have been robbed during the construction of the later hut-circle and the best preserved feature is a stretch of upright slabs marking the line of the inner wall-face. The entrance is on the SSE.

·5   NO 083 489   NO 04 NE 38
There are at least twenty-seven small cairns on the open moorland about 500 m SE of a group of sheep-pens that overlook the S bank of the Benachally Burn. The majority of the cairns, which measure up to 3 m in diameter by 0·4 m in height, lie on rising ground centred at NO 083 489, while a further six are visible amongst deep heather on almost level ground about 100 m to the N (NO 082 490).

·6   NO 092 481   NO 04 NE 24
A group of about forty small cairns, measuring up to 4 m in diameter, is strung out along a gentle NE-facing slope 550 m WSW of the farmstead of Dulater (no. 310·6). The majority of the cairns are situated in heather moorland below, and to the N, of a rough track, but those at the SE end are on slightly higher ground to the S of the track. The area of the cairns is also split by a wet gully, on the W bank of which there is a burnt mound (no. 169).

·7   NO 096 479   NO 04 NE 25
At least twenty small cairns, measuring up to 4 m in diameter, are situated on poorly-drained heather moorland immediately S of the rough track, and some 150 m SE of (·6).

·8   NO 092 469   NO 04 NE 33
A group of at least thirty-four small cairns, measuring up to 6 m in diameter, is situated on gently-sloping, S-facing rough pasture some 480 m SW of Seefar farmhouse.

·9   NO 090 470   NO 04 NE 34
At least forty-nine small cairns are situated on rough pasture 650 m W of Seefar farmhouse; they measure up to 5 m in diameter, and much of the area covered by the cairns has been disturbed by a network of trackways.

·10   NO 076 471   NO 04 NE 39
A group of at least twelve small cairns, measuring up to 4 m in diameter, survive on a N-facing slope 300 m SSE of (·4). They are sandwiched between an area of boggy ground to the N and an extensive plot of ridge-and-furrow cultivation which covers much of the summit and N slopes of Arlick.

·11   NO 066 465   NO 04 NE 26
A group of at least twenty-one small cairns is situated within sparse woodland 200 m W of Leduckie steading; they measure up to 5 m in diameter, and most lie on a gentle W-facing slope to the N of the farm track.

115   Craigton, hut-circle and small cairns
      NO 1245 5861   NO 15 NW 29
Situated at the foot of a prominent rock outcrop 1·2 km NW of Craigton steading, there are the remains of a hut-circle, which measures 9·5 m in diameter within a stony bank up to 2·6 m thick and 0·3 m high. The interior has been levelled into the slope, and there is an entrance (1·9 m wide) on the SE. There are up to thirty small cairns (up to 4 m in diameter) and several lengths of stony bank on the slopes below the hut-circle.

116   Creag Dubh-leitir, Glenfernate Lodge, hut-circles and small cairns
Five hut-circles, a group of small cairns, and a burnt mound (no. 167) are visible on terraces and rocky ridges along the SW face of Creag Dubh-leitir (see also no. 272).

·1   NO 053 651   NO 06 NE 38
Two hut-circles lie about 80 m apart on low ridges to the NW of an old stone dyke that runs up on to the SW face of Creag Dubh-leitir. The more westerly has an internal diameter of about 7·3 m, and the wall of the other has been reduced to little more than a scatter of stones with an overall diameter of 13·5 m.

·2   NO 052 654   NO 06 NE 39
Three hut-circles lie about 250 m to the NNW of (·1). Two are set tangentially, and are little more than platforms about 8 m in diameter levelled into the slope; the relationship between the two is unclear. The third hut-circle lies on a broad terrace to the SW; it measures about 9 m in internal diameter. At least four small cairns are visible to the S.

117   Creag na Bruaich, hut-circle and small cairns
      NO 1453 6689   NO 16 NW 42
This hut-circle is situated on a grassy terrace high up on the S flank of Creag na Bruaich. It measures about 12·5 m in internal diameter, and the entrance is on the SW. On the slope above the hut-circle there are at least ten small cairns, while a few more are scattered amongst the shieling-huts (no. 232·17) on a shelf 200 m to the W. An area of about 1·5 ha around the hut-circle is enclosed on the N, W and S by a stony bank.

118   Dalhenzean Lodge, small cairns
    NO 126 670   NO 16 NW 81
A group of at least six small cairns is situated on a terrace about 350 m WNW of the forestry plantation to the W of Corrydon Cottage.

119   Dalnaglar, hut-circles
    NO 150 642   NO 16 SE 2
The remains of three hut-circles and several sections of bank, together with a Pitcarmick-type building (no. 233), are situated 600 m SE of Dalnaglar Castle. The majority of the remains are in open ground, but the N hut-circle lies within a stand of trees. The site was partially excavated between 1958 and 1960 (Stewart 1964), and the results of that work are incorporated into this account.

The largest hut-circle (NO 1508 6424) measures 11 m in maximum diameter within a stony bank up to 2·2 m thick and 0·4 m high. The interior has been levelled into the gentle SW-facing slope and the entrance, which is not now visible, lay on the SW. Excavation of little more than a quarter of the hut-circle revealed few structural details, and the only finds were several hundred sherds of coarse pottery (which represent at least seven vessels), most of which were found outside the hut-circle.

In 1960 Stewart partially excavated a second hut-circle (NO 1501 6431) which lay on a low knoll some 80 m NW of the first. Much of the S side had previously been quarried, but excavation revealed a house measuring about 11 m in diameter within a boulder wall, the base of which measured 1·2 m in thickness. The finds comprised a few fragments of coarse pottery similar to those found at the other hut-circle.

The third hut-circle (NO 1500 6425) is situated about 65 m W of the first and was not excavated. It is in an extremely poor state of preservation and measures about 9·8 m in diameter within a bank which is barely discernible.

Stewart also excavated one of the field-banks. It comprised a loose core of boulders, on the N side of which two stone discs and a stone 'rubber' were found; in addition a small rim-sherd of coarse ware was found in the rubble of the bank.

120   Dalrulzion, hut-circles and small cairns
    NO 1224 5722 to 1281 5752   NO 15 NW 2
This group originally comprised nineteen hut-circles and a number of small cairns, but afforestation has obliterated eleven houses, and the remainder are now preserved in a narrow clearing. Three of the hut-circles (one double-walled and a tangential pair) were excavated in 1932 and c. 1945 respectively; their positions, however, were not recorded and it is not known if they are amongst the surviving remains. The present account includes information derived from the excavation reports (Thorneycroft 1933 and 1948) and OS record cards.

The easternmost of the surviving eight hut-circles (NO 1281 5752) measures 8·2 m in internal diameter and has a central scoop 5 m in diameter; the entrance is on the SE. About 450 m to the SW (NO 1240 5732) there is a second hut-circle; it measures 9 m in internal diameter with an entrance on the ESE. A short distance to the SW there are three pairs of hut-circles, each of which comprises a double-walled house with a single-walled house adjacent to its SE side. The E pair (NO 1231 5730) comprises a double-walled house (measuring 7·5 m in internal diameter by 14 m overall) accompanied by a single-walled house 11 m in diameter within a low wall. The central double-walled house (NO 1228 5726) measures 8 m in internal diameter by 16 m overall and its accompanying single-walled house is 8·5 m in internal diameter. The W

double-walled house (NO 1224 5722) measures 9 m in internal diameter and 17·7 m by 15·5 m overall; its outwardly-splayed entrance is on the SE. Immediately to the E there is a single-walled house which measures 11 m in internal diameter; the interior has been levelled into the slope, and the entrance is on the SSE.

Three further hut-circles, which were recorded by the OS, now lie within the plantation. One (NO 1207 5716) measured 17·5 m in diameter between wall centres, and is probably Thorneycroft's 'hut-circle T' (1933, 190). Two other hut-circles (NO 1205 5735) measured 10 m and 12 m in diameter respectively between wall centres.
— *Stat. Acct.*, 15 (1795), 519–20; Stuart 1868, 404; OS 6-inch map, Perthshire, 1st ed. (1867), sheet 42; Maclagan 1875, 80, plate 33.

121   Dirnanean, hut-circles, field-system and small cairns
A series of hut-circle groups are strung out along the hills flanking the valleys of the Allt Doire nan Eun and its tributaries. Most of the hut-circles lie at heights of between 400 m and 450 m OD and are situated high up on the crests and shoulders of the hills. One group (·10), at the head of the Allt Dubhagan, is even higher at almost 500 m OD, the highest recorded hut-circle in this part of Perth.

·1   NO 0773 6327   NO 06 SE 41
This hut-circle is situated on the SE flank of Creag na Ballaige 80 m NNW of the E corner of Creag na Ballaige Wood. Although its wall is barely discernible, the hut-circle measures about 9 m in internal diameter, and it is surrounded by an unusual square enclosure. The enclosure measures a maximum of 14 m across the interior, and at the entrance, on the SE, its wall unites with that of the hut-circle.

·2   NO 080 636   NO 06 SE 40
About 400 m NE of (·1) there are five hut-circles set on knolls and terraces on the SE flank of Creag na Ballaige. They range from 7·8 m to 11 m in internal diameter, and one shows two phases of construction. The northernmost of the hut-circles, which lies on level ground 150 m ENE of the summit of the hill, has a bank up to 3 m thick with traces of an internal ring-ditch. On a terrace to the SW of the central hut-circle there are at least two small cairns, a stony bank, and a later building (see no. 255·4).

·3   NO 082 638   NO 06 SE 39
At least five hut-circles and a thin scatter of small cairns are visible on the SW flank of Menachban. The westernmost of the houses is an enclosed pair; the hut-circle occupying the W half of the enclosure measures about 9·2 m in internal diameter, but the E half, which is levelled into the slope and has its own entrance, is apparently empty.

On the shoulder of the hill 100 m to the ESE, there are two hut-circles (one a double-walled example) and a later building (see no. 255·6). A further 100 m to the ESE there are two hut-circles set at the rear of a gently sloping terrace. The more easterly of the two measures 7·6 m in

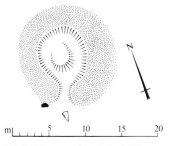

121·3 Dirnanean, hut-circle, 1:500

39

D

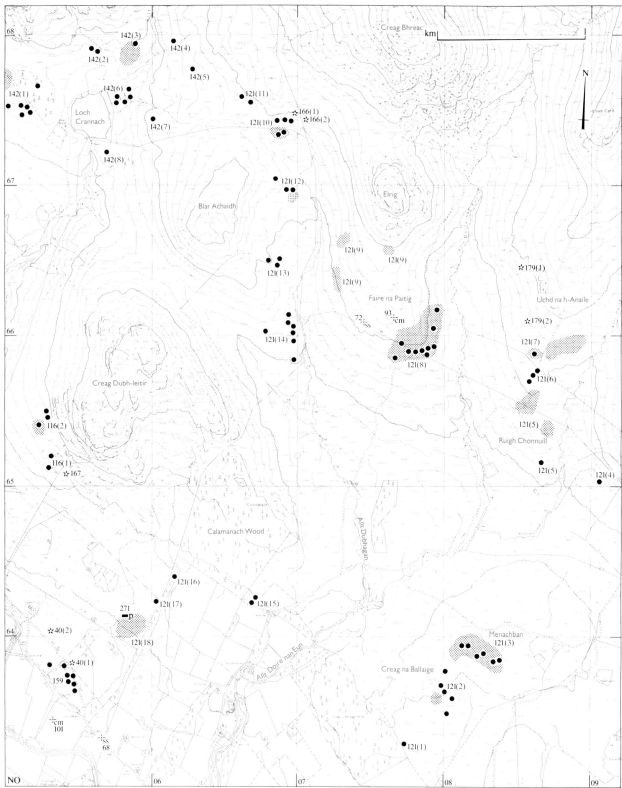

121 Dirnanean, 1:25 000

diameter within a low bank up to 3 m in thickness, and it
encloses an internal ring-ditch up to 0·3 m in depth; its
entrance was probably flanked by two large boulders, but
only one is still in position.

·4   NO 0904 6503   NO 06 NE 66
What may be the last vestiges of a hut-circle are situated
on a low rise 40 m SW of a farmstead (no. 255·16) on the
SW flank of Barr Salachaidh.

·5   NO 0861 6530   NO 06 NE 67, 40
A small hut-circle (about 6·5 m in internal diameter) is
situated on a low ridge 320 m N of the old sheepfold on
the S flank of Ruigh Chonnuil. What may be the remains
of a second are set on the summit of a knoll about 180 m N
of the sheepfold. A group of at least four small cairns lies
at the E end of a slightly higher ridge to the NE of the
first hut-circle, and a further fifteen are scattered around
the intersection of the track and fence 150 m to the NW.

·6   NO 086 657   NO 06 NE 11
The remains of three hut-circles are strung out over a
distance of 60 m on the level crest of the spur to the N of
the fence that crosses Ruigh Chonnuil: the first is
probably double walled (16·5 m in diameter overall), but
is has been severely robbed; the second, some 40 m to the
NNE, comprises a shallow ring-ditch (7 m in diameter
overall) surrounded by traces of a low bank some 2·5 m in
thickness; and the third, immediately NE of the second,
forms little more than a shallow circular depression about
8·2 m in diameter.

·7   NO 0859 6588   NO 06 NE 41
A circular area of disturbance on the crest of a knoll 120 m
N of (·6) probably indicates the position of a robbed hut-
circle. Two small cairns lie at the foot of the knoll to the
W and a further three are scattered to the E. Farther to
the E a group of at least twenty small cairns and two
banks extend SE from the track that mounts the S flank of
Uchd na h-Anaile.

·8   NO 078 659   NO 06 NE 16
A large group of hut-circles and stances for timber houses
extends from the S to the E flank of Faire na Paitig. Three
of the hut-circles fall within a new forestry plantation: two
lie on either side of the track at the gate through the deer-
fence, and the third is on an unploughed knoll 120 m to
the WSW. A fourth hut-circle is crossed by the deer fence
100 m WNW of the gate; it measures 12 m in internal
diameter and is notable for the step in its back scarp,
where the interior has been levelled into the slope on the
N.
   On gently sloping ground to the E of the gate there are
traces of at least five timber houses clustered around a
double-walled hut-circle. The latter measures 8·4 m in
internal diameter (17·1 m overall), and is unusual for the
shallow ring-ditch visible immediately within its inner
wall; on the SE the hut-circle appears to overlie a timber
house-stance. Four of the timber house-stances comprise
semi-circular scoops (7 m to 8 m overall), which lie on the
E half of the stance, with an entrance gully on the S; the
fifth is little more than a depression 8 m in diameter. Two
further hut-circles lie 130 m and 260 m N respectively of
the double-walled hut-circle; the more northerly is set on
a level terrace, is markedly oval, and measures 11 m by
9 m internally. A scatter of small cairns and a bank are
visible on the slopes between the houses and the forestry
plantation.

·9   NO 073 666   NO 06 NE 23–4, 43
A group of at least nine small cairns and a bank are
situated on a terrace on the SW flank of Elrig. Two more
small cairns and a group of five lie 150 m and 250 m
respectively to the S, and a group of at least three lie at
the foot of the S face of Elrig, 300 m to the E.

·10   NO 069 674   NO 06 NE 27
This group of hut-circles lies at about 500 m OD on the S
face of a spur of Creag Bhreac at the head of the Allt
Dubhagan. Two (one in a poor state of preservation) are
situated on a low knoll S of a fence, three others are
spread over a distance of 70 m across the slope above the
fence, and they range from 5·5 m to 9 m in internal
diameter. The westernmost of the upper hut-circles,
which is slightly oval and measures 9 m by 8·5 m internally,
differs from the rest in that it has an internal ring-ditch
and traces of a concentric outer bank around the uphill
side. In the vicinity of the two lower hut-circles there are
at least six small cairns and a bank. For a burnt mound
nearby see no. 166.

·11   NO 066 675   NO 06 NE 29
Two hut-circles are situated on low rises at the foot of the
slope on the N side of the saddle between Blar Achaidh
and the SW flank of Creag Bhreac. The more westerly
measures 7·7 m by 6·9 m internally and has traces of a
possible ring-ditch set immediately within its bank; the
other measures at least 6·3 m in internal diameter.

·12   NO 069 669   NO 06 NE 26
Three hut-circles are situated on the northernmost of the
gently-sloping spurs that project from the E flank of Blar
Achaidh. Two are set side-by-side, and the third (6·3 m in
internal diameter) lies 100 m to the WNW. Of the pair,
the more easterly has an internal diameter of 6·2 m, and is
deeply levelled into the slope; the more westerly
measures 7·4 m in internal diameter and has a ring-ditch
set immediately within its broad bank. A single small
cairn lies 100 m to the WNW, while three more are visible
at the foot of the slope to the SE of the other two.

·13   NO 068 665   NO 06 NE 25
This group of three hut-circles is situated on a spur on the
E flank of Blar Achaidh. The westernmost, which
measures 9·5 m in internal diameter and has traces of a
ring-ditch set immediately within its bank, is situated on
the crest of the spur. The other two lie on a terrace 80 m
to the E; one measures 9·8 m in diameter within a bank up
to 3 m in thickness, and it has an internal ring-ditch; the
other measures 8·2 m in internal diameter and has been
levelled into the slope.

·14   NO 069 660   NO 06 NE 44–6
The remains of at least five hut-circles are visible over a
distance of 170 m along a low ridge that forms the W bank
of the Allt Dubhagan at the foot of the SE flank of Blar
Achaidh. They are poorly preserved, and all but one are
overlain by shieling-huts (no. 255·34). The houses range
from 7·7 m to 9 m in internal diameter, and one (a semi-
circular scoop about 0·5 m in depth) is possibly the
remains of a timber house-stance similar to those at (·8).
Two more hut-circles are situated at the foot of the slope
150 m to the W and on a knoll 110 m to the S.

·15   NO 0669 6423   NO 06 SE 82
Two hut-circles are situated on terraces midway between
the Dirnanean sheep dip and the S corner of Calamanach
Wood. Set on opposite sides of a fence, they have both
been reduced to little more than shallow scoops about 8 m
in diameter.

·16   NO 0614 6439   NO 06 SE 64
This hut-circle, which has been reduced to little more
than a circular scoop 9·5 m in diameter by up to 0·5 m in
depth, lies on the S flank of a knoll in the gap between
Calamanach Wood and a shelter belt running along the
Dirnanean march dyke.

·17   NO 0603 6423   NO 06 SE 65
On the opposite side of the march dyke some 190 m SW of
(·16), there are the remains of a hut-circle, measuring
9·5 m in internal diameter, with its entrance on the SW.

·18   NO 058 640   NO 06 SE 102
A group of small cairns extends across a SW-facing slope
200 m SW of (·17).

122   Drumderg, hut-circles, field-systems and small cairns
Drumderg is a rounded, heather-covered ridge which lies

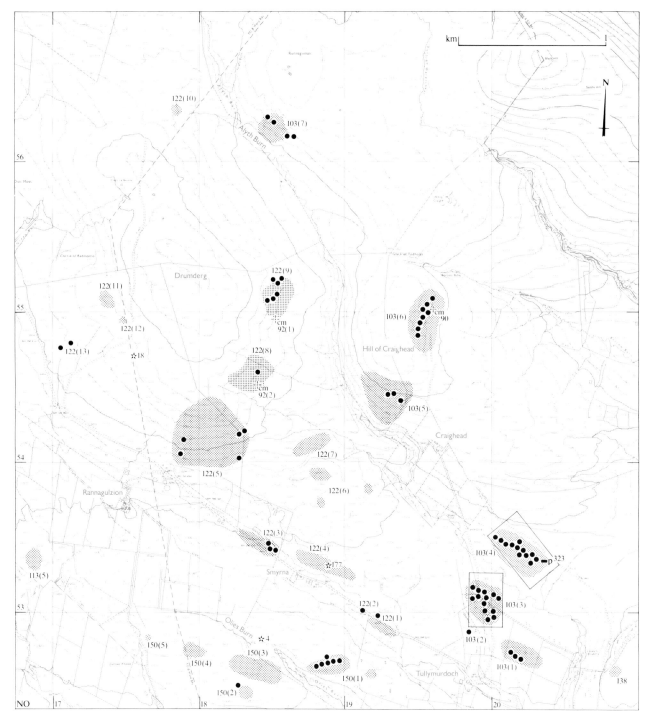

122 Drumderg, 1:25 000

between the Alyth Burn on the E and the Corrie of
Badmorris and Dun Moss on the W; its S side is crossed
by the public road from Alyth to Glenshee, and at its N
end there is an extensive area of bog. Evidence for
prehistoric settlement and land-use is extensive on the S
and SE slopes, while on the W it is more restricted, and
on the N side there is only one group of small cairns. At
least one burial cairn (no. 18) and two cupmarked stones
(no. 92·1–·2) are situated on the ridge.

·1   NO 1922 5297   NO 15 SE 24
Situated on a low knoll within a clearing in a conifer
plantation and immediately N of the public road 600m SE
of Smyrna cottage, there are the remains of a hut-circle.
It measures 9m in diameter within a heather-covered wall
2·5m thick and 0·3m high, and there is an entrance gap

(2m wide) on the SE. To the S of the road there are at
least eighteen small cairns measuring up to 4m in
diameter.

·2   NO 1912 5301   NO 15 SE 81
A hut-circle measuring 7·5m in diameter within a heather-
covered wall (2·5m thick and 0·2m high) is situated
between the S edge of the public road and a field wall
100m WNW of (·1).

·3   NO 185 534   NO 15 SE 18
A group of three hut-circles is situated on a low rise
immediately N of the public road 220m NW of Smyrna
cottage. The E hut-circle is either double walled or multi-
period and measures 10·8m in diameter within a wall
between 1·4m and 2·6m thick and 0·2m high; the inner

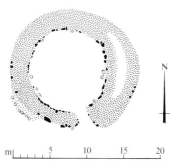

122·3 *Drumderg, east hut-circle, 1:500*

face, which is composed of stones set on edge, is well preserved. The outer wall has an overall diameter of 16·6 m. Immediately to the W there is a second double-walled house, which measures 7 m in diameter within an inner wall with a well-preserved inner face of boulders and slabs set on edge. The outer wall (13·1 m in overall diameter) has been largely robbed; the empty sockets of several outer facing-stones are clearly visible, and there is an entrance (1·4 m wide) on the SSE. The third hut-circle, which is of single-walled construction, is situated a few metres N of the second and measures 9·7 m in diameter within a wall reduced to a turf-covered bank 3 m thick and 0·2 m high. There are no facing-stones visible and the entrance is probably situated on the SW. At least forty small cairns, measuring up to 5 m in diameter, are situated on either side of the public road to the W of the hut-circles. A low rubble bank, which appears to join on to the NW side of the third house, extends W along the S side of a stream gully and defines the N edge of the group. A similar bank runs E from the E hut-circle, but there are no cairns on this side.

·4 NO 189 533   NO 15 SE 8
A group of at least fifteen small cairns, measuring up to 5 m in diameter, occupies a terrace 100 m NE of Smyrna cottage. The cairns lie to the W and E of a burn, on the W of which there is a burnt mound (see no. 177). Also situated to the W of the burn, there are two curving sections of bank which form two tangential open-ended enclosures.

·5 NO 181 541   NO 15 SE 2
The remains of five hut-circles are disposed on the S-face of Drumderg within a field-system which comprises small cairns and stony banks and covers an area of about 15 ha.
   On the NE there are two hut-circles. The first (NO 1828 5418) is double walled and measures 9 m in internal diameter. The second hut-circle measures 6·5 m in diameter within a rubble wall measuring up to 1·5 m in thickness and 0·4 m in height. The inner and outer wall-faces are both defined by rows of non-contiguous boulders, and the entrance (0·9 m wide) is situated on the SSE. Attached to the NE arc there is a small circular structure measuring 2·9 m in diameter within a stone wall up to 1·1 m thick and 0·2 m high; the position of the entrance is uncertain.
   Situated 160 m to the S there is a third hut-circle (NO 1829 5402), which lies immediately below the break of slope in the SE corner of the field-system. It measures 10·2 m in diameter within a heather-covered bank 2·5 m thick and 0·5 m high; the interior has been levelled into the slope, and the entrance is probably on the SSE.
   Towards the W edge of the field-system there are two further hut-circles and a small enclosure (previously identified by the OS as a hut-circle, but which is probably of relatively recent date). The first hut-circle is situated in a natural hollow (NO 1787 5414), and on the date of visit

it was masked by deep heather. It is double walled (measuring 8·7 m in internal diameter), and the entrance is situated on the SE. A substantial stony bank passes close to the S edge of the hut-circle. The second hut-circle (NO 1787 5405) is situated on a narrow terrace towards the base of the hill and measures 10·2 m in diameter within a turf-covered bank up to 1·6 m in thickness and 0·2 m in height. Several outer facing-stones are present on the E, and the poorly-defined entrance lies on the SW.
   Although there is a thin scatter of small cairns to the N of the hut-circles, the main concentration lies in the area between the hut-circles. Some of these cairns are relatively large, and one, immediately S of the two NE hut-circles, measures 7·5 m in diameter. Several stony banks cross the area, including one which curves around the S side of the NE double-walled house and roughly defines the N limit of the cairns. Some of the banks are probably of prehistoric date; others, however, may be contemporary with the rig-and-furrow cultivation that encroaches on to the S part of the field-system.

·6 NO 18 53, 19 53   NO 15 SE 70
Situated on a series of ridges which descend from the E side of Drumderg, there are groups of small cairns at NO 1884 5392, 1884 5373 and 1916 5381 respectively. The groups contain up to twelve cairns, which measure 4 m in maximum diameter.

·7 NO 1876 5810   NO 15 SE 71
A group of at least thirty-seven small cairns (measuring up to 5 m in diameter) is situated on the northernmost of the low-lying ridges that lie on the SE slopes of Drumderg. On the W there is a plot of probable cord rig which measures 80 m from E to W by about 60 m transversely. It comprises a series of roughly parallel ridges (1·2 m from crest to crest), and it probably post-dates the phase of cairn construction.

·8 NO 1840 5459   NO 15 SE 19
Situated on the SE flank of Drumderg, there are the remains of a hut-circle (8·8 m in internal diameter). A stony bank, aligned NNE-SSW, abuts the NNE side of the hut-circle, and after a short distance its line is continued by a well-defined lynchet. Further lengths of stony bank and small cairns occur close to the hut-circle; many are poorly preserved, and on the date of visit they were obscured by deep heather. Situated about 80 m to the SSW, there is a semi-circular arc of stony bank, which forms half of an enclosure about 13·5 m in internal diameter; as the interior has not been levelled into the slope, the remains are probably not those of a hut-circle.

·9 NO 185 551   NO 15 NE 5
A settlement of at least six hut-circles and a field-system occupy the northernmost slopes on the SE flank of Drumderg. At the centre of the field-system there is a line of three hut-circles; the largest lies on the NE (NO 1851 5510) and is double walled, measuring 9·3 m in diameter with an entrance on the SE. On the SW a short length of bank links it to a single-walled structure, which measures 6 m in diameter within a wall 1·6 m thick and 0·6 m high with a poorly-defined entrance on the ESE. Immediately to the SW there are the possible remains of a small hut measuring about 5 m in internal diameter. The third hut-circle (NO 1848 5508) measures 7·7 m in diameter within a heather-covered wall 2·2 m thick and 0·5 m high. The interior has been levelled into the slope, and there is a probable gap for the entrance on the SE. A bank springs from the hut-circle wall on the SW and runs concentrically to the wall for a short distance before turning to the W to form an enclosure. A second bank springs from the E side of the entrance of the eastern hut-circle to form a court in

122
122·9

front of the houses before looping downhill to define part of a second enclosure, the E side of which is defined by a natural gully. The enclosure contains two strip-fields, broad plough-furrows (and one rig), two small cairns, and at least one lynchet. On the opposite side of the gully there is a further area of lynchets. There is no visible relationship between any of the hut-circles and the cultivation remains, and it is uncertain if any of the cultivation remains are contemporary with the hut-circles or the enclosure banks.

On the N there is a double- and a single-walled hut-circle and a hut-platform. The double-walled hut-circle measures 6·8 m in internal diameter by 15·2 m overall and has traces of an internal ring-ditch. Immediately NE of the outer wall and concentric with it, there is what may be a drainage gully (not shown on plan). The single-walled house lies 14 m to the SW; it measures 10·8 m in diameter within a particularly impressive inner wall-face of boulders and slabs. There is no outer face to the wall, and the core material has been built up against the inner face. Adjacent to the hut-circle there are the remains of a subcircular structure which, although identified by Thorneycroft (1933) as a tangential hut-circle, is probably a shieling-hut. Situated about 25 m to the NW, there is a platform, possibly the stance for a timber house, which is 7·4 m in diameter, with what may be an entrance on the S.

·10 NO 1785 5633   NO 15 NE 38
A short length of bank and six small cairns (measuring up to 4 m in diameter) are situated towards the northern foot of Drumderg.

·11 NO 1734 5512   NO 15 NE 36
A group of at least twelve small cairns (measuring up to 4 m in diameter) occupy a narrow terrace on the SW flank of the hill.

·12 NO 1747 5494   NO 15 SE 69
Situated about 150 m SE of (·11) there are three small cairns, the largest of which measures 4 m in diameter.

·13 NO 1713 5478   NO 15 SE 17
This hut-circle is situated on a low knoll within an area of poorly-drained moorland; it measures 9·4 m in diameter within a boulder wall 1·7 m thick and 0·2 m high, and immediately inside the wall there is an irregular ring-ditch which gives the interior a domed appearance. About 65 m to the WSW and situated at the base of an E-facing slope in a poorly-drained position, there is an enclosure measuring 12 m by 9·5 m within a stony bank 1·1 m thick and 0·2 m high; there is a possible entrance gap on the SE.

123 Drumderrach, hut-circle
      NO 2828 5082   NO 25 SE 41
This hut-circle is situated on the SW edge of an undulating S-facing terrace 630 m W of Bruceton farmhouse. It measures about 7·5 m in diameter within a wall which is reduced to a low grass-covered bank 1·8 m in maximum thickness and 0·2 m in height. Much of the S arc has been destroyed by erosion, and an exposed section shows that the wall is composed of rounded stones and earth.

124 Drumturn Burn, hut-circles, field-systems and small cairns
This major group of monuments is disposed on the slopes around the headwaters of the Drumturn Burn and its tributaries. See also nos. 288–9.

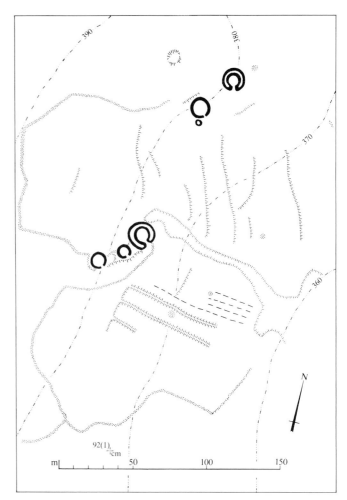

122·9 Drumderg, hut-circles and field-systems, 1:2500

·1 NO 151 577   NO 15 NE 16
A group of five hut-circles is situated on the SE flank of the Hill of Easter Bleaton 700 m NNW of Mill of Drumturn. Four lie within a conifer plantation and were not located on the date of visit. The OS record, however, that they were single walled and measured from 6 m to 8 m in internal diameter. The fifth hut-circle (NO 1529 5770) lies on the top of a low rise to the E of the plantation; it measures 7·3 m in diameter within a poorly-preserved heather-covered wall.

·2 NO 152 580   NO 15 NE 15
A group of four hut-circles and what may be a Pitcarmick-type building (no. 288·1) are situated in heather moorland 270 m NNE of (·1); three are comparatively small measuring from 5·6 m to 8 m in diameter within low rubble walls, and the fourth, on the N edge of the group, measures 10·5 m in internal diameter. Where visible, the entrance gaps are located on the S or SE arcs.

·3 NO 1564 5836   NO 15 NE 11
Situated on a prominent rounded knoll on the E bank of the Drumturn Burn 450 m NE of (·2), there are the remains of an unusual circular enclosure. It measures 10·5 m in diameter over a slight bank (1 m thick and 0·1 m high) which encloses a ditch (1·5 m broad and 0·15 m deep). A gap in the bank on the ESE corresponds with a break in the ditch, and within the interior there is a spread of stones. The date and purpose of the enclosure are unknown, but it may be an unusual house type or a burial monument. Immediately NNE of the enclosure

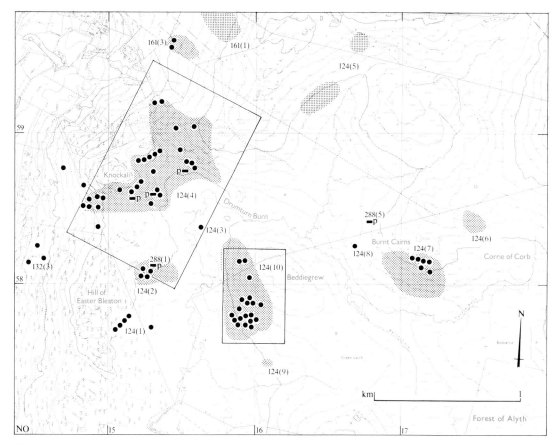

124 Drumturn Burn, 1:25 000

there are the poorly-defined footings of a structure which measures about 5 m in diameter overall.

·4   NO 15 58   NO 15 NW 13, NE 12–14
This complex of hut-circles, field-banks and small cairns lies on the W and S flanks of Knockali and extends across a saddle to the slope beyond. Amongst the cairns and field-banks there are three Pitcarmick-type buildings (A-C, see no. 288·2–·4) and a small enclosure of unknown date and purpose (D). At least thirty hut-circles have been identified, four of which are double walled. Most of the single-walled hut-circles, which range from 4·5 m to 12·8 m in internal diameter, are dispersed, but they include a row of five (E) set along the back of a narrow terrace on the SE flank of Knockali. The interiors of all five have been levelled into the slope and their walls have prominent boulder faces; one has an internal ring-ditch about 3 m in breadth by 0·2 m in depth. On the slope above the row, there is a low stony bank which extends NE to form one side of a trackway leading down into the saddle to the E. In front of the hut-circles there is a courtyard which was probably approached along a second trackway from the W. Of the other single-walled hut-circles, one on the SW flank of the hill is overlain by a double-walled hut-circle (F). The double-walled hut-circles range from 7·7 m to 9 m in internal diameter; two of them (F and G) have concentric inner and outer walls, but the two on the SE flank of the hill (H and J) are eccentric, with overall diameters of 18 m by 15 m and 17·2 m by 14 m respectively. The field-banks around the hut-circles are of more than one period of construction. Some form large enclosures and trackways, but others are probably no more than linear clearance heaps. The small cairns are scattered haphazardly amongst the enclosures and there is no detectable relationship between the two. In places, the enclosures have been extensively cleared of stone, but elsewhere, particularly in the saddle to the E of

124·4C

124·4A

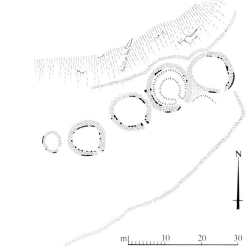

124·4A   Drumturn Burn, hut-circles (E), 1:1000

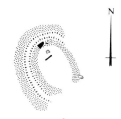

124·4B   Drumturn Burn, enclosure (D), 1:500

Knockali, the ground is littered with uncleared boulders. In several cases relationships between hut-circles and field-banks can be established. At E, the row of hut-circles and the banks appear to be integral, while two other hut-circles (K and L) have small enclosures attached. The enclosure at K, however, is also attached to the enclosure around the Pitcarmick-type building (A). Elsewhere field-banks simply butt on to hut-circles (e.g.

45

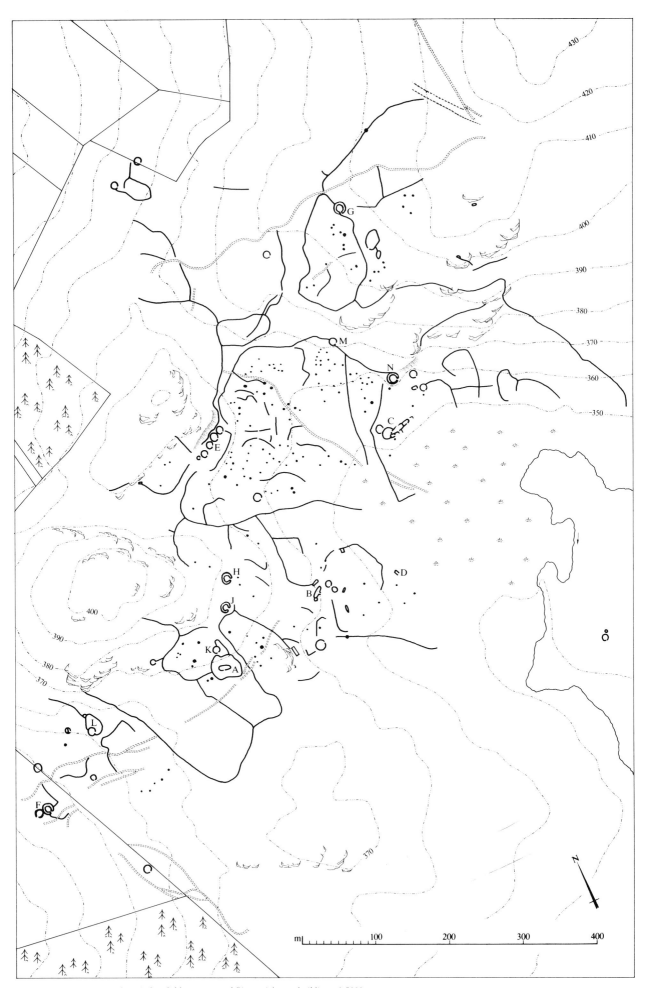

124·4C Drumturn Burn, hut-circles, field-systems, and Pitcarmick-type buildings, 1:5000

M); such relationships suggest that the hut-circles were built first, but they may still be broadly contemporary with one another. In two instances (G and N), however, banks can be seen overlying the outer walls of hut-circles. Despite the observation of these relationships, it is not possible to relate the cairns and banks to any one period of occupation. The enclosure (D), which is set at the foot of the slope below the Pitcarmick-type building (B), measures 6·2m by 3·2m within a wall 1m in thickness by 0·3m in height. On the uphill side the wall is flanked by a shallow ditch with an external bank. There is a wide entrance on the S, and a stone slab (1m by 0·15m and 0·35m in height) has been set on edge within the interior. The date and purpose of the enclosure are unknown.

·5   NO 164 592   NO 15 NE 19, 42
Situated on a gentle SE-facing, heather-covered slope, there is a group of at least twenty small cairns. A smaller group is situated below a trackway some 300m to the NE (NO 167 596).

·6   NO 175 584   NO 15 NE 43
The vestiges of a field-system are situated on the N side of the Corrie of Corb. It comprises two small cairns and a number of low stony banks.

·7   NO 171 581   NO 15 NE 3
A group of six hut-circles is situated high up on the S flank of Burnt Cairns, a spur of Cairn Gibbs, which rises from the N bank of the Corrie Burn at the mouth of the Corrie of Corb. Four of the hut-circles are strung out over a distance of 100m along a terrace immediately below the rocky crest of the spur. The westernmost is a massive structure, measuring 7·5m in diameter within a wall up to 4m in thickness by 0·9m in height; the second is about 7·5m in internal diameter and has traces of an external drainage ditch around its N side. The third is the more westerly of a pair of houses, and measures up to 7·6m in diameter within a severely robbed wall; the fourth, the more easterly of the pair, is double walled, with diameters of 9·8m internally and 19·5m overall, and traces of an external drainage ditch are visible around the N side.

The remaining two hut-circles lie on the slope below the terrace; one measures 6·2m in internal diameter, and the other, some 60m to the ESE, 8·5m by 7·7m internally. The field-system extends down the hill from the hut-circles and comprises three enclosures and a group of small cairns, the latter concentrated on the slopes immediately below the hut-circles. The lower of the enclosures is significantly larger than the others and extends to at least 6ha. The field-system is traversed by a series of hollow trackways.

·8   NO 1668 5825   NO 15 NE 9
A small circular enclosure lies at the foot of a rocky knoll low down on the W flank of the ridge known as Burnt Cairns. It measures about 7·3m in diameter within a low bank of large boulders, and there is an entrance on the W. Set slightly S of the centre of the interior, there is a mound about 2·8m in diameter by 0·3m in height.

·9   NO 1606 5746   NO 15 NE 31
A group of at least six cairns, measuring up to 3m in diameter, is situated on the SW flank of Beddiegrew.

·10   NO 160 579   NO 15 NE 10
One of the most extensive groups of hut-circles and field-systems known in NE Perth occupies the SW flank of Beddiegrew. Most of the hut-circles are situated towards the S end of the field-system, and are disposed in three tiers, two of which appear to be related to trackways leading between the fields.

The middle tier is strung along the trackway that leads down to the westernmost of the double-walled hut-circles (A), which has an overall diameter of about 16m but has been severely disturbed by stone-robbing. The establishment of this trackway appears to predate the construction of an enclosed pair of hut-circles (B), whose

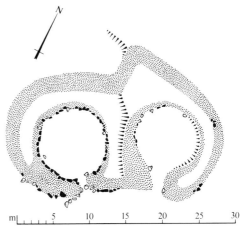

124·10A Drumturn Burn, hut-circles (B), 1:500

outer wall dog-legs to meet the bank along the SW side of the track. The westernmost is perhaps the best-preserved hut-circle on the site, with an internal diameter of 9·5m and an almost complete ring of inner facing-stones; the other measures 9·3m by 8m internally, and the interiors of both are terraced into the slope on the E. Immediately to the E there is a pair of smaller hut-circles (C), which appear to have been constructed side by side across the line of the track. Their interiors measure 7·3m in diameter and 4·6m by 3·8m respectively. To the SE the trackway continues between an unusual double-walled hut-circle (D) and the lynchet at the bottom of a field to the NE. The inner wall of (D), which is 6·9m in diameter,

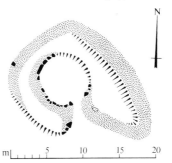

124·10B Drumturn Burn, hut-circle (D), 1:500

lies eccentrically within the outer wall, the gap between the two walls measuring up to 7·2m on the E side of the entrance.

The uppermost tier includes four double-walled hut-circles (E to H), with internal diameters ranging from 6·6m to 9·3m, and overall diameters from 15·4m to 16·5m. The interiors have all been terraced into the slope, and a series of inner facing-stones (slabs up to 0·7m high) is visible in E and F. The inner wall of G lies eccentrically within the outer, and on the W the two walls merge, giving a combined thickness of about 2·4m; on the E, however, there is a gap from 2m to 4·3m wide between the two, and this outer annexe appears to have been terraced into the hillside. On the slope above G there is a shallow platform (J); it measures about 8m in diameter, and is probably the stance for a timber house. Some distance to the N there is a double-walled hut-circle (K)

47

124·10C   Drumturn Burn, hut-circles and field-system, 1:2500

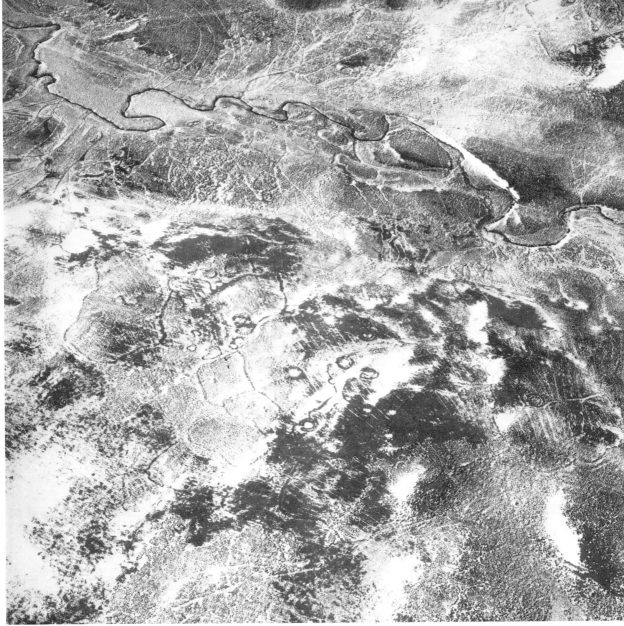

124·10D Drumturn Burn, hut-circles and field-system, aerial view from NE

set on a terrace overlooking the southern part of the site; it measures up to 7·9 m in internal diameter by 14·2 m overall, and many of the inner facing-stones of its inner wall (boulders up to 1·3 m long by 0·6 m high) are still visible. Yet further N, there are two more hut-circles (L), with internal diameters of 8·3 m and 11·5 m; the latter is very poorly preserved.

The field-system is divided into a series of large enclosures bounded by thick banks of cleared stones and low lynchets. To the SE there are wide gaps between the outer fields, probably left to provide access to the two trackways which lead down to double-walled hut-circles. Both trackways seem to have gone out of use in the course of the site's history, since not only is the lower one blocked by the construction of hut-circles (C), but the other one is blocked at H. The relationships of the hut-circles to the lower trackway suggest that there is considerable chronological depth to the prehistoric use of this hillside, and it is likely that the varying states of preservation of the hut-circles reflect the robbing of some to provide materials for the construction of others. Within most of the fields there are traces of widely-spaced

grooves, but these are probably the remains of rig-and-furrow cultivation of relatively recent date, since they appear to obliterate a hollowed trackway which cuts through some of the banks at the N end of the field-system. Other evidence of later activity is provided by the small huts and enclosures at the foot of the hillside.
— Mackenzie 1831; RCAHMS Survey of Marginal Lands.

125   Easter Riemore, hut-circles
      NO 052 490   NO 04 NE 41–2
The remains of two hut-circles are situated on a low, rocky rise 80 m NNW of the farmstead of Easter Riemore (no. 312·1). The W hut-circle (NO 0527 4901) is double walled and measures 7·8 m in diameter within a wall 1·2 m thick and 0·3 m high. Stretches of the inner face are formed by small upright slabs, and the entrance (1·4 m wide) is situated on the SW. On the NW, the outer wall (1·1 m thick by 0·2 m high and 15 m in overall diameter) is partially overlain by a later building.

The second hut-circle (NO 0529 4902), which lies 15 m to the NE, measures 11·5 m in diameter within a wall

49

defined partly by an outer face of large boulders but mostly by a turf-covered bank up to 1·5 m thick and 0·4 m high; the entrance is on the SW. At least ten small cairns, measuring up to 4 m in diameter, are situated on low-lying, but relatively well-drained, ground on the slopes below the hut-circles.

126 Glen Derby, hut-circles and small cairns
Glen Derby is bisected by the western boundary of the survey area and only the monuments in the E half of the valley are described in this volume. The monuments comprise a series of hut-circles and groups of small cairns which are disposed on the drier ridges and knolls of the otherwise poorly drained valley bottom and on the more gently rolling upper slopes. The upper slopes on the N side of the valley have been afforested recently, and in this area descriptions of the sites have been taken from the OS records. Along the S side of the valley the sites are described from E to W and on the N side from W to E.

·1   NO 066 590   NO 05 NE 14
A group of four single-walled hut-circles, measuring from 5·2 m to 8 m in internal diameter and with entrances on their E or SSE sides, is situated on the summit of a NE-SW aligned ridge 750 m SW of Croft of Cultalonie. A number of small cairns lie in the vicinity of the hut-circles and, situated between the hut-circles and the steep edge of a terrace to the N, there is an area of pasture which appears to have been cleared of all surface stone.

·2   NO 0641 5921, 0641 5923   NO 05 NE 7, 13
The remains of two hut-circles, measuring 6·4 m and 7·3 m in internal diameter respectively, are situated on the S edge of the crest of a prominent heather-covered knoll immediately S of the Balnald Burn. The larger hut-circle has a wide entrance-gap on the SE. A group of small cairns is situated on the slope to the SE of the hut-circles, and its S edge is defined by a stony bank which cuts across the saddle between the cairns and higher ground to the S. A further group of cairns occupies a low ridge 250 m to the W (NO 0615 5915).

·3   NO 0574 5935   NO 05 NE 4, 8
Situated on a low knoll within an area of poorly-drained ground immediately N of the Balnald Burn, there are the remains of a hut-circle. It measures 5·6 m in diameter internally, and the entrance gap is probably on the ill-defined E side. About 200 m to the NNE and bisected by the modern track, there is a group of small cairns (NO 0585 5953). A further group of small cairns lies to the WSW (no. 248).

·4   NO 057 598   NO 05 NE 9
Five hut-circles and numerous small cairns have been recorded on a series of terraces and a gentle S-facing slope within a recently-created forestry plantation. The wasted remains of only four of the hut-circles were identified on the date of visit, the fifth having been destroyed by forestry ploughing, and the following description is based on OS records. There is a row of three hut-circles on a narrow terrace (NO 0574 5985). Two are double walled with entrances on the SE, and they measure 7·8 m and 8·7 m in internal diameter respectively. The third was single walled, measuring approximately 9·5 m in internal diameter and abutted the SSW side of the central hut-circle; it was noted by the OS as being of light construction, and is not now visible. About 50 m to the ESE and on the S side of the modern forestry track, there are the possible remains of a third double-walled hut-circle (NO 0579 5983), which measures 9·2 m in internal diameter. A further 20 m to the NE, and

on the same narrow terrace, there are the remains of a single-walled structure, scarped into the rear of the S-facing terrace; it measures about 7·3 m in internal diameter with an entrance on the S. Little now survives of the small cairns and stony banks that the OS recorded lying to the W and E of the hut-circles.

·5   NO 0605 6007, 0603 6004   NO 06 SE 21
Two hut-circles (about 10·5 m by 8 m and 7·5 m in internal diameter respectively) were recorded by the OS amongst a group of small cairns situated close to the crest of the ridge. On the date of visit a few fragmentary cairns were noted within the area delineated by the OS, but neither of the hut-circles was located.

·6   NO 0609 5980, 0617 5984   NO 05 NE 10
On the slopes below (·5), and similarly badly disturbed by forestry ploughing, there are two hut-circles (about 10·5 m and 9 m in internal diameter). Little can now be seen of the small cairns that lay close by; a forestry track, however, runs across at least two stony banks a little to the N of the easternmost hut-circle.

·7   NO 0609 5951, 0607 5950   NO 05 NE 11
The remains of two hut-circles are situated on the W side of Tom Liath, a heather-covered promontory which extends from the N side of Glen Derby immediately S of the track. The larger of the hut-circles lies on the top of the promontory; it measures 10 m in diameter within a wall 1·7 m thick and 0·3 m high, and there is an entrance gap on the S. The second hut-circle is situated immediately to the SW. It measures 7·2 m in diameter within a bank 1·1 m thick and 0·2 m high, and the entrance is probably on the SSE; the interior has been levelled into the slope. To the NW there is an area of gently-sloping SW-facing ground, which appears to be stone-free and is defined on its N and NE sides by a stony bank extending from the N side of the lower hut-circle.

·8   NO 064 595   NO 05 NE 1, 12, 144
There are eight hut-circles on a ridge to the E of (·7). Six lie on the top of the ridge; five of them (NO 063 595) survive only as low banked enclosures 7 m to 9·7 m in internal diameter, but the sixth (NO 0631 5995) is more substantial and measures 8·4 m in diameter within a wall 1·6 m thick and 0·3 m high. The remaining two (NO 0648 5948 and NO 0651 5942) are on the SE flank of the ridge; they measure 8·2 m and 9 m in internal diameter respectively, and their entrances lie on the SE and SSE. Little can now be seen of the small cairns that the OS recorded around the hut-circles, and landscaping for a chalet development has all but obliterated a group of small cairns that the OS recorded between NO 065 596 and NO 067 599. A group of at least seven cairns, however, (NO 069 599) measuring up to 4 m in diameter survives in pasture at the E end of the ridge which defines the N side of Glen Derby.

127 Glenkilrie, hut-circles, field-system and small-cairns
These groups of hut-circles and small cairns extend along the NE side of the valley of the Ennoch Burn. Further hut-circles have been located on the spur overlooking Glenkilrie, around the steading at Dalnoid (no. 128), and in the headwaters of the valley beyond the Ashintully march dyke (no. 105).

·1   NO 128 621   NO 16 SW 78
Three hut-circles and two platforms are set in a line running down the slope immediately below the track leading from Glenkilrie. The hut-circles range from 11 m to 13·8 m in internal diameter, and the platforms measure

9·2m and 11m in diameter respectively. The interiors of the hut-circles have been levelled into the slope, and the lowest of them is notable for its stepped back-scarp, the lower step faced with large upright slabs. Two small cairns are visible on the slope to the SE and at least ten to the NW.

·2   NO 127 625   NO 16 SW 79
This group of small cairns extends up a shallow gully above the track some 300m to the N of (·1).

·3   NO 125 629   NO 16 SW 80
About twenty-five small cairns are scattered across the face of the SE spur of Lamh Dhearg. Amongst the cairns, and lying about 150m WNW of a clump of larch trees, there is a possible platform about 8m in diameter with a mound of stones on its N side. Two huts are also visible amongst the cairns (no. 277·10).

·4   NO 123 623   NO 16 SW 91, 130–1
Three hut-circles and a group of small cairns are situated on the SE spur of Cnoc Feanndaige to the N of the rocky spur overlooking the remains of the farmstead of Craigies (no. 277·12). The easternmost, which is the best preserved, is double walled and measures 9·2m in internal diameter; the outer wall lies eccentrically to the inner and the gap between the two varies from 2·4m to 4·2m. The remaining two hut-circles were probably set tangentially to each other, but an old field-wall obscures the junction between them. They measure 10·2m and 9·6m in internal diameter respectively, and the latter is enclosed by a wall up to 2·8m in thickness. On the slope below the hut-circles there is a scatter of small cairns and banks accompanied by a large rectangular structure, probably the remains of a building. Further scatters of cairns are visible on the slopes about 100m NW of the hut-circle and on a low ridge 250m to the SE. A cairn set on the crest of the spur 50m NNW of the hut-circles is probably a funerary structure (no. 74).

·5   NO 118 625   NO 16 SW 4
At least four hut-circles are situated between the central and westernmost clusters of the ruins of Craigies farmstead (no. 277·12). One is set on the crest of a knoll in the bottom of the valley, the second lies on a terrace about 100m to the WNW, and the other two are on the steep slope above them. They vary from 7·8m to 13m in internal diameter and, with the exception of the one on the knoll, which is the smallest, their interiors have been levelled into the slope to depths of up to 1·2m.

Apart from the burial cairn situated above the hut-circles (·4), and another to the S of Craigies (no. 15), further evidence of prehistoric activity in the valley is provided by a burnt mount (no. 170) which stands beside a burn 150m NNW of the hut-circles and platforms (·1).

128   Glenkilrie/Dalnoid, hut-circles, field-systems and small-cairns
These hut-circles and groups of small cairns are scattered over the rocky spur to the N of Glenkilrie and the knolls and terraces to the N of the steading at Dalnoid.

·1   NO 134 610   NO 16 SW 139
The remains of two hut-circles are situated some 550m NNW of Glenkilrie, and immediately S of farmstead no. 277·2. The N house (NO 1348 6103) lies on the front of a narrow terrace and measures 8·9m in diameter within a poorly-preserved wall. The second house (NO 1349 6097) is situated about 50m downslope to the S and is crossed by a modern stone dyke. It measures about 7m in diameter within a rear scarp (0·3m high) and a wall

which, apart from a sector on the NW (where there are several probable outer facing-stones), has been reduced to little more than a low stony bank.

·2   NO 1318 6113   NO 16 SW 82
A probable double-walled hut-circle is situated on a terrace immediately above the track leading up from Glenkilrie. It is exceptionally small, measuring 6·2m in internal diameter by 12·3m overall, but numerous facing-stones are visible and there is a well-defined splayed entrance on the SSE.

·3   NO 1311 6103   NO 16 SW 83
Situated on a terrace below and some 110m to the SW of (·1), there are the remains of an enclosed pair of hut-circles which are overlain by several rectangular buildings (no. 277·4). The NW hut-circle is the better preserved and measures 9·1m internally and 15m overall. The SE hut-circle measures at least 7·5m in diameter internally by 16·6m overall, but much of the interior and the outer wall at the rear of the houses have been masked by the later buildings. The entrance is on the S.

·4   NO 131 617 to 134 612   NO 16 SW 84–5
On the broad terrace 100m NE of (·2) there are the remains of at least one Pitcarmick-type building (no. 276·1), and to the NW of it there is a group of small cairns. Further clusters of cairns and banks are scattered along the line of the track between the burial cairn no. 21 and a point 200m NNE of the prominent rock outcrop known as Clach Sgorach.

·5   NO 135 615   NO 16 SW 86
On a low spur 200m NE of a track and 650m WSW of Dalnoid, there are two hut-circles (set 25m apart) within a group of small cairns. The hut-circles measure 6m and 6·5m in diameter respectively within banks no more than 1·4m in thickness by 0·2m in height. One of the cairns, which lies 15m SSE of the SW hut-circle, is exceptionally large, and measures 8m in diameter by 0·5m in height; another a little further to the E is 6m in diameter and 0·7m in height.

·6   NO 141 617   NO 16 SW 7
Four hut-circles are visible to the N of Dalnoid; two lie 100m apart in pasture on the E side of the road, and two (100m apart) in moorland to the W of the road. They range from 7m to 12m in internal diameter.

·7   NO 1437 6241   NO 16 SW 90
The remains of this hut-circle are situated on a terrace at the foot of the slope below the plantation on Creag an Lair. The hut-circle has been cultivated over and now forms little more than a shallow depression 9·5m in maximum diameter with traces of a low bank around its edge.

129   Hill of Alyth, hut-circles, ring-ditch houses, and small cairns
The remains of seven poorly preserved hut-circles, two ring-ditch houses, and a group of small cairns have been identified on the W and SW flanks of the Hill of Alyth.

·1   NO 228 502   NO 25 SW 19
Six of the hut-circles, together with a Pitcarmick-type building (no. 281), are disposed over a distance of 130m on a low rise between a wire fence on the W and the old drove road on the E, some 340m NE Whiteside steading. Beside the fence there is a pair of hut-circles measuring 12·5m and 9·5m in internal diameter respectively; the bank of the larger turns inwards on either side of the

entrance to form a deeply splayed passage comparable to those of double-walled hut-circles. A second pair, with internal diameters of 5·7 m and 11 m by 9·8 m respectively, lie on a terrace about 70 m further E; on the NW and SW sides of the smaller hut-circle there are traces of an outer bank linking it to the bank of the larger. On the crest of the rise to the NE of this pair there is a hut-circle about 6·5 m in internal diameter and, 7·5 m to the ESE of it, a double-walled example measuring 7·5 m in internal diameter and 16·3 m overall. There is a burnt mound (no. 172·1) adjacent to the old drove road about 100 m to the E.

·2   NO 224 502   NO 25 SW 29
About 300 m W of (·1) and to the WNW of a wrecked burial cairn (no. 26), there are two ring-ditch houses set 30 m apart. The larger, which is situated on the leading edge of a terrace, measures about 14·5 m in overall diameter and its entrance is on the SW. The other, which is better preserved, lies at the foot of the slope to the NW; it measures 12·5 m in overall diameter and the

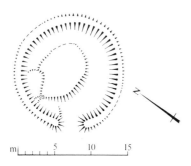

129·2 Hill of Alyth, ring-ditch house, 1:500

entrance, which is also on the SW, leads into the bottom of the ditch. The ditch is best defined to the S of the entrance, where it is up to 3·8 m broad by 0·3 m deep.

·3   NO 232 497   NO 24 NW 54
A group of about seven small cairns lies on the SW flank of the Hill of Alyth 400 m NW of Kirklandbank farmhouse. One of the cairns is much larger than the rest and measures 6 m in diameter by 0·3 m in height.

·4   NO 2340 4970   NO 24 NW 62
Immediately above the improved ground, 150 m E of (·3), there are traces of a hut-circle overridden by cultivation ridges. It measures about 16 m in overall diameter.

130   Hill of Cally, hut-circles, field-systems and small cairns

The Hill of Cally lies between Strathardle and Glenshee, and it extends SE from the foot of Balmyle Hill to the junction of the two valleys at Bridge of Cally. The slopes of the ridge steepen towards the SE, but the summit area is broad and relatively flat. Evidence of medieval and later settlement and land-use is restricted to two areas (see ·1 and ·3 below), and modern land improvements have encroached upon the prehistoric remains on the E and SE.

·1   NO 118 549   NO 15 SW 8
On the northernmost part of the ridge there is a linear settlement of hut-circles aligned NW to SE along the crest of a low rise. Six of the hut-circles are grouped into three
130·1 enclosed pairs, and they range from 9·2 m to 11·1 m in internal diameter, each having an entrance gap on the S or SW arc. A ring-ditch 3 m wide and about 5 m in internal diameter is visible in A. At the SE end of the group there

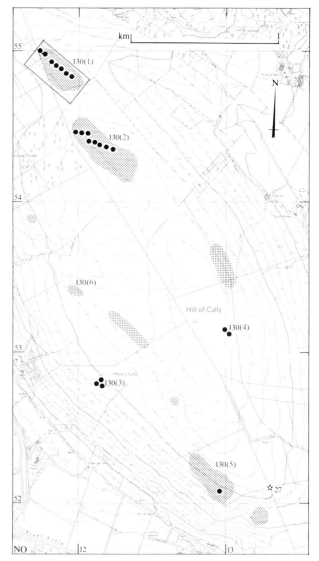

130 Hill of Cally, 1:25 000

are the remains of two single-walled hut-circles (9·2 m and 8 m in internal diameter), one of which is overlain by a field bank, which follows the crest of the rise to pass close to the entrances of the SE pair of hut-circles. It continues and blocks the access to the central pair.

The field bank, which also overlies two of the enclosed pairs, is one element of a multi-period field-system surrounding the hut-circles. The chronology of the field-system is unclear, but the wedge-shaped furrows probably represent the latest episode of cultivation and may be associated with a rectangular building which is situated on a narrow terrace on the W (no. 283). The furrows may have been superimposed on to a series of subrectangular plots defined by low terraces and stony banks, but the relationship of these and the small cairns to the hut-circles is impossible to ascertain without excavation.

·2   NO 121 543   NO 15 SW 9
Situated towards the NW end of the ridge 400 m SSE of (·1) and immediately E of Blackcraig Forest, there is a linear settlement of eight hut-circles aligned NW to SE over a distance of 250 m. At the NW end there is a hut-circle measuring 11 m in diameter within a wall with inner facing-stones visible on the SE and NE. The entrance is probably on the SW, and the interior, which contains a possible ring-ditch, has been terraced into the slope. From a point 6 m W of the hut-circle a rubble bank arcs around the N side and runs for a distance of about 40 m

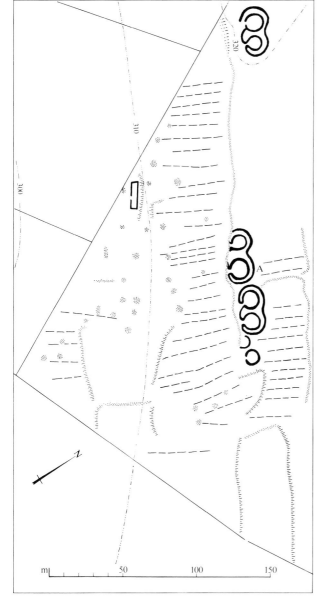

130·1 Hill of Cally, hut-circles and field system, 1:2500

third a short distance to the ENE (no. 283·2), may be contemporary with a large enclosed plot of rig-and-furrow cultivation which is situated about 70 m E of the hut-circles.

·4   NO 1299 5314, 1301 5312   NO 15 SW 13
Situated towards the E edge of the flat-topped summit area, there are two poorly-preserved hut-circles. Both lie on low natural rises, and they measure 11 m and 13 m in diameter respectively over walls which have been reduced to turf-covered banks measuring up to 2·5 m in thickness and 0·2 m in height. Both have single entrance gaps, on the S and SSW respectively.

·5   NO 1295 5208   NO 15 SW 11–12, 14, 23–5
This hut-circle (10 m in internal diameter) is situated at the SE end of a group of small cairns on the SW flank of the ridge. The interior is levelled into the slope and on the downhill side the wall is 1·5 m thick and 0·3 m high, but on the uphill side the space between the wall-faces forms a ledge running around the top of the back scarp and there is no trace of any core material. There is an entrance (1·9 m wide) on the S side, and a section of the wall on the E side is masked by field-clearance. The surrounding small cairns have suffered from relatively recent land improvement, but further groups of cairns survive on the S end of the ridge at NO 132 519, on the summit at NO 126 526 and NO 123 531 respectively, and on the E edge of the summit at NO 192 535. The latter group has been encroached upon by improvements on its W and S margins, but it still contains about eighty cairns measuring up to 5 m in diameter and 0·5 m in height. A final group of five cairns (the largest measuring 7 m in diameter and 0·7 m in height) is situated within poorly-drained rocky ground on the W flank of the ridge 300 m SE of Hillside farmhouse (NO 1168 5387).

·6   NO 1201 5339   NO 15 SW 22
A small field-system is situated on the SW face of a low ridge towards the W side of the Hill of Cally. It comprises a series of parallel banks running up and down the slope. The banks are 1·2 m thick and 0·2 m high and the longest is 45 m in length. The banks define narrow strip-fields comparable with those overlooking Loch Benachally (no. 310·15–·18), but here there is no evidence of later settlement in the immediate vicinity. About 45 m to the W there is a small cairn 5 m in diameter.

131   Hill of Drimmie, small cairns
NO 185 497   NO 14 NE 4
Two small cairns are visible above the road on the S flank of Hill of Drimmie.

132   Hill of Easter Bleaton, hut-circles
The remains of three groups of hut-circles are disposed on the NW and S flanks of the Hill of Easter Bleaton; the two at the S end survive within clearings in a forestry plantation but the NW group has been ploughed and planted.

·1   NO 148 569   NO 15 NW 7
Situated high up on the S face of the southern spur of the Hill of Easter Bleaton, there is a row of five hut-circles ranged at right angles to the contours. The uppermost (NO 1482 5698) is double walled; it measures 7·5 m in internal diameter by 13 m overall and the entrance is on the SSE. Below it, and levelled into the slope, there are two smaller houses (up to 5·5 m in internal diameter). At the SW end of the row there is an unusual pair of double-walled hut-circles. The NE house is 17·5 m in overall

before petering out 12 m N of a second hut-circle. This hut-circle measures 9·2 m in diameter and has an entrance on the S side and it has been levelled into the slope. Although the position of the bank around the two hut-circles may suggest comparison with enclosed pairs of hut-circles, it is likely that it is no more than a field-bank. The remaining hut-circles measure from 5·7 m to 11·6 m in internal diameter and, where visible, the entrances are on the S or SSW arc. In two examples the interiors have been levelled into the slope, but in none are there substantial remains of either inner or outer wall-faces. Close by there are a number of small cairns and stony banks.

·3   NO 1213 5279   NO 15 SW 20
Situated on a terrace on the SW flank of the hill 1·5 km S of (·2), there is a group of three hut-circles and two rectangular buildings (nos. 283·2). The largest of the hut-circles is double walled, measuring 8·6 m in internal diameter by 14·8 m overall with a widely-splayed entrance on the S. The poorly-preserved second hut-circle (4 m in internal diameter and with no apparent entrance) is situated 6·5 m to the E. Situated about 9 m SE of the first, the third hut-circle measures 4 m in diameter and has an entrance on the S. The two rectangular buildings, and a

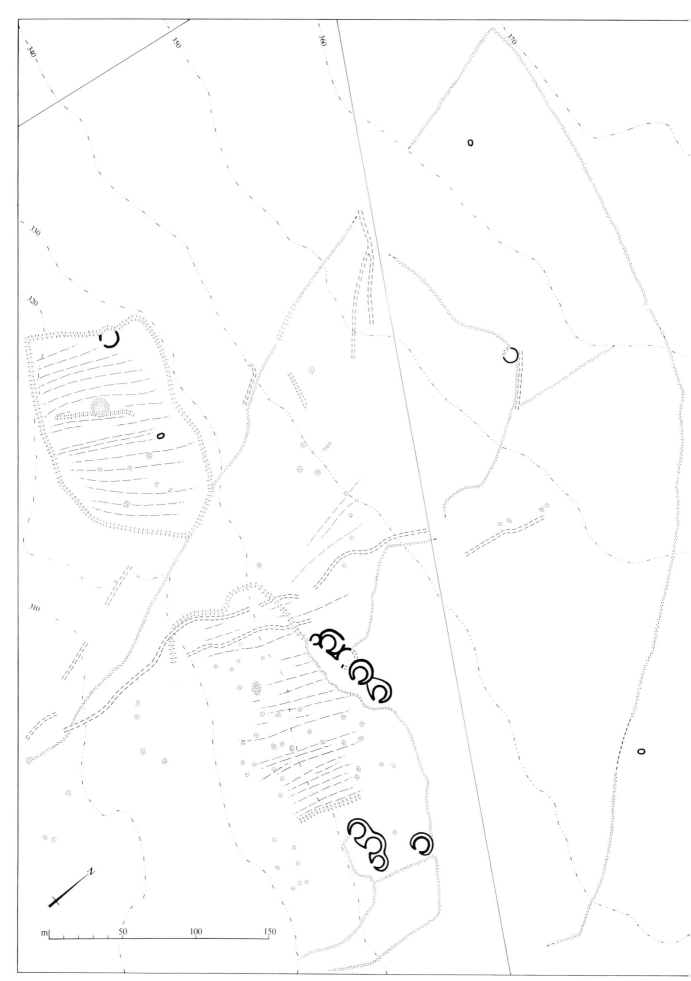

133A Hill of Kingseat, hut-circles and field-system, 1:2500

133B Hill of Kingseat, hut-circles, aerial view from SE

diameter by 9 m internally, with a ring-ditch in the interior and an entrance, 1·3 m wide, on the SSE; the other is 9 m in internal diameter with an entrance on the SE, but in this case the outer wall springs from the outer wall of the NE house.

·2   NO 145 570   NO 15 NW 8
The remains of two hut-circles are situated about 150 m WNW of (·1). The first (NO 1458 5698) measures about 9·1 m in diameter within a rubble wall 1·8 m in thickness and 0·3 m in height, and there is an entrance on the SSW. The second lies about 40 m to the NW (NO 1456 5702) and is double walled, measuring 7·8 m in internal diameter by 14 m overall. The inner wall is partially composed of slabs set on edge and the entrance is on the S.

·3   NO 145 581   NO 15 NW 9
The remains of two hut-circles are situated within a thick conifer plantation low down on the NW flank of the Hill of Easter Bleaton, and the following description is based on OS records. The SE hut-circle (NO 1457 5816) 124 measured 7·5 m in diameter within a boulder-faced wall (1·4 m thick) and had an entrance on the S. The second house (NO 1453 5824) was situated some 85 m to the NW and measured about 10·5 m in diameter between wall centres. A third hut-circle is situated on the crest of a knoll near the foot of the hill (NO 1445 5814); it measures about 8 m in internal diameter.

133   Hill of Kingseat, hut-circles, field-system and small cairns
NO 158 545   NO 15 SE 3

Situated on the lower SE slopes of the Hill of Kingseat 134 overlooking the Rough Burn, and in an area of moorland crossed by the Ashmore/Shieldrum march dyke, there is a group of remains which includes hut-circles, a field-system and small cairns, as well as traces of later settlement and agriculture (no. 284·1).

At the centre of the field-system there are two strings of hut-circles. The N group comprises the remains of what 133A have probably been four double-walled houses and a small hut. Three of the double-walled houses are well preserved, but the fourth has been reduced to an arc of walling on the W and a fragment of the E side of the entrance. This house is clearly earlier than its E, and probably its W, neighbour, but the chronological relationship of the other houses is uncertain. The small hut that overlies the W hut-circle wall is choked with field-gathered stones and may be of comparatively recent origin. To the S of the houses there is an embanked courtyard. The S group of hut-circles comprises three conjoined double-walled houses fronted by an embanked courtyard, while a fourth double-walled hut-circle lies a short distance to the NE. The only other prehistoric building within the field-system is a much reduced single-walled hut-circle, which lies to the N of the march dyke.

The field-system is enclosed on three sides by a stony bank, while the fourth side was probably formed by the steep-sided gully of the Rough Burn. What may be an original entrance through the enclosure bank can be seen on the N, and within the interior there is a series of minor divisions and small cairns (the latter lying in greatest numbers on the more steeply sloping ground to the S of the two strings of hut-circles). The area to the S of the march dyke has been disturbed by later activity, and there are traces of rig-and-furrow cultivation, four stretches of field-wall or linear clearance, and numerous hollowed trackways leading up from a ford across the Rough Burn. Also belonging to later phases of activity are two huts that lie close to the enclosure bank on the N.

To the W of the prehistoric field-system, and partially

55

E

overlying it, there is an irregular enclosure (probably of
late 19th-century date), which contains a single-walled
hut-circle and, at its centre, an indeterminate (but
probably prehistoric) mound, as well as traces of rig-and-
furrow cultivation, clearance cairns and a small enclosure.
On a terrace below the enclosure there is a group of at
least twenty-two small cairns (not shown on plan). To the
W the ground has been extensively cultivated, but a single
circular house-platform survives on the slopes above the
farmstead no. 284·1 (NO 1525 5484).

134   Hill of Kingseat/Saebeg, hut-circles and small cairns
A series of groups of small cairns and hut-circles is
scattered to either side of the public road that crosses
over the saddle between Hill of Kingseat and Saebeg.

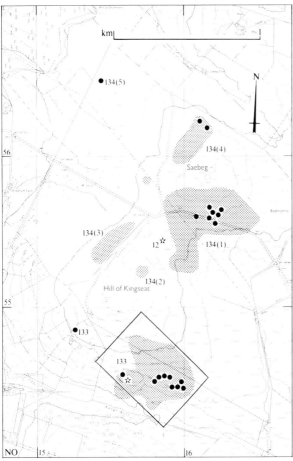

134 Hill of Kingseat / Saebeg, 1:25 000

·1   NO 162 556   NO 15 NE 2
The principal group of hut-circles is situated on the N side
of the road about 350 m ENE of Cairn Gleamnach
(no. 12). A large double-walled hut-circle, with an internal
diameter of 10·5 m, lies on the leading edge of a terrace
which overlooks a line of four hut-circles. The
easternmost is the best preserved; it measures 9 m by 8 m
internally, and a small pen or hut has been built on the W
side of its interior. The next building is 7·5 m in internal
diameter and is flanked by traces of a pair with internal
diameters of 5·5 m and 5·3 m respectively. Due S of the
pair, its N side clipped by the construction of the road,
there are the remains of a further hut-circle (8·3 m in
internal diameter), and what may be part of another is
visible on the S side of the road 130 m to the WNW. The
surrounding group of cairns covers an area of about 25 ha,
extending from the SE flank of Saebeg across the E slopes
of the saddle and on to the NE flank of Hill of Kingseat.

·2   NO 157 552   NO 15 NE 27
A group of about fifteen small cairns, the largest only 2 m
in diameter, is situated on a terrace 250 m SSW of Cairn
Gleamnach (no. 12).

·3   NO 155 554   NO 15 NE 28
About sixty small cairns extend along the gentle NW-
facing slope below an old stone dyke on the NW flank of
Hill of Kingseat. There are traces of broad cultivation
ridges amongst the cairns, and three small huts are visible
at the SW end of the group (no. 284·2).

·4   NO 161 561   NO 15 NE 8, 29
Two hut-circles are situated 50 m apart on the N shoulder
of Saebeg. The NW house is double walled, measuring
7·5 m in internal diameter by 14·8 m overall; its walls have
been severely robbed, but on the S they coalesce on
either side of the entrance, forming a bank 4·3 m in
thickness. The second hut-circle is about 8 m in internal
diameter, and there are possible traces of a third
immediately to the SW. To the S of the two hut-circles
intermittent traces of a stony bank can be seen enclosing
an area of about 1 ha. Beyond this enclosure a thin scatter
of cairns extends towards the SW, ending in a cluster of at
least six about 80 m E of the track leading to Corb. A
further 200 m to the SW at least two more cairns are
visible 80 m below the track (NO 1574 5583).

·5   NO 1544 5649   NO 15 NE 30
A heavily robbed hut-circle, its wall reduced to robber
trenches and three inner facing-stones, is situated on a
low ridge 60 m W of the stone dyke that runs along the
foot of the NW flank of Saebeg. It measures 10·5 m in
internal diameter.

135   Hill of Persie, hut-circles
The remains of eight hut-circles and two groups of small
cairns have been identified on the rocky E flank of the
Hill of Persie.

·1   NO 132 559   NO 15 NW 3
Four hut-circles are spread over a distance of 170 m
between an old dyke and a shallow gully high up on the
face of the hill, while a further three can be seen on a
rocky knoll to the NE. The best preserved is the
uppermost of the hut-circles; its interior, which has been
levelled into the slope on the NW, measures 9·5 m in
diameter, and a few outer facing-stones protrude from its
bank. The other hut-circles have been severely robbed
and reduced to little more than shallow scoops or
platforms ranging from 8·5 m to 10·8 m in diameter. On
the slopes below the three to the NE of the gully there is a
scatter of irregular clearance heaps.

·2   NO 1336 5551   NO 15 NW 59
What may be the remains of a double-walled hut-circle,
measuring 9·6 m by 8·8 m internally, is situated on a knoll
200 m N of a pond. The outer wall of the hut-circle is
clearly visible on the E and N but no trace of it survives
on the W.

·3   NO 135 552   NO 15 NW 33
A scatter of small cairns (up to 6 m in diameter) extends
SE from the burial cairn no. 30. Amongst the cairns there
are traces of a rectangular building and two enclosures
(no. 301·2).

136   Invereddrie, hut-circles
NO 1351 6783   NO 16 NW 28
Two hut-circles are situated on a terrace 250 m SW of

Invereddrie farmhouse. The better preserved, which is on the leading edge of the terrace, measures 9·8 m in internal diameter, but for much of its course the wall has been reduced to little more than an external scarp 0·4 m high. All that can be seen of the other, some 16 m to the NE, is a low mound from 0·2 m to 0·4 m high, with a flat top 11 m in diameter.

137 Invereddrie/Westerton, hut-circles and small cairns
A number of hut-circles and groups of small cairns are disposed around the edges of a large natural amphitheatre about 1 km NE of Invereddrie steading. Much of the area is covered with peat, and the hut-circles are restricted to well-drained knolls and terraces.

·1   NO 135 691   NO 16 NW 56
Situated on a SW-facing terrace about 600 m E of Westerton farmhouse and just below the head-dyke, there are at least two severely robbed hut-circles. The first is double walled (NO 1356 6914), measuring 9 m in diameter internally by 17·8 m overall and there is an outwardly-splayed entrance (2·3 m wide) on the S. The second hut-circle lies on a low knoll 30 m to the SSE (NO 1359 6911) and measures 11·5 m in diameter overall; a slight depression on the S side may indicate the position of an entrance. At least twelve small cairns (measuring up to 5 m in diameter) are situated immediately to the N and E of the hut-circles.

·2   NO 135 694   NO 16 NW 55
Situated in a slight depression between a low knoll to the SW and gently rising ground to the NE, there is a probable hut-circle, which measures 7·8 m in diameter within a low stony wall. Numerous small cairns (up to 7 m in diameter) are situated on improved ground to the NW and SW, and to the SE there are a number of narrow plots defined by low stony banks up to 30 m in length.

·3   NO 1409 6911   NO 16 NW 72–3
The remains of a hut-circle, which measures 12·5 m in diameter within a heather-covered rubble wall 1·3 m thick and 0·1 m high, are situated immediately S of a rough track about 1·1 km E of Westerton farmhouse. Much of the interior and the wall on the S and SW have been destroyed by a small quarry.
   A group of small cairns is situated 360 m NE of the hut-circle (NO 1430 6946).

·4   NO 146 687   NO 16 NW 71
Situated on a low rise on the S edge of high moorland, there are the remains of a hut-circle (NO 1459 6875) which measures 10·5 m in diameter within a low turf-covered wall up to 2·7 m thick and 0·2 m high. The entrance, which is on the SSW, leads into a shallow ring-ditch.
   A second hut-circle (NO 1464 6878) is situated on a gentle SW-facing slope about 50 m to the ENE of the first; it measures 6·5 m in diameter within a low heather-covered wall and there is an entrance on the SW. A number of small cairns are visible close by, and a further group of small cairns lies on a low rise about 150 m to the SSW.

·5   NO 149 701   NO 17 SW 88
The remains of two hut-circles are situated on the S side of a shieling-group on the E side of the mouth of the Green Glen (no. 286·11). The uppermost of the hut-circles (NO 1493 7012) measures 5 m in diameter within a low wall up to 2 m thick and 0·2 m high. The interior has been levelled into the slope and there is an entrance on the S. Situated about 60 m to the SW there is a second hut-circle

(NO 1488 7008), which measures about 10 m in diameter within a low wall 1·7 m thick and 0·2 m high. There are several possible outer facing-stones close to the entrance on the S side. See also no. 286·7–·8 for some possible small cairns at the head of the Green Glen.

·6   NO 1517 6998   NO 16 NE 9
The remains of a hut-circle are situated on a low rise on the W side of the track which leads into Gleann Carnach. It measures 9·1 m in diameter within a low wall; the N and E sides are poorly preserved and there is no indication of the entrance, but on the W there are several possible outer facing-stones.

·7   NO 1529 6976   NO 16 NE 8, 23
A probable hut-circle, which measures 8 m in diameter within a turf-covered wall (1·8 m thick and 0·1 m high), is situated on a low promontory ridge at the mouth of Gleann Carnach. Sections of the wall have been destroyed, but on the E of the interior there is a shallow ring-ditch which extends from the entrance on the SE to a point on the N. Several small cairns and short lengths of stony bank are scattered across the stony, S-facing slope about 100 m NE of the hut-circle.

138 Kinkeadly, small cairns
      NO 2082 5261   NO 25 SW 28
A group of four possible small cairns is situated on the N flank of a low rise immediately above the coniferous plantation on the steep E bank of the Alyth Burn.

139 Lair, hut-circles and small cairns
A number of hut-circles and small cairns are disposed around the E and S flanks of Torr Lochaidh, a largely afforested hill situated NW of Lair.

·1   NO 143 641   NO 16 SW 52
The remains of at least seven hut-circles and a burnt mound (no. 178) are disposed along the top of, and at the base of, a terrace on the E flank of Torr Lochaidh (between NO 1427 6427 and NO 1435 6404) immediately E of the public road (A93). The houses lie in improved pasture and all are poorly preserved; they measure from 7·5 m to 11 m in diameter within low walls and, where visible, the entrances are situated on the SSW or SE arcs.

·2   NO 1402 6380   NO 16 SW 6
This hut-circle is situated on a narrow terrace 480 m NNW of Lair cottage; it measures 9·5 m in diameter over a grass-covered wall up to 2·1 m thick and 0·2 m high, and the position of the entrance is uncertain.

·3   NO 1388 6381   NO 16 SW 47
Two hut-circles are situated on the W side of a slight rise 130 m W of (·2). The first measures 9·4 m in diameter within a stony wall 1·7 m thick and 0·2 m high; the position of the entrance is uncertain and the only other feature visible is a slight scarp on the E side of the interior. The second lies 21 m to the ENE (NO 1391 6382). It is 11·7 m in diameter within a wall 1·5 m thick and 0·1 m high; the entrance is on the SSE, and the rear of the interior is levelled into the slope. See also no. 2.

190·3

·4   NO 13 64   NO 16 SW 34, 39, 43, 135
Four groups of small cairns lie on moorland to the NW, W and S of (·3). To the N of the Allt Corra-lairige there is a group of at least three cairns (NO 140 635), while 300 m NW of (·3) there is a group of four cairns in an area of rig-and-furrow cultivation (NO 137 640; see also no. 291·14). To the S of the burn, 150 m SW of three Pitcarmick-type

buildings (no. 290·1), there are at least three cairns and two lengths of bank (NO 137 635), and there are traces of a scatter of cairns to the WNW of another Pitcarmick-type building (no. 290·2) on the E flank of Lamh Dhearg 600m further to the WNW (NO 130 637).

·5 NO 140 647   NO 16 SW 100
Situated some 800m N of Torr Lochaidh there are two groups of small cairns which lie on E-facing terraces on the N and S banks of the Allt Coire Lanard. Each group comprises about six cairns (up to 3m in diameter), and at the N edge of the NW group there is a low rubble bank.

140 Loch Benachally, hut-circles, field-systems and small cairns
Loch Benachally is an artificially dammed loch situated at the S end of the valley of the Craigsheal Burn. To the E the valley shares a low watershed with the Baden Burn (see no. 106) but on the W and N it is enclosed by high, craggy hills. The hut-circles, field-systems, and small cairns are described from SE to NW along the W side of the valley, and from NW to SE along the E side.

·1 NO 072 497   NO 04 NE 11
This group of six hut-circles, two circular structures, and a surrounding field-system are situated on the S shore of Loch Benachally, and they extend from a broad terrace on the NE to the hillslopes on the SW.

Four of the hut-circles lie on the terrace. Two have single walls, and measure 7·8m and 8·5m in internal diameter respectively. The remaining two are double walled: the more easterly measures 8·4m in diameter internally by 15·1m overall, and the entrance, which is on the S, leads into an enclosure (21m by 9·3m) on the SE of the hut-circle; the W hut-circle lies immediately E of the single-walled hut-circles and measures 10m internally by 16·7m overall with an entrance (1·9m wide) on the SSE.

To the SW, on a higher terrace, there is a pair of houses and an associated enclosure. The earliest element lies on the W and comprises a hut-circle 10·5m in diameter within a wall 0·8m thick and 0·2m high with an entrance on the S; immediately to the E, and probably later, there is a second hut-circle (7·3m in internal diameter with a well-defined inner face of slabs laid on edge). Springing from the NE arc of the first hut-circle there is an enclosure bank which almost entirely encloses the second house and links the entrances of the two houses. A further short stretch of bank links the E side of the entrance passage of the W house to the W side of the entrance of the E house. To the SW there are the remains of two further circular structures, possibly shieling-huts, measuring 3·6m and 6·5m in diameter respectively; both have stone walls with entrance gaps on the ESE, but only the smaller has a well-defined inner face.

·2 NO 0530 5009   NO 05 SE 19
This double-walled hut-circle measures about 7·6m internally by 14m in diameter overall. The entrance (1·7m wide) is situated on the SSE, and it has a distinct outward splay. Several small cairns lie on the slopes below the hut-circle.

·3–·5 NO 06 50, 06 51   NO 05 SE 11, 25, 36
Situated on the NW side of the loch, there are two groups of small cairns (·3) NO 0637 5077, (·4) NO 0616 5113. A further group (·5) occupies steeply sloping ground (NO 0600 5085), and at the W end of this group there is a stony bank which forms a U-shaped enclosure, open on its E side.

·6 NO 0512 5180   NO 05 SE 35
Situated within the valley of the Allt Lochan a' Chait, there is a group of about twenty small cairns measuring up to 3m in diameter.

·7 NO 0532 5178   NO 05 SE 34
About 200m E of (·6), there is an area of strip-fields comprising a series of seven roughly parallel stony banks which measure up to about 40m in length and are about 6m to 9m apart.

·8 NO 0604 5204   NO 05 SE 12
This particularly interesting group of three hut-circles is situated on the SE flank of Spurn Hill. On the SW there is a double-walled house, which measures about 7·5m in diameter internally by 17m overall and has an entrance on the SE. Lying 10m to the NE, there is an unusual double-walled house; it measures 8m in diameter internally with an entrance on the SE. From the N side of the entrance the outer wall is concentric with the inner wall, but on the W, instead of completing the circuit, it turns abruptly and joins the outer wall of the SW house. On the SE, the outer wall swings in a gentle arc away from the entrance, and again links on to the outer wall of the SW house. To the NE of the entrance, and in part overlying the line of the outer wall, there is a single-walled hut-circle 8·5m in diameter with an entrance on the ESE. The sequence of construction of this group is therefore clear: the SW house was the first to be built; it was followed by the central house (which could have been occupied contemporaneously); and finally the single-walled house was built (presumably superseding the central house).

There are three subrectangular buildings, probably shieling-huts, lying on top of the houses (no. 246·1), and on the slopes to the SE a number of small cairns and banks are visible.

·9 NO 0603 5220   NO 05 SE 13
Situated on the E flank of Spurn Hill 130m N of (·8), there is a hut-circle, which has been levelled into the slope. It measures 9·5m in diameter within a wall 1·5m thick and 0·2m high, and there is a poorly-defined entrance gap on the E.

·10 NO 0638 5230   NO 05 SE 14
A group of three hut-circles is situated on a rocky rise on the E side of the Craigsheal Burn. Two of the hut-circles measure up to 10·5m and 11·7m in internal diameter and have entrances on the S and SE sides respectively; the former is partly overlain by the footings of a subrectangular structure (no. 246·3). The third hut-circle is double walled and measures up to 9·7m in diameter internally and about 15m overall. Several inner and outer facing-stones are visible, including a small upright boulder on the W side of the entrance (1·8m wide), which is situated on the SSE. The hut-circles are partially enclosed by a stony bank which rises out of boggy ground to the SW and runs past the SE side of the hut-circles to peter out a short distance to the NE; a subrectangular structure (no. 246·3) abuts the S side of this bank immediately SE of the hut-circles. Situated on the gentle slope to the S, there is a group of about twenty small cairns; a kidney-shaped enclosure (measuring about 55m by 25m within a low bank) lies about 150m NNW of the hut-circles.

·11 NO 0663 5200   NO 05 SE 15
A double-walled hut-circle, measuring 10m in internal diameter and 16m overall, lies on a terrace on the E side of the valley. There is an entrance on the S, but any other features were masked by a thick growth of heather on the

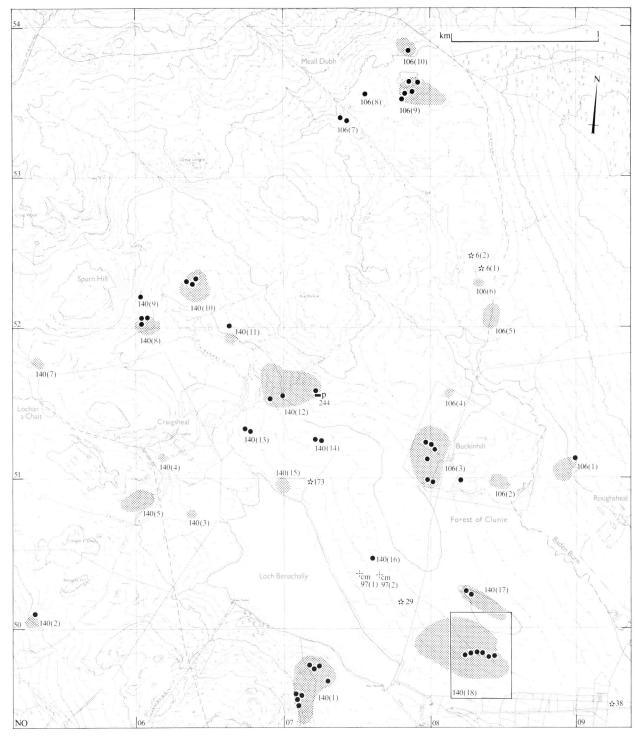

140 Loch Benachally, 1:25 000

date of visit. Situated on a low knoll immediately to the SW, there are the footings of three subrectangular buildings (no. 246·4), and on the slope below, there is a scatter of at least ten small cairns.

·12 NO 070 515   NO 05 SE 16
Situated on a gentle, SW-facing slope on the E side of the valley about 600 m N of Loch Benachally, there are three hut-circles and a field-system comprising small cairns and stony banks. The E hut-circle (NO 0721 5158) sits upon a low knoll at the rear of a broad terrace and measures 16·7 m in overall diameter. The interior is largely masked by a Pitcarmick-type building (no. 244). About 210 m to

the W there is a double-walled hut-circle (NO 0701 5155) which has been levelled into the SW-facing slope. It measures about 10 m in internal diameter and about 22 m by 18·8 m over the outer wall, which ranges from 1·4 m to 4 m in thickness. Situated a further 70 m to the W, there are the poorly-preserved remains of a hut-circle (NO 0690 5153) measuring 9·3 m in diameter within a low wall. The hut-circles lie towards the S edge of the field-system, which comprises small cairns and stony banks.

·13 NO 0675 5132   NO 05 SE 17
The remains of two hut-circles are situated on a low rise 300 m N of Loch Benachally: one measures 13·6 m in

140·18 *Loch Benachally, hut-circles and field-system, 1:2500*

internal diameter and has an entrance (about 3 m wide) on the SE; the other, lying immediately to the E, is double walled with an entrance (2 m wide) on the SSW, and measures 8·2 m in internal diameter and 16 m overall.

·14 NO 0722 5125   NO 05 SE 7
A pair of hut-circles is situated on a knoll on an otherwise featureless SW-facing slope, about 420 m NE of Loch

Benachally. The W hut-circle lies on the highest part of the knoll and measures about 8·2 m in diameter within a low stony bank about 2 m thick; there is a possible entrance gap on the SE. The second hut-circle, situated about 10 m to the ESE, measures about 7 m in diameter within a low stony bank about 1·8 m thick, and it, too, has a probable entrance on the SE.

·15 NO 0699 5100   NO 05 SE 28
Situated about 350 m SW of (·14) and close to the NE
shore of Loch Benachally, there is a group of about
twenty small cairns.

·16 NO 0760 5046   NO 05 SE 9
A poorly-preserved hut-circle is situated on the summit of
a low ridge 300 m E of Loch Benachally; it measures 8 m
in diameter within a low stony bank and has a probable
entrance on the ESE. A stony bank springs from the SE
side of the hut-circle and extends in a SE direction for a
short distance before petering out close to several possible
clearance cairns. OS surveyors also identified a double-
walled hut-circle 250 m to the SSE, but all that was visible
beneath deep heather on the date of visit were two
hollows. For nearby cupmarks and a cairn see nos. 29, 97.

·17 NO 0825 5023   NO 05 SE 18
Situated on the crest of a whale-backed ridge to the NE of
the Loch Benachally Dam there are two hut-circles and a
scatter of small cairns. The W hut-circle measures about
11 m in diameter internally and may be of double-walled
construction, but all that is visible in the interior is an
enclosure of more recent date. To the E there are the
wasted remains of a double-walled house; all that survives
of the inner wall are the butts of the hair-pin terminals at
either side of the entrance. The outer wall is not circular,
but splays towards the W house; this suggests that the E
house may originally have formed the E portion of a pair
of houses, the W element of which is now overlain by the
surviving W hut-circle. An arc of probable field-bank
springs from the W wall of the W house, and the scatter
of small cairns (up to 5 m in diameter by 0·3 m in height) is
disposed along the crest of the ridge.

·18 NO 083 498   NO 04 NE 10
This group of hut-circles, which is situated on open
moorland to the ENE of Loch Benachally Dam, is
disposed along the contour immediately above a break in
slope. There are five tangential large hut-circles, which
are flanked by two free-standing houses and four small
(and probably secondary) huts, and to the E an isolated
large hut-circle with an attached enclosure. The tangential
houses range from 11·3 m to 7 m in diameter and the three
to the W have internal scarps, suggesting that they may
have been double walled. The two flanking large houses
both have internal grooves within the walls, and may
either be of multi-period construction or double walled.
An arc of bank springs from the W side of the entrance of
the W house to form a yard in front of the line of houses;
before it joins the field-bank there is a gap which
probably marks the position of an original entrance.

The field-system comprises two major elements: a large
field to the N and W of the houses and a smaller field to
the S. Neither field is completely enclosed, but both
probably used the stream at the bottom of the slope to
form their SW side. On the NE of the larger field there is
a subdividing bank that runs NNE from a hut-circle, and
to the E of its junction with the main bank there is an
original entrance.

The small cairns and linear clearance heaps are
scattered to the N, W and S of the houses, but they are
entirely absent from the plot formed by the subdivision.
Later activity is represented by traces of rig-and-furrow
cultivation to the N, W and S of the houses, and to this
period may also belong the zig-zag section of bank to the
N of the hut-circles.

141 Loch Charles, hut-circles and small cairns
Loch Charles occupies the floor of a shallow basin high up
(350 m OD) in the hills that form the W flank of

Strathardle, and on the S-facing slopes to the N and E of
the loch there are numerous groups of hut-circles.

·1 NO 083 545   NO 05 SE 2
The westernmost group of hut-circles is situated on
gently-sloping ground to the NNW of the loch. Near the
foot of the slope there are two hut-circles set side by side,
each measuring about 9·7 m in internal diameter. To the
NW there is a line of three hut-circles; the central hut-
circle is the most substantial, and it probably post-dates
the hut-circle to the E. The other two hut-circles have
been reduced to little more than platforms. Midway
between the row of three and the pair there is what may
be another hut-circle, but it is obscured by deep heather.
About fifty-four small cairns are scattered around the hut-
circles. Later use of the site is indicated by the presence of
rectangular huts (see no. 293·3).

·2 NO 084 547 to 090 545   NO 05 SE 3
A number of hut-circles are spread, singly and in clusters,
round the low rim of the basin to the NNE of the loch.

Three (a pair and an outlier) are situated in the angle
between the Pitcarmick/Woodhill march dyke and a
triangular plantation (NO 086 546). The pair comprises a
double-walled house (10·7 m in diameter internally by
17·5 m overall) which is overlain by the single-walled
house on the N (8·2 m in internal diameter with an
entrance on the SSW); the outlier, which is 10 m to the
SSE, has been reduced to little more than an oval hollow
measuring 7·5 m by 6·5 m with an entrance on the SSW.

From the NE angle of the triangular plantation there is
a line of at least six hut-circles extending to the NW.
Immediately N of the plantation there are two, which
have been reduced to platforms 9·5 m in diameter; about
40 m to the NW there is a twin double-walled house (the
W half measures 7·6 m in diameter internally and the E
8·2 m). On the E the outer wall is incomplete, and
originally it may have extended to the SE to include a
shallow depression (possibly the remains of a third
house). A further hut-circle (12 m in internal diameter)
lies immediately to the NW and it is overlain by the W
half of the double-walled house.

On a rocky ridge 100 m to the NW (NO 086 547) two
hut-circles are visible (both measure about 10 m in
internal diameter). In the angle between the E side of the
plantation and the march dyke there is a ploughed down
hut-circle (8 m in internal diameter); a second (10 m in
internal diameter) lies 70 m to the S, and at least one more
(9·5 m in internal diameter) is visible on the crest of a
knoll a further 60 m to the ESE.

Two more are set on a knoll on the N side of the march
dyke. The interior of the better preserved example
measures about 9 m in diameter and has been levelled into
the crest of the knoll; the other lies immediately SW and
measures 7·5 m in internal diameter. On the NE flank of
the same knoll there is what may be another hut-circle
which survives as little more than an overall platform
measuring 8·8 m by 7·5 m.

On the S side of a shallow gully to the SE of the knoll
and immediately NE of the march dyke, there is a
heather-clad hut-circle measuring 7·3 m in internal
diameter, and 50 m to the SE a second measures about 7 m
in diameter internally. A thin scatter of small cairns is
visible around the hut-circles, and several banks can be
seen to the N and W of the plantation.

·3 NO 091 544   NO 05 SE 4
To the SE of (·2) the rim of the basin descends gently
towards the burn that drains the loch; at least three hut-
circles are visible on the spur thus formed. The
easternmost (11 m in internal diameter) lies on the S side
of the track leading down to Woodhill; the other two lie

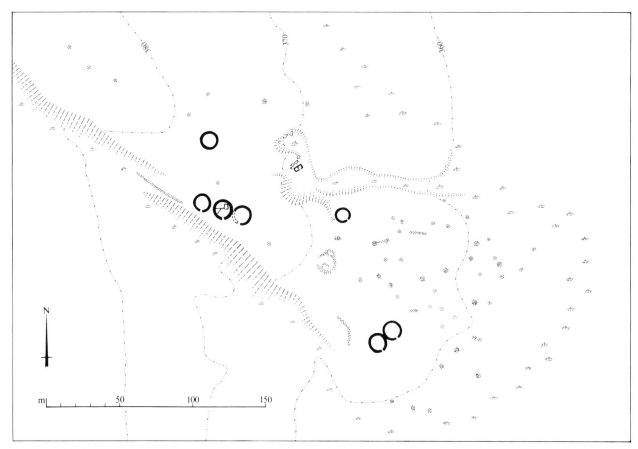

141·1 Loch Charles, hut-circles, 1:2500

on the N side of the track and have been heavily robbed
and little more than stony rings, 16m and 11·8m in overall
diameter respectively, now survive. There are several
small cairns and rickles of stones in the vicinity of the hut-
circles.

142 Loch Crannach, hut-circles, field-systems and small cairns

121 A number of hut-circles are to be found both singly and in
groups around Loch Crannach. The loch, which is
artificial, lies at a height of about 415m OD in a natural
basin, and the hut-circles extend up the flanks of the
surrounding hills to heights of 470m OD.

·1 NO 051 675   NO 06 NE 47–8
This group of hut-circles is situated on the ridge that
forms the rim of the basin to the W of the loch. It
comprises a compact cluster of four hut-circles (two of
them tangential), a fifth on a rocky knoll 100m to the W,
and a sixth in a forestry plantation 150m to the NNE.
They range from 6.2m to 10m in internal diameter, and
the interiors of five of them have been levelled into the
slope. The entrances of the tangential pair are on the
SSW. To the N there is a cluster of small cairns (NO 050
677), and to the W, outside the area covered by this
volume, three further hut-circles.

·2 NO 0559 6790   NO 06 NE 49
Two hut-circles lie 17m apart on gently sloping ground
300m due N of Loch Crannach. Measuring 8·7m and 10m
in internal diameter respectively, they form little more
than shallow hollows enclosed by low stony banks.

·3 NO 0588 6794   NO 06 NE 50
This double-walled hut-circle is situated on the fringe of a

group of small cairns on the low ridge that forms the W
bank of the Allt a' Choire Charnaich. The hut-circle,
which measures 9·3m in internal diameter and 17m
overall, is notable for the concentric ring-ditch visible
within its interior. At least ten small cairns and two banks
are scattered across the broad crest of the ridge to the S of
the hut-circle.

·4 NO 0614 6796   NO 06 NE 55
There are traces of a shallow platform (8m in diameter)
levelled into the gentle slope to the E of the Allt a' Choire
Charnaich 260m E of (·3).

·5 NO 0628 6777   NO 06 NE 51
This hut-circle lies on the E flank of a knoll. It measures
about 7·3m in internal diameter.

·6 NO 058 676   NO 06 NE 54
A group of five hut-circles is situated in a small plantation
on the E bank of the loch. Two lie on the E side of the
plantation; both measure about 8m in internal diameter
with entrances on the SSW, and there are traces of a
shallow ring-ditch within the N house. The third hut-circle
lies on a terrace to the S of the plantation; it is about 8m
in internal diameter but is poorly preserved and is
overlain by a shieling-hut (no. 273·14). The remaining two
are situated side by side in the middle of the plantation, a
little further down the slope; they measure 7·4m and 8m
in internal diameter respectively, both have internal ring-
ditches, and entrances facing SW.

·7 NO 0600 6744   NO 06 NE 52
This hut-circle lies 180m SE of the plantation. It measures
7·3m in diameter within a bank from 2m to 3·6m in
thickness, and the entrance is on the WSW. Immediately
within the bank there is a ring-ditch.

·8 NO 0568 6722   NO 06 NE 53
There are traces of a hut-circle with an internal diameter of 10 m amongst the fallen trees and branches at the W end of the plantation.

143 Mains Moss, hut-circles
These hut-circles are situated in small clearings in a new forestry plantation on a ridge that lies between Mains Moss and Hatton Moss.

·1 NO 193 509   NO 15 SE 37
On the SE flank of the ridge there are the remains of four hut-circles disposed in two pairs about 70 m apart. All of the hut-circles have, to some extent, been levelled into the slope, and all have entrances in the SE. The NE pair (NO 193 509) measure 9 m and 8 m in diameter respectively within walls which have been reduced to turf-covered banks up to 4·5 m in thickness and 0·2 m in height.
    The SW pair (NO 192 509) measure 8·5 m and 7 m in diameter respectively within walls reduced to banks up to 3·4 m in thickness and 0·4 m in height. Both hut-circles have been robbed, possibly to build the enclosure bank that surrounds an extensive plot of rig-and-furrow cultivation immediately to the SE.

·2 NO 1873 5061   NO 15 SE 7
This possible hut-circle (previously identified as a cairn), which sits on a terrace on the SW flank of the ridge 600 m to the WSW, has been reduced to a low mound (16 m in diameter overall) with a shallow depression at its centre.

144 Mains of Creuchies, hut-circle
NO 1970 5153   NO 15 SE 53
There are traces of a probable hut-circle (about 9 m in internal diameter) in the gateway at the junction between a fence and a stone dyke 180 m ENE of the stone circle no. 79.

145 Mains of Mause, hut-circles and small cairns
The remains of several groups of hut-circles and small cairns have been found around the head of the Morganston Burn on the W side of Glen Ericht. The hut-circles and cairns are disposed around the edge of a natural amphitheatre at the centre of which there is a reservoir, and the sites are described here from N to S.

·1 NO 154 500   NO 15 SE 34–5
Situated at the edge of heather moorland and about 80 m NE of the Military Road, there are the poorly-preserved remains of three hut-circles. The first (NO 1544 5005) measures 10 m in internal diameter with an entrance on the SE; the second lies immediately to the E and measures 7 m in diameter internally by 11 m overall, and the third, about 20 m to the SE (NO 1547 5003), is probably double walled, measuring 7·5 m internally by up to 15·8 m overall. Situated 13 m to the E there is a robbed cairn which measures 6·5 m in diameter over a low rim; it is probably part of a field-system, faint traces of which survive in the improved field to the NE of the hut-circles.

·2 NO 1550 4973   NO 14 NE 70
A group of at least ten small cairns (measuring up to 5 m in diameter) is situated on a gentle S-facing slope about 150 m NE of the reservoir.

·3 NO 15 49   NO 14 NE 68–9
Two small groups of cairns (NO 1564 4907 and NO 1529 1429), measuring up to 5 m in diameter, are situated 450 m SE and 120 m SSW respectively of the reservoir.

·4 NO 1557 4924   NO 14 NE 71
Situated on a narrow terrace on a gentle NE-facing slope, there are the remains of a hut-circle which measures 9·3 m in diameter within a turf-covered wall spread up to 2·6 m in thickness and 0·3 m in height. Surviving facing-stones indicate an original wall-thickness of about 1·5 m, and the entrance is probably on the ESE. Several small cairns are scattered throughout the area of heather moorland to the N and W.

·5 NO 1581 4921   NO 14 NE 67
The remains of this hut-circle are situated in improved pasture about 240 m E of (·4). It measures 6 m in diameter within a turf-covered wall up to 2·3 m in thickness and 0·2 m in height; a robber trench is visible around most of the perimeter, and an entrance gap is situated on the E.

146 Middle Mause, small cairns
During the 19th century numerous groups of small cairns were removed from the fields around Middle Mause. Their approximate former extent can be recovered from the first and second editions of the OS 6-inch map (Perth, 1867, sheet 52; 1901), and a thin scatter of cairns still survives beyond the modern head-dyke to the W.

·1 NO 1649 4887   NO 14 NE 22
The second edition of the OS 6-inch map depicts an area immediately to the E of the Haer Cairn (no. 23) as the 'site of several cairns', and the first edition shows a single cairn 180 m to the S (Name Book, Perth, No. 11, p. 52).

·2 NO 1675 4884   NO 14 NE 22
Several cairns lay in the vicinity of the urn burials (no. 56) found on a low rise 300 m to the ENE of (·1), but they were removed about 1840 (Name Book, Perth, No. 11, p. 52).

·3 NO 161 485   NO 14 NE 22
The second edition OS map identified an area 300 m WSW of (·1) as the 'site of numerous cairns'.

·4 NO 163 479   NO 14 NE 21
The first edition OS map shows a group of cairns in a field of rough pasture 250 m W of Hilltown of Mause, but they were removed before the second edition was prepared, and the area is now under the plough. By 1864 a number of cairns had been removed from the field to the W, where a bronze axe (now lost) was also discovered (Name Book, Perth, No. 11, p. 59).

·5 NO 155 481 to 158 481   NO 14 NE 21
A thin scatter of small cairns extends over the crest of a low hill immediately W of the improved fields. One of the cairns (NO 1581 4813), which was depicted on the first edition map (Name Book, Perth, No. 11, p. 59), is larger than the rest and measures about 7·5 m in diameter by 0·3 m in height.

Although no hut-circles were recorded in the vicinity of these groups of small cairns, it is likely that the majority were produced as a result of field clearance. The Reverend James Playfair, however, discovered 'burned bones' in a 'tumulus' near the Haer cairn (*Stat. Acct.*, 19 (1797), 370), and some of the cairns, particularly the larger examples (·1 and ·5), may be funerary.

147 Middleton Muir, hut-circles, field-systems and small cairns
The groups of hut-circles, numerous field-systems and clusters of small cairns, taken together with the burial

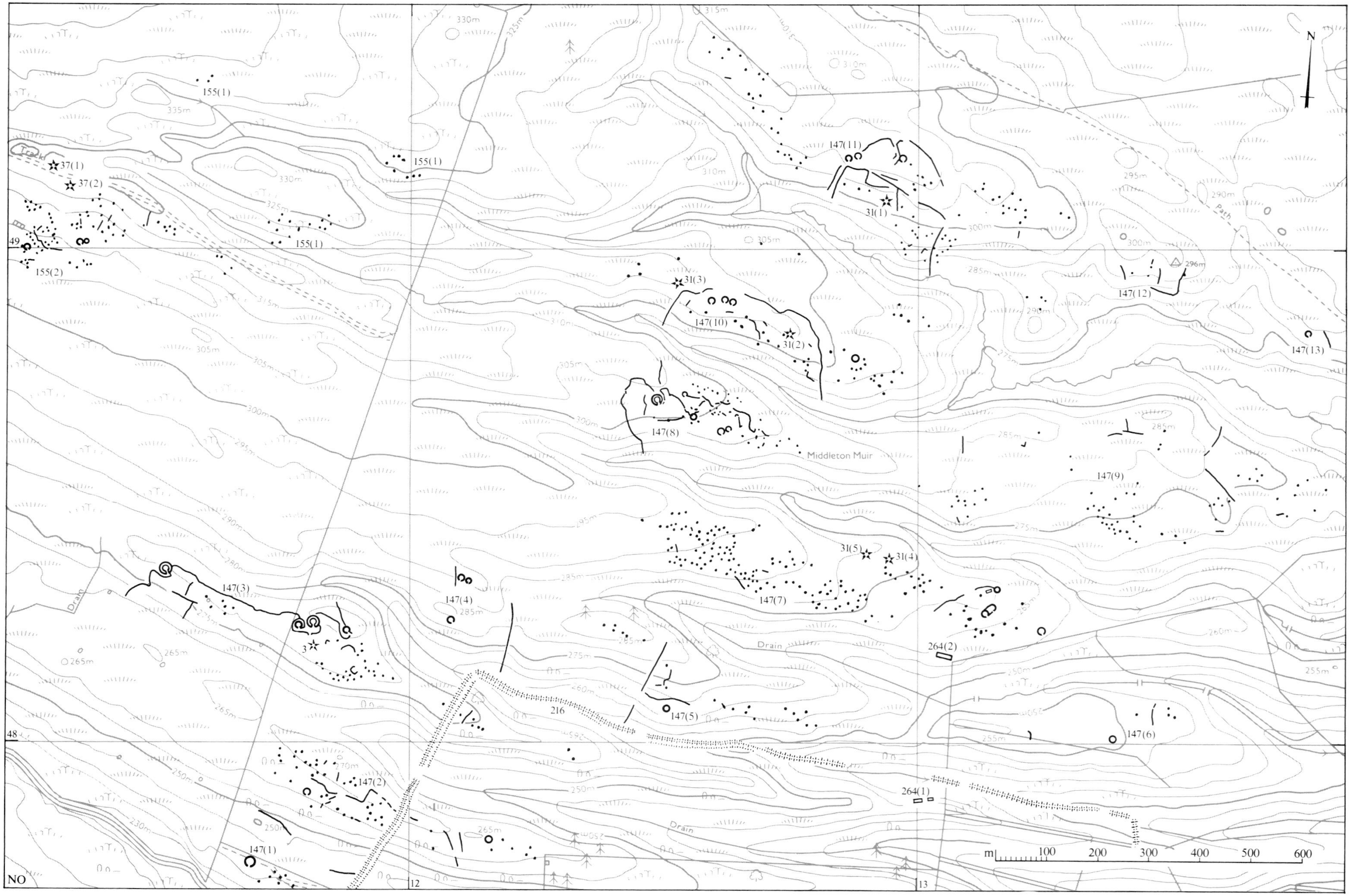

N

Middleton Muir

Drain

Drain

Drain

Path

147(13)

147(12)

147(11)

147(9)

147(10)

31(1)

31(2)

31(3)

31(4)

31(5)

147(7)

147(8)

147(6)

147(5)

147(4)

147(3)

147(2)

147(1)

264(1)

264(2)

216

155(1)

155(1)

155(1)

155(2)

37(1)

37(2)

49

3

13

12

NO

48

m   100   200   300   400   500   600

147 Middleton Muir 1:10000

cairns (no. 31) and the ring-cairn (no. 3), which are disposed over Middleton Muir, constitute one of the most extensive assemblages of prehistoric remains in North-east Perth. Middleton Muir rises northwards from the Lornty Burn (200 m OD) to a height of 315 m in a series of parallel ridges, which have given the country a marked WNW–ESE grain. Medieval and later ploughing has been restricted to the southernmost of the ridges, particularly within the medieval deer park known as the Buzzart Dikes (no. 216); doubtless the prehistoric settlements extended eastwards towards the modern farm of Middleton, and Pennant notes that 'in certain parts within [the deer park] are multitudes of tumuli' (1776, 453), a description that can hardly be sustained by the sparse scatter of hut-circles and small cairns visible there today.

·1 NO 116 477 to 120 476   NO 14 NW 26, 31
There are five hut-circles strung out along the lowest of the ridges on the N side of the Lornty Burn. They are in
149 varying states of preservation, and, working from E to W along the ridge, they measure 7·5 m, about 16 m, 10 m by 9 m, 6·2 m and 15 m in internal diameter respectively. The last is notable for the inturned wall-terminals on either side of the entrance. In the areas between the hut-circles there are traces of stony banks cutting across the axis of the ridge, one of them partly overlain by the park pale, and to the E of the westernmost hut-circle there is a scatter of small cairns.

·2 NO 117 479 to 122 477   NO 14 NW 14
On the ridge to the N of (·1) and W of the deer park earthwork, there is a substantial hut-circle measuring 10·7 m in internal diameter. About thirty small cairns are scattered along the ridge to either side of the hut-circle and there is at least one low stony bank. To the E of the earthwork the scatter of cairns peters out amongst possible traces of rig-and-furrow cultivation, and there is what may be a second hut-circle, now reduced to little more than an earthen ring-bank with an overall diameter of 12 m.

·3 NO 114 483 to 119 481   NO 14 NW 4
A more complex group of hut-circles is situated on the E
147·3 side of the Middleton/Laighwood march dyke, where it crosses over the ridge to the N of (·2). It comprises a single-walled hut-circle occupying the summit of the ridge, a double-walled hut-circle some 50 m to the WNW, and a probable ring-ditch house adjacent to the march dyke. The single-walled hut-circle measures 11 m by 10 m internally and is skirted by a trackway on the W and S. The double-walled hut-circle has been severely robbed, but several facing-stones are visible, and it measures 11·3 m in diameter internally and 20 m overall, with a deeply splayed entrance on the S. The ring-ditch house measures 9·5 m in overall diameter and, where best defined, its ditch is 3·8 m broad and 0·3 m deep. It is unlikely that all these structures are of the same date and detailed examination of the bank that forms the outer side of the trackway around the single-walled hut-circle, suggests that it overrides the outer wall of the double-walled hut-circle and encloses the ring-ditch house. From there the bank extends for a distance of 230 m along the N side of the ridge to a fourth hut-circle (a double-walled example measuring 9 m in diameter internally and 19 m overall), and then dog-legs down the slope. Two banks and a scarp to the SE of the hut-circle suggest the presence of fields at this end of the ridge, and there is a scatter of small cairns a little farther down the ridge to the ESE. A further scatter of cairns lies to the S of the main group of hut-circles, most of them set along the leading edge of the ridge, so that they appear on the skyline when viewed from lower ridges to the S; most are between 2 m

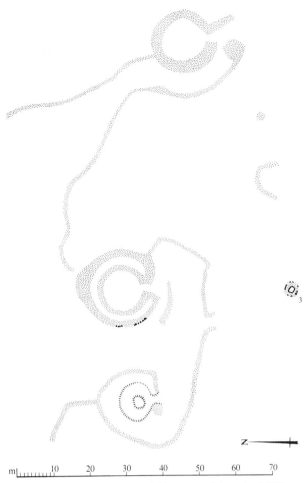

147·3 Middleton Muir, hut-circles, field-system, and ring-cairn, 1:1000

and 3 m in diameter, but on the E there are two larger examples measuring 5 m and 6 m in diameter respectively. Finally, to the E of the deer park, a stony bank, surrounded by a thin scatter of probable small cairns, cuts across the axis of the ridge.

·4 NO 1209 4824, 1211 4833   NO 14 NW 18
To the E of the main group of hut-circles described in (·3) and on a low rise that forms the shoulder of the adjacent ridge, there are the remains of a hut-circle marked by little more than an irregularity in the surface of the heather. It measures about 8·5 m in diameter internally and its entrance is on the SE. On the crest of the ridge 70 m to the N, there is a pair of hut-circles set side by side. Although the lines of their inner wall-faces are clearly marked by a series of slabs (up to 0·5 m in height), the outer faces, and consequently the chronological relationship between the two houses, have been obscured by stone-robbing. Unlike the areas around the majority of other hut-circles, there is little trace of stone clearance, but a possible bank crosses the ridge immediately to the W of this pair, and on the E side of a shallow gully to the E of the single hut-circle a short length of another is visible.

·5 NO 124 482 to 127 480   NO 14 NW 19
Continuing ESE from the hut-circles described in (·4), there is a group of six small cairns situated on the crest of a local summit. Immediately to the SE of them a stony bank cuts across the ridge and probably drops into the gully on the SW. Another bank runs along the side of the ridge, and on a low rise to the S of it there is a probable hut-circle with an internal diameter of 8 m and an

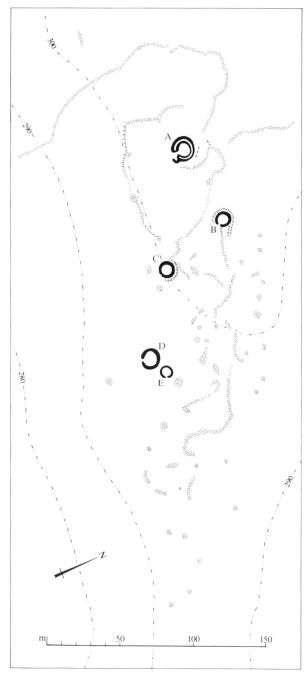

147·8A Middleton Muir, hut-circles and field-system, 1:2500

building (no. 264·2). Two of the hut-circles have been severely robbed, the easternmost reduced to an oval platform 9·5 m in maximum diameter, and the northernmost to an earthen ring-bank about 7 m in internal diameter. The third hut-circle, which has an internal diameter of about 8·5 m, has been incorporated into the WSW end of an oval enclosure measuring 21·5 m by 10·5 m within a ruinous stone wall. There are two entrances in the SE side of the enclosure, the southern one leading into the interior of the hut-circle. Immediately W of the northernmost hut-circle there is a small subrectangular hut measuring 9·5 m by 6 m overall. The relationship of the cairns to the hut-circles is not known, but a rickle of stones that runs up to the W side of the northernmost hut-circle may well overlie its wall, which is significantly more stony at this point.

·8   NO 124 486 to 127 486   NO 14 NW 7
The five hut-circles of this group show considerable variation in the details of their construction. The westernmost (A) is a double-walled hut-circle measuring 8 m in diameter internally and 16·5 m overall; outside the deeply-splayed entrance, which is on the S, there is a

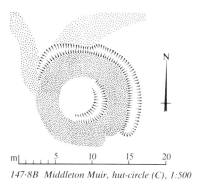

147·8B Middleton Muir, hut-circle (C), 1:500

small annexe. The next hut-circle (B) to the E measures 7·5 m by 6·7 m internally, and there are traces of a shallow ditch immediately outside its bank. The third hut-circle (C) is an unusual structure, measuring 6·5 m in diameter within a wall 3 m in thickness by 0·4 m in height, with traces of a possible entrance on the SSE. It has a ditch outside the wall, and there is a shallow ditch around the SE side of the interior. About 50 m to the E there is a pair of hut-circles; the westernmost (D) measures 8·5 m in internal diameter and has an entrance on the SE, while the other (E) has been reduced to little more than a low mound with an overall diameter of 9·5 m.

Around the hut-circles there is a field-system which can be divided into two sections. To the W, and centred on the double-walled hut-circle, there is a series of banks which block access along the ridge and form at least one enclosure. To the E, a group of cairns and linear clearance-heaps straggle along the crest of the ridge; several of the cairns are of considerable size, and the largest, which lies immediately NE of the easternmost hut-circle, is a mound 7 m in diameter. The relationship of the hut-circles to the cairns and banks is far from clear. The arrangement of banks to the NE of the double-walled hut-circle, however, suggests that they respect its presence. There is also some evidence to suggest that banks have been robbed, leaving low scars (dashed on fig.), while on the NE the gap between the two walls of the hut-circle is filled with stones, perhaps indicating that stone-clearance continued after its abandonment. Two clearance heaps also run up to C, but without excavation the sequence between the clearance and the surrounding ditch cannot be ascertained.

entrance on the ESE. Two clusters of small cairns are situated on a terrace to the E of this hut-circle.

·6   NO 1338 4801   NO 14 NW 16, 83
What may be a hut-circle, reduced to an earthen ring-bank about 15·5 m in overall diameter, is situated on the crest of a low knoll within the area of the improved fields to the E of (·5). On the shoulder of the ridge to the NE of the hut-circle there is a stony bank and at least four small cairns (NO 134 480), while 160 m to the W there is an arc of bank (NO 1322 4801), which has previously been described as the remains of a second hut-circle.

·7   NO 124 484 to 132 482   NO 14 NW 17
The largest group of cairns recorded on Middleton Muir extends for a distance of about 850 m along the ridge to the N of (·4–·6). Midway along the group there are two burial cairns (see no. 31·4–·5), while at the E end there are at least three hut-circles and a substantial rectangular

·9 NO 130 485 to 137 485   NO 14 NW 27
Scattered down the ridge to the E of (·8), there are a series of small cairns and occasional lengths of bank. Most of the cairns lie in two clusters on the drier slopes that form the leading edge of the ridge, but others are scattered along the crest.

·10 NO 126 489   NO 14 NW 20
Across the gully from (·8) there is a hut-circle group with three houses set on the crest of the ridge and a possible platform dug into the E slope of a low knoll 250m to the ESE. The westernmost measures 14m by 12·5m internally, its low bank turning inwards on either side of the entrance on the S. The other two are set side by side, and almost certainly represent sequential construction. The E hut-circle, which measures 10·5m in internal diameter, is the more complete of the two, and probably the later, but what are possibly two separate lines of inner facing-stones within the thickness of the wall may indicate that it is itself of multi-period construction. The W hut-circle probably measured about 11·5m in internal diameter, and may have been linked to the earlier phase of the E hut-circle by short walls on the N and S. The area around the hut-circles has been enclosed by a long bank, the ends of which rest in the bottom of the gully to the S. A plan of the W end of this enclosure has been published by Feachem (1973, 343) but the site was probably surveyed under deep heather, and, now that the heather has been burnt off, most of the terraces running along the slope can be seen to be natural features. Within the enclosure there is a probable burial cairn set on the crest of a knoll, while to the WNW, overlooking the hut-circles, there is a second, reduced to a low stony mound (see no. 31·2–·3). A thin scatter of cairns lies beyond the enclosure, particularly in the vicinity of the possible house-platform, which measures about 9m in diameter.

·11 NO 129 492   NO 14 NW 21, 82
Three hut-circles lie within a field-system to the NE of (·10). The largest, which is about 9·5m in internal diameter, is situated on the summit of a knoll, while the other two (8·8m and 6·5m in internal diameter respectively) lie a short distance to the W. Again there appears to be an extensive enclosure around the hut-circles, with a trackway running up to the largest house from the N. At the point of contact between the enclosure bank and the hut-circle, the hut-circle wall is markedly more stony, and the bank probably post-dates the hut-circle; a similar relationship may exist with the easterly of the other two hut-circles. Within the enclosure there is a secondary enclosure bank with its ends stretching into the gully to the S. Unlike the other banks, however, it is composed of earth and small stones, and runs in straight sections with sharp angles; it may thus be of comparatively recent date, possibly associated with the phase of occupation attested by a rectangular building which lies 30m SSE of the large hut-circle. On the slope below the hut-circles there is a possible burial cairn (see no. 31·1) but its position is unlike any of the other cairns on Middleton Muir, and it may be no more than clearance on to a natural mound. Small cairns, however, are scattered along the ridge to both the WNW (NO 126 493) and ESE.

·12 NO 134 489   NO 14 NW 49
Further along the ridge to the ESE of (·11) there are traces of banks running up and down the slope below an OS triangulation station. The lower end of the easternmost bank rests on a terrace, which, although possibly a natural feature in origin, undoubtedly marks the bottom of a field.

·13 NO 1377 4883   NO 14 NW 25
This hut-circle lies on the SW shoulder of the ridge 300m ESE of the OS triangulation station. Although its bank has been levelled on the W, enough survives to indicate that the interior measured about 9m in diameter; the entrance is on the S. There is no evidence of stone clearance in the vicinity, but a stony scarp, no more than 0·3m high, drops obliquely down the slope to the E.

·14 NO 148 481   NO 14 NW 3
To the E of (·13) there are two more hut-circles. They lie on the crest of a low rise on the S side of the Glasclune Burn, some 100m E of Carnashach Wood. Both are about 9·5m in internal diameter. The area has been extensively cultivated, and they are in a poor state of preservation. The wall of the W hut-circle is joined tangentially by a bank which runs in a gentle arc towards the E house.

Although a certain degree of pattern is apparent in the layout of some of these major hut-circle groups on Middleton Muir, there is clear evidence to suggest that the landscape represents successive periods of occupation. The existence of a ring-cairn and at least six burial cairns within the area illustrated suggests that occupation on some of these ridges may date from the Late Neolithic or Early Bronze Age. Indeed, there is little apparent relationship between the hut-circles and the groups of small cairns, which may well be of considerably earlier date. As has been shown, however, there is also evidence to indicate that wherever field-banks come into physical contact with hut-circles the banks are likely to be of later date. Nevertheless, the banks either block access along ridges, e.g. (·3) and (·8), leaving funnels leading up to individual hut-circles, or form large enclosures resting on the bottom of a gully; the latter appears to be a variation of the former, and at the northernmost site there is again a trackway leading up to the back of a hut-circle. The chronology of the hut-circles is unknown, and no useful stratigraphic relationships are visible on Middleton Muir. The single ring-ditch house at (·3), however, can be compared with cropmarks in Fife and Tayside which have been dated to the first half of the 1st millennium BC.

148 Moss of Cochrage, hut-circles and small cairns
Two groups of small cairns and hut-circles are situated on the hill that rises from the S bank of the River Ardle at Bridge of Cally. Most of the flank of the hill has been afforested, and it is likely that other prehistoric settlements have been destroyed on the lower slopes.

·1 NO 139 510 to 143 510   NO 15 SW 30
The northern group of cairns, which extends along the shoulder of the hill between the Military Road and a birch wood, contains up to ten hut-circles. To the W three are set in a line running up the crest of a rocky ridge beside the road; all have been heavily robbed, with the smallest reduced to little more than a platform, but enough survives to show that they measured 7·8m, 6m and 10·2m in internal diameter respectively. A possible fourth, 6m in internal diameter, lies beneath a small stone pen immediately to the S; half of a fifth is visible on the S side of the road to the SW, and half of a sixth can be seen on the opposite side of the road a further 110m to the ESE. At least three others, their walls reduced to little more than stony swellings, are situated at the E end of the group of cairns. Two of them, which lie 25m and 50m S of the SE corner of the birch wood, measure 6·5m and 7·5m in internal diameter respectively. The third, situated at the foot of a natural scarp some 20m to the W, measures 8m in internal diameter; around its S half there are traces

of a concentric outer wall reduced to a low scarp enclosing an area of 17·8 m across. Immediately to the W and below some large boulders, a hollow (7 m in diameter with traces of a stony bank on its W side) may mark the position of another hut-circle. A further 15 m W along the foot of the scarp, there is what appears to be an arc of ditch 2·3 m broad, which is only visible where its outer lip has been cut back into the slope; it may indicate the position of a ring-ditch house with an overall diameter of at least 10·2 m.

·2   NO 1375 5052   NO 15 SW 10
Only one hut-circle (10 m in internal diameter) is visible within the second group of cairns, which lies to the N of the Moss of Cochrage, just outside Blackcraig Forest. Most of the cairns lie in a strip of forestry ploughing adjacent to the boundary dyke, but a few extend into some fields of rig-and-furrow cultivation to the E. Several short lengths of bank, one of which runs up to the NE side of the hut-circle, are also visible amongst the cairns.

149   Muir of Gormack, hut-circles, field-system and small cairns
The Muir of Gormack is an area of rough pasture lying to the S of the Lornty Burn, and it forms the southernmost of the ridges that are such a conspicuous topographical feature of Middleton Muir. As on the ridges of Middleton Muir (no. 147), the Muir of Gormack contains a remarkable concentration of settlement remains, which are here described from E to W.

·1   NO 132 470   NO 14 NW 68
At least two hut-circles, and what may be a third, are situated on a low rise immediately W of the improved fields at the E end of the Muir of Gormack. All have been severely damaged by rig-and-furrow cultivation; the two westerly houses measure about 9·5 m in internal diameter, while the easternmost, which has been reduced to little more than a shallow depression and is now overgrown with gorse bushes, is about 10·5 m.

·2   NO 1329 4720   NO 14 NW 67
This hut-circle, which measures about 10·8 m in internal diameter, is situated within a group of cairns and field-banks at the eastern extremity of the Muir of Gormack. Immediately SE of the hut-circle there are traces of a two-compartment rectangular building some 16·8 m in overall length, and there are also slight remains of rig-and-furrow cultivation in the gaps between the cairns.

·3   NO 127 473   NO 14 NW 65
At least two hut-circles are set on a low rise 50 m W of the fence that divides the Muir of Gormack into two. Both have been severely robbed, and the easterly was partly obscured by a cattle feed-bin on the date of visit; they measure 6·5 m and 8 m in internal diameter respectively. The E side of the easterly house is possibly overlain by a third hut-circle (8·5 m in internal diameter). There is a scatter of cairns and banks to the S and W of the hut-circles.

·4   NO 125 473   NO 14 NW 64
This group of six hut-circles is disposed over a distance of 100 m on a gently SE-facing slope. The best preserved (A) measures 8·8 m in internal diameter, and twenty-eight inner facing-stones are visible around the N half of the wall. On the NW, where the interior has been levelled into the slope, little core-material can be seen behind the inner face, but to the S the wall increases in thickness (up to 3 m by 0·4 m in height) to form club-shaped terminals on both sides of the entrance. A second hut-circle (B), which measures about 9·1 m in internal diameter, has had a wall 3 m thick, faced internally with upright slabs and externally with low boulders; like many of the double-walled hut-circles, it has a deeply-splayed entrance passage. From E to W, the remaining hut-circles measure 4·5 m, 7 m, 5·6 m and 6·8 m in internal diameter respectively. The stone clearance heaps around the hut-circles appear to be divided from those of the neighbouring field-system by a long stony bank which extends from the top of the slope to the bottom. The most notable features of the clearance to the E of the bank are

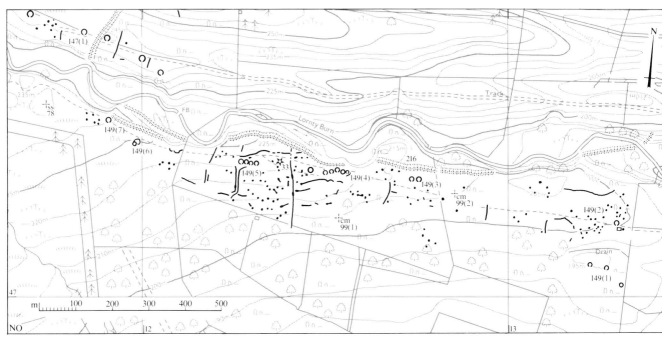

149, Muir of Gormack, hut-circles, 1:10000

9·4–5 Muir of Gormack, hut-circles and field-system, 1:2500

the broad spreads of stones that are visible in some of the natural hollows in the slope.

·5 NO 122 473   NO 14 NW 61–2
This group of hut-circles comprises a row of four with internal diameters ranging from 8·3 m to 9·5 m. One of the hut-circles (C) is of considerable interest, for there is evidence of a medial wall-face, indicating at least two periods of construction. In its latest phase this hut-circle measured 8·4 m in internal diameter and the wall was

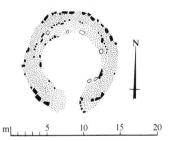

149·5 Muir of Gormack, hut-circle (C), 1:500

2·8 m in maximum thickness. The hut-circles are set so close together that it is unlikely that they are all contemporary. In its final form hut-circle C, the best preserved of the four, is probably later in date than either of its immediate neighbours. One of the hut-circles (D) may also overlie a hollow way, which approaches it from the NE. This trackway cuts through the field-banks to the E, while another, flanked by low banks, runs up to the hut-circles from the S. Numerous small cairns and a burial cairn (E; see no. 33) lie between the embanked trackway and the bank marking the E side of the field-system, and to the W there is at least one, and probably two, cleared fields, extending as far as a group of cairns immediately

beyond a stone dyke. On the edge of the scarp to the N of the cairns there is an irregularly shaped enclosure measuring 13 m by 6 m within a stony bank; its date and purpose are unknown.

·6 NO 1197 4741   NO 14 NW 60
About 130 m WNW of the stone dyke at the W end of the Muir of Gormack, there is an enclosure which may incorporate the remains of a hut-circle. The enclosure measures 18 m by 13·5 m internally, and its bank curves inwards on the S to either side of the entrance. The hut-circle has been reduced to little more than a roughly circular hollow about 7·5 m in diameter set within the curve of the bank on the W side of the entrance.

·7 NO 1190 4747   NO 14 NW 59
The westernmost of the hut-circles on the Muir of Gormack is set on a low rise immediately S of the park pale (no. 216), at the W extremity of its S side. A modern trackway cuts across the centre of the hut-circle, which measures 11·8 m in internal diameter. At least six small cairns are visible to the W.

As on Middleton Muir, the existence of a possible burial cairn (no. 33), two cupmarked stones (no. 99) and a four-poster stone circle (no. 78) amongst the settlement remains, shows that prehistoric use of the Muir of Gormack may have begun as early as the third millennium BC. Some of the clearance heaps, which are fairly randomly disposed across the area, may also be of this date, but the hut-circles are probably considerably later. Although none of the hut-circle groups can be dated, their overall distribution, particularly in the central section, points to an orderly distribution, involving regularly spaced settlements, each with its own area of arable ground on the S-facing slopes below. The evidence of multi-period construction in group (·5), however,

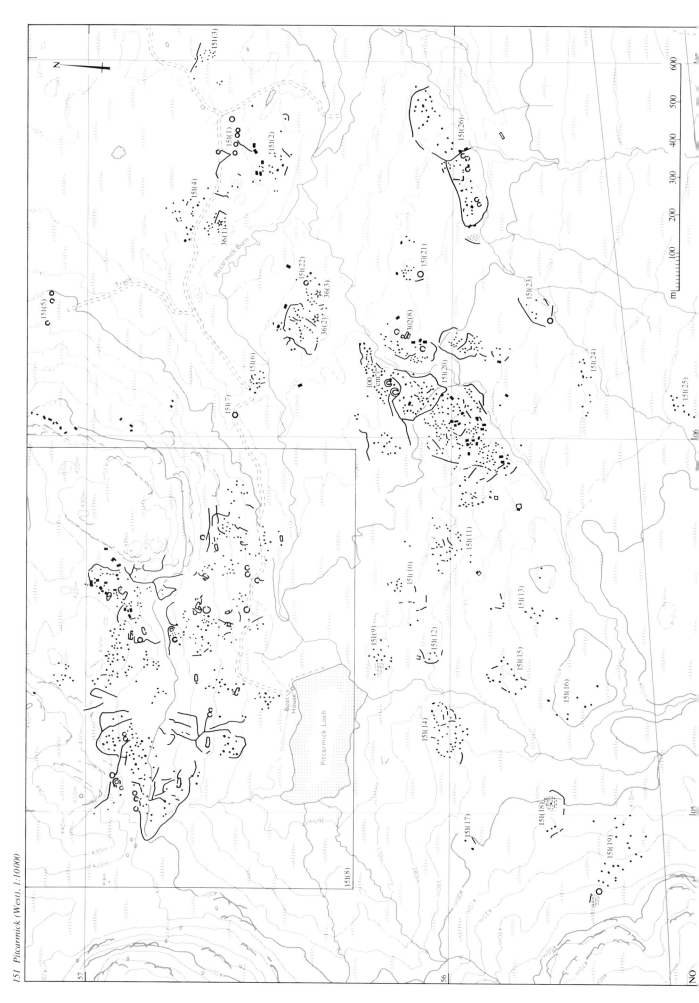

151 Pitcarmick (West), 1:10000

suggests that each group developed separately. Apparently absent from the groups are examples of double-walled hut-circles; hut-circle B of group (·4), however, with its thick wall and deeply splayed entrance, and the wrecked westernmost hut-circle of group (·5), again with traces of a deeply-splayed entrance and thick bank, may well indicate hut-circles of this type.

150 Olies Burn, hut-circles and small cairns

Olies Burn is a minor tributary of the Alyth Burn and rises in moorland about 1 km WSW of Smyrna cottage.

122 Situated on a low ridge on the N side of the deep stream gully, there is a group of six hut-circles within a field-system, and on the S side of the stream there is a solitary hut-circle and three groups of small cairns.

·1   NO 189 526   NO 15 SE 25

This group of hut-circles is disposed in a line of five with a sixth lying immediately to the N. The W hut-circle (NO 1883 5265) has been terraced into the slope and may be of double-walled construction. It measures 8 m in diameter within a wall 3 m thick and 0·2 m high; on the N there is an internal scarp (0·5 m high) and the wall bifurcates to form two distinct banks 3·7 m apart. About 20 m to the ENE there is a small hut-circle (NO 1886 5266) 7 m in internal diameter with an entrance on the S. Tangential to the E arc there is a double-walled hut-circle which measures 8·2 m in internal diameter by 15·3 m overall and has an entrance (1·2 m wide) on the S. A fourth hut-circle lies a few metres further to the E; it measures 6 m in internal diameter and its entrance is on the SSE. The easternmost hut-circle (NO 1890 5266) is double walled and measures 8·2 m in diameter within a wall 0·9 m thick and up to 0·4 m high; the inner face, which is composed of upright stones, is almost complete, but the outer facing-stones are well preserved only on the S, close to the entrance. The outer wall (1·7 m thick and 0·4 m high) measures 18 m in overall diameter. The sixth hut-circle (NO 1889 5268), a little to the N of the line of five, measures 9·5 m in internal diameter and is probably of multi-period construction. The interior has been terraced into the natural slope, and on the N the wall divides into two banks (1·6 m apart and about 1 m thick and 0·2 m high); the entrance is on the S.

The hut-circles lie within a field-system comprising numerous small cairns and several short lengths of stony bank. A smaller group of cairns (NO 1917 5257) is situated on broken ground 250 m E of the hut-circles.

·2   NO 1828 5250   NO 15 SE 58

This hut-circle is situated on a low rise 280 m SE of Olies Burn, and measures 10·7 m in diameter within a wall reduced to a stony bank 1·8 m thick and 0·2 m high. There is a probable entrance gap on the SSE, and in the S half of the interior there is a shallow ditch measuring about 2·3 m in breadth. Around the hut-circle there are faint traces of rig-and-furrow cultivation, and a short distance to the SE there are at least eight cairns, measuring up to 2 m in diameter.

·3   NO 1821 5265 to 1857 5257   NO 15 SE 82

Situated immediately S of Olies Burn there is a group of about thirty-five cairns, measuring up to 5 m in diameter, which are scattered along the crest of a low ridge (see also no. 299).

·4   NO 1788 5277 to 1804 5274   NO 15 SE 60

A group of about thirty cairns, measuring up to 4 m in diameter, is situated on the S crest of a low ridge some 800 m SW of Smyrna cottage and 200 m W of (·3).

·5   NO 176 528   NO 15 SE 61

Situated on a low rise at the W end of the ridge to the S of the Olies Burn, there is a group of small cairns. On the W flank of the group there is a particularly large cairn measuring 7 m in diameter by 0·5 m in height.

151 Pitcarmick (West), hut-circles, field-systems and small cairns

The valley of the Pitcarmick Burn is situated on the W side of Strathardle some 8 km NW of Bridge of Cally; it extends E from Pitcarmick Loch, an artificial reservoir, to Pitcarmick steading, a distance of 3 km. The head of the valley forms a natural amphitheatre around the loch, *151* which is overlooked by the craggy summits of Creag-nam-Mial (560 m OD) on the S and Creag na h-Iolaire (450 m OD) to the N. Much of the valley is covered with varying depths of peat (up to 3 m immediately E of the loch). The hut-circles and small cairns in the W part of the valley are described from E to W along the N side of the Pitcarmick Burn, and from W to E along the S side.

·1   NO 068 566   NO 05 NE 5

A group of six hut-circles is situated on a low rise 1·4 km E of Pitcarmick Loch. Five of the houses range from 5 m to 8·2 m in internal diameter; the sixth is considerably larger, measuring 15·8 m in diameter overall, and may have been double walled. The houses, and several banks which lie close by, were masked by deep heather on the date of visit but, where visible, the entrances were on the S or SSE arcs.

·2   NO 067 564   NO 05 NE 49

A group of small cairns and several stony banks occupy the terrace immediately below and S of (·1).

·3   NO 069 566   NO 05 NE 52

About 100 m E of (·1) there is a group of small cairns, the NE edge of which is marked by a stony bank.

·4   NO 065 567   NO 05 NE 27

A group of about forty small cairns and several short lengths of bank occupy a terrace about 100 m NW of (·1). On the S edge of the group there is a probable burial cairn (no. 36·1).

·5   NO 063 571   NO 05 NE 112

Situated on a terrace 400 m NW of (·4), and overlooking an area of raised bog almost immediately to the E, there is a group of three hut-circles. The westernmost (NO 0629 5711) measures 9 m in diameter within a wall (1·3 m thick and 0·2 m high) which has slab-built inner and outer faces; the entrance (1·4 m wide) is situated on the SE. About 50 m to the ESE there is a second hut-circle (NO 0635 5709) which measures 8 m in internal diameter and has an entrance on the SSW, and situated 10 m to the E there are the poorly-preserved remains of a third hut-circle measuring 8·5 m in diameter within a low wall.

·6   NO 061 565   NO 05 NE 55

Situated 400 m SW of (·4) and on a stony slope to the S side of the track up the valley, there is a group of small cairns and banks.

·7   NO 0605 5659   NO 05 NE 51

The remains of a hut-circle, which is bisected by the modern track, are situated on the edge of a narrow terrace about 70 m NW of (·6). It measures 8·5 m in diameter within a wall 2·7 m thick and 0·2 m high; short stretches of inner and outer facing are visible, and the entrance has probably been destroyed by the track.

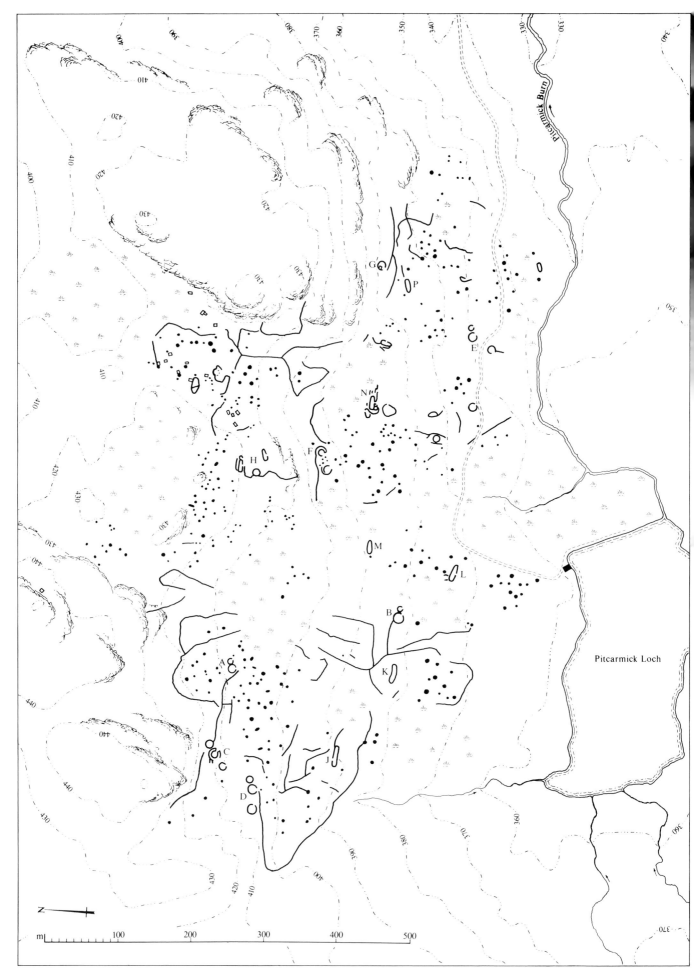

151·8 *Pitcarmick (West), hut-circles, field-system, and Pitcarmick-type buildings, 1:5000*

Immediately N of (·6) and (·7) the ground rises steeply in a series of rocky slopes and terraces before opening out on to a succession of gentler slopes and broader terraces to the N and NE of Pitcarmick Loch. Situated within this area there is an extensive field-system containing at least nineteen hut-circles as well as eight Pitcarmick-type buildings (no. 302·1–·7; H–P on fig.) and numerous probable shieling-huts (no. 307·7–·8).

The majority of the hut-circles occur either in pairs or groups of three and range in internal diameter from 4·1 m to 12 m. Two of the pairs comprise large and small hut-circles (A, B), but in both cases they appear to represent sequential, rather than contemporary, development. There are at least three groups of three hut-circles (C–E), one of which includes a double-walled example. There is a more complex group of hut-circles at (F); in its original form the group may have comprised three hut-circles enclosed by a single wall, but the site has been badly disturbed, and only two of the houses are now clearly defined. The W hut-circle is of at least two phases, and the outer wall of the E house is overlain on its N and E by a field-bank. The interiors of many of the single-walled houses have been levelled into the slope. (H) is a platform with a rear scarp and front apron, and (G) is an artificial terrace with an impressive front scarp that has been revetted with large boulders.

The surrounding field-system comprises small cairns, linear clearance heaps and stony banks. Many of the banks define the edges of cleared ground, but there are also curvilinear enclosures and, NW of (B), broad strip-fields. Where there is any visible stratigraphic relationship between the features, the banks appear to either abut (B) or overlie (F and G) hut-circles. In several instances the banks are likely to be contemporary with Pitcarmick-type buildings (e.g. H and J) and some may be associated with the shieling-huts.

·9–·18   NO 05 56   NO 05 NE 30, 34, 60–6

The S side of the valley, where the landscape is more open, is characterised by a series of low knolls and ridges. To the S and SE of Pitcarmick Loch many of the knolls and ridges are littered with uncleared boulders, but at least ten groups of small cairns have been identified. In themselves the cairns are unremarkable, but amongst two of the groups (·9 and ·18) an intense moorland fire has burnt off the thin layer of surface peat to reveal traces of cord rig with the furrows set about 1·2 m apart. In the case of (·9) there are two settings of rig meeting at right angles. Further plots of cord rig have been identified at (·19) and (·26).

·19 NO 0487 5554   NO 05 NW 9

This oval hut-circle measures 8 m by 7·2 m within a low wall. To the NW and situated between the hut-circle and a stony bank, there are traces of cord rig cultivation.

·20 NO 061 561   NO 05 NE 23, 139

Occupying a series of knolls and ridges about 800 m SE of
151·20 Pitcarmick Loch, there is a group of hut-circles accompanied by a field-system that covers an area of about 12·5 ha. Also included within the area are a cupmarked boulder (no. 100), two Pitcarmick-type buildings (no. 302·8), and numerous shieling-huts and associated enclosures (nos. 308·3–·5).

Two of the hut-circles lie close together towards the NW edge of the field-system (NO 0614 5617 and 0612 5615 respectively). The former is double walled and measures 10 m in internal diameter. The inner wall is interrupted by a gap on the NE, and the outwardly-splayed entrance is on the SE. The outer wall (16·5 m in overall diameter) has a slab-built outer face. Situated 20 m

to the SW there is a second double-walled house; it measures 8·9 m in internal diameter by 15·6 m overall, and the entrance is on the SE. Much of the outer wall has been robbed, and on the W the wall merges with an enclosure bank.

The third hut-circle (NO 0623 5608) is situated to the SE on the opposite side of a gully. It measures 9·4 m in diameter within a stony wall which has slab-and-boulder built inner and outer faces, and the entrance is on the S. The interior is occupied by a shieling-hut. Situated about ·60 m SE of the W hut-circle and about 15 m from a stream, there is a setting of upright slabs which has been set into a gentle E-facing slope. The slabs, two on each side, form a funnelled setting 2 m wide at the open E end and 1 m wide at the W. The structure measures 1·7 m in length from E to W and the tallest slab is some 0.6 m high; its date and purpose are unknown.

·21 NO 0643 5609   NO 05 NE 28

Situated on the W side of a low knoll about 170 m E of (·20) there is a hut-circle which measures 7 m in diameter within a low wall. The entrance is on the S, and to the N and E there are at least fifteen small cairns and a short length of bank.

·22 NO 0640 5640   NO 05 NE 54

Situated on a low, stony rise within an area of poorly-drained moorland, there is a hut-circle, a group of small cairns, several stony banks, two burial cairns (see no. 36·2–·3), and several later buildings. The hut-circle measures 6·7 m in diameter within a stony wall, and the entrance is on the ESE.

·23–·25 NO 06 55   NO 05 NE 56–8

To the S of (·20) there are three clusters of small cairns. One of them (·23) contains slight traces of a circular enclosure, possibly a robbed hut-circle, measuring 8 m in internal diameter.

·26 NO 067 559   NO 05 NE 29

On a low ridge 1·3 km ESE of Pitcarmick Loch there are two large enclosures, which contain five hut-circles and at least sixty-six small cairns. The hut-circles all lie within the W enclosure and are divided between a pair and a group of three. The pair measure 8·8 m and 5·8 m in internal diameter respectively, and both have been badly disturbed by rig-and-furrow cultivation. The remainder are equally poorly-preserved and measure 9 m, 10 m and 8 m in internal diameter. All have entrances in the S or SSE arcs, and two are overlain by the remains of shieling-huts (no. 308·1).

At least two other shieling-huts are integral with the cross-wall between the enclosures, both of which contain remains of rig-and-furrow cultivation. The turf-covered enclosure banks have built faces characteristic of medieval or post-medieval field-dykes. Almost certainly earlier than the enclosure, however, is a plot of cord rig cultivation which is situated 50 m SW of the W enclosure. Only visible where the peat has been burnt off, the ridges are up to 1 m wide (furrow to furrow) by up to 16 m long.

152   Pitcarmick (South), hut-circles and small cairns

These hut-circles and groups of small cairns are situated high up on the S side of the valley of the Pitcarmick Burn   153
close to its junction with Strathardle.

·1   NO 0832 5548   NO 05 NE 127

About 200 m W of the plantation above Dalnabreck a track passes through a group of at least five cairns. Four lie to the S of a dyke and the fifth to the N.

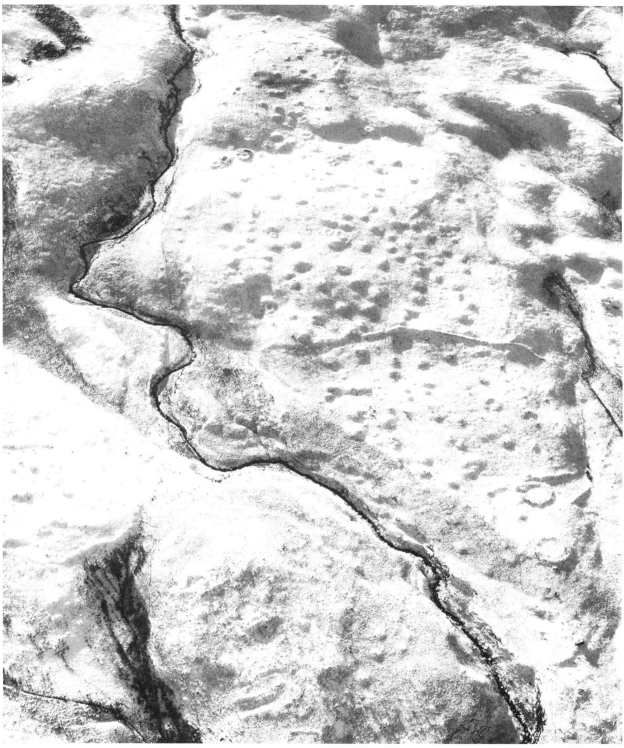

151·20 Pitcarmick (West), hut-circles, field-system, and Pitcarmick-type buildings from NE

·2   NO 0799 5519   NO 05 NE 128
Four small cairns are situated on the SE flank of a low rise 400m to the SW of (·1) and 250m S of the track. There are traces of a small rectangular enclosure on the crest of the rise.

·3   NO 076 553   NO 05 NE 129
Fifteen small cairns lie 100m S of the track 300m WNW of (·2).

·4   NO 0779 5556   NO 05 NE 130
A hut-circle lies within a group of small cairns to the N of the track 250m NNE of (·3). The hut-circle (6·7m in

internal diameter) is situated at the top of a gentle N- and E-facing slope. About twelve cairns are scattered across this slope and there are a further five to the WNW on the opposite side of a gully.

·5   NO 079 559   NO 05 NE 118, 131
Several clusters of small cairns extend down the hillside on the E side of a prominent gully to the N of (·4). The uppermost group comprises ten cairns, and at the W end of the group there are traces of a circular structure (NO 0780 5578), possibly a hut-circle, measuring 8·5m in diameter over a low stony rim. Two small cairns are visible farther down the slope; below them are two small

cairns accompanied by three banks, which possibly mark the edges of a field; at the foot of the slope there are at least six more, and on a knoll to the NNE a group of three.

·6   NO 0767 5576   NO 05 NE 132
To the W of the gully described above, there is a hut-circle (9 m in internal diameter) set on a terrace on the N side of a low rise. Immediately to the SE there is a possible ancillary structure measuring 2·5 m across its interior, and on a lower terrace 50 m to the NNW there is an oval hut-circle measuring 12·3 m by 11 m internally.

·7   NO 074 557   NO 05 NE 133
Two hut-circles are situated 150 m W and 300 m WSW of (·6); they measure 7 m and 5·8 m in internal diameter respectively. To the S and W of the E hut-circle there is a cluster of twenty cairns extending to the E bank of a small burn, where there is also a burnt mound (no. 175·2). To the NW there is a further cluster of eight cairns on the W bank of the burn, and a thin scatter extends to the SW.

·8   NO 0722 5617   NO 05 NE 72
This hut-circle lies in the bottom of the valley about 300 m NNW of the NW cluster of cairns described in (·7). Set on a low knoll, it measures about 7·3 m in internal diameter.

·9   NO 070 554   NO 05 NE 134
About fifteen small mounds are situated on a gentle NW-facing slope. Small stones protruding from some of them suggest that they are probably cairns.

153   Pitcarmick (East), hut-circles, field-systems and small cairns

The remains of several hut-circle groups and field-systems are situated on either side of the Allt Cul na Coille at the eastern edge of the high moorland above Pitcarmick House. With the exception of the southernmost group, the hut-circles lie in deep heather on broken ground and are generally poorly preserved; they are described from N to S.

·1   NO 078 576   NO 05 NE 31
A group of three hut-circles is situated on a terrace below the craggy E face of Creag Mholach. Two of the houses (NO 0776 5762) are tangential and measure 8 m and 7·8 m in diameter respectively within low walls; each has an entrance on the S arc. The third hut-circle (NO 0780 5756) is situated about 50 m to the SE and measures 8 m in internal diameter.

·2   NO 082 575   NO 05 NE 92
At least thirteen small cairns (measuring up to about 4 m in diameter) are situated on either side of a rough track 150 m NNW of Dalvey Cottage.

·3   NO 083 573   NO 05 NE 101
About four small cairns (measuring up to 3 m in diameter) are situated in pasture about 80 m E of Dalvey Cottage.

·4   NO 076 571   NO 05 NE 20
A group of five hut-circles is situated on a narrow ridge on the S side of the Allt Cul na Coille. They measure from 8·2 m to 11·5 m in diameter within low walls; only one (NO 0764 5715) displays both inner and outer facing-stones. All of the entrances are located on the SSE or ESE arcs, and one house (NO 0764 5711) is partly overlain by the remains of a small turf-built structure.

The hut-circles lie within a field-system comprising small cairns and banks but these were obscured under a thick cover of heather on the date of visit.

·5   NO 0732 5728   NO 05 NE 81, 122
At least eleven small cairns (up to 4 m in diameter) are situated within a saddle between the Allt Cul na Coille and an unnamed burn to the S. A further ten cairns (NO 068 575), measuring up to 3 m in diameter, lie close to the N bank of the Allt Cul na Coille.

·6   NO 074 569   NO 05 NE 19
Situated in undulating broken ground 1 km NW of Pitcarmick House, there are the remains of at least eight hut-circles which lie within a field-system comprising small cairns and banks. All the hut-circles are single walled and range from 7·3 m to 12·5 m in internal diameter; where visible, the entrances are on the SSE or E arcs.

The OS records the discovery of the broken, or unfinished, base of a bee-hive or bun-shaped quernstone embedded in the wall of one of the hut-circles (NO 0754 5695); another house (NO 0757 5698) is partially overlain by one of the numerous subrectangular structures in the area (see no. 305·5).

·7   NO 075 567   NO 05 NE 6
A group of five hut-circles is cut by a rough track 950 m WNW of Pitcarmick steading. The N hut-circle (NO 0754 5679) stands alone on the top of a knoll; it measures 9·2 m in diameter within a turf-covered wall and the entrance is on the SE.

Situated on a low rise on the S side of the track, there is a row of three tangential hut-circles which measure 10·7 m, 8·8 m and 8·8 m in internal diameter respectively. Their entrances lie on the E or SE, and all display several inner and outer facing-stones. The remains of the fifth hut-circle (NO 0764 5664) are situated on a fairly steep E-facing slope about 100 m E of the row of three. It measures about 4·5 m in internal diameter with an entrance on the S, and the interior has been levelled into the slope.

A number of small cairns (measuring up to 4 m in diameter) are scattered around the buildings, and there are also several lengths of curving bank close by.

·8   NO 0830 5668   NO 05 NE 135
At least six small cairns (up to 3 m in diameter) are situated immediately N of a sheepfold about 650 m E of (·7) and some 350 m WSW of Pitcarmick House.

154   Pitcarmick (North), hut-circles, field-systems and small cairns

The valley of the Allt Cul na Coille lies to the N of the Pitcarmick Burn (see nos. 151–3) and is separated from Glen Derby (see no. 126) to the N by an undulating ridge which rises steeply from Cultalonie and extends westwards for a distance of 3 km. The crest of the ridge is occupied by a series of hut-circle groups accompanied by field-systems and small cairns, as well as by large areas of rig-and-furrow cultivation. The remains are here described from E to W.

·1   NO 076 583   NO 05 NE 32
The remains of two hut-circles lie close together on a grassy terrace immediately E of the head-dyke and 420 m WSW of Cultalonie steading. The NE hut-circle (NO 0769 5835) measures up to 9 m in diameter within a poorly-preserved wall, and the second, which lies 7 m to the SW, is about 7 m in diameter internally with an entrance on the SE. A group of about twenty small cairns is situated on a well-drained promontory about 100 m to the SE of the hut-circles.

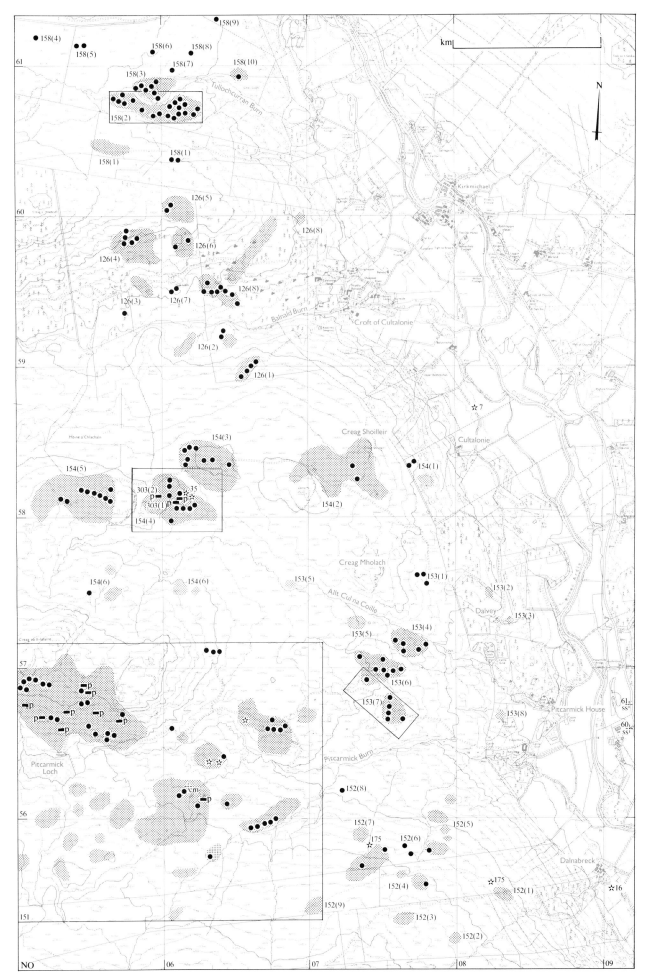

158(4)
158(5)
158(6)
158(8)
158(9)
158(7)
158(10)
158(3)
Tullochcurran Burn
158(2)
61
158(1)
158(1)
158(1)
60
126(5)
126(8)
126(6)
126(4)
126(8)
126(3)
126(7)
Balnald Burn
Croft of Cultalonie
126(2)
59
126(1)
Creag Shoilleir
☆ 7
Móine a' Chlachain
Cultalonie
154(3)
154(1)
154(5)
303(2)
☆ 35
p
p ☆
303(1) p
154(1)
58
154(4)
154(2)
Creag Mholach
154(6)
154(6)
153(5)
Allt Cul na Coille
153(1)
153(2)
Dalvey
153(3)
153(4)
153(5)
57
153(6)
p
p
p
153(7)
153(8)
p
p
p
p
Pitcarmick House
p
p
61 SS
60 SS
Pitcarmick Loch
cm
p
Pitcarmick Burn
152(8)
56
152(7)
152(5)
175
152(6)
☆
175
152(4)
Dalnabreck
152(1)
☆ 175
☆ 16
152(9)
151
152(3)
152(2)
NO
06
07
08
09

153 Pitcarmick, Glen Derby, Tullochcurran, 1:25 000

·2 NO 073 583   NO 05 NE 18

Two hut-circles and a field-system comprising several hundred small cairns and a few short stretches of stony bank occupy an area of undulating moorland between Creag Shoilleir and another, but unnamed, rise to the SW. The first hut-circle (NO 0730 5833) lies on a gentle SW-facing slope and measures 12 m in diameter within a low wall with a splayed entrance on the SSE. The second (NO 0733 5825) is situated on the summit of a low rise and measures 12 m in diameter within a low wall 1·4 m thick and 0·1 m high.

·3 NO 062 584   NO 05 NE 16

Situated about midway along the ridge, there are eight hut-circles and a field-system comprising small cairns and short stretches of stony bank. The easternmost of the hut-circles (NO 0645 5835) is the best preserved, despite its location within a large plot of rig-and-furrow cultivation. It measures 10·7 m in internal diameter and the entrance (2·6 m wide) is on the S side. The inner edge of the wall is defined by a series of vertically-set slabs, and intermittent stretches of the outer face are also visible. Situated on the summit of the rise that forms the highest part of the settlement, there are the remains of two double-walled hut-circles (NO 0628 5838 and 0633 5838). Both have been disturbed by the construction of an earth-and-stone wall which crosses them from E to W. They measure 17·4 m and 16·9 m in diameter overall respectively, and both have an entrance on their S arcs.

The remains of three further hut-circles are situated on a low rise at the NW edge of the field-system (NO 0618 5846). The W hut-circle is little more than a platform (6 m in diameter) which has been terraced into a gentle NW-facing slope. The central hut-circle measures about 8 m in diameter within a wall 1·7 m thick and 0·2 m high; it has an entrance on the S, and within the interior there are two large slabs, one vertical (0·6 m high) and the other leaning, which do not seem to have formed part of any wall fabric. The third hut-circle, which lies immediately to the E, measures 8·3 m in diameter within a wall 2 m thick and 0·2 m high, and there is an entrance gap on the S side.

In the SW corner of the area there are two hut-circles (NO 0616 5836). They are situated on a low rise and measure 9·8 m and 8·4 m in diameter respectively within walls measuring up to 2 m in thickness; their entrances are in the S arc.

·4 NO 061 581   NO 05 NE 17

Situated about 200 m SW of (·3) and on the S bank of a minor stream, there is a complex sequence of monuments, which includes burial cairns, hut-circles, field-systems and small cairns, as well as a series of buildings some of which are of Pitcarmick-type (nos. 303·1; 306·3–·4).

There are nine hut-circles ranging from 7·2 m to 12·5 m in internal diameter. Of particular interest is a double-walled hut-circle (A), where the outer wall has been extended to embrace what may be the stance for a timber round-house or a yard. The most complex of the hut-circles (B) comprises two superimposed buildings, the E element of which is itself multi-period. The earliest building is on the W (9·6 m in internal diameter), and its NE arc has been overlain by the wall of the later which, in its first phase, measured 12·5 m in internal diameter, but was subsequently reduced in size to measure 10·2 m in diameter with the construction of an additional arc of wall on the NE. Later phases of settlement are represented by three Pitcarmick-type buildings (C and D), a series of rectangular buildings, and several shieling-huts.

Surrounding the hut-circles and later buildings there is a sequence of cultivation remains, which includes clearance cairns, field-banks, and cultivation rigs. The clearance of stone into heaps probably marks the first phase of agricultural activity on the site, but it is clear that this practice continued over a long period as several of the cairns are set on the top of field-banks. Two of the cairns (E) are exceptionally large and are probably burial cairns (see no. 35). What may be the earliest fields are a series of rectilinear enclosures on the S. Much of the site is obscured by rig-and-furrow cultivation (not shown on plan), some of which has been fitted into existing plots, while elsewhere it is probably contemporary with the construction of some of the late field-banks (F and G). In the absence of excavation it is not clear which, if any, of the cultivation remains are associated with the Pitcarmick-type buildings.

·5 NO 055 581   NO 05 NE 15

Situated at the W end of the ridge, there are nine hut-circles, several stony banks and an extensive area of small cairns. Eight of the hut-circles are disposed in pairs, with each pair comprising one large and one small building. Three of the pairs lie in a rough line along the crest of the ridge, while the fourth is situated some way to the SW.

The E pair (NO 0558 5813) consists of a double-walled house (8·5 m in internal diameter by 16·4 m overall) accompanied by a large hut-circle (12 m in internal diameter), and both have their entrances on the S. The second pair (NO 0553 5815) lies about 15 m to the NW; they measure 10·5 m and 8 m in internal diameter, and the entrances are on the SSE and S respectively. A substantial bank abuts the S side of the smaller hut-circle. The W pair is situated a further 35 m along the ridge (NO 0547 5817); the larger measures 11 m in internal diameter, while the smaller is 8·5 m in internal diameter, and both have entrances on the S. About 140 m to the SW (NO 0583 5811), the fourth pair is situated on a low rise; the larger hut-circle is 11 m in internal diameter, and within the interior there is a ring-ditch which extends anti-clockwise from the entrance on the SE to peter out in the W arc. The smaller hut-circle measures 8·7 m in diameter within a wall 2 m thick and it has an entrance on the S. Situated about 70 m NE of the E pair of hut-circles, there are the remains of a poorly preserved hut-circle which measures 8 m in internal diameter.

·6 NO 0549 5750   NO 05 NE 104–5, 107, 145

Situated some 600 m S of, and on the opposite side of the valley from (·5), there are the remains of a hut-circle which sits on a N-facing terrace. It measures 7·8 m in diameter within a stony wall (1·4 m thick and 0·5 m high), and has an entrance on the SE. A group of at least seven small cairns (NO 056 576) lies on a stony ridge some 200 m to the NE. A second group of at least five small cairns (NO 056 574) is situated on a low ridge some 150 m to the E, and a third group (NO 061 575), which comprises at least thirteen cairns measuring up to 3 m in diameter and several lengths of stony bank, lies on the E side of a low rise some 600 m to the E.

305

154·4B

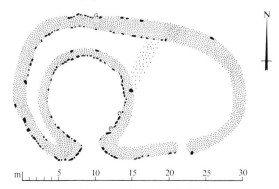

154·4A *Pitcarmick (North), hut-circle (A), 1:500*

154·4B Pitcarmick (North), hut-circles, field-system, and buildings, 1:2500

155 Ranageig, hut-circles and small cairns
The area of Ranageig is defined as that part of the N side of the valley of the Benachally Burn which runs from the margins of improved ground W of Ranageig to the heather-covered ridges at the W end of Middleton Muir (see no. 147). Extensive medieval and later settlement (no. 310) has effectively destroyed most of the prehistoric settlement between Ranageig and Loch Benachally, but numerous hut-circles, small cairns and field-systems survive on the poorer soils to E of Ranageig steading. The sites are here described from E to W.

·1 NO 11 49, 12 49   NO 14 NW 30
The E end of the area is marked by several low ridges (aligned WNW–ESE) which run into Middleton Muir; on the crests and S-facing slopes of two of the ridges on the N side of the track there are three groups of cairns at NO 1160 4935, 1180 4905 and 1200 4916 respectively. In addition, there are traces of cairns on the improved ridge (NO 1147 4905 to 1165 4895) along which the modern track runs.

·2 NO 11 49   NO 14 NW 32
Situated on a low knoll to the S of the modern track and the two burial cairns (no. 37), there are two poorly-preserved hut-circles set side by side. They measure 9m and 9·5m in internal diameter respectively. About 50m to the WNW, there is a D-shaped structure measuring 4·6m by 3·6m within a rubble wall 0·9m thick and 0·2m high; a possible entrance is situated in the SE corner. The remains of a third hut-circle (NO 1124 4900) are situated a further 50m to the SW; it measures 8·2m in diameter within a wall 1·6m thick and 0·3m high. The wall incorporates a stretch of rock outcrop on the N, and there is a possible entrance some 3·7m wide on the SSE. The hut-circles lie within an area of small cairns and stony banks, the W edge of which has been truncated by a later farmstead (no. 310·4).

·3 NO 110 494   NO 14 NW 23
About 400m to the NW of (·2) and on the N side of the track, there are three hut-circles and an enclosure, as well as numerous small cairns and short lengths of stony bank occupying about 10ha of hill-slope. On the SW (NO 1071 4939) there is a double-walled hut-circle which measures 10·2m in internal diameter with an entrance (1·2m wide) on the S. On the E, a small circular structure (possibly a hut-circle), which measures 4m in diameter within a wall 1·4m thick and with an entrance 1·3m wide on the SSE, overlies the line of the outer wall of the hut-circle.

About 210m to the E (NO 1093 4941), there is a well-preserved hut-circle measuring 9·4m in diameter within a wall which is up to 2·2m thick and 0·5m high; there is an entrance (1·1m wide) on the SSE. The outer face of the wall consists of an almost complete row of boulders which have been set on edge or upright; on the NW a section of about 4·5m has been robbed, and on the NE there is a displaced boulder which bears on its upper surface eleven cupmarks (up to 55mm in diameter and 15mm in depth). The N half of the hut-circle is occupied by a later subrectangular building. About 130m to the ENE (NO 1107 4945) there is a double-walled hut-circle which is about 8m in internal diameter and 18m by 15m overall; the entrance (1m wide and outwardly splayed) is situated on the SSW. The remains of an enclosure (previously identified by the OS as a hut-circle) are situated about 80m to the NNW (NO 1104 4954); it measures 17·4m by 12·4m within a turf-covered bank (up to 1·9m thick and 0·2m high) and is overlain on its E side by a small subrectangular structure measuring about 2·1m by 1·6m within turf-covered walls. Although there is a break in the wall on the N side of the enclosure, the original entrance (3m wide) is on the S side. A prehistoric field-system lies to the NW and NE of two later farmsteads (no. 310·1, ·3), the field-walls of which overlie the earlier system.

·4 NO 10 49   NO 14 NW 24, 55
Situated 130m WNW of Ranageig farmhouse and immediately N of the modern track, there is a poorly-preserved double-walled hut-circle measuring 8·8m in internal diameter and 15·7m overall. It has an entrance (1·3m wide) on the SSW, and from the N side of the hut-circle a low stony bank runs N before turning NW; this bank forms the E side of a field-system comprising small cairns and rectangular plots defined by low stony banks. It is not clear, however, whether this field-system (which is overlain by field-banks associated with the later farmsteads), is contemporary with the hut-circles, or of later date, perhaps associated with the Pitcarmick-type building (no. 309) which partly overlies a second double-walled hut-circle. The second hut-circle (NO 1026 4947), which lies 90m N of the first, measures 9·3m in internal diameter by 16·4m overall. The entrance (1m wide) is situated on the SSW, and on the E the outer wall bows outwards to form an enclosure 7·6m in internal diameter with an entrance (2·2m wide) on the S.

156 Seefar, hut-circles and small cairns
·1 NO 103 472   NO 14 NW 72
The remains of three hut-circles are disposed along the 292m contour line on the SE flank of an unnamed ridge 640m ENE of Seefar farmhouse. The S hut-circle (NO 1035 4716) is situated on the line of a rough track in heather moorland and measures 8·5m in diameter within a featureless rubble wall; the entrance (2·2m wide) is on the SE. Situated within the improved field to the NE, there are two further hut-circles (NO 1036 4721 and 1037 4727), which measure 9·3m and 8·9m in internal diameter respectively. Both have entrances on the SE, and the interior of the latter has been levelled into the slope. The poorly-preserved remains of a number of small cairns are scattered throughout the field to the E of the hut-circles.

·2 NO 108 473   NO 14 NW 71
The remains of a hut-circle and three groups of small cairns are situated on parallel ridges 450m E of (·1). The hut-circle lies at the W end of the N group, which contains at least ten cairns. It measures about 11m in internal diameter and the entrance is on the SE. On the two ridges to the S there are thirty-three and four cairns respectively, the largest about 5m in diameter. On the middle ridge, the W part of which has been improved, there are about thirty-three cairns measuring up to 5m in diameter, and on the S ridge there are four cairns measuring up to 5m in diameter.

·3 NO 111 471   NO 14 NW 74
Situated on the upper edge of improved ground 800m NNW of Cairns steading and 800m E of (·1), there are the remains of two hut-circles. The W house (NO 1116 4712) has been reduced to little more than a platform on the steep S-facing slope. It measures 10·5m in internal diameter, and the entrance is on the SE. The E house (NO 1121 4710) is situated on a low knoll and measures 10·7m in diameter within a low turf-covered bank.

A single cairn (NO 1125 4704), measuring 7·4m in diameter and 0·3m in height, lies to the SE of the hut-circles in a field of well-formed cultivation ridges.

·4 NO 118 466   NO 14 NW 10
In the 19th century 'a great many' cairns were removed from the fields to the E of Cairns.
— Name Book, Perthshire, No. 42, p. 21.

157 Shaw's Croft, hut-circles

·1 NO 149 621 NO 16 SW 76

The remains of five hut-circles, all of which have, to varying degrees, been levelled into the slope, are situated on either side of the public road N of Shaw's Croft cottage. On the W side of the road some 40m NNW of the cottage, there is a hut-circle (NO 1486 6207) which measures 7·7m in diameter within a low, turf-covered wall 2m thick and 0·2m high. On the E side of the road, and immediately N of a small wood, there is a line of three hut-circles (centred at NO 1491 6211), which measure 10m, 9·7m and 10·3m in internal diameter respectively. Only in the E hut-circle is there an entrance, marked by a shallow depression, on the SSW. A fifth hut-circle (NO 1496 6215) is set on a terrace above, and to the NE of the others; it measures 8·5m in diameter within a rubble wall 2·3m thick and 0·3m high. There is an entrance gap on the SW.

·2 NO 1495 6170 NO 16 SW 77

The remains of this hut-circle are situated in pasture immediately E of the public road about 320m SSE of Shaw's Croft cottage. It survives as a platform measuring 9·5m in diameter and there is a probable entrance gap in the front apron on the SSE.

·3 NO 150 617 NO 16 SE 9, 34

The remains of two hut-circles are situated on a craggy rise 320m SE of Shaw's Croft cottage and 80m ENE of (·2). The W hut-circle (NO 1503 6173) measures 9·8m in internal diameter and the E hut-circle (NO 1505 6173) 15·2m. Situated immediately N of the hut-circles there are a number of small cairns; a further group, measuring up to 5m in diameter, are situated on the N bank of an unnamed burn some 900m to the NE (NO 1580 6235).

·4 NO 1514 6142 NO 16 SE 33

This hut-circle is situated on the SE side of a low rise 90m SSW of Tomlia cottage and some 310m SSE of (·3). It measures about 10m in internal diameter, and the entrance is probably on the S.

158 Tullochcurran Burn, hut-circles and field-systems

The valley of the Tullochcurran Burn is the northernmost side-valley on the W side of Strathardle, and it is situated 1km NW of Kirkmichael. Much of the S side of the valley comprises relatively poorly-drained N-facing slopes, and 153 the settlement remains are largely restricted to a series of knolls and terraces along the N side of the valley and to a low ridge along the valley floor. Recent afforestation on the N side of the burn has severely damaged many of the hut-circles, to the extent that only basic overall measurements can now be taken, and some are so badly damaged that the records of the Ordnance Survey have had to be used. Two hut-circles and a group of small cairns on the S side of the valley are described first, followed by the large group of hut-circles on the valley floor; the individual hut-circles on the N side of the valley are described from W to E.

·1 NO 06 60 NO 06 SE 60–1

The two hut-circles on the S side of the valley are situated on a low rise 1km WSW of Tullochcurran Cottage and approximately half way up the side of the N-facing slope. The E hut-circle (NO 0610 6038) measures 12·5m in internal diameter, and there is a narrow entrance gap on the S. The second hut-circle (NO 0608 6038) lies immediately to the W and measures 8·4m in internal diameter, and its entrance (1·5m wide) is situated on the SSE side. About 250m W of the hut-circles there is a scatter of small cairns (NO 056 604).

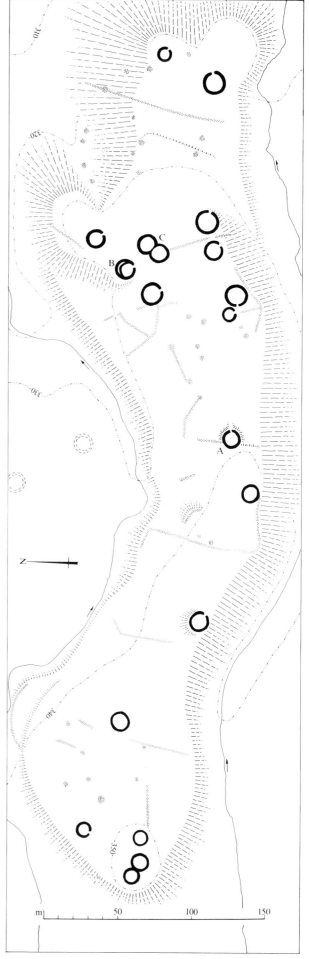

158·2 Tullochcurran Burn, hut-circles and field-system, 1:2500

·2 NO 060 607 NO 06 SE 11
A group of nineteen hut-circles is situated on a low, relatively flat-topped ridge 800m W of Tullochcurran Cottage and immediately S of the Tullochcurran Burn. The ridge measures 600m from W to E by up to 100m in width and, although the hut-circles occur on most parts of the ridge, there is a marked concentration towards the E end. On the ridge there are also a number of small cairns and several linear stone banks and lynchets.

The hut-circles vary in size from 6·7m to 12m in internal diameter. A few of the hut-circles have well-preserved boulder wall-faces, whilst others have been robbed. Some have been levelled into the slopes, and one (A) has been set on a platform with such a steep E face that a boulder ramp has been built to provide access to its entrance. One of the hut-circles (B) is probably multi-period, as may be the adjacent tangential pair (C).

·3 NO 059 608 NO 06 SE 12
Situated on a low rise immediately N of the Tullochcurran Burn, there is a group of five hut-circles which has recently been afforested. On the highest part of the rise, at the W end, there are the disturbed remains of a hut-circle (NO 0586 6087) measuring 9·3m in diameter within a stony wall; it originally had an entrance on the S side, but this is no longer visible. Immediately to the W, and at a slightly lower level, there is a platform measuring about 7m in diameter. Similarly placed to the SE, there is a small hut-circle, which measures 6·8m in internal diameter; it too originally had an entrance on the S side. To the NE side of the rise there is a hut-circle (NO 0592 6086), which measures 10·2m in diameter within a disturbed wall; immediately to the SW the remains of another may be indicated by a wall on the S and SE. On the SE side of the rise there is a hut-circle (NO 0596 6080) which measures 8·2m in internal diameter and has been levelled into the slope to a depth of 0·5m. A field-system comprising cairns and banks which lay to the E of the hut-circles has been destroyed by the recent ploughing.

·4 NO 0514 6117 NO 06 SE 19
The most westerly of the hut-circles on the N side of the valley is also one of the best preserved, despite having recently been ploughed and planted with conifers. It is situated on a narrow terrace and measures about 10m in diameter within a broad stony wall 2·7m thick and 0·6m high, and there is an entrance gap on the S side.

·5 NO 0547 6113 NO 06 SE 18
About 330m E of (·4) and situated on a narrow terrace, there are the poorly-preserved remains of a hut-circle, which measures about 9m in internal diameter. Some 40m to the W there is a house-platform measuring 12m in diameter.

·6 NO 0594 6110 NO 06 SE 17
This hut-circle is situated on a low rise on the NE shoulder of the valley; it measures about 9m in internal diameter.

·7 NO 0607 6096 NO 06 SE 13
This hut-circle, which measures about 9·3m in internal diameter, is situated on a low rise on the N bank of the Tullochcurran Burn; it is now barely discernible after recent forestry ploughing.

·8 NO 0620 6108 NO 06 SE 15
The remains of this hut-circle are situated on a prominent knoll low down on the NE shoulder of the valley; it measures about 11m in internal diameter.

·9 NO 0637 6130 NO 06 SE 16
Situated 270m NE of (·8) and on a prominent position on the N side of the mouth of the valley, there are the remains of a recently ploughed hut-circle, which measures approximately 11·5m in internal diameter. Abutting the NNW side, there are the stone wall-footings of a rectangular building (7m by 5m overall).

·10 NO 0653 6093 NO 06 SE 14
The easternmost hut-circle in the valley lies close to the N bank of the burn; originally it measured up to 8·8m in diameter within a stony wall. The OS recorded that the S half had been destroyed by the construction of an earth-and-stone dyke, and the N half, along with an adjacent group of small cairns, has been obliterated by recent forestry ploughing.

159 Tulloch Field, Enochdhu, hut-circles
NO 054 637 NO 06 SE 20
Six hut-circles are disposed along an old river terrace 330m NNW of Tulloch Cottage. The first (NO 0545 6373) lies on the top edge of the terrace and measures 9·3m in diameter within a low wall. To the SE there are two platforms (NO 0546 6369) which measure 8m and 8·8m in diameter respectively, and to the NW (NO 0539 6380) there is a further hut-circle, measuring 10·5m in internal diameter. *121*

The remaining two hut-circles are situated at the base of the terrace and have both been excavated. The more southerly (NO 0544 6370) revealed the remains of a timber house within a wall which measured 14·5m by 10m in internal diameter and up to 3·6m in thickness. The wall had a wide entrance on the SW, and charcoal from two arcs of post-trench produced C–14 dates of 3015 ±50 b.p. (GU–1147) and 3040 ±45 b.p. (GU–1148). Finds from the interior were limited to sherds of a bucket-shaped, coarse-ware vessel about 250mm high and 175mm in diameter.

The second hut-circle (NO 1543 6373) produced evidence of a double post-ring (3·5m and 7·6m in diameter respectively) within a low rubble wall about 12m in internal diameter and up to 4m in thickness. Additional features included a porch (defined by two post-holes) on the S, and internal pits, one of which produced a C–14 date of 2275 ±60 b.p. (GU–1489). Finds included numerous sherds of coarse pottery, possible fragments of quernstones, several possible quartz scrapers, a flint flake, and a fragment of what may have been a bronze pin.

At the NW end of the site, and situated on a low knoll, there are the remains of what may be a seventh hut-circle (NO 0530 6381). It measures about 10·5m in diameter within a turf-covered wall, and there is a wide gap on the NNE which opens on to a broad access ramp.

— *DES* (1976), 51; (*1977*), 30; (*1978*), 32; (*1979*), 45; (*1980*), 41; (*1981*), 48; (*1982*), 34; (*1983*), 36–7; Thoms 1979.

160 Welton of Creuchies, hut-circles and small cairns
The remains of several groups of hut-circles are visible between Hatton Moss and the Den of Welton. Much of the area has been reseeded in recent years and consequently most of the hut-circles are in a poor state of preservation.

·1 NO 205 495 NO 24 NW 61
This group lies to the SE of the track from Welton of Creuchies; it comprises a line of five ploughed-down hut-circles, the easternmost of which has been partly quarried away. They measure, from NE to SW, about 12m, 7·7m, 7m, 9m, and 5m in internal diameter respectively.

·2   NO 198 489   NO 14 NE 72

Two hut-circles are situated 25 m apart on the S side of the march fence between Welton of Creuchies and West Tullyfergus, 400 m N of the larger of the two Glendams reservoirs. The more westerly is set into the crest of a narrow ridge and it is 5·4 m in internal diameter; the other, which lies at the foot of the ridge, has been almost obliterated and probably measured about 9·3 m in internal diameter. Four small cairns are visible in the immediate vicinity of the hut-circles, and there are a further nine 150 m to the E (NO 200 489); the gap between the latter and the hut-circles has probably been cleared relatively recently. A larger group of cairns, numbering about thirty-five, extends along the low ridge on the N side of the march fence.

·3   NO 1967 4957   NO 14 NE 77

This hut-circle is situated on the SW side of a low rise 600 m NNW of (·2). It measures 9·6 m in internal diameter and the interior has been levelled into the slope on the NE. Although the area has been reseeded, a light scatter of cairns is visible around the hut-circle and across the gently sloping ground to the WSW. The remains of a small building lie immediately N of the hut-circle, and there is a group of Pitcarmick-type buildings 100 m to the E (see no. 326).

·4   NO 194 499   NO 14 NE 79–81

On the N side of a small valley to the N of the hut-circle and small cairns described above, there is a group of hut-circles and platforms. Midway up the slope from the burn, and 150 m NE of the march dyke (NO 1943 4976), there are traces of two platforms which have been almost obliterated by pasture improvements; they measure 7·7 m and 10 m in diameter respectively. On the crest of the ridge to the NNE, bisected by the fence-line, there is a row of at least four hut-circles and two platforms (NO 194 499); they range from 6 m to 10·5 m in diameter. Those to the N of the fence are relatively well-preserved, but the two to the S (one probably a double-walled hut-circle obscured by a modern clearance heap) have been largely destroyed by pasture improvements. The hut-circle immediately N of the fence probably overlies the hut-circle to the NW. The remains of two more double-walled hut-circles lie to the E (NO 197 499); they measure 10·5 m and 8·8 m in internal diameter.

·5   NO 2050 4999   NO 24 NW 58

This hut-circle lies to the W of the stone dyke that encloses the fields on the N side of the valley 650 m WSW of Welton of Creuchies; it measures 9·4 m in internal diameter. What may be the W arc of a second protrudes from beneath the stone dyke a short distance to the SE.

161   Whitehouse, hut-circles and field-systems

There are three groups of hut-circles to the S of Whitehouse, and a fourth in a forestry plantation to the E.

·1   NO 156 600   NO 16 SE 18

The principal group of hut-circles is situated on a low spur 400 m S of Whitehouse (Stewart 1964, 144). OS surveyors described the site in 1974; subsequently it was partially incorporated into an L-shaped shelter belt and at least six of the hut-circles were destroyed. Three of the surviving hut-circles lie within the area enclosed by the shelter belt: the first is set on the summit of a low knoll and measures 10·3 m in internal diameter; the second, which is situated at the edge of the shelter belt, 50 m to the S, is double walled and measures 7·5 m in internal diameter; and the third, which lies beside the other arm of the shelter belt, a

further 40 m to the ESE, measures 9·5 m in internal diameter and exhibits traces of an internal ring-ditch. The sites of the destroyed hut-circles, which include a row of three, lie in the trees to the SW. Two hut-circles are visible outside the SW arm of the shelter belt: the first (7·4 m in internal diameter) is set on a knoll immediately beyond the trees; the second (9·5 m in internal diameter) is situated on the leading edge of a terrace 100 m to the S, and it is accompanied by a small Pitcarmick-type building (no. 332). The other hut-circles are crossed by the outer fence of the SE arm of the shelter belt: one (10 m in internal diameter) lies in a gap in the trees, and the other two (6·5 m and 7·8 m in internal diameter respectively) are set side by side 40 m to the NW. What may have been another hut-circle was noted by Stewart within the shelter belt, a little farther to the N. Fragments of an extensive system of field-banks are visible around the hut-circles, and a scatter of small cairns extends for a distance of about 350 m up the hillside to the S of the shelter belt. Several deeply-hollowed trackways cut through the field-system.

·2   NO 151 602   NO 16 SE 32

These two hut-circles are set on a terrace overlooking the Old School House at Blacklunans 400 m WNW of (·1). One measures 8·5 m in diameter within a wall up to 3·1 m in thickness; the other, which lies 40 m to the S, is double walled and measures 6·7 m in diameter internally by 14·6 m overall.

·3   NO 154 595   NO 15 NE 21

Two hut-circles are situated 50 m apart at the lower end of a small field-system about 400 m SSW of the L-shaped shelter belt described in (·1). One is about 6 m in internal diameter, the other, which lies 50 m to the S and beneath the Drumfork march dyke, has been reduced to little more than a platform measuring 9 m in diameter. The field-system comprises a group of cairns which is partly enclosed by low field-banks.

·4   NO 1627 6053   NO 16 SE 5

A group of five hut-circles, one of which may have been double walled, was identified by Thorneycroft (1933, 188) 650 m E of Whitehouse steading. The site has now been afforested, but at least four single-walled hut-circles, and possibly a fifth, can still be identified beneath the trees.

SOUTERRAIN

162   Balloch, souterrain
   NO 2587 4987   NO 24 NE 18

Nothing is now visible of this souterrain which was discovered about 1790 on the crest of a terrace on the S side of the Hill of Loyal 470 m NW of Balloch farmhouse. The passage measured about 1·2 m in breadth by 1·8 m in height and was roofed with 'large broad stones', and was 'full of ashes'.
— *Stat. Acct.*, 6 (1797), 406; Name Book, Perthshire, No. 5, p. 50; Wainwright 1963, 170–1.

BURNT MOUNDS

163   Ashintully, burnt mound
   NO 1041 6220   NO 16 SW 99

This probable burnt mound is situated between two boggy stream-beds 60 m NW of the track leading into Coire a Bhaile and about 200 m NE of the improved fields to the N of Ashintully. Partly buried in peat on its uphill side,

124

105

the mound is probably crescent-shaped, measuring 7·5 m by 4·4 m and up to 0·5 m in height. Its open side faces downhill.

164 Burnside of Drimmie, burnt mound
NO 1722 5236   NO 15 SE 42
This burnt mound is situated on the N side of a boggy hollow in the gentle S-facing slope above the Burn of Drimmie, some 800 m NNW of Burnside of Drimmie. Crescentic on plan, it measures a maximum of 8·1 m across by 0·5 m in height, with its open side facing on to the boggy hollow.

165 Craigton, burnt mound
NO 1248 5843   NO 15 NW 28
A small burnt mound, measuring 8·5 m by 5·6 and 0·5 m in height, is situated about 1 km NW of Craigton steading; crescentic on plan, the mound opens on to a wet gully on the S.

166 Creag Bhreac, burnt mounds
What may be two burnt mounds are situated at a height of almost 500 m OD to the NE of the hut-circle group on the W spur of Creag Bhreac (no. 121·10). Like the examples on Uchd na h-Anaile (no. 179), these burnt mounds are set at exceptionally high altitudes.

·1 NO 0698 6747   NO 06 NE 30
The first, which comprises two mounds separated by a slight hollow, stands on the E bank of a burn 25 m W of the Dirnanean/Glen Fearnach march fence. The E mound is the larger (measuring 6 m by 4 m and 0·7 m), and the hollow between the two is 5·5 m long and 2·3 m wide.

·2 NO 0705 6745   NO 06 NE 31
The second lies 75 m to the ESE on the E bank of a small burn to the E of the march fence. It measures 4 m in diameter by 0·5 m in height and is composed of small fragments of stone.

167 Creag Dubh-leitir, Glenfernate Lodge, burnt mound
NO 0540 6511   NO 06 NE 37
This burnt mound is situated on the W side of a shallow gully at the foot of the SW face of Creag Dubh-leitir some 20 m S of an old stone dyke that runs up the flank of the hill. It measures 8·4 m by 4·8 m in diameter and 0·7 m in maximum height, and a hollow cuts across the centre of the mound.

168 Drumderrach, burnt mound
NO 2797 5076   NO 25 SE 42
This burnt mound is situated on the E side of a wet hollow on the S face of Drumderrach some 100 m NNW of the standing stone no. 69. The turf-covered mound measures 12·3 m by 11·2 m and 0·5 m in height; there is a slight depression (3·9 m wide and 0·2 m deep) at the centre of the mound, which may be edged on its N side by a row of small boulders.

169 Dulater, burnt mound
NO 0937 4813   NO 04 NE 23
This burnt mound is situated on the NW side of a wet gully at the E end of a group of small cairns (no. 114·6). Crescentic on plan with the hollow side opening on to the gully, the peat-covered mound measures 6·7 m by 5 m in diameter and up to 0·5 m in height.

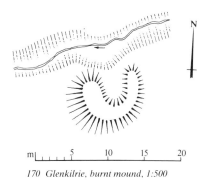

170 Glenkilrie, burnt mound, 1:500

170 Glenkilrie, burnt mound
NO 1279 6234   NO 16 SW 72
This U-shaped burnt mound is situated in moorland on the NE flank of Glenkilrie and lies on the S bank of a small stream below the track up the glen. It measures 11 m in maximum diameter and stands to a height of 0·8 m, with its open N end facing on to the stream.

171 Heatheryhaugh, burnt mound
NO 1890 5100   NO 15 SE 39
Situated on the S side of a wet gully 1·3 km SE of Heatheryhaugh farmhouse, there is a crescentic turf-covered mound measuring 9·8 m by 8 m and 0·5 m high; its open side faces on to the gully. What may be a second burnt mound underlies the NW end of an adjacent building (no. 280·1).

172 Hill of Alyth, burnt mounds
There are two burnt mounds on the Hill of Alyth, one high up on the W flank of the hill, and the other at the foot of the NW slopes beside the Bruckly Burn.

·1 NO 2298 5024   NO 25 SW 21
The first lies between the old drove road and a boggy sump about 100 m E of the hut-circles no. 129·1. Oval on plan, it measures 4·5 m by 3·5 m and 0·6 m in height.

·2 NO 2272 5066   NO 25 SW 24
The second, which is on the SE side of the Bruckly Burn, measures 8 m by 5·5 m and 0·6 m in height.

173 Loch Benachally, burnt mound
NO 0717 5097   NO 05 SE 45
This burnt mound stands on the NW bank of a burn 140 m NE of the NE shore of Loch Benachally. Pear-shaped on plan, it measures 10 m in length by up to 10 m in breadth at the broader NNE end, and it stands to a height of 0·9 m. There is an oval hollow at its centre.

174 Loch Charles, Woodhill, burnt mounds
Two burnt mounds are situated high up on the W side of Strathardle above Woodhill.

·1 NO 0880 5437   NO 05 SE 60
The first lies between a burn and a track 250 m ENE of Loch Charles. It measures 9·2 m by 5·6 m and 0·6 m in height, and a hollow runs through the centre of the mound, opening on to the burn on the S.

·2 NO 0936 5398   NO 05 SE 61
The second is situated beside a boggy stream-bed on the hillside about 700 m to the ESE of (·1). Crescentic on plan, it measures 7·5 m by 5 m and 0·6 m in maximum

height. The hollow in its open side faces SSE on to the stream-bed.

175   Pitcarmick, burnt mounds
Two burnt mounds are situated amongst the groups of small cairns and hut-circles high up on the flank of the hill to the SW of Pitcarmick (see also no. 152).

·1   NO 0823 5556   NO 05 NE 126
The first lies 70 m N of the track leading up from Dalnabreck and about 700 m W of the steading. Crescent-shaped on plan, it measures 8·5 m by 5·3 m and 0·5 m in height, and its open side faces NW on to a boggy stream-bed.

·2   NO 0741 5580   NO 05 NE 125
The second lies 850 m to the WNW of (·1) and overlooks the valley of the Pitcarmick Burn. It is crescent-shaped, measuring 9 m by 6·5 m and up to 0·9 m in height. Its open side faces W on to a small burn.

176   Rochallie, burnt mound
NO 1423 5065   NO 15 SW 29
This burnt mound lies on the E bank of a small burn 100 m NNW of the easternmost corner of the forestry plantation to the N of the Moss of Cochrage. Crescentic on plan, it measures a maximum of 8·3 m across by 0·5 m in height, and its open side faces SSE on to boggy ground beside the burn.

177   Smyrna, burnt mound
NO 1888 5330   NO 15 SE 51
This small burnt mound is situated on the W side of a burn 200 m ENE of Smyrna cottage and at the E end of a group of small cairns (no. 122·4). It is crescentic on plan, measuring 9·7 m by 4·9 m and up to 0·5 m in height, with the U-shaped hollow side facing SSE on to the burn.

178   Torr Lochaidh, burnt mound
NO 1432 6430   NO 16 SW 60
This burnt mound is situated on the E side of a boggy hollow on the NE flank of Torr Lochaidh and approximately 100 m E of the A93 public road. Crescentic on plan, with a hollow on its W side, it measures 7·5 m by 4·5 m and up to 0·5 m in height.

179   Uchd na h-Anaile, burnt mounds
Two burnt mounds have been located at heights of 470 m and 490 m OD respectively on the SW flank of Uchd na h-Anaile.

·1   NO 0855 6610   NO 06 NE 17
The first lies beside a spring at a major break in slope some 200 m NW of the track that mounts the S face of the hill. Crescentic on plan, it measures 9·3 m by 6·5 m in diameter and 1 m in height, and its open side faces N on to the small burn that issues from the spring.

·2   NO 0851 6646   NO 06 NE 18
The second lies beside another spring immediately W of the mouth of a gully some 350 m to the N. It too is crescentic on plan and measures 6·5 m by 3·5 m and 0·6 m in height; its open side faces NW on to the spring. A shieling-hut lies 30 m to the E.

180   Welton of Creuchies, burnt mounds
There are five burnt mounds strung along the tributaries of the unnamed burns that drain the area of rough pasture to the WSW of Welton of Creuchies.

·1   NO 2056 4995   NO 24 NW 57
This burnt mound is situated at the edge of a field of improved pasture 600 m WSW of Welton of Creuchies steading. Roughly crescentic on plan, it measures 11·2 m by 6·3 m and 0·6 m in height, and the hollow in its SE side opens on to a burn. The N side of the mound has been clipped by cultivation, revealing a mass of small fragments of stone set in a matrix of black earth.

·2   NO 2044 4988   NO 24 NW 56
A crescent-shaped burnt mound is situated 130 m to the WSW of (·1) and on a tributary of the same burn. Measuring 9·2 m by 8·2 m and 0·4 m in height, it faces W, opening on to the burn.

·3   NO 1970 4979   NO 14 NE 78
About 730 m further up the tributary from (·2), there is a crescent-shaped burnt mound measuring a maximum of 8·7 m across by 0·7 m in height. The hollow on its open side faces S on to the burn.

·4   NO 2020 4943   NO 24 NW 59
This burnt mound is situated on the N side of a shallow boggy gully, which drains into the Den of Welton to the E. It is crescent-shaped, measuring about 10·5 m across by 0·6 m in height, and the hollow in its open side faces WSW.

·5   NO 2023 4938   NO 24 NW 55
Situated on a low rise 50 m SE of (·4), there is a burnt mound. It is bilobate on plan, measures 14·2 m by 8·2 m overall, and stands to a height of 0·4 m. The unusual form of the mound suggests that it comprises two elements: a standard crescent-shaped burnt mound on the E, and an oval mound on the W.

RING-DITCHES

181   Clayhills, ring-ditch
NO 2087 4612   NO 24 NW 43
Aerial photography has revealed the cropmarks of what may possibly be a double ring-ditch situated on a low knoll about 45 m S of Clayhills. The inner ring is less

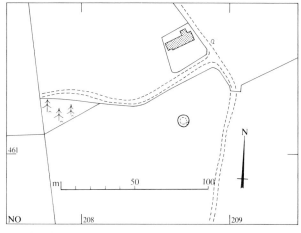

181 Clayhills, ring-ditch, 1:2500

121

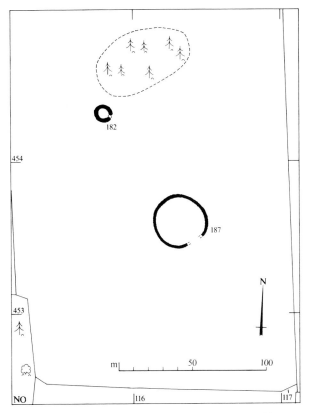

182 Wester Tullyneddie, ring-ditch and enclosure (no.187), 1:2500

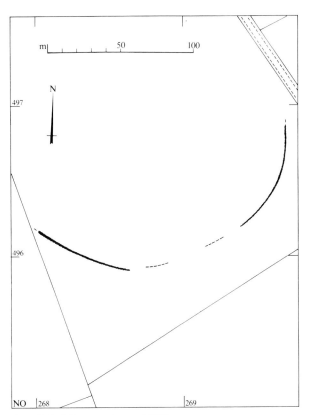

184·1 Balloch House, enclosure, 1:2500

clearly defined than the outer, which measures about 8 m in overall diameter; between the rings on the SE arc there are two indeterminate markings, possibly pits.

182 Wester Tullyneddie, ring-ditch
NO 1158 4543   NO 14 NW 39

The cropmark of what may be a ring-ditch was recorded by aerial photography on the flank of a low hill 700 m NNW of Wester Tullyneddie and 65 m NW of enclosure no. 187. It has an internal diameter of about 8 m and surrounds a rock outcrop, now partly obscured by field-gathered stones.

MISCELLANEOUS ENCLOSURES

183 Badkeirie, enclosure and hut
NO 1755 5748   NO 15 NE 6

This enclosure, which was previously recorded as a hut-circle (Thorneycroft 1933, 188), is probably an old sheepfold. It measures 13 m by 12 m within a stony bank 1 m in thickness by 0·5 m in height and there is a narrow entrance on the S. A small rectangular hut (5·6 m by 3·6 m overall) lies about 150 m to the SW.

184 Balloch House, enclosures
·1 NO 2690 4960   NO 24 NE 50

A cropmark in the form of an intermittent arc measuring about 180 m along the chord and 53 m in depth was revealed by aerial survey in gently undulating ground 170 m NE of Balloch House. The feature appears to indicate the course of a ditch defining the SE portion of an enclosure which may extend some distance into the adjacent fields.

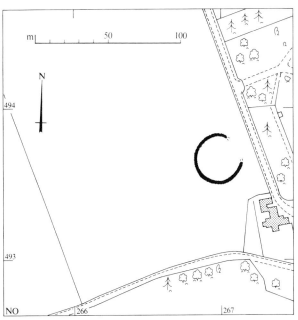

184·2 Balloch House, enclosure, 1:2500

·2 NO 2670 4936   NO 24 NE 61

A light-toned cropmark defining all but the NE quadrant of what is probably a circular enclosure was recorded 85 m SW of Balloch House. It is situated on gently rising ground and measures about 30 m in internal diameter.

185 Barry Hill, enclosure
NO 2654 5027   NO 25 SE 26

The remains of this enclosure are situated on a gentle SE-facing slope about 300 m ESE of the fort on Barry Hill (no. 102). Prior to its partial destruction in 1854 it

measured 32 m by 30 m within a wall accompanied by an external ditch, and there were entrances on the N and S respectively. All that can now be seen is a 30 m arc of the wall which measures 3·9 m in thickness. The outer face has been reduced to a basal course of massive blocks (up to 1·4 m long and 0·6 m high), while the inner face is built of smaller boulders; a stretch of intermural wall-face is visible on the E. Amongst the core material there is a small boulder with vitrified stone adhering to it. This, however, may have been gathered from the nearby fort; an iron pintle is also wedged between the stones of the wall-core. Amongst the stone finds made in 1854 were a number of querns and a steatite cup (RMS, AQ 22).
— *Stat. Acct.*, 1 (1791), 509; Wise 1859.

186   Mains of Mause, enclosure
NO 1662 4974   NO 14 NE 40
Vertical photography taken by the RAF in 1949 has revealed a subrectangular enclosure situated on a low flat-topped knoll 100 m SW of Mains of Mause. The enclosure measures about 64 m by 30 m within a ditch at least 4 m in average width, whose course may be traced without interruption on all sides but the N. There are faint traces of what may have been an outer circuit lying some 10 m outside the main ditch on the E, S and W, and it is possible that on the N it was extended to enclose an annexe.

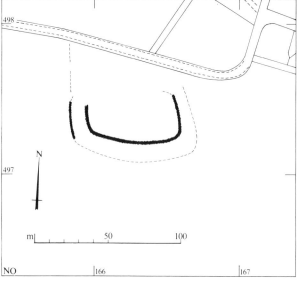

186 Mains of Mause, enclosure, 1:2500

187   Wester Tullyneddie, enclosure
NO 1163 4536   NO 14 NW 35
Aerial survey has revealed the cropmark of a near-
182 circular ditched enclosure 600 m NNW of Wester

Tullyneddie and 65 m SE of ring-ditch no. 182. The enclosure, which lies on a low rounded knoll, has an internal diameter of about 33 m, and there is a gap some 10 m in width on the SE arc.

ECCLESIASTICAL MONUMENTS

(See also no. 209)

188   Alyth, old parish church, chapel and burial-ground
NO 2448 4879   NO 24 NW 6, 17
About 120 m ENE of the present parish church (1839) there are the remains of its predecessor, which stood on a terrace close to the centre of the old town. The remaining fabric includes a portion of the N wall and aisle arcade (25·4 m long overall) suggesting on plan, a church with a square-ended choir, a nave and aisle(s) of three bays, and a N aisle chapel or sacristy. The surviving, but remodelled, fragment of the N wall is medieval and incorporates a plinth, a blocked round-headed doorway and window-opening, and, towards its E end, aumbries and a sacrament house; the aisle arcade is probably of late 15th- or early 16th-century date. A skewput bearing an armorial escutcheon, and a lintel (dated 1629), are set in the wall of the burial-ground beside the N gate. There are a number of 17th- and 18th-century gravestones. A church dedicated to St Moluag is on record by 1352. In 1727 it is said to have been '49 and ½ foot (15·09 m) in breadth and 50 (15·24 m) in length, abstracting from the Quire, and stands on two rows of pillars'. No visible remains survive of a chapel dedicated to St Ninian that is alleged to have stood on the N side of the burial-ground.
— *Stat. Acct.*, 6 (1793), 402; *NSA*, 10 (1845), 119; Macfarlane 1908, 109; Mackinlay 1914, 160; Scott 1925, 249; 1950, 471; Meikle 1933, 29–44; Cowan 1967, 6; Webster 1982, 148, no. 121.

188B Alyth, old parish church, south aisle arcade from SW

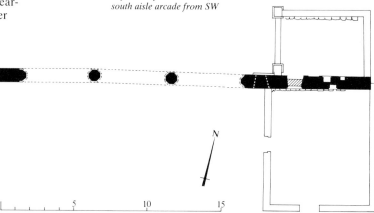

188A Alyth, old parish church, 1:250

189 Alyth, Pictish symbol stone
NO 2432 4875   NO 24 NW 14

In 1887 a Class II symbol stone was discovered when
ground was levelled in front of the manse at Alyth (NO
2450 4885). The stone (a slab of grey schist 1·37 m long,
0·45 m wide and up to 0·13 m thick) now stands in the
porch of Alyth High Kirk. The front bears a Latin cross
with an unusual tenon at the base of the shaft; the arms
and shaft of the cross are decorated with interlace and
there are spirals in the angles between the arms. On the
reverse there is a Pictish carving comprising a fragmentary
double-disc and Z-rod symbol.
— Allen and Anderson 1903, iii, 286; Coutts 1970, 52.

189B Alyth, Pictish symbol stone

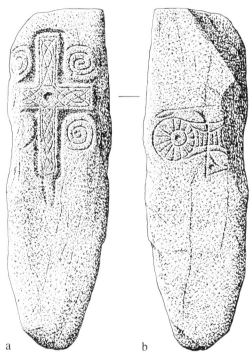

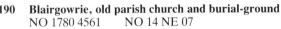

189A Alyth, Pictish symbol stone, 1:15

190 Blairgowrie, old parish church and burial-ground
NO 1780 4561   NO 14 NE 07

There are no visible remains of the medieval parish
church which stood on the site occupied by the present
church (1824). Within the burial-ground there are a 17th-
century graveslab and a number of 18th-century
gravestones. The church is on record by 1207.
— *Stat. Acct.*, 17 (1796), 199; *NSA*, 10 (Perth), 925; Scott 1950, 472–3;
    Cowan 1967, 18–19.

191 Bruceton, Pictish symbol stone
NO 2898 5039   NO 25 SE 17

191A, B This Class I Pictish symbol stone (up to 1·40 m high,
0·25 m thick and 0·80 m wide) stands in a field 400 m S of
Bruceton farmsteading on the haughland of the River
Isla. On the S face it bears two symbols: an arch and the
'Pictish beast'. Macfarlane records the discovery of
human bones on the haugh, while Stuart notes that about
1841 a number of 'coffins' were found less than 18 m from
the stone (no. 47·2).
— Stuart 1856, 34, pl. III; Allen and Anderson 1903, iii, 282–3;
    Macfarlane 1906, 114.

192 Chapelton, chapel
NO 1188 4597   NO 14 NW 8

All that can now be seen of this chapel, the site of which
is largely obscured by field-clearance, is a fragment of its
E wall-footings. According to Dixon (1925, 94) the

191A Bruceton, Pictish symbol stone, 1:15

191B Bruceton, Pictish symbol stone

building measured about 11·6m by 5·5m over walls 0·7m in thickness; the entrance was possibly in the N wall. In the 19th century skeletal remains were discovered on the W and a 'font-stone' bearing the date 1511 is said to have been found on the E.

— *Stat. Acct.*, 9 (1793), 260; Name Book, Perth, No. 41, p. 22; Scott 1950, 348.

193 Drumfork, chapel and burial-ground
NO 1488 5953   NO 15 NW 4
This chapel stands within its walled burial-ground 270m S of Drumfork House. It is rectangular on plan (9·2m from WNW to ESE by 5·2m transversely over stone walls 0·8m thick and up to 1·5m high), and has an entrance-doorway central to the SSW wall; a lintel wrought with a mitred-chamfer and bearing the date 1668 lies to one side. There are a number of 18th-century gravestones.

— Meikle 1933, 83.

194 Kirkmichael, old parish church and burial-ground
NO 0812 6010   NO 06 SE 22
There are no visible remains of the medieval parish church of Strathardle, which probably stood on or close to the site occupied by the present church (1791). Within the burial-ground there is a 17th-century gravestone alongside others of 18th-century date and later. The church is on record in 1189.

— *Stat. Acct.*, 15 (1795), 515; Scott 1925, 163; Cowan 1967, 190.

195 Rattray, old parish church and burial-ground
NO 1897 4569   NO 14 NE 53
There are no visible remains of the medieval parish church which stood on or close to the site now occupied by the present church (1820). Within the burial-ground there are a number of 18th-century gravestones, the

Whitson of Parkhill mortuary enclosure and beside it that of the Rattrays of Craighall. The prebend of Rattray is on record in 1169.

— *Stat. Acct.*, 4 (1792), 149; *NSA*, 10 (Perth), 246; Scott 1923, 170; Cowan 1967, 169; *Third Stat. Acct.*, 27 (Perth), 311.

196 St Fink, chapel and burial-ground
NO 2146 4722   NO 24 NW 9
There are no visible remains of the chapel which stood due E of the present farmhouse at St Fink. Within the existing burial enclosure there is a fragment of an 18th-century gravestone. The burial-ground has been disturbed more than once; in the 18th century a number of skulls were dug up ('each enclosed between four square stones'), while in the 19th century, the removal of the chapel foundations was accompanied by the discovery of 'human bones and urns . . . two small coins and three bottles of a globular shape'. The chapel, dedicated to St Findeach, was the property of Coupar Abbey.

— *Stat. Acct.*, 19 (1797), 359; Name Book, Perth, No. 9, p. 7; *NSA*, 10 (Perth), 1188; Rogers 1880, 207; Scott 1950, 472.

197 Spittal of Glenshee, chapel and burial-ground
NO 1091 7017   NO 17 SW 11
The site of a chapel of 18th-century or earlier date is indicated by a rectangular depression (14·4m from WNW to ESE by 5·3m transversely and up to 0·3m deep) on the SE side of the walled burial-ground within which the present church (1831) now stands. There are a number of 18th-century gravestones. The chapel is depicted on Brown's 1808 survey, where it is shown as unroofed, and the 'Chapel-crofts' are on record in 1615. There is no documentary evidence to support the view that there was a medieval hospital at Spittal.

Pont (*c.*1600) and Gordon (1636/48) depict another chapel to the S of Spittal, which bore the name 'Chapel of Glenshy', but this chapel is otherwise unattested and there is no field evidence to indicate its presence.

— *Stat. Acct.*, 15 (1795), 515; Brown 1808; Cowan and Easson 1976, 197.

198 Steps of Cally, chapel and burial-ground
NO 1274 5161   NO 15 SW 6
There are no visible remains of a chapel which is said to have stood either within or immediately to the W of the walled burial-ground at Steps of Cally. The earliest surviving gravestone bears the date 1767. A chapel, dedicated to St Mary, is on record by 1542.

— Name Book, Perth, No.11, p. 24; Rogers 1880, 207; Scott 1950, 472.

CASTLES, TOWER-HOUSES AND ISLAND-DWELLING

199 Ashintully, tower-house
NO 1017 6123   NO 16 SW 2
This 16th-century, stepped L-plan tower-house stands within its policies 2·5km NE of Kirkmichael. The main block consists of three principal storeys and has a four-storeyed accommodation and stair-wing extruded on the SW. The entrance-doorway, above which there is an heraldic panel, is in the S re-entrant angle; the lintel is dated 1583. There are a number of horizontal gun-loops. Stobie (1783) depicts the tower as ruinous. It was restored, altered and extended in the late 18th or early 19th century, and was further added to in the late 19th century. Part of a dormer pediment is incorporated in the S wall of an adjacent stable-block.

255

199A, B

— *NSA*, 10 (Perth), 787; MacGibbon and Ross 1892b, 222–6.

199A Ashintully, tower-house from S
  B Ashintully, tower-house, entrance doorway and armorial panel

A

B

200 Balloch, castle and dovecot
NO 2629 4957   NO 24 NE 24

There are no visible remains of a castle which stood on, or close to, the site now occupied by Balloch farmsteading, but a number of dressed stones incorporated in the fabric of the steading may have come from it. A dovecot stood some 100 m to the N (NO 262 496). The castle is said to have been the seat of the Rollo family; 'Belouch' in the lordship of 'Alicht' is on record by 1470. Stobie (1783) gives the name as 'Ballock' and depicts and annotates it 'Castle in ruins'.

— Name Book, Perth, No. 5, pp. 49, 86; OS 6-inch map, Perthshire, 1st
  ed. (1867), sheet 53.

201 Bamff, tower-house
NO 2216 5147   NO 25 SW 3

The SW corner of Bamff House (built 1828 and remodelled in 1844 by William Burn) is formed by a well-preserved late 16th-century tower-house. It is rectangular on plan, and stands four storeys and an attic in height. Two horizontal gun-loops are incorporated at ground-floor level; the entrance-doorway has probably been on the NE and the stair most likely in the E angle. The vaulted basement which is divided into two compartments, was originally served by a draw-well. The Ramsays have been in possession of Bamff since the reign of Alexander II (1214–49).

— NSA, 10 (Perth), 1116–17; Macfarlane 1906, 112; SRO, GD 83/707;
  NMRS, PTD/34.

201 Bamff, tower-house from SW

202 Blackcraig Castle, tower-house
NO 1081 5345   NO 15 SW 33

Incorporated at the rear of Blackcraig Castle, a mansion of 1856, there are the remains of a substantial tower-house. It stands three storeys in height and has a stair-tower extruded on the NW; the masonry is of lime-

mortared random rubble and is readily distinguishable from the 19th-century ashlar superstructure of the mansion. Blackcraig was probably the property of the Maxwells who were in possession of the barony of Ballmacreuchy by 1550 (*Retours*, Perth, No. 9).

202 Blackcraig Castle, tower-house incorporated within a 19th-century
  mansion from SW

203 Corb, castle and buildings
NO 1648 5682   NO 15 NE 1, 22

All that remains of this castle is a low grass-covered mound measuring 18 m by 12 m (A). In its immediate vicinity, though not tightly grouped, there are at least five buildings, all reduced to their turf-covered wall-footings and ranging in size from 10 m by 5 m to 27 m by 6 m overall.

'Koirb' appears on Pont's map (c.1600), and on Stobie's map (1783) the castle is depicted as ruinous. It is said to have been a hunting seat of the Scottish kings or of the earls of Crawford (*NSA*, 10 (1843), 1118), but from the 17th century until the middle of the 18th century it was the property of the Rattray family (Marshall 1881, 223–4).

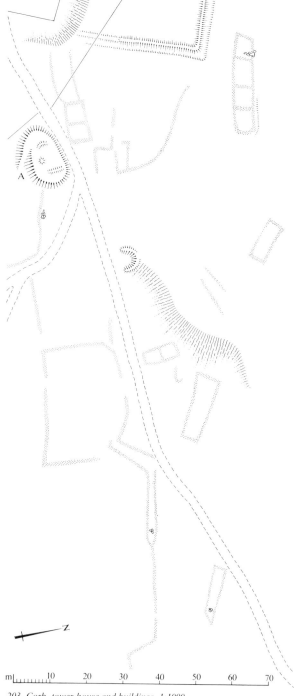

203 Corb, tower-house and buildings, 1:1000

204 Craighall, castle
NO 1750 4815   NO 14 NE 18

Craighall occupies a commanding and precipitous promontory overlooking at the River Ericht. All that can be seen of the medieval castle is a portion of what may be a D-shaped tower at the northern tip of the promontory, re-utilised in the extension to the 19th-century mansion; the masonry has been pierced to provide a number of window-openings and a buttressed support for a first-floor balcony. A pediment (dated 1614) and a mural monument with a half-length effigy (c.1640) commemorating Bartholomew Somerville, which are also incorporated in re-use, are said to have been brought from Edinburgh University by Baron James Clerk-Rattray. The Rattrays were in possession of Craighall by the first half of the 16th century. The author of the *Statistical Account* stated that 'there are round towers at each side of the house and the vestiges of a ditch'.
— *Stat. Acct.*, 4 (1792), 150; Douglas 1798, 274–6; *NSA*, 10 (Perth), 241–2; Miller 1890, 101–7.

205 Drumlochy, tower-house
NO 1576 4694   NO 14 NE 17

All that can be seen of the late 16th- or 17th-century tower-house of Drumlochy is a fragment of the S wall of the main block and part of a circular tower which was extruded on the W. The surviving wall, which is of mortared rubble masonry, measures 8·2 m in length, 0·8 m in thickness and up to 3·6 m in height. There are two blocked window-openings and a key-hole gun-loop. A number of moulded stones are incorporated in the ruinous walls of an adjacent steading. Drumlochy was the property of the Heron family.
— *NSA*, 10 (Perth), 899; MacGibbon and Ross 1889, 458.

206 Glasclune, tower-house
NO 1541 4700   NO 14 NE 37

The ruins of Glasclune, built about 1600, are prominently sited 140m ESE of Mains of Glasclune steading. The visible remains comprise two detached elements (once

206 Glasclune, tower-house from SW

possibly joined). On the S there is a portion of an L-plan block, two storeys and a garret in height. It has a stair-turret in the NW re-entrant and a corbelled round at the corresponding angle. The fragment of an accommodation wing stands 23 m to the N; it has a stair-turret and a three-storeyed tower extruded on its NE side. A walled courtyard extended to the W. In the 17th century Glasclune belonged to the Blairs.
— *Stat. Acct.*, 17 (1796), 478; *Retours*, Perth, No. 680; *NSA*, 10 (Perth), 915; MacGibbon and Ross 1892a, 46–7.

207 Inverquiech, castle
NO 2780 4964   NO 24 NE 17

This castle occupies a precipitous promontory at the
confluence of the Burn of Quiech and the River Isla; the
neck of the promontory is in part cut by a steep-sided
natural gully (18 m wide by up to 4·8 m deep). All that
remains visible are portions of the E and N walls. The E
wall, of which there are two fragments, stood at least two
storeys in height. The N fragment incorporates a
garderobe, a drain and what may be the robbed remains
of a ground-floor fireplace; that on the S has a postern
and a plinth. To the S the spread of structural debris can
be traced for at least 38 m and may indicate the extension
of a wall round the perimeter of the promontory. The
castle is on record in 1296 but was ruinous in 1394.

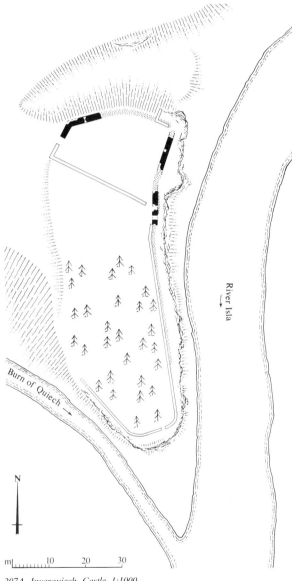

207A Inverquiech, Castle, 1:1000

Nothing is known of the castle's later history, but the
presence of a wide-mouthed horizontal gun-loop in the N
wall indicates that it was later refortified.
— Jervise 1853, 286; Warden 1885, 105; MacGibbon and Ross 1892, 394;
    Macfarlane 1906, 112.

208 Kingseat, tower-house
NO 1474 5450   NO 15 SW 34

Central to the S wing of Kingseat House (19th century)

207B Inverquiech Castle, the east wall

there are the remains of what may be a small tower-
house. These consist of a block (7·1 m by 4·8 m over walls
0·6 m thick) two storeys and an attic in height, which is
characterised by the use of granite dressings and an
irregularity in the spacing of its windows; to the rear, at
second-floor level, there are a number of tusking-stones.
A gun-loop and four iron yetts, which have been
incorporated in the garden walls at Kingseat, probably
came from this or some other fortified house. Kingseat
appears on the maps of Pont (*c*.1600) and Roy (1747–55,
sheet 18/4), and a mansion is depicted by Stobie (1783).

209 Laighwood, castle, chapel and burial-ground
NO 0774 4568   NO 04 NE 1

A mound in a field to the SE of Laighwood farmhouse is
said to be the site of the castle of Bishop William Sinclair   *217*
(1309/10–1337). It has been reduced and spread by
ploughing, and measures about 63 m by 55 m and is up to
2 m high. The author of the *Statistical Account* noted the
presence of 'two vaults and a small part of an under
gallery, with two loop-holes, pointing towards the draw-
bridge [on the N]', the remains of later buildings on the W
and SW sides of the castle, and the fact that it 'appears to
have been fortified on all sides by ditches filled with
water.' A chapel and burial-ground are said to have
adjoined the S side of the castle, and in the 18th century
some skeletal remains were found there.
— *Stat. Acct.*, 9 (1793), 66; Name Book, Perth, No. 16, pp. 8, 12.

210 Loch Beanie, island-dwelling
NO 1601 6867   NO 16 NE 22

This small island, which appears to be largely artificial,
lies towards the centre of the loch, about 100 m from its S   *286*
shore. It is roughly square on plan and formed almost
entirely of boulders and small stones. On the date of visit,
however, less than a third of the surface area was visible
above water. On the W the rubble slopes gently from the
surface, but on the ESE it pitches more steeply; a marked
intake on this side may have served as a boat-landing.
Towards the edge of the island there are fragmentary
traces of what may be walls. Pont (*c*.1600) depicts a   *p.6*
mansion on the loch and annotates it 'Loch Sesatut,
sumtyms ye dwelling of ye chief man of Glenshy and
Strathardle', while Gordon (1636/1647) notes 'L. Sesatur
ye old chief dwelling of Glens[hie]'; it does not appear,
however, on Roy (1747–55, sheet 18/4).

211 *Newton, tower-house from SW*

B

211 Newton, tower-house
NO 1716 4526   NO 14 NE 2

This well-preserved Z-plan tower-house, probably of late
16th-century date, stands within its policies on the W side
of Blairgowrie. Its main block, which is three storeys and
an attic in height, has a stair-wing extruded on the E and
a round-tower corbelled square on the W. The
repositioned entrance-doorway, protected by a horizontal
loop, is in the S re-entrant of the E wing. With the
exception of the W wing the main block is unvaulted.
Although the tower was later remodelled and extended, it
retains some early 18th-century interiors.
— MacGibbon and Ross 1887, 293–4; MacDonald 1899, 20, 136; Dunbar
    1966, 66, 78.

212 Whitefield, tower-house
NO 0897 7168   NO 06 SE 1

This 16th-century stepped L-plan tower-house stands on a
255 slight rise 1·2 km WSW of Ashintully (no. 199). The main
block has stood to at least three storeys in height and has
a three-storeyed stair-tower extruded at the W angle. The
internal and external detail is well executed and the tower

212B *Whitefield, tower-house from SE*
  C *tower-house, detail*

is well provided with horizontal gun-loops. A hood-
moulded panel-niche (dated 1577 on sill) is set above the
entrance-doorway in the SE re-entrant. The basement is
vaulted and divided into two compartments (that on the E
being the kitchen), with a corridor on the S, and a mural
service-stair in the W wall. A scale-and-platt staircase
(ceiled with a groined vault) provided access to the first-
floor hall, from which a turnpike, corbelled out over the
NW re-entrant, communicated with the floors above and
a chamber over the main stair.

On the S side of the tower there are some
indeterminate earthwork remains whose date and purpose
are unclear, and further to the S there are traces of what
may be an original causeway (A on fig.). Whitefield was
built for the Spaldings. It was altered in the late 18th
century and was abandoned by the early 19th century
when the tower was partly demolished to provide
materials for a neighbouring steading.
— MacGibbon and Ross 1892b, 222–6.

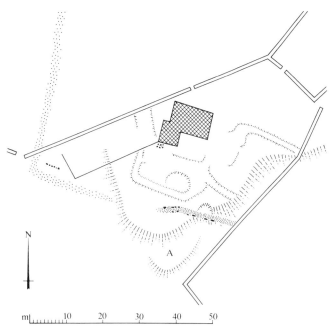

N

A

m | 10   20   30   40   50

212A *Whitefield, tower-house, 1:1000*

MEDIEVAL EARTHWORKS

213 Bamff, earthwork
NO 2275 5169   NO 25 SW 33

This earthwork is situated in woods on the edge of a scarp, 600 m ENE of the tower-house of Bamff (no. 201). Roughly oval on plan, it measures 90 m from NNE to SSW by at least 43 m transversely within a V-shaped ditch. The ditch is best preserved on the NNE, where it is 4·3 m broad and 1·2 m deep; around the S and SE it has been reduced to a terrace 4 m broad, and on the W all visible remains have been removed by ploughing. The date and purposes of the earthwork are unknown, but its proximity to the tower-house of Bamff may be significant.

214 Blairgowrie, motte
NO 1785 4544   NO 14 NE 3

There are no visible remains of the flat-topped conical motte that stood about 170 m S of Blairgowrie old parish church (no. 190). The authors of the *Statistical Accounts* record respectively that it consisted of strata of earth and gravel, and that it was about 200 yards (182 m) in circumference. In 1838, when it was removed, 'a circular excavation, about three feet (0·91 m) in diameter, and six feet (1·83 m) in depth, which had been dug far down into the hard gravel, and afterwards filled up with a black unctuous looking mould, intermixed with ashes and pieces of burnt wood,' was found at the centre of the space formerly occupied by the mound.
— *Stat. Acct.*, 17 (1796), 207; *NSA*, 10 (Perth), 914.

215 Lady Lindsay's Castle, Craig Liach, earthwork
NO 1772 4887   NO 14 NE 23

Lady Lindsay's Castle is a medieval earthwork occupying a sheer-sided promontory on the W bank of the Ericht gorge 700 m N of Craighall and immediately S of a rock pinnacle known as Craig Liach. A ditch (up to 4 m broad

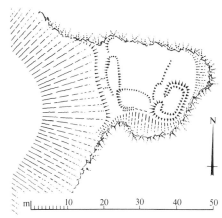

215 Lady Lindsay's Castle, earthwork, 1:1000

and 1·6 m deep) with a low internal bank (up to 3·5 m thick) cuts partway across the neck of the promontory (22 m by 18 m), which is overlooked by higher ground immediately to the W. On the SE there are the remains of a rectangular building (7·1 m by 5·1 m over turf-covered walls 1·1 m thick) with an entrance in its W wall. A subrectangular scooped depression (8·4 m by 4 m), to the W, may indicate the site of a second building or enclosure. Although the site takes its name from Janet Gordon of Huntly (died 1489/91), wife of Alexander Lindsay, there is no documentary evidence to confirm her presence on this site.
— *NSA*, 10 (Perth), 901–2; MacDonald 1899, 133–4; Paul 1906, 23–4; 1907, 530.

DEER PARKS

216 Buzzart Dikes, deer park
NO 1268 4766   NO 14 NW 2

The earthwork known as 'Buzzart Dikes' encloses an area of about 86 ha on Middleton Muir. Although once identified by antiquarians as a Caledonian camp and

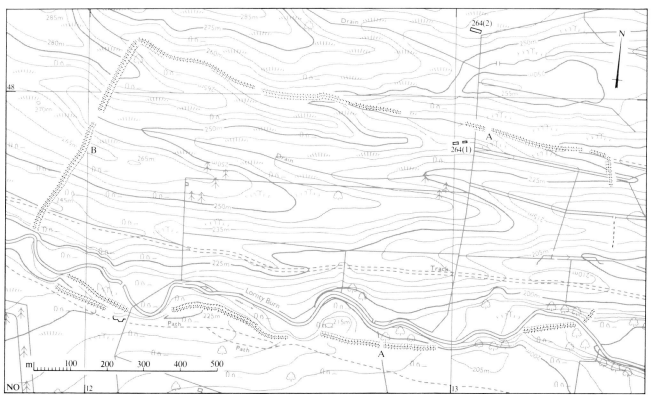

216 Buzzart Dikes, deer park, 1:10000

associated with the battle of Mons Graupius, it has been convincingly interpreted as the remains of a medieval deer park (Crawford 1949, 76–7). On the E the earthwork has been obliterated by cultivation, but most of the perimeter elsewhere survives intact. It comprises a bank (up to 1·4 m high) and internal ditch (up to 1·2 m deep), and where best preserved on the W it measures about 10·1 m in overall width. The course of the earthwork is as described by Childe and Graham (1943, 45–9), but at the SW corner the present survey has recorded a second line of bank and ditch cutting across the haughland on the S side of the Lornty Burn. The purpose of the latter feature is unclear and it may merely represent the reconstruction of an eroded section, but in conjunction with an enclosure, which overlooks the haughland at this point, it is possible that both fulfilled a specialised function. No evidence of an original entrance is apparent, but the perimeter is cut by hollowed trackways at two points (A on fig.) and another track is overlain by the earthwork itself (B on fig.). For buildings in proximity to the deer park see no. 264.

217   Laighwood, deer park
NO 0728 4584   NO 04 NE 2

This deer park is about 156 ha in extent and straddles the Lunan Burn. All that can be seen of the stone wall which enclosed it, known as the Pict's Dyke, is a fragment of the plinth on its SE side. It is probable, however, that the

wall extended to the W and N. In the middle of the S side there is what may be an original gate flanked by out-turned wing-walls. In the reign of Robert II (1371–90) the land enclosed was granted to the Earl of Moray. The park pale is said to have been demolished about 1760 and its materials reused in the wall which replaced it; according to the author of the *Statistical Account*, the original wall was up to 2·1 m high and 1·2 m thick at the top. For a castle which stood within the park, see no. 209. Stobie (1783) annotates his map 'Park of Laighwood' and 'Laighwood Castle in ruins'.

— *Stat. Acct.*, 9 (1793), 257–8; Name Book, Perth, No. 16, p. 7; Atholl Muniments, 13, v, iil.

MEDIEVAL BURGHS

Excluded from this list are Balnakilly, Balnald and Dalnagairn in the parish of Kirkmichael, which, although chartered (1510–11), do not appear to have been established. In 1615 Spalding of Ashintully was granted the privilege of holding a weekly market in the burgh of barony of Kirkmichael, to be held on the lands of Balnakilly and Balnald. Alyth possessed a mercat cross (1670), but did not become a burgh until 1875.

— Small 1900, 23; Spalding 1914, 44; Pryde 1965, nos. 190, 198, 199; Adams 1978, 26; *Third Stat. Acct.*, 27 (Perth), 224.

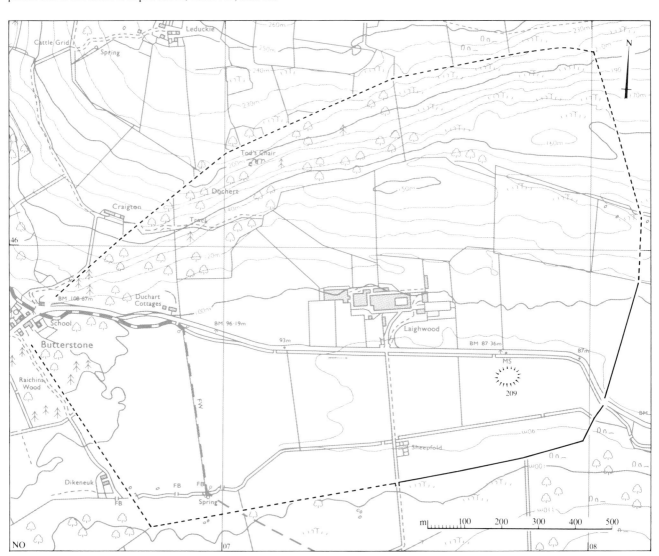

217 Laighwood, deer park, 1:10000

218 Blairgowrie, burgh
NO 17 45   NO 14 NE 64
In 1634 Blairgowrie was erected a burgh of barony, and in 1929 it was united with Rattray (a burgh of 1877); see also nos. 190, 214.
— Pryde 1965, 69, no. 331; *Third Stat. Acct.*, 27 (Perth), 312.

219 Kirkmichael, burgh
NO 07 06   NO 06 SE 27
In 1511 Kirkmichael was erected a burgh of barony; see also no. 194
— Spalding 1914, 44; Pryde 1965, 56, no. 197; Adams 1978, 26.

MEDIEVAL AND LATER SETTLEMENT

(See also nos. 102; 103·6–·7; 109·2; 114·2–·3; 122·9; 124; 130·1; 133; 140·1; 147·7; 147·11; 149·2; 155·3; 158·9; 183)

220 Alyth Burn, building
NO 1808 5644   NO 15 NE 37
A two-compartment building, adjoined on the N by an enclosure, is situated on a low ridge 130 m W of the confluence of the Alyth Burn and the Thief's Burn.

221 An Dun, farmstead
NO 1446 6562   NO 16 NW 23
This farmstead occupies a sheltered position at the edge of a terrace at the foot of An Dun and is overlooked by a ridge of higher ground immediately to the W. It consists of three buildings, which are on the same alignment together with a yard (within which there is a stone-walled enclosure) and a kiln. The buildings are all reduced to the lowest courses of their stone walls and range from 7·3 m by 3·8 m to 15·2 m by 5 m overall, the largest being a two-compartment building. The farmstead is depicted and named 'Altbui' by Roy (1747–55, sheet 18/4); it is 'Auldvuie' on the maps of Stobie (1783) and Ainslie (1794).

222 Ashintully, Pitcarmick-type building
NO 1084 6249   NO 16 SW 14
This building is situated close to the edge of a broad natural terrace. It measures 25 m by 8·1 m at its widest point over a bank 2 m in thickness and 0·2 m in height, though it narrows to 6·2 m and 6·7 m respectively at either end; the E half of the building is scooped to a depth of

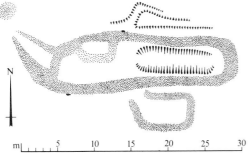

222 Ashintully, Pitcarmick-type building, 1:500

0·4 m. Immediately to the S there is a D-shaped enclosure measuring 6 m by 3·5 m within a bank 1·1 m thick and 0·2 m high, whilst to the N a roughly rectangular depression

(not shown on plan) 0·5 m in depth and measuring 14·5 m by 4·7 m may be the remains of an earlier building. The purpose of the two banks which spring from the corners of the building on the W is unclear.

223 Ashintully, farmsteads and buildings
On the margins of improved fields and in pasture around the tower-houses of Ashintully and Whitefield (nos. 199 and 212) there are the remains of a number of farmsteads. Most of the area lay within the barony of Ashintully, erected in 1615 (Spalding 1914, 44), but with the exception of (·1), which lay within the barony of Dounie, and (·12), none of the sites can be identified with lands in the barony recorded prior to the early 18th century. Nos. ·1–·12 are shown on the accompanying map.

·1   NO 0851 6159   NO 06 SE 8
This farmstead comprises five buildings and four pens clustered at the foot of a rocky knoll, whilst what may be a further building and pen lie to the N. The buildings have been largely reduced to their stone wall-footings and range in size from one of a single compartment measuring 11 m by 5·1 m overall to one of at least four compartments and measuring 25·5 m by 4 m overall; one is adjoined by an enclosure and another has traces of a raised walkway along its WSW wall. About 100 m to the N, on opposite sides of an unnamed burn, there are a kiln and what may be three retting pools.
   The farmstead is probably 'Edenarnochkie', depicted on Stobie's map (1783), which lay within the barony of Dounie, where it is recorded in 1629 (*Retours*, Perth, No. 367) and 1510 (Atholl Muniments).

·2   NO 0859 6178   NO 06 SE 80
Situated 200 m NNE and upslope of (·1), with which it may have been associated, there is a farmstead of five buildings, their walls reduced to stone footings or low banks. The two larger buildings lie parallel to each other across the slope; one is of three compartments and measures 12·1 m by 3·4 m overall, the other is of two compartments and measures 13·5 m by 4·3 m overall with an outshot at its ESE end. To the WNW, and on opposite sides of a yard, there are a two-compartment building (measuring 9·5 m by 3·5 m overall) adjoined by an open-sided structure, and an apparently open-sided building measuring 8·7 m by 4·5 m overall. The fifth building stands alone and measures 10·2 m by 4·4 m overall, whilst at the foot of crags 39 m to the NNW there is a small rectangular enclosure.

·3   NO 0905 6171   NO 06 SE 79
The remains of two buildings lie immediately adjacent to the ruinous tower-house and steading of Whitefield (no. 212). The larger, which is of two compartments, measures 23·3 m by 6·2 m over stone wall-footings and has an outshot at its E end; the smaller (NO 0909 6168) is of a single compartment measuring 16 m by 6·5 m over a low bank and has an outshot at its SE end.

·4   NO 0897 6195   NO 06 SE 38
This farmstead comprises three single-compartment buildings, all reduced to their turf-covered wall-footings. Two of the buildings are set end-on to each other, the larger measures 13·4 m by 5·8 m overall and has an outshot at one end, the smaller measures 7·7 m by 4·6 m overall; the third building is set at right angles to them and measures 14 m by 6·2 m overall.

·5   NO 0898 6195   NO 06 SE 134
This farmstead comprises four buildings and an enclosure set on the edge of marshy ground 260 m N of Whitefield

Castle. The farmstead is named 'Croitnuash' on the first edition of the OS 6-inch map (Perthshire, 1867, sheet 32) where it appears as ruinous. Stobie (1783) also records a farm of this name, but it is unclear whether it applies to this farmstead or (·4).

·6   NO 0924 6236   NO 06 SE 37
Situated on low-lying ground on the W bank of the Allt Menach there is a farmstead. Two buildings, both reduced to their turf-covered wall-footings, are set on opposite sides of a yard; the larger, which is of three compartments, measures 27·5 m by 5 m overall, the smaller, which is of a single compartment, measures 9·7 m by 5 m overall. Some 16 m to the ENE a third building lies on the ENE side of an enclosure; it is of a single compartment and measures 10·5 m by 5 m overall.

Although named 'Balnald' on both the modern OS 1:10,000 scale map and the first edition OS 6-inch map (Perthshire, 1867, sheet 32), this is probably the farmstead of 'Burnside' depicted on Stobie's map (1783). Roy's map (1747–55, sheet 18/4) also depicts a farmstead named Burnside, but it is difficult to reconcile his location of the site with either Stobie's map or with the OS maps. 'Easter Burnside of Ashintully' and 'Wester Burnside of Ashintully' are on record in 1719 and 1743 respectively (Spalding 1914, 226, 244–5).

·7   NO 0942 6232   NO 06 SE 34
On the E bank of the Allt Menach, on gently rising ground a little above the valley floor, there is a farmstead comprising at least one building, two enclosures and a kiln-and-chamber. The building, which is of a single compartment, measures 10·7 m by 5·5 m over a low bank and its SW end adjoins one of the enclosures. Immediately to the N what may be a second building, measuring 15·2 m by 6 m over a low bank, forms the SW side of the second enclosure.

·8   NO 0934 6263   NO 06 SE 70
Lying beneath the Ashintully/Balvarran march dyke, 320 m NNW of (·6), there are the remains of a two-compartment building measuring 14 m by 6 m over a low bank.

·9   NO 0974 6256   NO 06 SE 35
Situated at the old head-dyke on the SW flank of Cnoc an Daimh, 480 m upslope from the Allt Menach and immediately NE of a modern plantation, there is a farmstead comprising seven buildings, a kiln-and-chamber and a pen, all, with the exception of the kiln, reduced to their stone wall-footings. The buildings appear to form two units, one (A) being ranged around a yard, whilst the other (B) lies 24 m to the NNW. What may be the principal building of the farmstead is adjoined by the head-dyke; it is of two compartments and measures 18·6 m by 5·3 m overall; immediately to the SE there is a pen. The other buildings vary in size from 6·5 m by 3 m overall to 15·9 m by 4·8 m overall. The purpose of C, an artificial platform with a slightly dished top, is unknown.

·10 NO 0981 6247   NO 06 SE 33
Some 20 m above the old head-dyke, 90 m SE of (·7), there is a single-compartment building measuring 11·7 m by 5 m over stone wall-footings.

·11 NO 0980 6236   NO 06 SE 36
This farmstead is situated 200 m SSE of (·7), immediately below the old head-dyke which turns down to adjoin it and allow access to the hill above. It comprises five buildings (all reduced to their stone wall-footings), a kiln and a pen or enclosure. The two largest buildings, (A and B), are set at right angles to each other (A) parallel to the

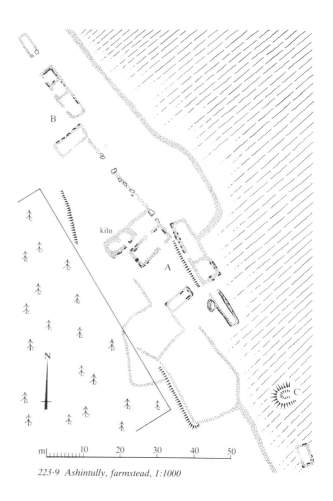

223·9 Ashintully, farmstead, 1:1000

contour, (B) being across it. Building (A), which may be the principal building of the farmstead, has been terraced into the slope; it is of at least four compartments and measures 31·5 m by 5 m overall. A roughly rectangular platform (C), measuring 8·8 m by 6·3 m, lies 42 m to the SE. To the S of B there is a pit of unknown function.

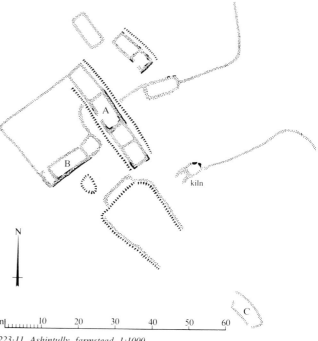

223·11 Ashintully, farmstead, 1:1000

223·12 Ashintully, fermtoun, 1:1000

·12 NO 1021 6210   NO 16 SW 31
From (·9) the old head-dyke follows the contour to the S spur of Cnoc an Daimh where, immediately above the improved fields, there is a fermtoun. The buildings, which have all been reduced to their stone wall-footings, are disposed in two clusters 50m apart. Within the westerly cluster buildings (A) and (B) and buildings (C) and (D) appear to represent separate units, each with a yard area; the two larger buildings, (A and C), measuring 17·5m by 4·9m and 17·1m by 4·5m respectively overall. A kiln-and-chamber lies on the E fringe of the cluster; E is probably a pen. The easterly cluster (NO 1034 6214) comprises an irregular grouping of buildings and yards, the largest building (F) measuring 15m by 5·2m overall.

The remains are clearly to be identified with the settlement of 'Brae' depicted on Stobie's map (1783). The lands of 'Easter' or 'East Brae of Ashintully' are on record in 1719 and 1743 respectively (Spalding 1914, pp. 226, 244–5), and Roy's map (1747–55, sheet 18/4) depicts 'Braes of Essentilly'.

·13 NO 0955 6106   NO 6 SE 89
About 600m WSW of Ashintully Castle there is a farmstead comprising seven buildings and a kiln-barn, their walls reduced to little more than stone footings. Four of the buildings are ranged around a yard, the largest, situated on the NW side, being of four compartments and measuring 26·3m by 4·7m overall. The remaining buildings vary in size from 10·4m by 3·8m to 16m by 6m overall. The kiln-barn is to the S of the yard, two of the other buildings to the SE, whilst the final building lies at the E corner and, together with those on the NW and NE sides of the yard, forms the S side of an enclosure. The farmstead may be that named 'Little Whitefield' on Stobie's map (1783).

·14 NO 0911 6081   NO 06 SE 91
The farmstead of 'Seana Bhaile', depicted as ruinous on the first edition of the OS 6-inch map (Perthshire, 1867, sheet 32), is situated midway between Craig Dally and the plantation on Tom an t-Sabhail. It comprises two buildings set at right angles to each other, the larger, which measures 18·7m by 5·4m overall, with an adjoining yard.

'Easter Shannavaill' is on record in 1712 (Spalding 1914, 221–2), whilst Roy's map names 'W^r Shanwell', 'Mid Shanwell' and 'E^r Shanwell'. On Stobie's map (1783) only 'Shenvail' appears, though a little to the N of the present position.

·15 NO 0925 6069   NO 06 SE 90
At the foot of a low knoll to the NE of Craig Dally there is a building, measuring 15m by 5·5m over a low bank, adjoined on the SW by a probable yard. The yard is linked to a more extensive field-system and on its NW side there is what may be a platform.

·16 NO 0977 6011   NO 06 SE 78
Situated on a terrace on the E bank of the Allt Menach, at the foot of Milton Knowe and immediately E of the ruinous buildings of the mill of Moulinuarie, there are two L-plan buildings now reduced to their stone wall-footings. The principal ranges of each are of two compartments and measure 15·3m by 7·3m and 15m by 6·8m respectively overall; the subsidiary ranges are both of a single compartment and measure 9m by 5·6m and 10m by 6m overall. The easterly building is adjoined on the N by a rectangular yard, and there are also what may be a third building, measuring 8·3m by 4·2m over stone wall-footings, and a square platform up to 0·4m high and 4·8m across.

The remains are probably those of a steading associated with an earlier phase of the adjacent mill which, together with Over and Nether Weries, is on record in 1615 (Spalding 1914, 45). It presumably served the barony of Ashintully and must be that sometimes referred to as the Mill of Ashintully (Spalding 1914, 223). It appears on Stobie's map (1783) as the mill of 'Wierie', but whilst the first edition of the OS 6-inch map (Perthshire, 1867, sheet 32) shows roofed buildings, it is unclear whether or not the mill was still functioning as such at that date.

·17 NO 1056 5994   NO 15 NW 65
A building is situated at the foot of the unnamed rocky hillock which lies to the E of Milton Knowe; it measures 18·2 m by 5·7 m over stone wall-footings and has an outshot at its E end.

·18 NO 1096 6084   NO 16 SW 98
On the lower slopes of Creag nam Brataichean, overlooking the road to Ashintully Castle, there is a farmstead comprising a three-compartment building adjoined by a rectangular enclosure; the building measures 17·6 m by 4·4 m over stone wall-footings and has an outshot at its E end. Some 30 m to the SSE, partly within a plantation, there are the remains of what is probably a second building, whilst 70 m to the NW there is another rectangular enclosure.

224   Ashmore, mills
On the haughland to the W and SW of Ashmore House there are the remains of two mills.

·1   NO 1417 5332   NO 15 SW 35
The first, which lies beside the Black Water, has been substantial (17 m by 5·7 m over walls reduced to a bank of rubble 1·8 m thick and 0·7 m high); on its S side there is another structure, possibly a building (8·7 m by 5·4 m overall). The lade (up to 3·3 m wide and at least 1·4 m deep) can be traced to its origin some 300 m to the NNE (NO 1427 5355).

·2   NO 1422 5316   NO 15 SW 35
At the foot of the slope to the SW of Ashmore House there is what may be a horizontal mill. The building has been let into the slope and measures 10 m by 4·5 m over turf-covered stone walls 0·8 m in thickness and up to 0·7 m in height; the entrance was at the ENE end of the NNW wall. The wheel-pit was at the WSW end of the building and both the lade and tail-race are well defined. Water appears to have been collected in a pond some 30 m to the NW of the mill. A mill is depicted by Stobie (1783), but it is unclear which of these two sites is meant.

225   Baden Burn, shielings
The remains of at least six shieling-huts are disposed over a series of ridges and knolls on the E bank of the Baden Burn, 1·3 km N of the farmstead of Buckinhill (no. 310·13). A further six are situated at the top of the valley.

·1   NO 0835 5238   NO 05 SE 42
The southernmost hut lies immediately WSW of a cairn (no. 6·1) and measures 8·7 m by 5·2 m overall.

·2   NO 083 524   NO 05 SE 41
Some 100 m NNW of (·1) there is a row of three huts. That on the S (NO 0830 5245) is oval on plan, measures 5·6 m in overall length and has an annexe or the remains of an earlier structure on its W side. The second hut is of two compartments and measures 9·8 m by 4·5 m overall, whilst the third (NO 0832 5250) measures 6·5 m by 3·8 m overall.

·3   NO 0853 5259   NO 05 SE 40
About 230 m ENE of (·2), close to the lowest of a line of grouse-butts, there is an oval hut measuring 5 m by 4·4 m overall; what is probably a second lies 12 m to the N.

·4   NO 0801 5291   NO 05 SE 39
A single hut lies 600 m NW of (·3) and measures 9·3 m by 4·8 m overall. There is a small pen 27 m to the WSW.

·5   NO 0776 5360   NO 05 SE 31, 33, 49
On a low heather-covered ridge at the foot of Meall Dubh there are the remains of five shieling-huts. Three of them, the largest measuring 9·5 m by 3·5 m overall, are situated on the E side of a saddle, whilst the others lie 100 m W (NO 0766 5358) and 250 m WSW (NO 0753 5351) respectively. On a narrow terrace overlooking the ridge, 130 m to the NNW (NO 0770 5373), there is a sixth hut and a small pen.

226   Balchrochan, farmstead
NO 0786 5871   NO 05 NE 48
A farmstead, its buildings standing to a maximum height of 0·7 m, is situated on a terrace 380 m SSW of Balchrochan. Two of the buildings are set at right angles to each other and are adjoined on the SE by an enclosure, in the E corner of which there is a possible kiln. The larger building, which appears partly roofed on the first edition of the OS 6-inch map (Perthshire, 1867, sheet 32), is of three compartments, measures 20·4 m by 5·6 m overall and has a small outshot at each end; the smaller, on the NE, is of a single compartment and measures 9·8 m by 5·1 m overall. About 15 m to the SW, on the opposite side of what is probably a yard, there is a second three-compartment building measuring 15·6 m by 4·9 m overall, a clamp at its N corner; immediately to the W, on the same alignment, lies a fourth building, measuring 12·5 m by 5·9 m overall. To the S of these buildings there is a second enclosure adjoined on its S side by a building measuring 5·1 m by 3·5 m overall.

The remains are possibly to be identified with the settlements of either 'Uppertown' or 'Tomgarrour', depicted on Stobie's map (1783). 'Tommagarrour' appears on Roy's map (1747–55, sheet 17/2).

227   Balnabroich, Pitcarmick-type buildings
At least six Pitcarmick-type buildings occur within the cluster of small cairns and hut-circles at Balnabroich (see no. 108; D on fig.). Along with several other rectangular buildings, these can be loosely divided into two groups, located respectively in the NW and SE area of the cluster.

·1   NO 099 575   NO 05 NE 45
The NW group comprises two Pitcarmick-type buildings set on opposite sides of the burn, and a subrectangular building which lies further to the N on the NW side of a burn. The principal Pitcarmick-type building is crossed by a modern track 40 m E of a stone dyke; it measures 30 m in length overall by a maximum of 8·5 m in breadth. The SE end, which may incorporate an outshot with a separate entrance, narrows to 4·5 m in breadth. The whole of the interior has been levelled into the slope, and the SE end of the main building is more deeply hollowed than the rest. Immediately upslope a subsidiary scarp, which runs the length of the NE side, cuts through an earlier building which measures 20 m in overall length. The interior of the earlier building has also been levelled into the slope, and there are traces of a drainage-ditch along the NE side.

The second Pitcarmick-type building measures 15 m in

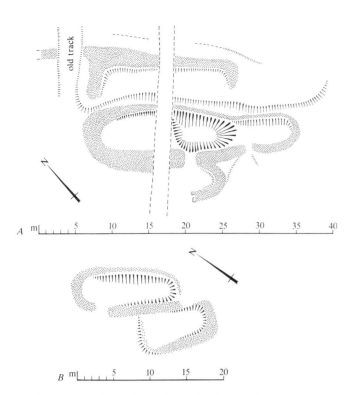

227·1A, B Balnabroich, Pitcarmick-type buildings, 1:500

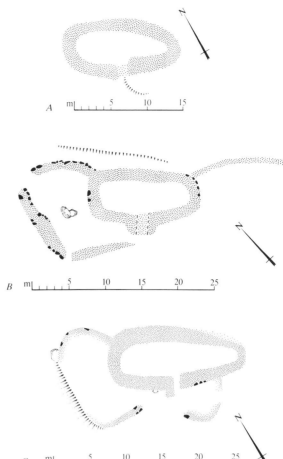

227·2A, B, C Balnabroich, Pitcarmick-type buildings, 1:500

overall length by 6m in maximum breadth, and there is a shallow depression at the SE end of the interior. Immediately to the S there is what is either another building or a small annexe. A subrectangular building to the N measures about 12m by 5m overall and there is a drainage-ditch along its NE side.

·2 NO 106 569   NO 15 NW 46–50, 58
Four Pitcarmick-type buildings are disposed around the edges of a natural basin. Two lie on a low ridge to the NW of the burn that drains the basin, 40m and 90m respectively SE of a burial cairn (no. 9·3). The

227·2A westernmost is a bow-sided structure, narrowing markedly towards the SE end; it measures 16·3m by a maximum of 8m over earthen walls spread to a thickness

227·2B of 2m and standing to a height of 0·3m. The E building is narrowed only slightly towards one end and measures 15·6m by a maximum of 7·4m overall. Its wall consists of an earthen bank with an external stone kerb, but only a few of the kerbstones are visible. There is a poorly defined entrance on the SW, and thickening of the wall at this point suggests the presence of a porch. An enclosure bounded by a stone-cored wall is attached to the NW end of the building, and there are traces of a low bank springing from its E corner. About 40m to the S and on the SE bank of the burn, there is a small building (12·2m by 6·6m overall) and another lies on a rocky ridge a further 130m to the SE. The latter is open ended on the SE, measures at least 16m by 6m overall, and has an

227·2C entrance in its SW side. The third Pitcarmick-type building is situated on a low ridge 200m to the ESE; it measures 19m by a maximum of 8·5m overall and narrows towards the SE. There is a small annexe on the S side of the entrance and an enclosure springs from the NW end of the building. The fourth Pitcarmick-type building is situated in deep heather on a slope 200m to the NNW. It is a substantial structure, measuring about 23·5m by a maximum of 10m over walls up to 1·6m in thickness and 0·6m in height, and its interior has been deeply scooped into the slope. A subsidiary wall at the N end of the interior raises the possibility that the building itself stood

within the main enclosing wall. There is a small annexe immediately NW of the entrance and an enclosure on the SE. The remains of another small rectangular building (10·6m by 5·4m overall) lie 40m to the SW.

228 Balnoe, farmstead, building and shieling
NO 1401 6535   NO 16 NW 89–90
At the foot of the slope beside the A93, and in part incorporated in a later fank, there are fragments of the farmstead of Baile Nodha, which is depicted as roofed in 1867. Adjacent to the W wall of the fank the remains of what may be a kiln-and-chamber are visible and to the NNW there are the wasted remains of a number of shieling-huts. Upslope, about 140m SSW of the fank and set to the rear of a terrace (NO 1398 6517), there are the remains of a building (10m by 4·5m overall) which incorporates an upright boulder at its W angle. Roy (1747–55, sheet 18/4) depicts a farmstead and names it 'Newloim'; it is 'Balino' on the maps of Stobie (1783), Ainslie (1794) and Thomson (1825); the lands and town of 'Balno' are on record in 1719 (Spalding 1914, 226).
— OS 6-inch map, 1st ed. (1865-7), sheet 24.

229 Balvarran, farmsteads, mills, buildings and shielings
The house of Balvarran (NO 0735 6203), formerly known as Easter Inverchroskie (Roy 1747–55, sheet 17/2) or Inverchroskie (Stobie 1783), stands 280m SE of the Inverchroskie Burn and 200m upslope from the floor of Strathardle. Although largely of 18th-century date, the house incorporates an earlier marriage-lintel above the central ground-floor window of the S front; the lintel, which has been recut, bears the date 1641. The modern

255

Inverchroskie, which lies 1 km to the NW (NO 0662 6271), was formerly known as Wester Inverchroskie (Roy 1747–55, sheet 17/2; Stobie 1783). Both 'Inner-Chrosky' and Wester 'Innerchrosky' appear on Pont's map (c.1600).

In 1608 Lady Anna Stewart inherited a half-part of the lands of Inverchroskie and 'Chapeltoun' (*Retours*, Perth, No. 184), whilst in 1642, amongst the inheritance of John Robertson of Straloch, were a third-part of the lands of Easter Inverchroskie (*Retours*, Perth, No. 519), a half-part of the lands of Inverchroskie with pendicles called 'Auchintepall' (Auchinchapel) and 'Menach', and a half-part of the mill of Inverchroskie (*Retours*, Perth, No. 520).

The mill of Inverchroskie lies on the E side of the River Ardle, 700 m to the S (NO 0723 6131). It appears on the maps of Roy (1747–55, sheet 17/2) and Stobie (1783), and on the first edition of the OS 6-inch map (Perthshire, 1867, sheet 32) a sawmill and a flour mill are depicted.

To the ENE, E and SE of the house, on the SW flank of Whitefield Hill, there are the remains of five farmsteads, and over the same area on Stobie's map (1783) there are symbols representing perhaps three settlements, at least one of those on the S bearing the name 'Auchinchapel'. It may be that the Chapeltoun inherited by Lady Anna Stewart in 1608 and Auchinchapel are the same place and are to be identified with one or both of farmsteads (·1) and (·2).

·1 NO 0805 6174   NO 06 SE 83
This farmstead comprises three heavily robbed buildings, their walls reduced to little more than low stony banks. The two larger buildings, both of two compartments, are set parallel to each other and measure 21·7 m by 5·7 m and 15·7 m by 4·8 m overall respectively, the latter being adjoined on the SW by a small yard; the S side of the yard is formed by the third building, which is of a single compartment and measures 9 m by 5 m overall. On the adjacent hillside there is an extensive system of field banks.

·2 NO 0781 6180   NO 06 SE 77
Lying in a narrow strip of badly-drained ground traversed by a modern fence there is a farmstead comprising four single-compartment buildings and a kiln with chambers on both its uphill and downhill sides. Three of the buildings are set parallel to the contour and range in size from 10·8 m by 5·1 m to 13·9 m by 5·5 m overall; there are traces of raised walkways along the downhill sides of two of them, and the largest has what is probably an outshot at its NW end. The fourth building is set across the contour and measures 6·2 m by 4·4 m overall.

·3 NO 0791 6210   NO 06 SE 76
This farmstead comprises a single-compartment building measuring 8·7 m by 4·8 m over stone wall-footings, an enclosure and a kiln.

·4 NO 0786 6218   NO 06 SE 74
A single-compartment building measuring 12·9 m by 4·8 m over stone wall-footings is adjoined on the N by an irregularly-shaped enclosure; a small rectangular enclosure lies to the NW of the building.

·5 NO 0806 6224   NO 06 SE 75
A single-compartment building measuring 13 m by 4·9 m over stone wall-footings is adjoined on the W by a rectangular enclosure.

·6 NO 0905 6395   NO 06 SE 46
A four-compartment building lies 180 m N of the ruinous 19th century cottage of Menachmore, immediately E of the modern track. It measures 33·5 m by up to 6·1 m over turf-covered wall-footings, though it narrows at either end to 4·5 m and 4·7 m respectively, and there is a lateral outshot close to the NNW end. See also no. 255·9.

·7 NO 0916 6335   NO 06 SE 24
The mill of Moulnanean is situated on the Allt Menach, 100 m below its origin at the confluence of the Allt a' Bhuirich and an unnamed burn. The mill-building is on the W bank of the burn, it measures 11·4 m by 4·1 m over stone wall-footings and the wheel-pit is at the W end, fed by a lade which springs from the Allt a' Bhuirich 420 m to the NE (NO 0941 6370); the purpose of an artificial gully immediately N of the building is uncertain. The kiln and steading which accompany the mill are on the E bank of the burn. The steading comprises three buildings ranging in size from 11·9 m by 4·9 m to 21·4 m by 4·8 m over walls reduced to their lowest courses.

Both mill and steading appear on Stobie's map (1783) and are probably to be identified with the mill of 'Morecloich' depicted on Roy's map (1747–55, sheet 18/4). It may have formed part of a small estate associated with the tower-house at Whitefield (no. 212), formerly known as Morecloich, which was purchased by David Spalding from his brother, the Laird of Ashintully, in 1665 (Spalding 1914, 77).

On slight knolls 120 m and 160 m respectively to the NE there are single-compartment buildings, that on the SW (NO 0927 6343) measuring 7 m by 4·1 m over walls reduced to their lowest courses, that on the NE (NO 0928 6346) measuring 8·6 m by 4·6 m over stone wall-footings and with traces of what may be an outshot or an earlier building at the NNW end.

·8 NO 0983 6346   NO 06 SE 47
Some 640 m ENE of the mill of Moulnanean, to the E of the Balvarran/Ashintully march dyke, there is a group of at least five shieling-huts. The largest, of two compartments, is rectangular on plan and measures 9 m by 4·8 m over stone wall-footings. Two low mounds may be the remains of further huts.

·9 NO 0960 6365   NO 06 SE 48
On the S side of the unnamed burn to the NE of the mill of Moulnanean there are two shieling-huts. One is subrectangular and measures 6·5 m by 3·4 m over stone wall-footings; it has an outshot at its NW end and is adjoined on the SW by a small enclosure. The second appears as a roughly rectangular mound 0·4 m high measuring 8·8 m by 5 m.

·10 NO 0972 6403   NO 06 SE 23
On the W flank of Cnoc a' Chaorainn, 200 m upslope from the Allt a' Bhuirich, there is a farmstead. What may have been the principal building is partly overlain by a sheepfold, but was probably at least 23·7 m in overall length. Immediately adjacent to it there are the remains of two possible buildings, whilst some 50 m to the S (NO 0971 6398) there is a large kiln-and-chamber, and 50 m to the ENE (NO 0979 6404) there are three single-compartment buildings ranged around a yard and measuring 10·1 m by 4·8 m, 8·6 m by 4·4 m and 14·4 m by 4·4 m respectively over walls reduced to little more than their stone footings. A further two buildings lie beyond the head-dyke 200 m to the ENE (NO 0991 6408) and 200 m to the E (NO 0992 6401); they measure 11·8 m by 4·6 m and 12·3 m by 4·4 m respectively over stone wall-footings. Within the head-dyke there is a well-preserved system of rectilinear embanked fields.

The farmstead is named 'Ruigh a' Chaorainn' on the modern OS 1:10,000 scale map, 'Ruidh a' Chaorruinn' on the first edition OS 6-inch map (Perthshire, 1867, sheet

32) and 'Rechurle' on Stobie's map (1783), whilst Roy's map (1747–55, sheet 18/4) depicts 'Richarrel'. In 1710 Charles Spalding, feuar of Morecloich, granted to David Spalding of Ashintully the liberty of pasturage of cattle upon the lands of 'Richirrell' and on the 'Allanmoor' (Spalding 1914, 221).

·11 NO 0991 6453   NO 06 SE 53
On the edge of a scarp dropping steeply to the Allt a' Bhuirich there are three shieling-huts. The largest, which is subrectangular and measures 8·2 m by 4·9 m over a low bank, occupies a mound up to 0·4 m high.

·12 NO 0948 6437   NO 06 SE 50
On a terrace a little above the valley floor there is a farmstead comprising three buildings and two enclosures, all reduced to their wall-footings. Two of the buildings are set on opposite sides of a yard. The larger, on the SW side, is of two compartments and measures 17·7 m by 4·5 m overall; it also forms the chord of a D-shaped enclosure on the SW. The smaller, on the NE side of the yard, is of a single compartment and measures 14·7 m by 5·4 m overall. The third building lies to the NW; it is of a single compartment measuring 14·3 m by 5·2 m overall, has an outshot at its SSE end and is adjoined on the WSW by a rectangular enclosure.

It is probable that either this or (·13) is the farmstead of 'Bardsallachaig' depicted on Stobie's map (1783).

·13 NO 0950 6451   NO 06 SE 51
Some 120 m N of (·12) there is a farmstead comprising three buildings, two enclosures and a possible pen. Two of the buildings are set end-on to each other, though on slightly different alignments, and form the N side of an enclosure; they measure 13·8 m by 5·3 m and 8·1 m by 5·1 m respectively over banks up to 0·4 m high. The WSW end of the smaller building abuts a rectangular enclosure, at the lower NW end of which there is third building, adjoined by a field-bank and measuring 10·4 m by 5·6 m over a bank up to 0·6 m high.

·14 NO 0962 6450   NO 06 SE 52
Situated 50 m NW of the modern track there are two buildings. The larger is of two compartments and measures 13·3 m by 4·4 m over stone wall-footings, it has an outshot at its NW end and what may be an outshot or an independent structure at its SE end; the smaller is of a single compartment and measures 10·4 m by 5·1 m over turf-covered wall-footings. Some 70 m to the NE (NO 0967 6459) there is a roughly oval shieling-hut measuring 8·6 m by 5·6 m over turf-covered wall-footings.

·15 NO 0968 6481   NO 06 SE 54
About 200 m upslope from (·14) there is a single subrectangular shieling-hut measuring 5·4 m by 4·5 m over a low bank.

·16 NO 0980 6501   NO 06 NE 3
Two rectangular shieling-huts are situated 340 m upslope from a modern hut and measure 5·6 m by 3·8 m and 8·4 m by 5·1 m respectively over stone wall-footings. A further 80 m to the WNW (NO 0970 6504) there is a group of three huts, two rectangular and one oval, ranging in size from 6·3 m by 4 m to 7 m by 4·4 m over banks up to 0·4 m high.

·17 NO 0993 6514   NO 06 NE 57
A rectangular shieling-hut measuring 7·2 m by 4 m over a bank 0·2 m high lies 180 m NE of (·16).

·18 NO 1035 6601   NO 16 NW 79
In Coire Bhuraich, on the E bank of the westerly of the two burns which come together to form the Allt a' Bhuirich, there is a group of five shieling-huts, together with two small enclosures. The huts range in overall size from 6 m by 2·9 m to 9·4 m by 4·3 m, the largest being of two compartments. In 1642 John Robertson of Straloch inherited a half-part of the shielings of 'Corrievurich' (*Retours*, Perth, No. 520).

·19 NO 1064 6582, 1070 6574   NO 16 NW 80
Situated 300 m and 390 m respectively to the SE of (·18) there are a further two rectangular shieling-huts, each adjoined by a small enclosure. The larger hut is of two compartments and measures 9·7 m by 4·7 m overall; the smaller is of a single compartment measuring 9 m by 5 m overall, with traces of what may be an outshot or an earlier hut at the E end.

230 Blackhall, farmsteads
·1 NO 1442 5622   NO 15 NW 42
Immediately S of the public road and 110 m SE of Blackhall farmhouse, there is a farmstead comprising a two-compartment building (measuring 14 m by 4·7 m over wall-footings 0·8 m thick and 0·4 m high) with an L-shaped enclosure on its NE and SE sides. Immediately S of the building and adjacent to the enclosure wall, there are the footings of a slight structure (7·5 m by 2·8 m overall), and a few metres SE of the enclosure wall there are three small cairns.

·2 NO 1451 5604   NO 15 NW 61
This farmstead is situated in rough pasture 300 m SSE of Blackhall farmhouse; it comprises a rectangular building (8·1 m by 5·1 m over walls 0·9 m thick and 0·6 m high) with a small outshot at its S end, and three enclosures. The enclosures are attached to the N and E sides of the building, and the northernmost contains the remains of lazy-bed cultivation.

231 Borland, farmstead
·1 NO 1529 6140   NO 16 SE 29
This farmstead is situated on a terrace 480 m NNE of Borland and comprises a well-preserved building adjoined on the SW by an enclosure. The building measures 9·8 m by 5·3 m over clay-bonded walls up to 1 m high, and at its NW end there is an outshot into which a small lade runs. About 35 m to the ENE a building measuring 6·7 m by 4 m over turf-covered wall-footings lies at the SE corner of a yard, and a further 35 m to the ESE (NO 1535 6141) there is a building measuring 7·3 m by 4·3 m over turf-covered wall-footings. Another building lies immediately above the head-dyke 120 m E of the farmstead; it is of two compartments and measures 15·6 m by 5·4 m over walls up to 0·6 m in height.

·2 NO 1578 6130   NO 16 SE 30
About 40 m upslope from the head-dyke on the S face of Tom Bealaidh, about 500 m to the ESE of (·1), there is a building, measuring 8·4 m by 3 m overall, adjoined on the NE by an enclosure.

232 Broughdearg, farmsteads, buildings and shielings
Between the steadings of Broughdearg and Dunmay (unoccupied) there are several farmsteads and buildings, while disposed to either side of the Allt Coire na

Ceardaich and towards the head of Coire na Ceardaich, there are a number of shielings. Another farmstead and four buildings lie to the N of Broughdearg.

·1 NO 1355 6750   NO 16 NW 30

This farmstead is situated on a broad terrace overlooking the haughland of the Shee Water, about 450m NNW of Broughdearg. The buildings have been reduced to their turf-covered wall-footings, and the two largest (A and B) are connected to form a range 37m in overall length, with a drainage gully along its E side and three pits, probably middens, on its W side. The remaining buildings vary in

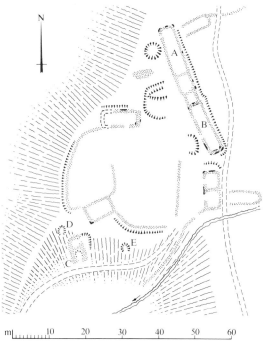

232·1 Broughdearg, farmstead, 1:1000

size from 6·5m by 3·5m to 8·4m by 4·6m, whilst the kiln (C), which is set into the face of the terrace, has a chamber on its uphill side. The purpose of two small pits (D and E) is unclear. The track which crosses the E side of the site from N to S is modern, but that which ascends the scarp-face on the S may be contemporary with the farmstead.

The remains may be those of the farmstead of 'Balinauld', depicted on the maps of Stobie (1783), Ainslie (1794) and Thomson (1825).

·2 NO 1364 6748, 1366 6745   NO 16 NW 32–3

On a terrace 370m N of Broughdearg steading, there are the remains of two rectangular buildings. Both are reduced to their turf-covered stone wall-footings and measure respectively 8·9m by 3·9m and 8·2m by 4·3m overall. The first possesses an outshot (4·7m by 3·6m overall); the second has a yard on the E.

·3 NO 1365 6720   NO 16 NW 66

On relatively level and poorly drained ground 120m NNW of Broughdearg steading, there are the wasted remains of a building. It measures 7·3m by 5·3m over a low bank spread up to 1·2m in thickness, and on the N there is an outshot (4m by 2·7m overall). About 80m to the NW (NO 1360 6727), there is a building (8·7m by 4·4m overall) with an enclosure attached.

·4 NO 1377 6710   NO 16 NW 31

Some 70m ENE of Broughdearg steading, within trees,

there are the turf-covered stone wall-footings of three buildings, the largest of which measures 9·8m by 5·5m overall.

·5 NO 1389 6705   NO 16 NW 34

To the ESE of (·4), on a shoulder of the hill, there are two probable shieling-huts which are set parallel to each other. They measure 7m by 4·1m and 5m by 4·3m overall respectively; the latter has been disturbed by a dog's grave at its SSE end.

·6 NO 1400 6680   NO 16 NW 38

Beside the modern field-wall to the SSE of (·5), there are two buildings; the first, a two-compartment building (16·9m by 5m overall), the other 15m to the NNW, of one (5·8m by 3·7m overall). A third building lies to the N (NO 1400 6685) but is severely wasted (7·4m by 4m overall).

·7 NO 1410 6666   NO 16 NW 39

At the margin of the unimproved ground to the SE of (·6) there are the remains of a farmstead which includes buildings on two sides of a yard. Both ranges are reduced to their turf-covered stone wall-footings and measure respectively 7·7m by 4m (building and outshot) and 15·8m by 5m overall (the latter a two-compartment building and outshot, with a drainage-hood to its rear). On the SE side of the yard there is a stance for what may be another building (3m by 2·4m overall), whilst to the ESE (NO 1414 6666) there are the boulder-footings of a building measuring 7m by 4·5m overall. The farmstead is depicted on the maps of Roy (1747–55, sheet 18/4), Stobie (1783) and Ainslie (1794) but is unnamed.

·8 NO 1439 6633   NO 16 NW 44

This farmstead comprises buildings on two sides of a yard. The larger of the two is now overlain by the modern field-wall; it is a two-compartment building, which has been set end-on to the slope, and measures 19·8m by at least 4·5m over turf-covered stone wall-footings 1·3m in thickness. Its neighbour to the NNE (10·3m by 4·8m over turf-covered stone walls up to 1·5m high) has a drainage-trench to its rear.

·9 NO 1443 6628   NO 16 NW 43

On the slopes immediately to the NNE of the unoccupied 19th century steading at Dunmay, there are the remains of a farmstead which consists of at least five buildings and a kiln. Incorporated in a modern field-wall, now followed by a deer fence, there are the well-preserved remains of a two-compartment building (20·2m by 6m over stone walls 1·2m thick and up to 2·1m high) with an outshot on the S (8·8m by 3·6m overall). Downslope and adjoining the old head-dyke, there is an open-ended rectangular structure (possibly a potato store), which has been partially set-back into the slope. It measures 7m by 3m over stone walls 0·7m in thickness. To the SSE there is an open-fronted building (10·2m by 5·7m overall), whose SE end-wall has been buttressed by a masonry addition. The wasted remains of a kiln are let into the slope to the SSE, and on the same alignment there are the wasted remains of another building (13·5m by 5·4m overall) with a pen at right angles to it. The lands of 'Dalma' are on record in 1608 ('Dumma' 1642, *Retours*, Perth, Nos. 184, 515). Roy (1747–55, sheet 18/4) depicts the farmstead of 'Dunmor'; it is 'Dunmie' on the maps of Stobie (1783), Ainslie (1794) and Blackadder (1825).

·10 NO 1440 6441   NO 16 NW 45

On a terrace beside the Allt Coire na Ceardaich there are the well-preserved remains of a round-ended, two-compartment building (13·5m by 4·8m over stone walls

1 m thick and 0·5 m high) with an entrance central to its W wall. The floor-level at the S end of the building has been slightly lowered and a byre-drain issues from the S end of the W wall; the E wall is slightly bowed and there are traces of what may be cruck-slots. Immediately to the S there are a small enclosure and, beyond it, the wasted remains of a second building (10 m by 4·6 m overall).

·11   NO 1443 6648   NO 16 NW 46
On relatively level, if poorly-drained ground, in a loop of the Allt Coire na Ceardaich and beside the modern track, there are the remains of a probable farmstead consisting of three unusual conjoined buildings (A, B, C). The walls

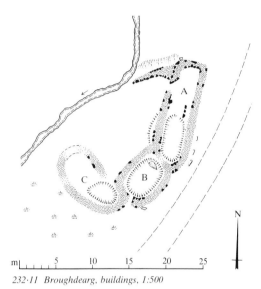

232·11 Broughdearg, buildings, 1:500

of A are irregular and there is a thickening on the S, possibly caused by slumping. The N side of the entrance passage is sharply splayed. The floor-level at the S end of the building has been slightly lowered, and this is particularly pronounced near to the end-wall; the purpose of a line of three stones to the NNE is unclear. A break in the end-wall may have served to provide access to B, which is roughly oval on plan. It too has a hollowed interior and there is a probable entrance on the SW; the W jamb-wall is integral with the end-wall of C. This is a roughly oval but more severely wasted structure. It has an entrance-doorway near the middle of its NE wall and a partially scooped interior. An open area to the NE may have served as a yard. A baffle-wall and associated gully connecting (A) to the burn may have served to deflect run-off.

·12   NO 1435 6651   NO 16 NW 36
Some 70 m to the WNW of (·11), at the foot of a rock-strewn gully, there are the well-preserved remains of a rectangular building (8·8 m by 3·9 m over stone walls 1 m thick and 0·5 m high) with an entrance-doorway central to its SW wall; a dyke extends upslope from its NW end-wall.

·13   NO 1445 6655   NO 16 NW 47
Beside the track and to the W of the Allt Coire na Ceardaich, to the ENE of (·12), there are the remains of another building (7·9 m by 4·5 m over stone walls 1·1 m thick and up to 0·5 m high).

·14   NO 1451 6662   NO 16 NW 48
On the left bank of the Allt Coire na Ceardaich, on the crest of a low ridge, there are the remains of a round-

ended building (14·4 m by 4 m over heather-covered stone wall-footings 0·8 m thick).

·15   NO 1427 6658   NO 16 NW 37
Some 230 m W of (·14), towards the edge of a terrace which has been partially cleared of stone, there are the remains of a farmstead comprising buildings on two sides of a yard, with a large adjoining enclosure on its NE side, on the perimeter of which there is another building. The principal building (11·8 m by 4·5 m over turf-covered stone walls 1 m thick and 0·5 m high) is round-angled and was latterly subdivided by the insertion of a cross-wall; at the NW end of its N wall there is a well-built subcircular annexe or outshot, which was entered from the principal building. The two remaining buildings measure 9·8 m by 3·8 m and 10·9 m by 4·3 m overall respectively. The latter is round-ended and narrows towards the NNW; it was probably of two compartments and has an annexe at its SE end (2·6 m by 4·8 m overall).

·16   NO 1426 6680   NO 16 NW 69
On a spur above (·15), there are the remains of a shieling group comprising buildings (A, B) on two sides of a yard. The remains can be divided into two phases; to the earliest belong the fragment of what may be a subrectangular building (C) to the ESE of B and the yard-wall which springs from its SSE angle. The principal building (A) is round-angled and was latterly subdivided;

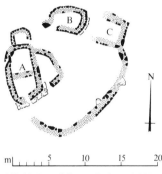

232·16 Broughdearg, shielings, 1:500

an intake in the external facing towards the N end of the W wall suggests it may have been remodelled more than once. It was provided with a pen on the N and an annexe on the E; the position of the entrance is not clear and a break in the S end-wall may be a drain. Building B is subrectangular on plan and has an entrance at the W end of its S wall.

·17   NO 142 668   NO 16 NW 35
Directly upslope from (·16), there are at least five probable shieling-huts and a number of small cairns. The huts are roughly oval and all are reduced to their turf- or heather-covered stone wall-footings (some more wasted than others) and range from 6 m by 4·6 m to 8·0 m by 5·5 m overall. The first (NO 1423 6684) occupies a slight rise and immediately to the ENE there are at least four small cairns; in broken ground and almost concealed by heather (NO 1427 6687), there are the remains of a further three huts. Situated on a shelf, a little upslope (NO 1432 6689), there is another and to the WNW there is a building (9·1 m by 5·5 m overall) and, close by, three small cairns.

·18   NO 1470 6706   NO 16 NW 41
Some 400 m ENE of (·17), on a knoll in the lee of a boulder, there are the remains of a building (6·7 m by 3·5 m overall), a hut (5·3 m by 3·7 m overall) and a pen.

H

·19 NO 1473 6720   NO 16 NW 67
To the NNE of (·18), in the lee of a boulder, there are the
remains of a round-angled building (5·7m by 3·8m
overall) and a pen.

·20 NO 1476 6723   NO 16 NW 40
On the nose of a spur upslope from (·19), there are the
wasted remains of a rectangular building (6·7m by 3·8m
overall), together with what may be either a hut or a pen
(4·1m by 3·9m overall).

·21 NO 1476 6727   NO 16 NW 68
On a terrace overlooking (·20), and in the lee of a number
of large boulders, there are the remains of a round-angled
stone-built hut (5·3m by 4·1m overall), which overlies an
earlier turf-built hut (6·5m by 4·4m overall). Immediately
upslope, the remains of a further three probable huts are
visible, which range from 4·6m by 3·6m overall to 8m by
4m overall.

·22 NO 1541 6710   NO 16 NE 6
Some 650m ESE of (·21), at the head of Coire na
Ceardaich (515m OD), there are the remains of a further
shieling. It consists of a hut (6m by 3·6m over stone walls
0·9m thick and 0·4m high), which partially overlies traces
of what may be an earlier turf-built hut (6·9m by 6·3m
overall); a spur-wall extends 8·6m from the N angle of the
hut towards a small stone-walled enclosure, which is set
back a little upslope.

233   Cairns, buildings
      NO 1134 4704, 1114 4716   NO 14 NW 73, 75
To the NW of Cairns steading there are the remains of
two buildings. Both are reduced to turf-covered stone
wall-footings and measure respectively 26m by 6·5m and
8·7m by 4·7m overall; the first is of three compartments.

234   Cambs, fermtoun
      NO 1141 7032 to 1152 7024   NO 17 SW 46–8
The remains of this fermtoun are disposed over the slopes
and terraces to the rear of the 19th-century cottage at
Cambs. They comprise at least fifteen buildings, together
with their yards, and a kiln. The buildings are all reduced
to turf-covered wall-footings and range from 6·1m by
4·3m to 16·9m by 4·7m overall. Beside the modern track
and to the rear of the cottage (NO 1145 7026) there are
three buildings, one of which is open-ended; another is
overlain by the wall of a 19th-century enclosure. Upslope
(NO 1141 7030) there are three yards, attached to which
there are at least four buildings (one of three
compartments); the head-dyke connects with the
uppermost yard. An irregularity in the head-dyke (NO
1145 7033) indicates the site of a building which stood
end-on to another. At right angles to the latter there is a
two-compartment building with an outshot on the SE and
a yard to the SW. To the NNE (NO 1146 7035) there are
the remains of what has been a substantial building,
represented now only by its wasted end-walls; a further
building lies immediately to the SE (NO 1148 7034). To
the E of Cambs Cottage there are the remains of a
building and yard, while to the SE (NO 1146 7026) there
are the wasted remains of a two-compartment building.
Another two-compartment building (possibly overlying
the remains of an earlier building) has been set across the
opening to a natural hollow, which is skirted on the NE
by an earlier track. To the N there is a yard and on the E
(NO 1152 7024) a kiln; upslope (NO 1159 7023) there are
traces of what may be another building.
   The 'town and lands of Cammis' are on record in 1599
and formed part of the barony of Wemyss; by 1621 they

formed part of the barony of Ashintully. In 1700 the lands
were disponed to Patrick McIntosh, passing in 1727, by
marriage, to the Farquharsons of Binzean. By 1811
Cammis constituted part of the Invercaulds estate. The
fermtoun is depicted by Roy (1747–55, sheet 18/4); it is
'Cambus' on Stobie (1783) and Ainslie (1794) but
'Cammis' on Brown's 1808 survey, by which date it was
largely abandoned. Brown, however, conveys
considerable detail both for the settlement and its
surrounding arable, pasture and meadowland; the field to
the S is named 'Well Field'.
— Michie 1901, 74, 216–17, 349–52.

235   Carnashach Wood, buildings
·1   NO 1464 4802   NO 14 NW 51
In Carnashach Wood and 450m NW of Middleton, there
is a three-compartment building measuring 18·6m by
6·4m over clay-bonded stone walls standing to a
maximum height of 1·5m at the gables.

·2   NO 1459 4822   NO 14 NW 44
About 200m N of (·1) there is a farmstead, its principal
building (A) being of three compartments and measuring
22m by 5·5m over stone wall-footings. Immediately to the

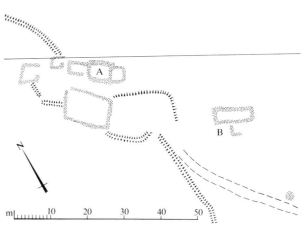

235·2 Carnashach Wood, farmstead, 1:1000

NW and WNW respectively there are two small structures
of uncertain purpose, and on the SW there is an enclosure
adjoined on the S by the remains of what may be a
second. A second building (B) lies 24m to the ESE and
measures 11·3m by 5·6m over stone wall-footings.

·3   NO 1397 4842   NO 14 NW 57
At the W end of Carnashach Wood and overlain by a field
dyke, there is a building measuring 8·8m by 5·2m over
stone walls reduced to their lowest courses. There is an
outshot at the E end of the building and the remains of a
fireplace in the W end-wall.

236   Clachavoid, mill
      NO 1454 6404   NO 16 SW 150
The site of a mill, which is depicted by Stobie (1783), is
probably indicated by a spread of rubble on the
haughland to the NW of Clachavoid steading; the
haughland has been cultivated and there is no trace of a
lade.

237   Cloquhat, farmsteads and buildings
Numerous ruined buildings and farmsteads are situated
on moorland belonging to the present farm of Cloquhat.
Those to the W of the Leapit Burn – Quichim (NO 1561

5306), Donnet's Hillock (NO 1597 5367), Mossend of Clayquhat (NO 1648 5365) and Garbert of Clayquhat (NO 1639 5295) – are shown roofed on the first edition of the OS 6-inch map (Perthshire, 1867, sheet 42), the last only now falling into disrepair. However, a series of unroofed buildings, described here, is shown extending along the NE side of the burn to the SE of Mossend of Clayquhat. These may be broadly contemporary with the farms still occupied in 1867, but a further three buildings, (·2) and (·5), not depicted on the first edition map and now reduced to their turf-covered wall-footings, may be earlier in date.

Of the farmsteads abandoned both before and after 1867 only Garbert of Clayquhat appears to correspond accurately with any of those depicted in this area on Stobie's map (1783), although it may be that one or both of (·4) and (·6) can be identified with two sites shown to the E of the burn. It is probable that the name 'Gallahills' refers to the more southerly of these, but it is unclear whether the name 'Turffdrum' applies to the other or to a settlement further to the N.

·1 NO 1647 5357   NO 15 SE 66
The westernmost of the buildings, which is of two compartments and measures 9·7 m by 5·7 m over turf-covered wall-footings, is situated on the E bank of the Leapit Burn, 70 m S of Mossend of Clayquhat. On the same side of the burn there is a small lade and, to the W and N of the building respectively, there are two retting pools.

·2 NO 1671 5335   NO 15 SE 73
The next ruin to the SE (NO 1662 5341) was still roofed in 1867, but about 90 m beyond it, immediately to the SW of an old turf and stone dyke, there is a three-compartment building measuring 18·3 m by 4·7 m over turf-covered wall-footings.

·3 NO 1663 5331   NO 15 SE 74
On a low ridge 90 m SW of (·2) there is a two-compartment building measuring 14·2 m by 5 m over walls up to 1 m high.

·4 NO 1673 5325   NO 15 SE 75
Some 100 m SE of (·3), on a low ridge, there are the remains of a farmstead. Its principal building, of five compartments, measures 36·6 m by 5 m over walls up to 1·2 m in height, and along its SW side there is a boulder-kerbed plinth up to 2·3 m wide. Between the plinth and a stone-walled enclosure to the SW there is a narrow yard, while to the SE there are the remains of a rectangular structure sunk into the slope and a two-compartment building measuring 8 m by 4·3 m overall. The structure measures 5·6 m by 2·3 m internally, and there is an entrance in its SSW end, but its purpose is unknown.

·5 NO 1688 5322   NO 15 SE 76
The remains of a two-compartment building measuring 12 m by 5 m over turf-covered wall-footings, its W end clipped by the construction of an old turf-and-stone dyke, lie 120 m E of (·4). On the S side of a low knoll 70 m to the N (NO 1688 5330) there is a building measuring 10·5 m by 6 m over low stony banks.

·6 NO 1691 5316   NO 15 SE 77
About 170 m ESE of (·4), immediately W of the improved fields, there is a farmstead comprising a four-compartment building measuring 25·4 m by 5·6 m over walls up to 0·8 m high, with a possible enclosure on its NW side.

·7 NO 1703 5318   NO 15 SE 78
Immediately SE of a pen attached to the NE side of a modern stone dyke, and probably set in the S corner of an enclosure, there is a building measuring 13·4 m by 4·2 m over walls up to 0·5 m high.

238 Cnoc Liath, farmstead
     NO 1362 6639   NO 16 NW 75
On the terrace and lower slopes to the SSE of Cnoc Liath Cottage, both within and to the foot of the modern plantation, there are the remains of a farmstead which consists of at least three buildings. The first, which is set end-on to the slope and is in part overlain by the boundary fence, is of three compartments (16·9 m by 4·9 m over stone walls reduced to their lowest courses) and has an adjoining pen. Within the plantation and at right angles to this building there is a second, which is remarkably well preserved (18 m by 5 m over turf-covered stone walls 0·8 m thick and up to 0·8 m high), while immediately to the E there is a third (11·6 m by 5·7 m over turf-covered stone walls up to 0·9 m high). Towards the edge of the terrace, to the NNE of the first building, there are the remains of what may be a stance, a kiln (with a baffled flue) and a hemispherical depression perhaps also a kiln. The remains are probably to be identified with the farmstead of 'Knocklia' which is depicted by Stobie (1783) and Ainslie (1794).

239 Coire Lairige, buildings
     NO 1095 6984   NO 16 NW 57–60, 74
On the right bank of the Allt a' Choire Lairighe 50 m to the SE of Logie, and depicted by Brown (1808), there are the remains of a building and enclosure; the building measures 12·4 m by 4·8 m overall. Upslope (NO 1085 6963) there are paired enclosures, and beyond these (NO 1075 6933), on the NE side of the modern head-dyke and beside an old turf-dyke that extends downslope for a distance of about 130 m, there are the remains of a building (8·8 m by 5·5 m overall) with an enclosure on its N side. Another building lies 240 m to the W (NO 1051 6928); about 210 m to the NNW (NO 1038 6945) there is an enclosure. Disposed over an area of gently sloping ground between the cottage at Leanoch Mhor and the Allt a' Choire Lairighe there are a series of long fields containing rig-and-furrow cultivation and lynchets. There are now no visible remains of the farmstead of Balln Ault (Stobie 1783), which stood on the site now occupied by the house at Logie; Balln Ault is shown as abandoned on Brown's 1808 survey.

240 Corrydon, farmsteads
·1 NO 1305 6698 to 1306 6707   NO 16 NW 22, 64
Scattered over an area of rough ground to either side of the Allt a' Choire Dhomhain, there are the remains of a farmstead comprising at least eight buildings and two enclosures. The buildings are all reduced to their turf-covered stone wall-footings (some are severely wasted) and range from 6·3 m by 3·5 m to 14 m by 4·2 m overall; the last is a two-compartment building. Astride the burn (NO 1305 6698) there are the wasted remains of what may be a horizontal mill (6·2 m by 4·8 m overall). Upslope and beyond the modern head-dyke (NO 1301 6703), there are the heather-covered remains of a further two buildings (6 m by 4·7 m and 5·5 m by 4·3 m overall respectively). The lands of 'Corridon' in the barony of Balmachreuchie are on record in 1674. The farmstead is depicted by Roy (1747–55, sheet 18/4) but is unnamed. It appears as

'Corrydon' on the maps of Stobie (1783) and Ainslie (1794), and was in part still roofed in 1865.
— Spalding 1914, 74–5; Atholl Muniments, 23, xii, 3.

·2   NO 1320 6676   NO 16 NW 76
On relatively level ground to the NW of Corrydon Cottage, there are the remains of a farmstead consisting of three buildings. The largest of these (of two compartments and reduced to the lowest courses of its stone walls) measures 17·9 m by 4·6 m overall; a later stone-walled enclosure has been abutted against its NW end-wall. The farmstead is depicted but not named by Roy (1747–55, sheet 18/4); it appears as 'Claggan' on the maps of Stobie (1783) and Ainslie (1794).

241   Cothole, Garbet, farmstead
NO 0827 4659   NO 04 NE 35
The farmstead of Garbet is situated 400 m NNW of Cothole and comprises five buildings, an enclosure or pen, and a kiln; the buildings range in size from 5·4 m by 4·3 m to 24·1 m by 5·1 m over stone walls standing to a maximum height of 1·9 m. Garbet appears on Stobie's map (1783).

242   Craigend, Pitcarmick-type building and building
NO 0731 4847   NO 04 NE 37
Situated in rough pasture about 100 m NNE of Craigend cottage, there are the remains of a Pitcarmick-type building, which lies parallel to the contour on a gentle S-facing slope, and measures 15 m by 6·6 m over a turf-covered wall (2 m thick and 0·4 m high). The interior has been levelled into the slope and the entrance is midway along the S side. There is an enclosure (11 m by 9·8 m) on the SE, and on the NW a level platform projects from the end-wall of the building.

310

A building situated 27 m to the WNW, measures 8·7 m by 6·6 m over a wall reduced to a heather-covered bank up to 2 m thick and 0·3 m high. The interior has been levelled into the S-facing slope and there is an entrance on the SW; a stony bank abutting the SW corner of the building may be associated with further banks which lie to the SW and W.

243   Craighead, shieling
NO 2076 5431   NO 25 SW 31
On the ESE flank of the Hill of Craighead there are five contiguous fields, within which there are traces of rig-and-furrow cultivation. Adjacent to the E boundary of the westernmost field, and overlying the rigs, there are the wasted remains of at least four huts. These range from 6·9 m by 4·5 m to 8·5 m by 5·2 m over turf-covered wall-footings spread up to 1·1 m in thickness; the first has an outshot on the W (3·1 m by 4·5 m overall). Adjoining the field boundary there are a pair of enclosures (that on the SSW incorporates what may be a pen), while some 20 m to the WSW of the huts there is another.

244   Craigsheal, Pitcarmick-type building
NO 0721 5158   NO 05 SE 16
On the SW flank of the Rie Meikle, some 970 m ENE of Craigsheal (no. 245), there are the remains of a
140 Pitcarmick-type building which overlies a hut-circle (no. 140·12). It measures 21·3 m in overall length and varies from 5·5 m in width at the NW end to 6·5 m at the centre and 5 m at the SE end; there is an entrance in the SW side. About 170 m to the SE there is a group of six buildings with a series of narrow strip-fields (no. 310·18).

245   Craigsheal, laird's house and fermtoun
NO 0631 5118   NO 05 SE 23, 50, 58–9
Situated 530 m NW of Loch Benachally there are the remains of a laird's or tacksman's house accompanied by a small fermtoun. The house (A) is gable-ended and rectangular on plan, measuring 14 m by 7 m over clay-bonded walls, and formerly stood two storeys in height,

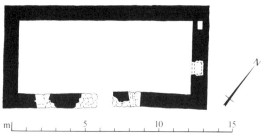

245A Craigsheal, laird's house, 1:250

though the side walls are now reduced to their lower courses and the interior is choked with rubble. At ground-floor level there is an entrance-doorway central to the SE wall and flanked by two splayed window-openings, whilst in the NE gable there is a lintelled fireplace and, at the N corner, a flue, suggesting the presence of an oven now concealed by rubble. At first-floor level, in the NE gable, there are a scarcement, a fireplace and a mural press.

With the exception of the two which flank the house, the buildings of the fermtoun, which include a kiln-barn (B), lie about 100 m upslope and are generally well-preserved. Of particular note is C, a three-compartment building measuring 18·5 m by 6 m over clay-bonded walls; it has a window-opening in its SE wall, close to the SW end, a paved walkway on its SE side, and an outshot at its NE end. Immediately to the N what is probably a small building (D) overlies an earlier building which has been reduced to turf-covered stone wall-footings. Situated on a terrace 200 m WNW of the fermtoun (NO 0601 5131) there is a single shieling-hut measuring 8·8 m by 4·2 m overall.

Craigsheal was amongst lands inherited by Thomas Tyrie of Drumkilbo in 1635 (*Retours*, Perth, No. 451), and what may be the policies of the house appear on Roy's map (1747–55, sheet 17/2). By the late 18th century, however, it was ruinous (Stobie 1783), though the fermtoun may have continued in occupation into the 19th century.

246   Craigsheal Burn, shielings
To the N of the laird's house and fermtoun of Craigsheal (no. 245) the hills form a natural amphitheatre on the N and E sides of which are disposed at least twelve shieling-huts.

·1   NO 0604 5204   NO 05 SE 12
Three shieling-huts, the largest measuring about 5 m by 3 m overall, overlie a pair of double-walled hut-circles (no. 140·8).

·2   NO 0603 5224   NO 05 SE 67
On a narrow SE-facing terrace 25 m NNE of a hut-circle (no. 140·9), there is a shieling-hut, measuring 5·9 m by 4·7 m overall, adjoined on the S by an oval enclosure. A second hut lies 15 m to the ENE, and a second enclosure 10 m to the N.

·3   NO 0637 5229   NO 05 SE 14
Two shieling-huts are situated on a prominent rocky knoll

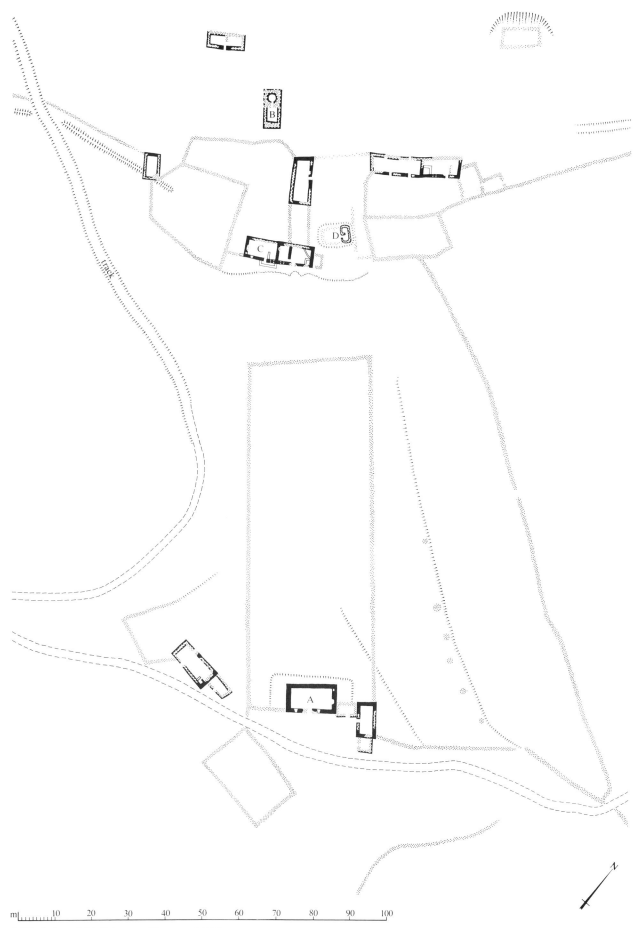

245B Craigsheal, laird's house and fermtoun, 1:1000

on the E bank of the Craigsheal Burn. One lies within the southernmost of three hut-circles (no. 140·10), is oval on plan, and measures 8·4 m by 7·4 m overall. The other, some 40 m to the NE, abuts a stony bank and measures 8·5 m by 4·2 m overall.

·4   NO 0662 5198   NO 05 SE 68
On a low knoll immediately SW of a double-walled hut-circle (no. 140·11) there are three shieling-huts, the largest measuring up to 8 m by 4 m overall.

·5   NO 0700 5171   NO 05 SE 37
The westerly of two shieling-huts measures 9·2 m by 3·8 m overall, the easterly, which is oval on plan, measures 5·6 m by 3·6 m overall.

247   Craigton, farmsteads and buildings
On the afforested E flank of the subsidiary summit of Cnoc Eirionnaich there are the remains of two farmsteads and at least four buildings.

·1   NO 1252 5848   NO 15 NW 27, 64
About 1 km NW of Craigton steading there are the remains of a farmstead comprising three buildings and a kiln. The buildings are all reduced to turf-covered stone wall-footings and range from 7·2 m by 4·9 m to 17·1 m by 5·6 m overall. The farmstead of 'Leadmore' is depicted by Stobie (1783). To the NW (NO 1242 5858), there are the wasted remains of a building measuring 6·8 m by 4·2 m overall.

·2   NO 1254 5832   NO 15 NW 25, 26
Some 150 m S of (·1) there are the remains of a building and enclosure. The building measures 10·4 m by 5 m overall. To the SE (NO 1266 5822) there is another building (8·2 m by 4·9 m overall).

·3   NO 1258 5803   NO 15 NW 23, 24
At the edge of the afforested area to the SW of (·2), there are the remains of a farmstead comprising a building and outshot, two kilns, and four enclosures. The building measures 21·8 m by 5·4 m over stone walls 0·8 m in thickness and up to 2·1 m in height and is in re-use as a sheepfold. The farmstead of 'Ballaqhuarey' is depicted by Roy (1747–55, sheet 18/4); it is 'Belecharry' on Stobie (1783). Some 380 m to the SE (NO 1292 5780) there are the turf-covered stone wall-footings of a two-compartment building (14·8 m by 4·6 m overall).

248   Creag a' Mhadaidh, buildings
NO 0550 5941   NO 05 NE 95–6
On the S flank of Creag a' Mhadaidh there are the remains of two buildings and a possible enclosure. Both buildings are reduced to their stone wall-footings and measure 13·6 m by 5·9 m and 16·3 m by 4·7 m overall respectively; the first is round-ended and has an entrance central to its S wall. To the SSW there are a series of small strip-fields and traces of rig-and-furrow; about 50 m to the NE (NO 0555 5944), there are the remains of another building (7 m by 4·5 m overall).

249   Creag nam Mial, building
NO 0575 5444   NO 05 SE 29
At the foot of the NE flank of Creag nam Mial there is a building measuring 11 m by 5 m over stone wall-footings.

250   Croft na Coille, Balnabroich, farmsteads
To the E and NE of the cottage at Croft na Coille there are the remains of five farmsteads.

·1   NO 0997 5720   NO 05 NE 39, NO 15 NW 51
This farmstead stands at the edge of a plantation and beside the modern head-dyke; it comprises three buildings ranged with a yard. The buildings range from 8·1 m by 4·9 m to 26·3 m by 5·7 m overall; the last of these is of three units. To the S there is what may be a potato store (4·3 m by 1·4 m internally) and to the W, partially within the plantation, there are the remains of an enclosure. A kiln lies 50 m to the NW, and 150 m to the SE (NO 1007 5705) there are the wasted remains of another building (11 m by 7·8 m overall).

·2   NO 0986 5748   NO 05 NE 43
Beside a burn to the NNW of (·1), there are the remains of a farmstead comprising six buildings ranged with a yard; the largest measures 10·9 m by 6·2 m over stone wall-footings up to 1·2 m in height. Immediately to the N there is what may be a pen and to the NW, beside the burn, there is a kiln.

·3   NO 0974 5757   NO 05 NE 41
About 140 m NW of (·2), there are the remains of a farmstead which consists of three buildings and an enclosure. The buildings range from 8·6 m by 5·1 m to 15·1 m by 5·5 m overall; two have outshots and one has opposed lateral entrances. The southernmost of the buildings has been incorporated into a later enclosure.

·4   NO 0960 5771   NO 05 NE 40
Some 160 m NW of (·3) there is a farmstead comprising a building adjoined on the S by an enclosure. The building, which is of two compartments and an outshot, measures 21·4 m by 5·7 m over stone walls up to 2·5 m high at the W gable. A second building measuring 6 m by 3·5 m over stone wall-footings lies in the SE corner of the enclosure.

·5   NO 0952 5747   NO 05 NE 42
About 240 m SSW of (·4) and beside a stream, there are the remains of a farmstead which consists of two buildings. Both are reduced to the lowest courses of their stone walls and measure respectively 20 m by 5·8 m and 5·1 m by 3·9 m overall; a hollow in the bank of the stream immediately to the SE may mark the site of a kiln.

251   Croft of Cultalonie, building
NO 0703 5926   NO 05 NE 97
In trees, some 300 m WSW of Croft of Cultalonie, there are the stone wall-footings of a building measuring 6·9 m by 4·5 m overall.

252   Dalhenzean, farmsteads
·1   NO 1295 6744   NO 16 NW 20
This farmstead lies in broken ground to the W of Dalhenzean Lodge and consists of three buildings grouped with a yard. All are reduced to turf-covered stone wall-footings and range from 9·2 m by 4 m to 13·1 m by 4·9 m overall; the last is a two-compartment building. Some 20 m to the SW and situated on a slight rise, there are the remains of a turf-built hut (6·2 m by 3·8 m overall). The lands of 'Dalhinzean' are on record in 1730 (Atholl Muniments, 23, xii, 3) and the farmstead of 'Dalhingan' is

depicted by Roy (1747–55, sheet 18/4), Stobie (1783), Ainslie (1794) and Thomson (1825).

·2 NO 1296 6725   NO 16 NW 21, 63
This farmstead lies at the margin of the unimproved hill-grazings; it is remarkably well preserved and consists of three buildings, two of which are ranged with a yard. On the N side of the yard and set end-on to the slope, there is a two-compartment building (14·7 m by 4·6 m over stone walls 0·8 m thick and 0·9 m high); the yard is masonry-revetted on its downslope side. On the SW there is a three-compartment building (12·7 m by 5·4 m over stone walls 0·8 m thick and 0·9 m high), which has a byre-drain central to its E compartment. The third building, to the ESE and downslope from the yard, lies beside an old track. It is rectangular (10·1 m by 6 m over stone walls 0·7 m thick and up to 1 m high) and there is a cruck-slot at the N end of its W wall; on the S there is what may be a byre-drain. Close to the first building there is a freshwater spring. Upslope (NO 1291 6722) there are the remains of a building (6·5 m by 3·7 m overall) and yard, and at the SSE corner of the yard, and levelled with the slope, there is a hut (5·6 m by 3 m overall). The farmstead is that of 'Tomsnadarg' which is depicted both by Stobie (1783) and Ainslie (1794).

253 Dalnaglar, Pitcarmick-type building
    NO 1508 6421   NO 16 SE 31
This building stands beside a hut-circle (no. 119) within a clearing at the SW corner of a forestry plantation some 650 m SE of Dalnaglar House; the clearing has itself

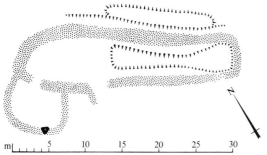

253 Dalnaglar, Pitcarmick-type building, 1:500

recently been planted. There appear to have been two entrances in the SW wall; one has a marked out-turn, the other opens directly to the enclosure. Towards the SSE end of the same wall there is the suggestion of a third break, and this too may be original. Outside the NE wall there is a drainage-gully and beside it a low mound, which, though probably artificial, is of uncertain origin; it may be no more than coincidence that the mound and scooped floor-level of the interior appear to correspond. The building appears on Stewart's plan of the Dalnaglar settlement (1964, 135, fig. 2) but was not excavated.

254 Dalvey, buildings
    NO 0835 5747   NO 05 NE 99–100
Close to the track about 160 m NNE of Dalvey cottage there are the remains of a building and enclosure. The building measures 7·8 m by 4·9 m over turf-covered stone wall-footings; some 135 m to the NNW (NO 0831 5760), there are the remains of another (7·8 m by 4·2 m overall).

255 Dirnanean, farmsteads, buildings and shielings
Dirnanean is on record in 1530, when Small of Dirnanean

married a daughter of Spalding of Ashintully (Spalding 1914, 16), and on Stobie's map (1783) it is depicted by the mansion symbol. The present house (NO 0654 6350), however, appears to be of 19th-century date.

To the SE of the house, in the block of ground between the Allt Doire nan Eun and the Inverchroskie Burn, to the SW of Creag na Ballaige Wood, Roy's map (1747–55, sheet 17/2) shows, from N to S, 'Heathyfaulds', 'W.ʳ Inverchroskie' and 'Balln[ ]urlar', whilst Stobie's map (1783) shows 'Brae', 'W. Inverchroskie', 'Ardthroskie' and 'Balinular'. Most of this area has now been improved or planted with trees, but aerial photographs taken before afforestation show a small fermtoun, part of which survives (·1), and what are probably two single farmsteads (·2 and ·3). The sites are described from S to N, those to the E of the Allt Doire nan Eun first (·1–·27) and those to the W second (·28–·39).

·1 NO 0697 6265   NO 06 SE 84
The remains of this fermtoun lie on a terrace immediately W of the afforested area and comprise six buildings and an enclosure. With one exception the buildings are all reduced to turf-covered stone wall-footings and range in overall size from 5·7 m by 4·4 m to 11·5 m by 6 m, though the best-preserved building, which lies immediately within the afforested area, is of three compartments and measures 17·5 m by 5·8 m over walls up to 1·4 m high.

·2 NO 0745 6253   NO 06 SE 85
This farmstead appears to have comprised a rectangular enclosure, divided into two halves, with two possible buildings immediately to the NW.

·3 NO 0692 6346   NO 06 SE 32
The second farmstead is situated 300 m E of the Allt Doire nan Eun and comprises at least seven buildings, two of which are set at right angles to each other on adjacent sides of a yard. The buildings are all reduced to turf-covered wall-footings and they range from 7·3 m by 3·8 m, to 15·8 m by 4·6 m overall.

·4 NO 0796 6358   NO 06 SE 71
This building is one of three (·4–·6) defined by low banks, which are situated amongst the hut-circle groups to the NE of Creag na Ballaige Wood. The first lies on a terrace 50 m SW of the southerly of two hut-circles (no. 121·2). It measures 11 m in overall length and varies in breadth from 6 m at the SSE end to 6·7 m at its mid-point and 5·3 m at the NNW end.

·5 NO 0821 6363   NO 06 SE 69
The second building lies on a broad terrace 250 m to the W, it has rounded ends and measures 14·3 m in overall length, varying in breadth from 6·7 m at the N end to 6·5 m at its mid-point and 5·8 m at the S end.

·6 NO 0825 6384   NO 06 SE 42
The third building is situated adjacent to two hut-circles (no. 121·3) on the SW shoulder of Menachban. It measures 12·9 m in overall length and varies in breadth from 6·2 m at the N end to 6·4 m at its mid-point and 5·8 m at the S end. What may be another building, about 6 m square, lies 5 m to the NW.

Although the variation in the breadth of these buildings (·4–·6) is relatively slight, their shape is sufficiently distinct to set them apart from other rectangular buildings and shieling-huts. Similar buildings have been noted elsewhere (see introduction).

·7 NO 0851 6393   NO 06 SE 43
Adjoining one of the turf field-banks on the SE flank of Menachban there is a building measuring 7·8 m by 4·4 m

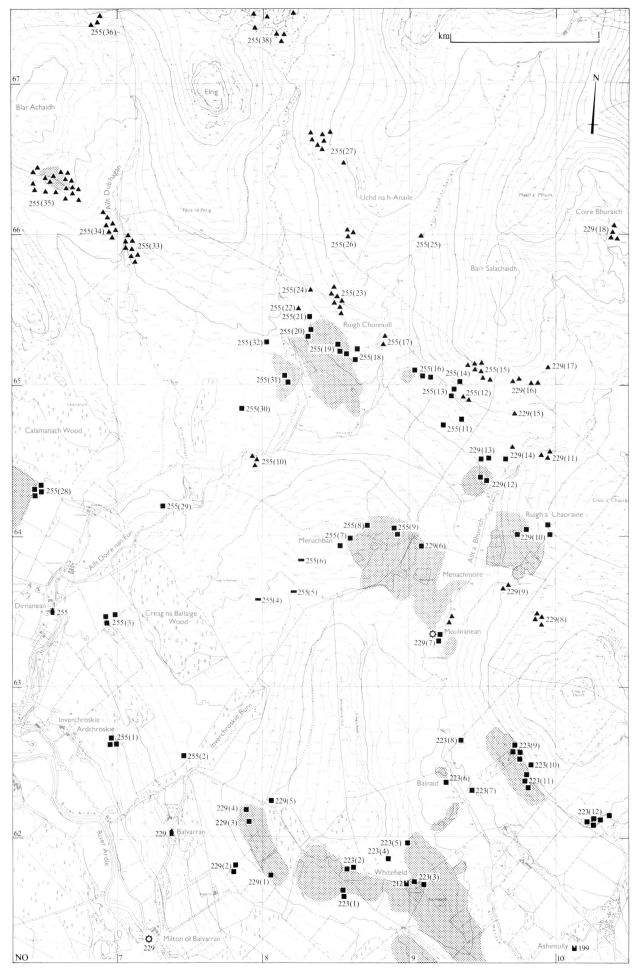

255(36)
255(38)
255(27)
Blar Achaidh
Elrig
Coire Bhuraich
Uchd na h-Anaile
Meall a' Mhuilt
255(35)
229(18)
255(34)
255(33)
Barr Salachaidh
255(26)
255(25)
Fàire na Pàitig
255(24)
255(23)
255(22)
255(21)
Ruigh Chonnuill
255(20)
255(17)
229(17)
255(32)
255(19)
255(18)
255(16)
255(14)
255(15)
255(31)
255(13)
255(12)
229(16)
Calamanach
255(30)
229(15)
Calamanach Wood
255(11)
255(28)
255(10)
229(13)
229(11)
229(14)
255(29)
229(12)
Cnoc a' Chaoir
Ruigh a' Chaoraine
255(8)
255(9)
229(10)
Menachban
255(7)
229(6)
Allt a Bhuirich
Allt Doire nan Eun
255(6)
Menachmore
229(9)
Dirnanean
255
255(5)
255(3)
255(4)
229(8)
Creag na Ballaige
Wood
229(7)
Moulnanean
Inverchroskie
Ardchroskie
255(1)
223(8)
223(9)
255(2)
Balnald
223(6)
223(10)
223(11)
223(7)
River Ardle
229(5)
229(4)
223(12)
229(3)
229(229)
Balvarran
223(5)
229(2)
223(4)
Whitefield
223(2)
223(3)
229(1)
212
223(1)
Milton of Balvarran
229
Ashintully
199

NO
7
8
9
10

255 Dirnanean, 1:25 000

over a bank 0·4 m high; it has an outshot at its ENE end. Some 60 m to the NE there are a further two buildings defined by low banks. The larger measures 10·6 m by 5·9 m overall and at its SW end an enclosure 7 m across has been scooped into the slope, the smaller measures about 10·2 m by 5·3 m overall.

·8   NO 0869 6407   NO 06 SE 44
A little below the summit of Menachban, on the E, a single-compartment building, measuring 13·9 m by 3·9 m over stone wall-footings, and what may be a second building or a pen, measuring 7·6 m by 4·8 m over stone wall-footings, are set at right angles to each other to form two sides of a rectangular enclosure adjoining a field-bank.

·9   NO 0889 6402   NO 06 SE 45
On the E slope of Menachban, 130 m W of the Dirnanean/Balvarran march dyke, there is a farmstead, its buildings reduced to stone wall-footings. The two larger buildings are set on the same alignment, almost end-to-end, and are both of at least two compartments. That on the NW measures 19·1 m by 4·3 m overall and has a yard on its SSW side, that on the SE measures 21·4 m by 5·3 m overall. A third building lies to the E and at right angles to the other two; it measures 11·3 m by 4·5 m overall, and is adjoined on the ESE by a rectangular enclosure in which there are traces of what may be cultivation ridges. At the SW corner of the enclosure there is a rectangular structure, possibly a fourth building, measuring 7·4 m by 6 m over a bank up to 0·5 m in height; another building lies 150 m to the ESE (no. 229·6).

The ruinous 19th-century cottage of Menachmore lies 300 m to the SE (NO 0904 6373) and the pendicle of 'Menach', inherited by John Robertson of Straloch in 1642 (*Retours*, Perth, No. 520), presumably lay in this area. John Campbell of 'Minnach' is on record in 1718 (Spalding 1914, 225), and 'Minnochs' appears on Roy's map (1747–55, sheet 18/4). No settlement of this name is shown on Stobie's map (1783), though there are several settlement symbols on the W side of the valley to the N of the mill of Moulnanean (see no. 229·6).

·10   NO 0793 6451   NO 06 SE 81
On a low spur immediately S of the Allt Doire nan Eun there are three shieling-huts measuring 4·5 m by 3·7 m, 10 m by 4·3 m and 13·4 m by 5·2 m respectively overall. Some 7 m NW of the largest hut there is a small enclosure.

·11   NO 0920 6473   NO 06 SE 55, 59
On the SW slopes of Barr Salachaidh, between the 400 m and 500 m contours, there are a number of farmsteads and shieling groups (·11–·16). The first farmstead comprises two single-compartment buildings set at right angles to each other to form two sides of a small yard. They measure 12·5 m by 4·6 m and 10·1 m by 4·7 m respectively over stone wall-footings, the larger having an outshot at its WNW end. A third building, measuring 10·8 m by 5·3 m over a bank 0·3 m high, lies 120 m to the ENE (NO 0932 6477), whilst 60 m to the E (NO 0928 6471) there are traces of what may be another building or an enclosure.

·12   NO 0936 6491   NO 06 SE 57
A low mound measuring 10·3 m by 4·5 m is probably the remains of two subrectangular shieling-huts; traces of what may be a third lie 10 m to the WNW.

·13   NO 0927 6497   NO 06 SE 58
This farmstead comprises five buildings and a pen, their walls reduced to turf-covered footings. Three of the buildings are ranged around a yard, those on the NW and

NE sides being of two compartments and measuring 16 m by 5·6 m and 11 m by 5 m respectively overall, the latter having an outshot at its SE end; the building on the SE side of the yard is of a single compartment and measures 7·9 m by 4·4 m overall. The fourth building lies immediately to the S, its NW end adjoining the bank which closes the yard on the SW, and is of a single compartment measuring 9·1 m by 4·9 m overall. The fifth building, which lies to the NE, is probably of two compartments and measures 9·7 m by 4·6 m overall.

·14   NO 0932 6502   NO 06 NE 2, 4
Incorporated within a stone dyke and adjoined on the NE by a small, semi-circular enclosure there is a building of two compartments and an outshot measuring 9·7 m by 4·4 m over stone wall-footings. About 140 m to the NW (NO 0921 6514) a line of four small, connected rectangular enclosures adjoins the same dyke on the NE, though their purpose is unclear.

·15   NO 094 651   NO 06 NE 5
Between NO 0937 6514 and NO 0956 6502 there are the remains of at least ten shieling-huts and a small enclosure. Both rectangular and oval huts are present, the smallest measuring 3·6 m by 3·4 m over a bank 0·3 m high, the largest, which is of two compartments, measuring 11·3 m by 4·9 m over stone wall-footings.

·16   NO 0902 6510   NO 06 NE 1
This farmstead comprises three buildings, three rectangular enclosures and a circular enclosure, their stone walls generally reduced to their lowest courses or footings, but in places standing to a maximum height of 1·2 m. The largest building, which is of a single compartment, measures 10·5 m by 4·7 m overall and its SE end is adjoined by the largest of the enclosures, which measures 15·1 m by 12·9 m internally. The remaining buildings lie 60 m and 80 m respectively to the SE; one is of two compartments and measures 10·2 m by 4·6 m overall, the other is of a single compartment and measures 7·2 m by 5·4 m overall. About 115 m to the SSW a building measuring 8·8 m by 3·3 m over stone wall-footings has been set into a low mound measuring 14·2 m by 10·2 m.

·17   NO 0882 6534   NO 06 NE 67
On the E bank of the Allt Coire an Laoigh, 300 m NW of (·15), there are a shieling-hut, measuring 8 m by 5·3 m over a bank 1·6 m thick, an enclosure incorporating a possible hut, and what may be another hut or a pen. On a narrow terrace 60 m to the S (NO 0881 6528) there is a hut measuring 7·4 m by 4·2 m over turf-covered wall-footings, 15 m to the W of which there is a small enclosure.

·18   NO 0855 6519   NO 06 NE 62
On the lower slopes of the S spur of Uchd na h-Anaile, in the angle formed at the confluence of the Allt Coire an Laoigh and the Allt Doire nan Eun, there are four farmsteads (·18–·21) together with a number of single buildings and a shieling group (·22–·7). The first farmstead comprises three buildings, their walls reduced to low banks or footings. Two of the buildings are set with their long axes across the contour; the better preserved, which is the smaller, measuring at least 11·5 m by 4·5 m overall; the larger, which lies immediately upslope and to the NE, measures 18 m by 5·7 m overall. The third building lies to the SE; it is set parallel to the contour, adjoined on the SW by a square enclosure 12·2 m across and measures 9 m by 4·3 m overall. Some 70 m to the NE (NO 0862 6523) and 45 m to the ESE (NO 0861 6516) there are two more buildings measuring 9·8 m by 4 m over

stone wall-footings and 10·7m by 3·8m over turf-covered wall-footings respectively, whilst 60m to the SE (NO 0861 6514) there is a kiln-and-chamber.

·19 NO 0851 6522   NO 06 NE 21
The principal building of this farmstead is set parallel to the contour; it is of at least three compartments (there are traces of a fourth compartment at the SSE end) and measures 29·6m by 6·4m over stone walls standing to a maximum height of 0·6m. The largest compartment, that on the SSE, is a byre with three lateral drains about 1m broad, and there is possibly a fourth drain in the central compartment. At its NNW end a second building is set across the contour, it measures 11·3m by 5·5m over stone wall-footings and is adjoined on the NW and SE by a large rectilinear enclosure, whilst to the NNE there is what may be a potato store measuring 9·4m by 3·4m over stone wall-footings. This is the farmstead of 'Ruidh Chonnuill' depicted as ruinous on the first edition of the OS 6-inch map (Perthshire, 1867, sheet 23). It is clearly the most recent of the farmsteads on Uchd na h-Anaile and its byre is post-Improvement in character. Stobie's map (1783) shows the two settlement symbols and the name 'Rinnaconer' here, but it is not known to which of the farmsteads they refer.

·20 NO 0833 6536   NO 06 NE 8–9
This farmstead comprises three buildings and a roughly rectangular enclosure; the buildings, all reduced to stone wall-footings, are set parallel to the contour with drainage gullies on their uphill sides. The largest is of a single compartment measuring 15·3m by 5·5m overall and has an outshot at its SSE end. The enclosure lies immediately downslope to the S, its axis across the contour, and measures 30m by 17m within a bank 0·4m high; its lower end is adjoined by the second building which is of a single compartment and measures 10·2m by 5m overall. The third building lies to the NW of the enclosure, about halfway down its length, it measures 12·2m by 4·5m overall and is of two compartments, that on the SSE containing what may be a lateral drain. At the foot of the slope, 110m to the SW (NO 0820 6526), there is a kiln.

·21 NO 0831 6545   NO 06 NE 61
Immediately SE of the modern track there is a farmstead comprising a two-compartment building, measuring 18m by 4·4m over stone wall-footings, adjoined by a small rectangular enclosure.

·22 NO 0823 6550   NO 06 NE 59
Some 60m to the NW of the modern track there are the remains of a building measuring 14·4m by 5m overall.

·23 NO 0850 6554   NO 06 NE 10
Between NO 0852 6548 and NO 0846 6561, to either side of a fence, there are seven shieling-huts or buildings and what may be a further two huts or small enclosures. The largest is of two compartments, that on the SSE appearing as a mound 0·4m high with a dished top which measures 12·5m by 4·8m overall; it lies to the SSE of the modern track, whilst the remainder lie to the N.

·24 NO 0832 6563   NO 06 NE 60
What may be the remains of a building, measuring 12·5m by 5·3m over stone wall-footings, are situated 130m W of shieling group (·23).

·25 NO 0906 6659   NO 06 NE 12
On the W bank of the Allt Coire an Laoigh, immediately WNW of a stone-walled enclosure, a subrectangular shieling-hut (6·9m by 3·9m over stone walls 0·6m high)

with an outshot at its ESE end, has been built upon a mound 13·5m in diameter and 1m high. The NW angle of the enclosure overlies what may be the remains of another hut, whilst amongst the outcrops and boulders to the S there are traces of subsidiary enclosures. On the E bank of the burn, some 20m to the NE, a pen has been constructed against a rock outcrop.

·26 NO 0860 6601   NO 06 NE 13
The slight remains of three rectangular huts ranging in overall size from 7·5m by 3·5m to 9·5m by 4·5m are situated 400m NNE of (·23).

·27 NO 0839 6660   NO 06 NE 19–20
About 250m NW of the crags on Uchd na h-Anaile there is a shieling group comprising seven rectangular huts, four small rectangular enclosures and five pens; the huts range in size from 6m by 4·8m to 9m by 5·2m overall. Some 150m to the SE (NO 0855 6647) there is at least one further hut.

·28 NO 0645 6429   NO 06 SE 31, 86
On the SW slope of Calamanach, immediately below Calamanach Wood, there is a farmstead comprising an irregular cluster of eight buildings reduced to little more than wall-footings and ranging in size from 6·5m by 4·8m to 16·5m by 6m overall. Two of the buildings form two sides of a yard, that on the NW having a possible kiln at its NE end, and that on the SW apparently overlying the W end of a third building. Two buildings immediately to the S also appear to be successive, while the easternmost building contains what is probably a lateral byre-drain. In the field to the W there are traces of rig-and-furrow cultivation, some of which take the form of terraces on the slopes.

·29 NO 0730 6419   NO 06 SE 87
On a gentle SW-facing slope above the Allt Doire nan Eun there is a building measuring 7·8m by 4·6m over stone wall-footings.

·30 NO 0784 6485   NO 06 SE 88
This farmstead lies in an area between the Allt Doire nan Eun and the Allt Dubhagan which has recently been ploughed for forestry. Formerly it comprised two buildings set on opposite sides of a yard, but following the ploughing only the more northerly building can be identified.

·31 NO 0815 6503   NO 06 NE 64
Situated on a low rise between the Allt Doire nan Eun on the E and the new forestry plantation on the W there is a farmstead comprising four buildings and a kiln-barn, their walls reduced to little more than their footings. Two of the buildings are set end-to-end to form a range 28m in overall length. That on the SSE, a byre with two lateral drains, forms the ENE side of a square yard 14m across, the SSE side being formed by the third building, which measures 18·9m by 4·8m overall. The kiln-barn and the fourth building lie immediately beyond the NW corner of the yard, whilst immediately N of the long range there is a row of three earlier buildings identified only by slight bands of stone; the yard may also belong to an earlier configuration of buildings on the site.
      The remains are probably those of the farmstead of 'Carroch' depicted on Stobie's map (1783).

·32 NO 0802 6528   NO 06 NE 68
Some 280m NNW of (·30), immediately within the new forestry plantation, there is a farmstead comprising two adjoining buildings forming the NW and part of the NE

sides of a yard entered from the SE. The buildings measure 7·8m by 4·4m and 10·1m by 5m respectively over stone wall-footings.

·33 NO 0708 6594   NO 06 NE 63
Disposed along the E bank of the Allt Dubhagan, from NO 0711 6582 to NO 0711 6601, there are up to fifteen shieling-huts and four small enclosures (a fifth enclosure lies 140m to the N, NO 0715 6616). Whilst the majority of the huts are rectangular on plan, ranging in size from 4·9m by 4·5m to 10m by 6m overall, at least three are oval. Up to seven of the huts, including the three described as oval, have funnel-type entrances.

·34 NO 0694 6607   NO 06 NE 56
On the W side of the Allt Dubhagan, disposed along the crest of a low, heather-covered ridge from NO 0697 6597 to 0693 6615, there are at least fourteen shieling-huts. Whilst nine of the huts are rectangular on plan, ranging in size from 4·6m by 3·6m to 13·2m by 5·8m overall, two are oval and three appear as low mounds up to 0·4m high. Dispersed amongst the huts there are five hut-circles (no. 121·14).

·35 NO 066 663   NO 06 NE 58
On the SE spur of Blar Achaidh there is a terrace about 150m long and up to 150m broad. On the terrace itself, but mostly just below it on the SW and SE slopes (NO 0641 6634 to 0674 6628), there is a shieling group comprising forty structures, the majority probably built of turf. Of these, nine are rectangular enclosures ranging in size from 5m by 4·4m to 13·2m by 8·3m internally (a single oval enclosure measures 7·8m by 6·4m). Most of the rest are rectangular or subrectangular huts ranging in size from 4m by 3·6m to 14m by 5·5m overall. Much of the area is enclosed by turf banks, within which there are traces of rig-and-furrow cultivation.

·36 NO 0686 6741   NO 06 NE 28
This shieling group comprises six huts and two small rectangular enclosures, one with an adjoining hut. The huts are all rectangular on plan and range in size from one of a single compartment measuring 6·3m by 3·3m to one of two compartments measuring 10·4m by up to 4·2m over stone wall-footings. Immediately adjacent to a second two-compartment hut there is a hut-circle, one of a group of five at this location (no. 121·10).

·37 NO 0704 6763   NO 06 NE 32
On the SW flank of Creag Bhreac there is a shieling-hut, measuring 6·7m by 6m overall, lying partly within a small circular enclosure. About 80m to the E (NO 0713 6762) there is a three-compartment building measuring 12·8m by 4m overall; its SE end overlies a low mound 10m across, which is probably the remains of an earlier turf-built hut.

·38 NO 080 674   NO 06 NE 33–5
On the craggy S and SE slopes of Creag Bhreac there are three shieling groups. The first lies on a terrace close to the foot of the hill, a little way above the modern track (NO 0812 6730), where there are the remains of six huts or buildings ranging in size from 5·2m by 3·7m to 16·7m by 4·8m overall. The second is situated on another terrace to the NW (NO 079 674) where there are six huts, ranging in size from 6·6m by 3·7m to 10m by 4·8m overall, and three enclosures. The third group is situated on the spine of a grassy ridge to the NE (NO 0821 6747) and comprises three huts, measuring up to 10·2m by 4m overall, and an enclosure.

·39 NO 088 682   NO 06 NE 36
At the head of the valley of Allt Doire nan Eun, on the lower slopes of Creag an Dubh Shluic (not shown on plan), there is a large shieling group, within which some chronological depth is visible, three of the huts having been constructed upon or sunk into earlier mounds.

Disposed across a terrace close to the foot of the hill there are eleven huts ranging in size from 4·7m by 3·5m to 9·7m by 3·6m overall; most are of a single compartment, some are adjoined by enclosures, and the largest (NO 0876 6821) overlies an earlier mound. On the E edge of the group (NO 0884 6823) there is a more substantial building measuring 10·4m by 3·7m overall, whilst on the SE edge of the terrace (NO 0887 6815) there are four closely-spaced huts measuring up to 5·7m by 3·5m overall.

Lying downslope from the main group, to the WSW, there are two further huts and two pens. The huts measure 6·2m by 4m and 9·4m by 4·6m overall respectively, and the smaller (NO 0867 6818), which has an enclosure at its NW end, has been constructed upon an earlier mound.

256   Drumfork, farmstead
NO 1491 5933   NO 15 NW 68
At the foot of the N flank of Knockali, 200m S of the chapel at Drumfork (no. 193), there is a farmstead comprising up to four buildings, together with their attendant enclosures and a kiln. Of the three principal buildings, the largest, a four-compartment range measuring 28·7m by up to 5·3m overall, lies on the S side of a yard. At the NE corner of the yard there is a two-compartment building, measuring 17·5m by 4·6m overall, and immediately to the NE of it a three-compartment building measuring 20·3m by 5·1m overall. The kiln lies 130m to the SW and, on the slope above, what may be the remains of another building are cut through by a drain.

257   Easter Binzian, farmstead
NO 1226 6890   NO 16 NW 16, 62
On a terrace at the foot of Creag Bhinnein, to the ESE of the cottage at Easter Binzian, there are the remains of a farmstead comprising at least five buildings and two yards. The buildings (three of which are commonly aligned) are all reduced to turf-covered stone wall-footings and range from 8·2m by 3·8m to 11·9m by 5·9m overall; one possesses an outshot. They appear to respect an old trackway (probably the Military Road) whose course may be traced more clearly in proximity to Slochnacraig (no. 317); to the NE of the farmstead the track is skirted by the old head-dyke. Some 130m to the WNW, upslope from the cottage at Easter Binzian, there are the remains of a two-compartment building (12m by 4·2m overall). A farmstead is depicted here by Roy (1747–55, sheet 18/4) but is unnamed. It is 'Balinauld' on the maps of Stobie (1783), Ainslie (1794) and Blackadder (1825), but 'Little Binzean' on Brown's 1808 survey.

258   Easter Bleaton, fermtoun
NO 144 586   NO 15 NW 22
This well-preserved fermtoun is situated 400m E of Easter Bleaton, on a W-facing terrace at the foot of Knockali and immediately above the floor of Glenshee. Extending over a distance of 800m from N to S (NO 1445 5890 to 1438 5812) there are at least fifty-two buildings, their walls reduced to the lowest courses or to stone footings,

258A, C

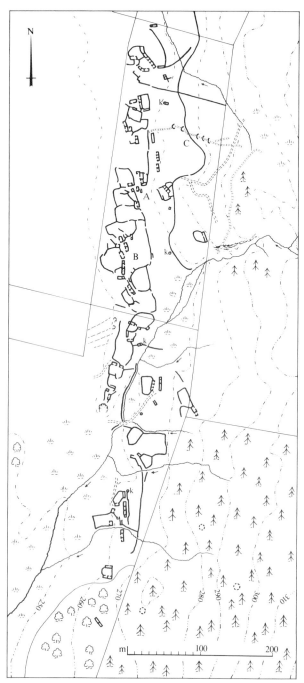

258A Easter Bleaton, fermtoun, 1:5000

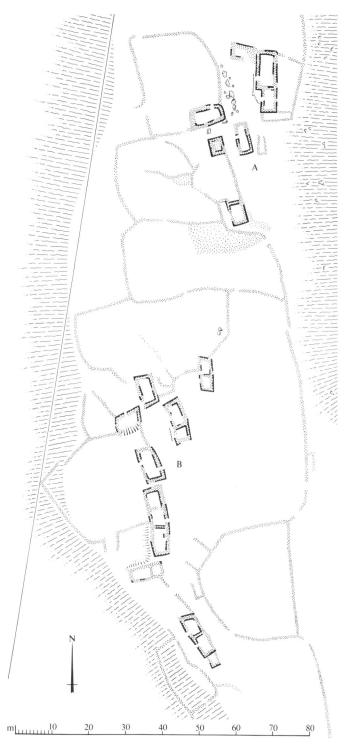

258B Easter Bleaton, fermtoun (detail), 1:1000

together with a series of attendant enclosures and four kilns (K on plan). From the disposition of the buildings it is possible to suggest the presence of at least eight units or farmsteads, perhaps reflecting the properties of individual tenants; two of the units are shown in detail (A and B on

258B fig.). On the slope above the N end of the site there is a line of five retting pools (C).

At least some of the remains, probably those at the S end of the site, are to be identified with 'up[per] Bleaton', depicted on Stobie's map (1783), though it is less clear whether the remains at the N end are to be identified with 'Torvack'.

259   Easter Dunie, farmstead and buildings
NO 0917 5842   NO 05 NE 140–41

To the E of Easter Dunie steading there are the remains of two buildings (one a building-and-outshot), and to the

ENE (NO 0952 5856) those of a farmstead comprising three buildings ranged with a yard with a fourth to the SE. The buildings are all reduced to turf-covered stone wall-footings; the largest measures 14·1 m by 4·6 m overall. The farmstead of 'Mid Dunie' is depicted by Roy (1747–55, sheet 18/4) and Stobie (1783); 'Maines of Douine' is on record in 1719 (Spalding 1914, 218).

260   Faulds, farmsteads and buildings
In the vicinity of the cottage of Faulds (NO 1397 5800) there are a number of farmsteads and buildings, described below from N to S.

258C Easter Bleaton, fermtoun, showing the northern half of the site, aerial view from S

·1   NO 1410 5826   NO 15 NW 54
Some 250 m NNE of the cottage and 20 m E of the track to Easter Bleaton there is a group of three buildings reduced to their wall-footings. All are of comparable size, the largest measuring 10·1 m by 5·8 m overall, and two have outshots. On the slopes to the N and NE there is a series of low lynchets which have developed from broad cultivation rigs.

·2   NO 1401 5804   NO 15 NW 52
About 60 m NE of the cottage there is a three-compartment building and a kiln; the building measures 14 m by 5·2 m over stone wall-footings.

·3   NO 1401 5797   NO 15 NW 39
A farmstead lies immediately SE of the cottage. It comprises a four-compartment building, measuring 21·7 m by 5·3 m over stone wall-footings, adjoined on the E by a roughly rectangular enclosure. Two smaller structures, the larger probably a building, adjoin the SW corner of the enclosure; they measure 7 m by 3·8 m and 2·9 m by 2·6 m respectively over stone wall-footings. These remains appear roofless on the first edition of the OS 6-inch map (Perthshire, 1865–7, sheet 33, and 1867, sheet 42), when they formed a part of the then ruinous farmstead of Faulds, depicted as 'Folds' on Stobie's map (1783).

·4   NO 1389 5784   NO 15 NW 40
Another group of three buildings lies 150 m SSW of the cottage. The largest, whose E wall displays a pronounced outward curve, is defined by banks up to 2·2 m thick and measures 18·5 m by up to 9·8 m overall. The second building lies 5·5 m to the W and measures 8·3 m by 4·8 m overall, whilst the third, which is bow-sided and measures 9 m by up to 5·4 m, lies 31 m to the W.

·5   NO 1386 5769   NO 15 NW 55
A single building lies 150 m S of (·4) and measures 8·3 m by 6·4 m over stone wall-footings.

·6   NO 1410 5755   NO 15 NW 53
On a knoll about 300 m ESE of (·5) there is a three-compartment building measuring 15·8 m by 4 m overall.

·7   NO 1412 5738   NO 15 NW 69
This farmstead comprises two buildings, reduced to their wall-footings, an enclosure and a kiln. The buildings, which measure 19·5 m by 5·5 m and 8·1 m by 5·3 m overall respectively, are adjoined on the W by the enclosure; the kiln lies immediately outside the N corner of the enclosure.

261   Finegand, Pitcarmick-type building
NO 1383 6606   NO 16 NW 88
Situated in a slight hollow at the edge of a terrace and end-on to a gully there are the wasted remains of what may be a Pitcarmick-type building. It measures 20·7 m in length and up to 7·1 m in width at its rounded NW end, narrowing to about 4·8 m towards the SE, over walls spread up to 1·4 m in thickness; the floor-level towards the SE end of the interior may be slightly sunken.

262   Finegand, buildings and huts
NO 1396 6611   NO 16 NW 82–7
Opposite Finegand steading, adjoining a track leading up the slope beside the A93, there are the robbed remains of a building (10·7 m by 4·9 m over turf-covered stone walls 0·8 m thick and up to 0·8 m high) which is shown as partially roofed on the first edition of the OS 6-inch map (Perthshire, 1867, sheet 24). Upslope, on a terrace beside the track (NO 1391 6613), there are the remains of a second building (10·4 m by 5·5 m overall), and on a knoll about 140 m to the W (NO 1377 6610) there is a third (10 m by 3·2 m over turf-covered boulder walls 1·1 m thick). The latter has an outshot at the S end of its W wall and there is also a low setting of stones at the foot of a boulder at the SE angle. On a terrace to the SSE (NO 1380 6606) there are the wasted remains of what is

probably a turf-built hut (9·6 m by 5·2 m overall) which, on its NW side, overlies the remains of another (9 m by 3·7 m overall). Towards the edge of a natural gully, immediately to the E, there are traces of what may be a Pitcarmick-type building (no. 261), while some 100 m to the SSE (NO 1384 6596) there are the wasted remains of another building (8·4 m by 4·8 m overall). In a hollow about 260 m SSE of this building (NO 1401 6575), there are the remains of a building (10·7 m by 5 m over heather-covered stone wall-footings 1·2 m thick) with what may be an outshot at its NW end.

263   Finegand, datestone
NO 1406 6623   NO 16 NW 9·1
A datestone of 1658 is incorporated in re-use in the fabric of the SSW gable to the ESE range of the steading at Finegand. Finegand, 'in the barony of Middle Dounie', is on record in 1561 (*Reg. Mag. Sig.*, ii, no. 3450) when it was the property of the McComies, later the M'Kenzies. It appears as 'Finninghand' on Pont (*c.* 1600) and 'Fenegeand' on Roy (1747–55, sheet 18/4), and a mansion is depicted by Stobie (1783).
— *Retours*, Perth, No. 367; Smith 1889; Michie 1901, 195; Miller 1929, 65–6; Atholl Muniments, 23, xvi.

264   Garry Drums, Middleton Muir, buildings
Buildings have been recorded at two locations on the ridges known as the Garry Drums (see also no. 147·11).   *216*

·1   NO 1300 4787   NO 14 NW 58
On the crest of a ridge and set end on to each other some 15 m apart, there are two buildings measuring 15·8 m by 6·5 m and 11·5 m by 4·9 m respectively over stone wall-footings.

·2   NO 1305 4817   NO 14 NW 50
Situated 300 m to the N, immediately NNW of the corner of a modern field wall, there are the remains of what may be a large building measuring 36·6 m by 8·7 m over a stony bank 1·9 m thick and 0·4 m high. There are two possible entrances in the SSW side and on the NNE side, and at either end there is an external drainage gully. Immediately to the W and about 40 m to the E there are traces of rig-and-furrow cultivation. The structure is unlike any of the other rectangular buildings recorded in NE Perth, and its date and purpose are unknown.

265   Gleann Beag, farmsteads, buildings, and shielings
Gleann Beag is a steep-sided, heavily-glaciated river valley which extends for a distance of 8 km from SSW to NNE. The visible remains principally comprise a series of farmsteads, together with extensive cultivation remains, and dispersed shieling-groups. Cultivable land on both sides of the valley is demarcated by a head-dyke, and this feature provides a common reference point for many of the farmsteads, which are sited either on or close to it.   *p.8* Much earlier occupation of the glen is represented by a prehistoric burial cairn (no. 20) and what may be a stone setting (no. 73). In this account, which focuses on the area between NO 1164 7131 and NO 1289 7384, the W side of the valley is described first (from SW to NE), followed by E side (from NE to SW). The present grazings are the property of the Invercauld Estate and are recorded in detail on Brown's 1808 survey, on which all the principal farmsteads are depicted.   *p.10*

·1   NO 1145 7154   NO 17 SW 59
Set in a shallow depression to the E of the track to Coire

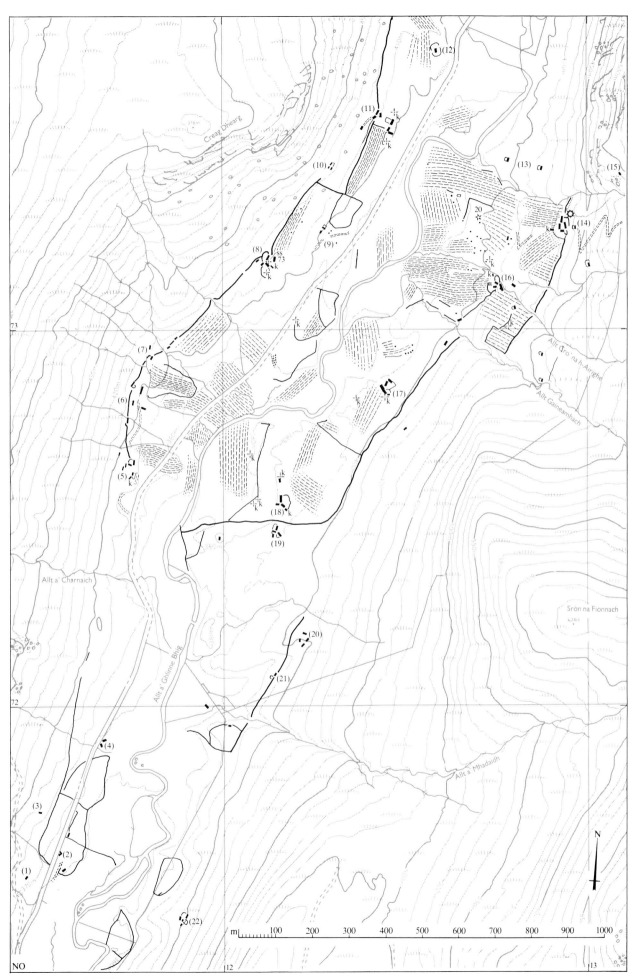

265 *Gleann Beag, 1:10 000*

Shith, there are the remains of what is probably a shieling-hut (8 m by 4·5 m over turf- and heather-covered stone wall-footings).

·2   NO 1154 7158   NO 17 SW 29
Beside the A93, on a terrace traversed by the Military Road, there are the remains of two probable buildings: one is of two compartments, and measures 9·4 m by 4·5 m over stone wall-footings about 0·8 m in thickness; the other, which has been truncated by road-widening, measures at least 7·5 m by 5·4 m overall.

·3   NO 1150 7172   NO 17 SW 60
On a terrace, upslope from the old head-dyke, there are the wasted remains of what may be a building (9·8 m by 4·6 m overall).

·4   NO 1167 7190   NO 17 SW 30
Beside the A93, and truncated by road-widening, there are the wasted remains of two buildings. The larger measures at least 11 m by 5·8 m over stone wall-footings spread up to 1·2 m in thickness.

·5   NO 1175 7264   NO 17 SW 13
Disposed across a terrace there are the remains of a farmstead comprising six buildings and a kiln. The buildings are all reduced to turf-covered stone wall-footings and range from 7·9 m by 4·3 m to 18 m by 5·4 m overall. At the centre of the group are two buildings on the E and S sides of a yard; one (on the E) is of three compartments and the other (on the S) possesses opposed lateral entrances. The yard is cut back into the old head-dyke, which extends along the break of slope at the rear of the terrace and clearly deviates to take in the farmstead. To the WSW of the yard there are two buildings, one with a drainage-bank to the rear. To the SSE of the first group there are the remains of a building with an entrance central to its W wall; on the E there is an adjoining enclosure. On the S side of the enclosure there is a pit (possibly of recent origin) and beside it the remains of a kiln-and-chamber. A track following the edge of the terrace is partially stone-revetted. On a terrace upslope from the head-dyke (NO 1171 7266), there are the remains of a building with what may be a drainage-hood on its uphill side; the entrance is in the SW *p.8* end-wall. The farmstead is depicted by Archer (1749) and is named 'Laganamer' by Roy (1747–55, sheet 18/4). It is 'Laginamer' on Stobie (1783) and 'Lag-na-mer' on Brown's 1808 survey. Near to the farmstead Brown depicts both arable and pasture.

·6   NO 1174 7276 to 1180 7295   NO 17 SW 14
Some 150 m N of (·5), and interrupting the head-dyke, there are the remains of a round-angled building (10·7 m by 4·1 m over turf-covered stone wall-footings 1 m thick) with an enclosure on its SW side. The angles of the building are secured by massive boulder underpinnings. To the NNE, and disposed across the slope and terrace, there are the remains of at least six buildings. All are reduced to either the lowest courses of their stone walls, or to their wall-footings. The first (NO 1175 7281) measures 8 m by 5 m overall and has a drainage-trench on its uphill side. About 20 m to the ESE, set end-on to the slope and skirted by the track from (·5), there are the wasted remains of a two-compartment building (13·8 m by 4·8 m overall), on the NNE side of which Brown (1808) depicts an 'Old Yard'. To the N (NO 1178 7284) there are the remains of a four-compartment building (23·3 m by 5·1 m overall); an arc of bank on the S may define the point at which the track from (·5) was directed past it. Abutting the head-dyke (NO 1175 7285), there is a two-compartment, round-angled building (15·5 m by 4·5 m

overall) with an entrance to each compartment on the E; these both open to an attached stone-walled enclosure. Some 70 m to the NE there is a building (7·6 m by 4·7 m overall) to which a second unit (5 m by 3·9 m overall) has been added on the NNE; this is levelled into the slope. Immediately to the W there is a hollow (about 2·5 m in diameter), the origin of which is uncertain. On a ridge of higher ground (NO 1180 7295) there are the remains of another building (7·9 m by 4·1 m overall).

·7   NO 1185 7295   NO 17 SW 100
Beside the burn and incorporated on the SE side of the head-dyke, there are the turf-covered remains of a building (7 m by 4·4 m overall), on the SE side of which there is a fragment of the NE angle of what may be a horizontal-mill; this is represented by a stony bank 1·5 m thick and 0·8 m high. A slab, set on edge, spans the burn at this point. A second building (NO 1187 1297), incorporated on the NW side of the head-dyke, measures 6 m by 4·4 m overall. The terrace immediately to the ENE is covered by rig-and-furrow cultivation.

·8   NO 1213 7318   NO 17 SW 15
This farmstead is depicted by Archer (1749) and is named 'Craigderay' by Roy (1747–55, sheet 18/4) and 'Craig-derig' by Stobie (1783). Some 350 m ENE of (·6), and disposed in a tight group towards the centre of the terrace, there are the remains of the farmstead of Craig Derg. It comprises at least five buildings, two enclosures, two kilns and a yard. With one exception the buildings are all reduced to turf-covered stone wall-footings and range from 9·7 m by 5·4 m to 12·4 m by 4·4 m overall. Central to this group are buildings on two sides of a yard; that on the NW, which is of two compartments with an entrance central to the SE wall, incorporates a large boulder orthostat at its S angle, together with a recumbent slab at the S end of the SE end-wall. Two further units have been added to the NNE end of the building. The building on the SW side of the yard incorporates a standing stone at the N angle of the NE wall, which appears to be aligned with a second stone 3 m to the ENE (see no. 73). A marked intake in the head-dyke provided a funnelled approach to the yard, but access was subsequently blocked; on the S the yard terminates in a mound of field-clearance. An oval enclosure adjoins the SSW side of the second building. Within it there are traces of cultivation and the remains of a kiln; beside the kiln there is a slight hollow (about 4·3 m in diameter) with a band of stone around its perimeter. To the ENE of the enclosure there are the remains of a kiln-and-chamber (8·4 m by 3·8 m overall). To the SW of the first building and at right angles to the second there is a third building. On the N the head-dyke angles away from the break of slope at the rear of the terrace and is drawn in, and back on itself, to form a secondary enclosure; on its WSW side there is an area of poorly-drained ground. Beside the head-dyke, immediately to the NW, there are the remains of a building with an entrance towards the W end of its S wall; a drainage-bank extends the length of the rear-wall. On an area of slightly raised ground, to the E of the main yard, there are the wasted remains of what may be a robbed, two-compartment building. The robber-trench is up to 1·5 m broad and 0·3 m deep; the interior of the structure is occupied by a low, turf-covered, rubble mound.

To the N of the farmstead, the head-dyke once more follows the rear of the terrace, over which there are extensive traces of rig-and-furrow, and a number of clearance cairns. The farmstead appears still to have been occupied at the time of Brown's survey (1808) on which ridged-fields are shown to the NE, SE and SW, taking in the land on both sides of the Military Road and descending as far as the valley floor and the terraces bordering the haughland.

·9 NO 1226 7325, 1227 7325   NO 17 SW 62
On a terrace to the ENE of (·8), there are the remains of two buildings. Both are reduced to turf-covered stone wall-footings and measure respectively 6·9 m by 5 m and 10·3 m by 5·8 m overall; to the NE of the second building there is a yard (8·2 m by 4·8 m internally). A track, probably the same as that noted in (·6), passes downslope of the buildings, and in the vicinity there are a few clearance cairns.

·10 NO 1230 7343   NO 17 SW 16
Some 230 m NE of (·8) the head-dyke reaches an area of unimproved ground and descends to a second terrace, which extends from NNE to SSW. Occupying a shelf, along the projected line of the head-dyke before it descends, on otherwise uncleared, boulder-strewn ground, there are the remains of a small farmstead comprising three buildings and a yard. The buildings are all reduced to either stone or boulder wall-footings, and range from 5·7 m by 4·3 m to 11 m by 4·3 m overall (the last, a two-compartment building); the yard is slightly hollowed. Brown (1808) depicts the farmstead, but does not give its name.

·11 NO 1244 7355   NO 17 SW 17
At the NNE end of the terrace referred to in (·10), there are the remains of the farmstead of Cloichiernoch (later Wester Craig Derg). The farmstead comprises at least three buildings, two enclosures and two kilns, and set on a narrow shelf on uncleared ground there are the remains of at least a further four buildings. The principal building, which is larger than the rest and more solidly built, measures 13·4 m by 5·3 m over boulder-footings up to 0·9 m in thickness and 0·7 m in height. It is set end-on to a dry water-channel and has an entrance-doorway central to its E side-wall. The turf-covered remains of the SSW end-wall are unusually thick. A well-formed, regular enclosure adjoins the NW side of the building; the interior is relatively stone-free and was once probably cultivated. The remaining buildings, which are all reduced to turf-covered stone wall-footings, range from 7·5 m by 3·7 m to 16·5 m by 4·4 m overall. Set apart to the S of the first building, there is a single unit formed by buildings on two sides of a yard (that on the NW is of two compartments). An enclosure extends to the edge of the terrace and incorporates a kiln; some 20 m to the N of the principal building there are the remains of a kiln-and-chamber. Over the terrace to the SSW of these buildings there are extensive traces of rig-and-furrow. Upslope, and interrupting the head-dyke, a second unit is defined by three buildings and a yard. The largest of these is of three compartments and has a drainage-bank to the rear. A track leads upslope to a fourth building, which lies some 30 m to the SW, and which also has a drainage-bank.

The farmstead of Cloicheruim is depicted by Archer (1749) and Roy (1747–55, sheet 18/5); it appears as 'Cloichiernoch' on Stobie's map (1783) and either 'Clow or Wester Craig-Derg' on Brown's survey of 1808. Miller (1929, 17) suggests the derivation of the name as Clachnahernan, or Clacherna 'the burial-place of the lairds'; but see (·12).

·12 NO 1258 7373   NO 17 SW 18
Towards the edge of the terrace 200 m NE of (·11), and central to a roughly oval enclosure, there are the remains of a subrectangular building. Although wasted by robbing, the building has been quite substantial (9·2 m by 5·6 m over boulder-footings up to 1·5 m thick); the entrance was probably towards the N end of the W wall.

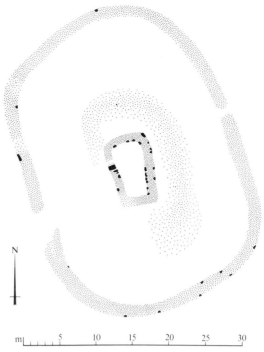

265·12 Gleann Beag, building and enclosure, 1:500

A crescentic rubble spread, on the N and E, is of uncertain origin but may be earlier. The enclosing bank is broken in two places (on the WSW and ENE respectively) and both may be original entrances. On the W the bank is cut by a plough-scar, the result of rig-cultivation over the adjacent area. Field-clearance may account for the thickness of the bank on the SSW. Both the building and enclosure are shown on Brown's 1808 survey, where the building appears as unroofed. Brown annotates it 'Clow-hairn' (Miller 1929, 17).

·13 NO 1277 7344, 1286 7342   NO 17 SW 19
Set apart, some 320 m ESE of (·11), on the W-facing slope below Creag Dubhaidh, there are the remains of two buildings both of which are depicted on Archer's survey of 1749. The first, which is round-angled with battered end-walls, was probably of two compartments (each entered independently) and measures 13·1 m by 5·2 m over stone walls 0·9 m in thickness and up to 1·2 m in height. On the W there is an attached stone-walled enclosure (11·3 m by 4 m internally) and on the E a drainage-bank. The building is shown as unroofed on the first edition of the OS 6-inch map (Perthshire, 1867, sheet 15). Although in a collapsed condition, the second building is remarkably well preserved. It is round-angled on plan and also has two compartments; the N end-wall is slightly battered. The building measures 15·2 m by 4·5 m over stone walls 0·9 m in thickness and 0·6 m in average height. The S end-wall, however, stands 1·5 m high (a doorway has been inserted on the W) and the W wall, which has collapsed internally, stood to a height of at least 1·8 m in eight courses. Two entrance-doorways are incorporated in this wall, and beside the S door there is a blocked window (0·3 m wide and 0·4 m high); opposed cruck-slots are visible at the N end of the building. On the W there is an attached stone-walled enclosure (10·3 m by 6 m internally), on the S side of which there are the wasted remains of what may be an earlier building (5·3 m by 3·6 m overall).

·14 NO 1292 7327   NO 17 SW 21
The farmstead of Cro na h-Airighe occupies a terraced area to the S of Creag Dubhaidh. It is the most northerly

J

265·14 Gleann Beag, Cro na h-Airighe, farmstead from NE

of the farmsteads disposed over the central portion of the valley and occupies a marginal position between the cultivated or cleared lower slopes and the higher hill-grazings beyond. The farmstead comprises at least six buildings and a yard, and there are a number of outbuildings, including a mill-site and three kilns. Some chronological depth is apparent in the farmstead, whose walls were partially rebuilt in the mid to late 19th century to provide a fank. The buildings are reduced either to their lowest courses, or to turf-covered stone wall-footings, and range from 8·7 m by 5·5 m to 16·8 m by 5 m overall.

Two buildings, one a two-compartment structure terraced into the slope at the foot of the yard, are set end-to-end with a drainage-trench extending their entire length on the E. To the S, and set slightly forward, there are the remains of a third building, while ranged on the side of the yard (end-on to the slope) there is a fourth. Levelled into the slope at the head of the yard (on the E), there is a two-compartment building, which connects on the S with the turf-and-stone head-dyke; a small enclosure (9·6 m by 11 m internally) has been formed in the angle between the head-dyke and the previous building. On the S, and also connecting with the head-dyke, there is an elongated subrectangular enclosure, at the NW corner of which there are the well-preserved remains of a kiln-and-chamber. An extension of the head-dyke to the N of the yard connects with the Allt Creag Dubhaidh. In the intervening ground, at the foot of a dry gully which drops from the crags above (from a height of 480 m OD), there is a probable mill-site. The head of the gully is canalised, and there are also traces of masonry-revetting and possible damming of the burn at NO 1308 7336; a wooden trough may have served to transfer water into the gully for its use as a lade. A second channel, probably the tail-race, extends from the mill-site to the burn.

Upslope from the yard there are the turf-covered footings of a building (9·5 m by 4·3 m overall) with a stone-walled enclosure attached to its S side; an adjoining structure on the N may be a pen. Immediately to the E, a track bifurcates and one branch leads upslope in a series of sweeping hairpins towards the remains of a further building (9·7 m by 4·2 m overall) and an enclosure; from there it climbs to the shielings around Creag Dubhaidh (·15). On the slopes below the farmstead and extending to the haughland, there are extensive traces of rig-and-furrow, numerous clearance cairns and a prehistoric burial-cairn (no. 20). Let into a low ridge (NO 1281 7326) there are the remains of a kiln with a baffle-wall attached to its flue. To the WSW (NO 1277 7324), and partially obscured by field-clearance, there are the remains of a building; SW of this there is a kiln (NO 1273 7318), and on the haughland to the NW of the cairn (NO 1263 7335), there is a stone-walled enclosure.

The 'shealing of Cro na choire' is on record in 1561, when it went with the farm of Finegand in Glen Shee (Atholl Muniments, 23, xvi). The farm is said to have belonged to the MacKenzies (later of Finegand), but from about 1640 it was tenanted by Alexander Ramsay (died 1702); the lands of 'Cronachoire' are on record in 1664 (Atholl Muniments, 23, xvii, 1). It was sold together with Gormel (no. 266) in 1770, and in 1780 became the property of Farquharson of Invercauld. In 1812 the decision was taken to clear the small-holdings in the valley to form a single grazing (Miller 1929, 17–21). It is possible that Cro na h-Airighe, which was the first to go, was already unroofed at this time (Brown 1808). Donald Ramsay, however, was apparently tenant in 'Cronaherie' until 1813 (headstone, Spittal burial-ground). The farmstead is depicted by Roy (1747–55, sheet 18/5), Archer (1749), Stobie (1783), Ainslie (1794), and Brown (1808).
— Smith 1808, i–ii, n. 16.

·15 NO 131 733   NO 17 SW 20, 79–82
There are at least eight shieling-huts clustered around the Allt Creag Dubhaidh to the ENE of Cro na h-Airighe. Three fall within the area covered by the map, one beside the burn and the other two (one adjoined by an enclosure) on a terrace 40 m to the N. A group of three more lies 30 m to the E, along with two outlying huts 30 m NNW and 60 m SSE respectively. The huts range from 4·1 m by 3·5 m to 8·7 m by 4·6 m overall. On the W flank of Carn Ait, about 250 m to the E (NO 1341 7331), there is a stone-walled enclosure with a subrectangular structure (9·7 m by 4·2 m overall), possibly a building on its N side.

·16 NO 1275 7311   NO 17 SW 23, 101–102
This farmstead is separated from its neighbours, on the N and S respectively, by the Allt Cro na h-Airighe and the Allt Gaineamhach. It occupies a position at the head of the cultivated lower slopes and comprises three buildings (A–C), two enclosures, a kiln (D) and a pen; the wasted remains of a fourth building (E) lie to the E. The

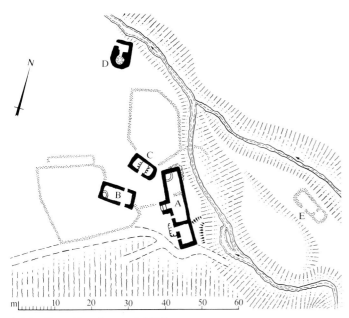

265·16 Gleann Beag, farmstead, 1:1000

principal building (A), probably a dwelling with byre attached, was divided into two compartments by an inserted cross-wall. It measures 16 m by 5 m over stone walls up to 1·3 m in thickness and 0·7 m in average height; the WSW wall, however, is well preserved and stands up to 1·8 m in height externally. The entrance-doorway, framed by a porch and approached by steps, was towards the SSE end of the WSW wall; beside it there is a window (through-splayed, square arrised and lintelled), 0·49 m wide and 0·42 m high. Latterly, a pen has been constructed in the NW corner of the building. The byre (on the SSE) is choked with field-clearance but the entrance is apparent at the NNW end of the WSW wall, and beside it a lintelled byre-drain emits from the wall; the entrance opens to a paved threshold or stance. Building B, probably a threshing-barn, has opposed lateral entrances; latterly, a pen has been constructed in the WSW corner. The adjoining enclosure has a pen on its NNW side. Building C, either a byre or store, has an entrance central to its SSW wall. To the interior, on either side of the doorway, the floor-level has been raised and is stone-revetted. The kiln (D) is well preserved. It has a bowl (at least 1·6 m deep in nine courses), which opens to a chamber on the N; the entrance was at the N end of the W wall.

Upslope there are other buildings. Within an area of rig-and-furrow (NO 1279 7305) there are the remains of a building and enclosure, while to the S (NO 1277 7300) there is a kiln. Still further upslope (NO 1287 7292 and NO 1287 7286 respectively), there are the remains of two buildings, each with an attached stone-walled enclosure. To the WSW of the farmstead, on the projected line of the old head-dyke, there are the remains of another building (NO 1264 7301). All are reduced to turf-covered stone wall-footings and are of roughly the same size (up to 9·4 m by 3·5 m overall).

The farmstead is depicted and named by Roy, 'Lagganagrien' (1747–55, sheet 18/5); it is 'Lagnagrien' on the maps of Stobie (1783) and Ainslie (1794), and 'Lag na craimh' on Brown's survey (1808).

·17 NO 1244 7283   NO 17 SW 24
To the SW of (·16) there are the remains of the farmstead of Sidh Chaluim, which comprise four buildings, two yards and a possible kiln. The principal building is square-angled and rectangular on plan (13·8 m by 6·1 m over clay-bonded rubble walls 0·7 m thick), and has an entrance-doorway central to its WSW wall (the lintel lies in two fragments to the exterior); the interior was subsequently consolidated by a masonry addition to the inner wall-face. The NNW end-wall (1·8 m high externally) is surprisingly thick and has a scarcement at first-floor level, probably for a loft. An outshot abutted on the NNW was subsequently rebuilt (perhaps as a bothy), reducing the original dimensions (4·3 m by 6·1 m overall) by 2 m; beside the door to the outshot there is a blocked window. A third unit (9·7 m by 4·8 m overall) with an entrance-doorway at the NNW end of its WSW wall, was added to the building on the SSE; a transverse byre-drain issues from the doorway.

On the NE, two buildings are ranged with a yard. The first (10 m by 5·3 m overall) has opposed lateral entrances and an outshot (5·1 m by 4·4 m overall) which is open-ended; its neighbour, to the W, was probably of two compartments (11·9 m by 4·9 m overall) and has an entrance-doorway at the S end of its WNW wall. A third building (5·1 m by 4·1 m overall), with an entrance at the S end of its WNW wall, is incorporated at the SSE corner of a subsidiary yard; adjacent to the NNE wall-face there is a low turf-covered mound. About 5 m to the S of the SSW angle of the principal building, the remains of what may be a kiln are represented by a low, turf-covered circular plinth (4·3 m in diameter and up to 0·7 m high). Some 180 m to the ENE (NO 1260 7295) and adjacent to the head-dyke, there are the remains of a building (9·6 m by 5·6 m overall) with an entrance towards the SSW end of its W wall, while to the SSE (NO 1249 7273) there are the remains of another building (7·9 m by 4·5 m overall). In the vicinity of the farmstead there are traces of rig-and-furrow, and, on a low spur to the WSW (NO 1236 7281), there are two hollows set 75 m apart (the larger 3·4 m in diameter and 0·8 m deep with upcast around its lip), which may be clamps, possibly for lime-burning.

The farmstead is depicted by Archer (1749) and is named 'Sihallion' by Roy (1747–55, sheet 18/4); it is 'Malcolm's Seat' on the maps of Stobie (1783), Ainslie (1794) and Thompson (1825). Brown (1808) depicts the farmstead, but the principal building is not shown, and he seems to have been uncertain of the name ('Schicluim' may be a later interpolation).

·18 NO 1216 7254   NO 17 SW 25
To the SW of (·17) there is the farmstead of Dail Bhreac, whose remains can be principally divided into two phases. The earlier comprises buildings ranged with a yard. The first (at least 6·9 m by 5 m overall) stands on the W side of the yard, which is terraced in two stages (19·9 m by 22·7 m and 17·4 m by 13·6 m respectively). Almost at right angles to it (on the SSE) there are the remains of another; this is round-angled and rectangular on plan (13·3 m by 4·7 m over turf-covered stone wall-footings 1 m thick) and possesses two entrance-doorways in its S wall. It is possible that the two buildings were at one time joined and that access between the two was facilitated.

Overlying the first building and extending further to the N there are the remains of a two-compartment rectangular building (10·8 m by 5·3 m over stone walls 0·7 m thick and up to 1·1 m high) to which a further unit (5 m square) has been added on the S. This building stands on the W side of a stone-walled enclosure (9·8 m by 24·2 m internally), which overlies the earlier yard. Let into the slope, immediately to the SSE, there are the well-preserved remains of a kiln-and-chamber, with an entrance central to its end-wall and one at the rear (the latter giving access to the kiln-floor). The wasted remains of what may be a pen or a building extend downslope from the farmstead.

To the N (NO 1215 7259) there are the turf-covered

121

remains of a building (7·4m by 5m over boulder wall-footings) with an entrance at the S end of its W wall and an outshot on the N (5m by 2·7m overall). Let into the slope at the rear there is a kiln. To the WSW (NO 1208 7254), and let into a morainic ridge, there are the remains of a further three possible kilns or clamps. A small kiln, now partially obscured by field-clearance, is let into the slope at the rear of the haughland (NO 1207 7266).

The farmstead is depicted by Archer (1749) and is named 'Dalvreachk' by Roy (1747–55, sheet 18/4); it is 'Dalbrach' on the maps of Stobie (1783), Ainslie (1794), and Thomson (1825), and 'Dalbreachd' on Brown (1808).

·19 NO 1215 7246   NO 17 SW 61
This farmstead, which lies to the S of (·18), comprises buildings on two sides of an elongated, subrectangular enclosure which has latterly been subdivided by the insertion of a third. A fourth building, detached from the enclosure, lies immediately to the SE and has a stone-walled yard attached to its SW side. The buildings are all reduced to their stone wall-footings and range from 5·3m by 2·3m to 13·4m by 4·5m overall; that on the ENE side of the enclosure had a central byre-drain. On a spur some 120m to the W there are the remains of one building (12·2m by 3m overall) overlying another (9·7m by 4·4m over stone wall-footings); this building alone is depicted by Brown (1808).

·20 NO 1222 7217   NO 17 SW 26
A group of at least four shieling-huts are tucked into a natural hollow some 300m SSE of (·19). All are reduced to turf-covered stone wall-footings and range from roughly 4m square to 10·6m by 4·3m overall; one is of two compartments, another has an outshot.

·21 NO 1214 7207   NO 17 SW 27, 57–8
To the SW of (·20), adjoining the W side of the head-dyke, there are the remains of a building (9·4m by 5m over turf-covered wall-footings). Immediately to the S, and respecting an original break in the head-dyke, there is an enclosure. On relatively low-lying ground, to the S of the modern fence (NO 1192 7205), there are the remains of a round-angled building (9·1m by 4·4m overall), with what may be an outshot at the SSE end of its WSW wall. Another building lies some 70m to the SE; it is incorporated on the N side of an enclosure defined by a low turf bank, and measures 10·3m by 5·3m overall.

·22 NO 1188 7143   NO 17 SW 28
Some 750m SSW of (·20), on a heather-covered knoll (400m OD), there are at least four shieling-huts and two enclosures. All are reduced to their wall-footings and range from 4·5m by 2·9m to 10·7m by 3·6m overall (the last divided into two compartments).

From an early date the grazings of Gleann Beag provided the shieling-grounds for farming communities resident in Glen Shee (cf. Robertson 1799, 68). The shieling of Gormel, on record in the 13th century, was associated with the farm of Finegand. In 1561 the same farm possessed the shieling of 'Cro na choire' (due S of Gormel). In 1562, however, the four merk land of Finegand simply went 'with the shealing in Glen Beag', and the same was the case in 1565 in respect to the lands of Binzian Mor. A similar arrangement may be reflected on Pont's manuscript map of about 1600, on which the name 'Allt-Ruy-na Vey' is applied to the E side of the valley; the township of 'Runahervie', on record in 1680, is situated some 2·4 km to the SE of Spittal in Glen Shee.

To judge from the most accessible documentary and map evidence, Cro na h-Airighe was the first of the farms to be brought under permanent cultivation. It appears to have been occupied by the MacKenzies (later of Finegand) but from about 1640 was tenanted by Alexander Ramsay (died 1702, and described as 'Grazier' on the headstone preserved in the burial-ground at Spittal). The lands of 'Cronachoire' are on record in 1664. By the time of Roy's Military Survey, settlement had extended to both sides of the valley and the principal farmsteads were all in place: on the NW (from SW to NE) Laginamer, Craig-derig, Cloichiernoch and Rhiedorrach; and on the SE (from NE to SW) Gormel, Cro na h-Airighe, Lag nan Cnaimhean, Sidh Chaluim and Dail Bhreac. There is one inconsistency and one omission: Roy reverses the farm-names for Cro na h-Airighe and Lag nan Cnaimhean (a simple error), and the farmstead of Dail Bhreac ('Dalvreachk') is named but not depicted, although its presence can reasonably be inferred. The picture was much the same in 1783 and 1794, although the form of the names had altered and one had been fully anglicised (Sidh Chaluim) 'Malcolm's Seat'.

Brown's survey of 1808 catches the valley at the height of its development, and provides a valuable insight into the extent and ordering of the pre-Improvement landscape. Both infield and outfield are shown accompanying their respective farms, along with the high hill and moorland grazings beyond the head-dykes. Changes, however, are apparent on both sides of the valley. On the NW, two new farmsteads are depicted: one to the NE of Craig-derig, the other 'Bardnalue' to the WSW of Rhiedorrach (nos. 265·8 and 267·1 respectively). Cloichiernoch is still shown as roofed but appears now under a different name 'Clow or Wester Craig Derg', which may point to a change in tenancy. In addition, Brown depicts the building and enclosure at 'Clow-hairn' (·12); the building is shown as unroofed but its function is not apparent. However, the evidence is probably best interpreted, as the name would imply, as the remains of 'The Lairds' Burial-ground', the precedessor, perhaps, to the chapel and burial-ground at Spittal.

On the SE side of the valley the buildings at Cro na h-Airighe are depicted but are unshaded, which would suggest that they were unroofed. This is in conflict with the Spittal headstone, which records that Donald Ramsay was in possession of 'Cronaherie' until 1813. Miller, however, notes the sale of Gormel and Cro na h-Airighe, by Colin MacKenzie in 1770, to a Mr Mackintosh who disposed of them ten years later to Farquharson of Invercauld, and it was upon his death that the trustees in 1812 decided to create a single large grazing from the small-holdings in the valley. This is consistent with the picture presented by Thomson in 1825. By this date Cro na h-Airighe and Lag nan Cnaimhean had been removed from the map, and, although only recently established, the farmstead of Bardnalue had also disappeared. What is perhaps surprising, in view of the decision taken in 1812, are the number of farmsteads that still remained in 1825. But these, too, were soon abandoned, for, by 1862 the pattern of desertion was complete and the house and steading at Rhiedorrach alone remained.

— Pont c.1600; *Retours*, Perth, No. 498; Roy 1747–55, sheets 18/4 and 5; Stobie 1783; Ainslie 1794; Brown 1808; Thomson 1825; Miller 1929, 19–20; Caird n.d., 7; Atholl Muniments, 23, xiii; xvi; xvi, 8; xvii, 5.

266 Gleann Beag, Gormel, farmstead
    NO 1330 7481   NO 17 SW 31–2
This farmstead comprises eleven buildings, two kilns, three enclosures and a pen, and its remains are disposed over a terrace at the foot of Meall Gorm and over a limited area of the adjoining haughland. Attached to the head-dyke (NO 1328 7473) there are the well-preserved remains of a round-angled, two-compartment building (11m by 4·5m over stone walls 1·1m thick and up to 1·3m

high in six courses), with a yard on its W side. The building overlies an earlier hut (at least 2·6m by 4·8m overall). To the N, and also attached to the head-dyke, there are two buildings (9m by 3·2m and 5·5m by 4·1m overall), one of which is overlain by another (6·6m by 4·3m overall). The nucleus of the farmstead is provided by buildings on two sides of a yard which connects with the head-dyke on the E. The principal building is of three compartments (14·8m by 5·5m over stone walls up to 0·9m thick and 0·8m high), the southernmost containing a central byre-drain; the entrance (at the S end of the W wall) has a porch and beside it a stone plinth. Its neighbour, which is probably earlier in date, measures 11·6m by 4·3m overall. On the S side of the yard there is a pen, and to the ENE (NO 1338 7486) an enclosure.

On the haughland, two natural knolls have been adapted as enclosures. On one (NO 1326 7480) there are the remains of a building measuring 9·2m by 4·6m overall, while on the other there are two buildings set at right angles to one another (8m by 4·9m and 9·2m by 4·9m overall respectively); the larger has opposed lateral entrances. A kiln has been let into the slope to the SSE (NO 1326 7474) and to the NW (NO 1322 7483) there are the well-preserved remains of a kiln-and-chamber. The haughland has been cultivated and there are a number of clearance-cairns in the vicinity. Some 400m S of the farmstead (NO 1314 7443) there are the remains of a building (8·7m by 5·2m overall) with a drainage-hood on the E; downslope, to the W of the head-dyke, there is a large stone-walled enclosure.

In the 13th century the shielings at Gormel went with the farm of Finegand, as they did in 1680. The farmstead of 'Gorumhul' is depicted by Archer (1749), Roy (1747–55, sheet 18/4), Stobie (1783), Ainslie (1794), Brown (1808) and Thomson (1825). In 1770 it was sold by Colin MacKenzie (of Finegand) to a Mr Mackintosh, who disposed of it ten years later to Farquharson of Invercauld.

— Smith 1899, i–ii, n. 16; Miller 1929, 17, 19; Caird n.d., 7; Atholl Muniments, 23, xvi, 8.

267 Gleann Beag, Rhiedorrach, farmstead, buildings and shieling
A farmstead and three buildings are visible to the W of the old road at Rhiedorrach; another building and a shieling lie 580m NW and 1·1 km WSW respectively.

·1 NO 1265 7404   NO 17 SW 94–7
The remains of the farmstead of Bardnalue (Brown 1808) occupy a terrace to the SW of Rhiedorrach and comprise buildings on three sides of a yard with a fourth to the SE. All are either severely wasted or reduced to their wall-footings and they range from 7m by 4·2m to 14·6m by 5·8m overall; the last is probably a two-compartment building and is overlain by a stone wall enclosing a field to the SW. To the W of Rhiedorrach (NO 1255 7409), and overlain by the modern field-wall, there are the remains of a building (13·2m by 3·7m overall) and a yard, on the NE side of which there is a pen. Beside the Allt Coolah (NO 1253 7403) there are the remains of a stone-walled enclosure. Another building (9·7m by 4·5m overall) occupies a terrace about 110m WNW of Rhiedorrach (NO 1263 7417), while less than 50m to the NNW (NO 1269 7416) there are the remains of a two-compartment building (17·3m by 3·7m overall) with an attached enclosure. There are no visible remains of the farmstead of 'Ridorach', which stood beside the Military Road, on or close to the site now occupied by the present house; it is depicted on the maps by Archer (1749), Roy (1747–55, sheet 18/5), Stobie (1783), Ainslie (1794), Brown (1808) and Thomson (1825), but is shown unroofed on the first edition of the OS 6-inch map (Perthshire, 1867, sheet 15).

·2 NO 1236 7458   NO 17 SW 98
This building has been levelled into the slope beside an unnamed tributary, close to its confluence with the Allt Coolah. It measures 8·5m by 4·5m over stone walls up to 0·8m in height in five courses; the entrance is at the ESE end of the WNW wall.

·3 NO 1174 7367   NO 17 SW 99
This remarkably well-preserved shieling-hut stands on the E flank of Creagan Bheithe (560m OD). Rectangular on plan, with rounded external angles, it measures 5·5m by 3·2m over rubble walls 0·6m in thickness; its W gable stands up to 1·6m high in twelve courses, and elsewhere its walls are 0·8m in average height. The entrance is at the S end of the E wall.

268 Gleann Beag, shielings
A series of shieling groups is situated at the head of Gleann Beag.

·1 NO 1293 7499   NO 17 SW 93
On the E flank of Creagan Dearg there are at least two buildings and an enclosure. One of the buildings (and also a possible third building) adjoins the enclosure, whose stone wall extends around a natural hollow in the hillside. The other building, which has a possible outshot at its SSW end, lies to the N. The two buildings measure 8·3m by 4m and 8·9m by 4·3m overall respectively.

·2 NO 133 752   NO 17 NW 5–10
In rough ground around the fank that stands at the confluence of the Allt a' Choire Dhirich and the Allt a' Ghlinne Bhig (NO 1335 7519 to 1347 7535), there are the remains of at least five buildings, two huts, a kiln and a pen. The huts and buildings are all reduced to their wall-footings (some more wasted than others) and range from 5·3m by 4m to 10·7m by 6·1m overall. Immediately to the S of the fank there are the wasted remains of a building and a pen; a further 20m to the SSW there is a second building, from which a bank extends NW to the Military Road, before turning to follow the road towards the fank. On the haugh to the E of the Allt a' Ghlinne Bhig, about 60m SSE of the fank (NO 1339 7517), there are two buildings, set parallel to each other 24m apart; one is of two compartments and both are overlain by the footings of a stone wall which extends upslope to the SSE.

On the bank of the Allt a' Choire Dhirich, to the E of the fank (NO 1340 7525), there are the remains of a building, while 50m to the NNE (NO 1341 7532) there is what may be a kiln. The peat-covered and wasted remains of two huts (probably bothies) are let into the crest of a conspicuous knoll (NO 1347 7535) a further 60m to the NE.

·3 NO 139 755   NO 17 NW 4, 11–14
This shieling group, which comprises at least five buildings, three enclosures and a pen, is situated on the SE side of the glen at the confluence of the Allt Choire a' Bhathaich and the Allt a' Choire Sheiridh. The buildings are all reduced to turf-covered stone wall-footings and range from 3·5m by 2·5m to 10m by 1·9m overall. At the centre of the group (NO 1390 7550) there is a double enclosure with two buildings, one of two compartments (possibly overlying an earlier structure), the other with a sunken floor. About 80m to the WSW there is a third building (NO 1382 7548), while beside the Allt Choire a' Bhathaich 40m E and 90m ESE respectively, there are a

further two buildings (NO 1395 7552 and 1398 7546). About 60 m SW of the latter on a hill terrace at the foot of Meall Gorm (NO 1392 7542), there are the remains of a building and an enclosure (the latter has a pen on its ENE side), and upslope there are the remains of another pen (NO 1397 7537).

·4 NO 1394 7562   NO 17 NW 3
This shieling occupies a grass-covered terrace at the foot of Creag nan Carn on the NW side of the glen. It consists of three huts, a building and a pen. The huts are all reduced to turf-covered wall-footings and range from 3·4 m by 2·8 m to 5·9 m by 2 m overall; one has a sunken floor. The building has two compartments and measures 10·8 m by 2·6 m within walls 0·8 m in thickness and 0·7 m in height. Beside the Allt a' Choire Sheiridh (NO 1404 7565) there is a stone-walled enclosure. This is the shieling of 'Ru Cloich' ('Lechory' on Roy's map; 1747–55, sheet 18/5), which is shown as abandoned on Brown's 1808 survey, and belonged to the hill ground of Rhiedorrach.

·5 NO 144 752   NO 17 NW 16
Five shieling-huts are strung out over a distance of 100 m along the S flank of Leacann Dubh (known as the Middle Ridge). Subrectangular and rectangular on plan, they range from 5 m by 3·9 m to 10·8 m by 3·6 m over stone wall-footings. The two easternmost huts are set end-to-end; adjacent to one there is an irregularly-shaped mound, and by the other there is an enclosure.

·6 NO 1464 7522   NO 17 NW 16
Two subrectangular huts (the larger 9·2 m by 4·3 m) and a pen lie 150 m to the E of (·4). Two more huts are situated 80 m NW (NO 1458 7527) and 240 m NE (NO 1486 7535) respectively.

·7 NO 1480 7508   NO 17 NW 17
A group of four huts is situated on the SE side of the glen 200 m SE of (·5). The uppermost is particularly well preserved (5·7 m by 4·2 m over walls up to 1·1 m high in six courses) and has what is either an outshot or the remains of an earlier building on its SSW side. The other three range from 7·3 m by 3·2 m to 9·7 m by 4·1 m overall; one has been dug into the slope and its rear wall – no more than a masonry revetment of the backslope – still stands to a height of 1·1 m.

269 Gleann Fearnach, Allt Linne a' Bhuirein, shielings
NO 051 693   NO 06 NE 86
Three shieling-huts are situated immediately SE of an enclosure on a terrace on the N side of the Allt Linne a' Bhuirein (510 m OD). One of the huts is turf-built with a funnel-shaped entrance and the other two are rectangular. The more northerly of the latter is grass grown and probably overlies a second turf hut with a funnel-shaped entrance, but the other is stone built with two compartments and an outshot at its SE end. What is probably a fourth hut is situated on the N bank of the stream 40 m to the SW, and others can be seen further down the glen to the W, outside the area of survey.

270 Gleann Fearnach, Coire Domhain, shielings
NO 052 709   NO 07 SE 44
This group of shieling-huts is situated at the head of the Allt Ruigh nan Eas on the N side of Coire Domhain (600 m OD). The main group comprises at least twelve huts strung along a narrow terrace. Six of them are stone-built with walls up to 0·6 m high, and they range in shape from subcircular to rectangular; of the rest, which are of much slighter construction and wholly grass-grown, three

are overlain by stone-built huts. Outlying huts occur 70 m to the W (NO 051 710) and 100 m to the NNW (NO 051 711).

271 Gleann Fearnach, Creag Dubh-leitir, Pitcarmick-type building
NO 0582 6411   NO 06 SE 125
On the S flank of Creag Dubh-leitir and levelled into the slope, there are the remains of a Pitcarmick-type building. *121* It is round-ended and measures 13·5 m by up to 6·7 m over walls spread up to 1·5 m in thickness. The entrance is central to the SSW wall, which is thicker at this point, and was provided with a baffle (3·1 m long overall); the floor-level at the ESE end of the building seems to be slightly sunken. A drainage-bank extends the length of the rear-wall and hooks round the end of the building to form an enclosure on the WSW side of the entrance. Close by there is a scatter of small cairns (no. 121·18).

272 Gleann Fearnach, Creag Dubh-leitir, fermtouns, farmsteads, buildings and shielings
At the mouth of Gleann Fearnach, disposed over the slopes and terraces on the S flank of Creag Dubh-leitir and bounded on the E by the Dirnanean march dyke, there are a series of small fermtouns, farmsteads and shielings, together with a number of other buildings, one of which is of Pitcarmick type (no. 271).

·1 NO 0512 6421   NO 06 SE 118
Immediately to the NW of Castle Pirnie Cottage and flanked by two enclosures, there are the wasted remains of what has been a sizeable building (13·5 m by 6·2 m over turf-covered stone wall-footings) together with a number of linear clearance-heaps. The remains may be those of the farmstead of Balnacoine which is named and depicted by Roy (1747–55, sheet 17/2), Stobie (1783), Grainger (1818) and Douglas (1826).

·2 NO 0526 6404   NO 06 SE 120
Beside the track 150 m SSE of the cottage, there are the remains of a small fermtoun comprising at least seven buildings and a kiln-and-chamber. The buildings seem to be randomly disposed: one has an adjoining enclosure with a pen on its NW side, and another is fronted by a yard. With the exception of two, all are single-compartment structures and these range from 9 m by 4·7 m to 13·8 m by 4·9 m over stone wall-footings about 0·9 m thick. The building which gives on to a yard is a two-compartment structure (12·2 m by 4·8 m overall), which lies at the centre of the fermtoun; it has a drainage-trench to the rear and the entrance is central to its SW wall. Immediately to the W there are the remains of a substantial three-compartment building (19·2 m by 5·8 m over turf-covered stone wall-footings up to 1 m thick and 0·4 m high); this has a drainage-trench to the rear and an entrance central to its SSE wall, and at its W end there are traces of what may be an earlier building. To the SW of the yard and adjoined by a later dyke, there is a building (13·8 m by 4·9 m overall) with an outshot at its NW end (8 m by 4·9 m overall); entrances to both are in the SW wall. To the ENE there are the remains of a probable burial cairn (no. 40·2) and extending over the terrace to the rear of the fermtoun there are at least fifteen small cairns, clearance-heaps and traces of rig-and-furrow.

·3 NO 0535 6392   NO 06 SE 117, 122
On either side of the track about 100 m SE of (·2), there are the remains of a small fermtoun. This comprises six buildings, three enclosures and a kiln. The principal

building (14·1 m by 5·1 m over turf-covered stone wall-footings 0·9 m thick and up to 0·5 m high) stands on the NE side of the track and is aligned with the contour. To the SW and at right angles to it, there are the wasted remains of what may be another (6·6 m by 4·4 m overall); the kiln lies immediately to the S. A little upslope there are the remains of a building (9·4 m by 4·3 m overall) with a slightly sunken interior, to which an open-fronted outshot (6·8 m by 3·1 m overall) and a further unit (4·5 m by 5 m overall) have been added on the NW. A low turf-covered bank connects this building with a two-compartment building (12·5 m by 5 m overall) immediately to the SSE. To the S beside the track there is a building (8·4 m by 4·3 m overall) and an enclosure; a dyke springs from the latter and extends to (·2). On the SW side of the track there are the remains of a substantial four-compartment building (20 m by 4·3 m over turf-covered stone wall-footings 0·7 m thick and up to 0·4 m high) with entrances to three of the compartments in the SW wall; at the NW end of the same wall, there is a midden-hollow. A number of enclosures lie to the SE and NW, and beside one there are the remains of a building (9·6 m by 5·1 m overall) with what may be a partially sunken store at its SSW end (2·6 m by 3·5 m overall). Close by there is a series of lynchets, some of which are within enclosures, and traces of rig-and-furrow. The remains, together with those described in (·2), are probably to be identified as 'Ballintuim' which is named and depicted by Roy (1747–55, sheet 17/2), Stobie (1783), Grainger (1818) and Douglas (1826). Upslope (NO 0546 6405) there are the wasted remains of a hut (5·5 m by 3·4 m overall) with an enclosure on its SW side. See also nos. 40·1, 159.

·4   NO 0555 6387   NO 06 SE 28
Disposed over a terrace to the ESE of (·3), there are the remains of what is probably a small fermtoun comprising at least twelve buildings and a kiln. The buildings are all reduced to turf-covered stone wall-footings and range from 6·6 m by 4·1 m to 19·3 m by 6·5 m overall. The largest building, which is round-angled and has two compartments, is one of a row of five buildings strung out on roughly the same alignment along a low ridge towards the rear of the terrace. Immediately to the SW and parallel with these buildings, there are three enclosures; two have accompanying pens. The kiln, which has chambers at both ends (12·5 m by 6 m overall), is situated adjacent to another building some 30 m to the SSE. Extending across the slope there are traces of rig-and-furrow cultivation.

·5   NO 0573 6393   NO 06 SE 29, 123
Strung out over a ridge of ground to the ENE of (·4), there are the remains of a fermtoun comprising at least nine buildings, three enclosures and two kilns. The buildings are all reduced to their turf-covered stone wall-footings and range from 6·2 m by 4·8 m to 16·1 m by 4·2 m overall (the largest is a two-compartment building). Three are distinguished by the provision of an ancillary structure set at right angles to the rear of the main compartment; the largest of these measures 5·9 m by 3·3 m overall. A series of lynchets extends downslope from the fermtoun and some are overlain by rig-and-furrow. The fermtoun of Kerrow appears on the maps of Roy (1747–55, sheet 17/2), Stobie (1783), Grainger (1818) and Douglas (1826). Upslope from the fermtoun (NO 0578 6400), there are the turf- and heather-covered remains of another building (9·2 m by 4·4 m overall).

·6   NO 0553 6351   NO 06 SE 131–2
At the corner of the field on the NE side of the public road NW of Tulloch, there are the remains of what may be a small fermtoun comprising at least six buildings;

these are grouped on either side of the track leading down from (·3). The buildings are all reduced to their turf-covered stone wall-footings and range from 6·8 m by 4·2 m to 11·3 m by 5·7 m overall. Two are set at right angles to each other at the junction between the track and a burn; the angle between the two buildings has been infilled by an outshot and to the SE there is a small enclosure. On the NW side of the burn, a building has been levelled into the slope at the head of another enclosure to which a further enclosure has been added on the SW. Upslope, to the ENE of these buildings (NO 0560 6355), there are the remains of a farmstead comprising four buildings ranged with a yard. The principal building, which has been levelled into the slope, is represented by a stance (12·3 m by 4·9 m overall); the others are all reduced to turf-covered stone wall-footings and range from 7·1 m by 4·1 m to 10·5 m by 4·1 m overall. On the WNW side of the yard there is a well-preserved plinth (3·9 m by 2·1 m overall and up to 0·3 m high in three courses). Collectively, the remains are probably to be identified as the fermtoun of Tomindoun which is depicted by Roy (1747–55, sheet 17/2); it appears as 'Tominturie' on the maps of Stobie (1783), Grainger (1818) and Douglas (1826).

·7   NO 0537 6358   NO 06 SE 130
On the S side of the A924, overlooking the burn to the WNW of (·6), there are the remains of a farmstead which consists of four buildings ranged with a yard. The principal building, which is of two compartments (16·5 m by 5·1 m overall), occupies the NE side of the yard and has a drainage-trench to the rear and an entrance central to its SW wall; the remaining buildings range from 5·2 m by 4 m to 12·3 m by 4 m overall. The yard has a slightly sunken interior and is drained on the SW by a gully; on this side there is an elongated pen and to the SE of the yard a quarry-scoop. A hollow track extends upslope from the burn to the NW of the farmstead. Stobie (1783) depicts the farmstead of 'Tulloch' but it is unclear whether the name should be applied to this site or to that of the present house (NO 0559 6335).

·8   NO 0561 6411   NO 06 SE 30
About 150 m to the NNW of (·5), there is the first in a series of farmsteads and buildings which are disposed over an area of unimproved ground that rises to the rear of the main terrace. Most of this area, however, lies within the tract of ground bounded by the old head-dyke which extends upslope from (·5); the course of the dyke is depicted by Grainger (1818) and Douglas (1826). The farmstead consists of a round-angled, two-compartment building (12·7 m by 5 m over turf-covered stone walls reduced to their lowest courses 0·8 m thick and up to 0·6 m high) with an outshot on the NW, which stands at the head of a double enclosure. Beside the mid-wall of the enclosure there are traces of another structure (8·4 m by 4·5 m overall), and to the SSW there are the remains of a two-compartment building (13·1 m by 4·5 m overall); to the SSW there is a D-shaped enclosure and to the WNW a pen. Extending upslope from the farmstead there is a series of well-preserved lynchets.

·9   NO 0554 6416   NO 06 SE 119, 127
Levelled into the slope to the NW of (·8), there are the remains of an unusual round-ended building (17·5 m by up to 6·7 m over stone walls about 1·2 m thick and up to 0·7 m high in three courses) which has been modified by the addition of a second unit at its ESE end (7·3 m by up to 5·6 m overall). This second unit has what may be the opening for a byre-drain central to its end-wall. The main compartment, which has a drainage-hood to the rear, has a possible entrance central to its SSW wall and another at the WNW end of the same wall, which opens in to an

enclosure. About 110m to the N (NO 0553 6428), there are the wasted remains of a three-compartment building and enclosure.

·10 NO 0539 6421   NO 06 SE 103
Beside the fence to the WSW of the last building mentioned in (·9), there are the remains of a building measuring 9·8m by 4·6m over turf-covered stone wall-footings 0·8m in thickness and 0·5m in height. This has an entrance central to its SSW wall, which opens in to a yard, and to the SSE there is an enclosure. A series of well-preserved lynchets extends upslope from the line of the fence; some are stone revetted.

·11 NO 0535 6444   NO 06 SE 106
Some 230m N of (·10) there are the turf-covered stone wall-footings of a building (8·6m by 3·8m overall) with a subdivided enclosure on its S side. Downslope, immediately to the S, there are the remains of a two-compartment building 10·8m by 3·9m over stone wall-footings 0·8m thick and 0·6m high) which has a drainage-bank to the rear and entrances to both compartments in the SSW wall. About 40m to the SE, beside a burn, there is a building (5·9m by 4·1m over heather-covered stone and boulder wall-footings 0·8m thick and 0·4m high) with an entrance central to its SW wall; more recently a pen has been constructed at its NW end.

·12 NO 0526 6448   NO 06 SE 104–05
On a heather-clad slope about 90m WNW of (·11), there are the remains of a shieling comprising two buildings and an enclosure. The larger of the two buildings measures 9m by 4·6m over stone walls 0·8m in thickness and 0·6m in height, and has an entrance central to its SSW wall. The second, immediately to the WSW, measures 6·6m by 3·8m overall; the enclosure, which is D-shaped, is attached to its SSW wall. Upslope (NO 0527 6452), there are the well-preserved remains of a two-compartment building (14·3m by 3·6m overall) with what may be either an earlier building or an additional two units at its WSW end (7·6m by 3·7m overall); the entrance to each compartment is in the SSW wall.

·13 NO 0529 6463   NO 06 SE 108
On a grass-covered terrace, beside a conspicuous boulder to the NNE of (·12), there are the remains of a round-angled two compartment building (10·5m by 3·6m over turf-covered stone wall-footings 0·8m thick and 0·5m high) with an outshot on the ESE. At the NE corner there is a pen and on the SSW a yard, on the ESE side of which there is a second building (8·9m by 4·8m overall) with an entrance central to its SSW wall; both the second building and an enclosure which adjoins its SSW side are integral with the old head-dyke.

·14 NO 0537 6485   NO 06 SE 109–10, NO 06 NE 65
Some 230m NNE of (·13), in the angle between the old head-dyke and a modern fence, there are the remains of a round-ended building (18·1m by 3·9m over turf-covered stone wall-footings 0·7m thick) with an enclosure on its S side; about 50m to the SSE (NO 0542 6477) there is a second enclosure. About 150m to the N of the round-ended building (NO 0534 6500), there are the remains of a building with an entrance on the W, measuring 11·3m by 6·5m over walls spread up to 1·4m in thickness. Close by there are two hut-circles (no. 116·1) and a burnt mound (no. 167).

·15 NO 0559 6461   NO 06 SE 111–12
Some 300m SE of (·14) and situated at the head of a series of broad strip-fields, there are the remains of a probable farmstead comprising a building (9·5m by 5m over turf-covered stone wall-footings 0·8m thick) with an enclosure on its S side. A circular stone-setting on the SW side of the building may be a stance. To the NE, occupying a low knoll (NO 0560 6467), there are the wasted remains of another building (7·5m by 4·7m overall).

·16 NO 0543 6453   NO 06 SE 107
About 160m WSW of (·15) there are the truncated remains of a two-compartment building with an adjoining enclosure on its SW side. The building measures 9·8m by 4·1m over turf-covered stone walls reduced to their lowest courses (0·8m in thickness and 0·5m in height).

·17 NO 0560 6448   NO 06 SE 113–16
Towards the head of the strip-fields to the S of (·16), there are the remains of two buildings which have been aligned with the contour. These measure 7·3m by 4m and 9·2m by 3·8m respectively over turf-covered stone wall-footings up to 1·1m in thickness and 0·4m in height; beside the larger of the two buildings there is a pen. To the SW (NO 0558 6444) there are the well-preserved remains of a round-angled four-compartment building with a stone-walled enclosure on its SSW side. The building measures 18·5m by 4·4m over turf-covered stone walls up to 1·1m in thickness by 1·1m in height in eight courses, and is noteworthy for the way in which a large earthfast boulder has been incorporated in the line of its NNE wall; the entrance was probably on the SSW. At the foot of a rock outcrop (NO 0562 6441) there are the remains of another building (6·5m by 3·9m over turf-covered stone walls 0·8m thick and 0·4m high), and to the SE, and peripheral to the strip-fields (NO 0575 6431), there is one more (7·6m by 3·8m overall).

·18 NO 0575 6410   NO 06 SE 126
Beside the burn some 200m to the S of the last building described in (·17) and levelled into the slope, there are the remains of two buildings and an enclosure. Both buildings are reduced to turf- and heather-covered stone wall-footings and measure 7·7m by 3·7m and 9m by 4·3m respectively overall.

·19 NO 0577 6404   NO 06 SE 124
To the SSE of (·18) there are the remains of two buildings which are connected by a bank; both are reduced to turf- and heather-covered stone wall-footings and they measure 9·7m by 4·3m and 5·2m by 3·6m overall. Immediately to the NW there are the remains of another building (10·8m by 3·9m overall) and this has an outshot at right angles to its main compartment (6·2m by 4·1m overall); the entrance is central to the SW wall.

·20 NO 0592 6410   NO 06 SE 128
On a ridge of higher ground to the ENE of (·19), there are the remains of two unusual buildings, whose walls are reduced to low banks between 1·5m and 3·3m in thickness. The first is round-ended and overall measures 18·5m in length by up to 8·6m in width on the SE, narrowing to 6·4m on the NW; the interior, however, is consistently 3·5m wide. There is an entrance central to the SW wall (at which point the wall is spread up to 3·3m thick) and possibly another opening into an enclosure at its NW end; another enclosure adjoins the SE end of the building. Immediately to the S and occupying a similar position (NO 0592 6405), there are the remains of another building which seems to be of similar character. It, too, is round-ended, but overall the building is more regular in shape (15·5m by 7·2m over walls up to 1·5m thick). The entrance was central to the WSW wall and at the NNW end of the building there is an enclosure; for another building, which may also be of this type, see (·9) above.

273 Gleann Fearnach, Loch Crannach, farmsteads and shieling

Within lower Gleann Fearnach there are extensive remains of pre-Improvement settlement and agriculture. Most of these settlements lie outside the area of survey, but a few have been identified on the slopes between Crannach, now a holiday house, and Loch Crannach, which lies in a natural basin about 1 km to the NW. A series of groups of shieling-huts occurs on terraces and knolls in the glen that extends a further 2 km to the NNE beyond the loch.

·1 NO 0507 6677   NO 06 NE 92–3
There are three buildings on the slope NE of Crannach. The northernmost, which is the largest (15 m by 5·3 m overall), is set into the angle between the foot of a lynchet and a field-bank, and the second lies 40 m to the SW. The third building is set immediately NE of what is probably a quarry-pit 50 m NE of Crannach (NO 0501 6667).

·2 NO 0544 6718   NO 06 NE 88
About 200 m SW of Loch Crannach the track leading to the boat-house cuts through the remains of a farmstead comprising three buildings, with a probable fourth building lying in a small enclosure immediately to the ESE and a fifth 80 m to the S. The farmstead appears to be integral with the surrounding pattern of fields enclosed by turf dykes.

·3 NO 0552 6729   NO 06 NE 89
A building some 33 m in overall length is situated along the N side of a small field immediately SW of the dam of Loch Crannach. The building, which has at least five compartments, is likely to represent more than one period of construction as the alignment of its axis changes slightly midway along its length.

·4 NO 0532 6736   NO 06 NE 91
Traces of two buildings (the larger 14 m by 4·2 m overall) lie within a turf-banked enclosure which forms part of the system of enclosed fields surrounding (·2) and (·3). A third building lies in the external angle between the enclosure and the adjacent field-dyke.

·5 NO 0513 6816   NO 06 NE 74
Two stone-built shieling-huts (the larger 9·8 m by 3·1 m overall) and two pens are situated on a terrace at the foot of some crags on the S spur of Creagan Uaine.

·6 NO 0539 6813   NO 06 NE 75
On gently sloping ground 250 m E of (·5) there are at least ten huts and four small enclosures. All the huts are rectangular and stone-built (up to 8·4 m by 3·7 m overall) and one occupies a low mound.

·7 NO 0561 6825   NO 06 NE 76–7
At the foot of the crags on the W flank of the SE spur of Creagan Uaine, there are three stone-built huts. Two are rectangular and one is oval; the larger of the rectangular huts (7 m by 4·7 m overall) occupies a low mound. An outlying hut lies amongst boulders some 150 m to the SE (NO 0572 6813).

·8 NO 0555 6899   NO 06 NE 84–5
A shieling-hut with a possible funnel-shaped entrance is situated in the saddle to the NE of Creagan Uaine; a small enclosure lies immediately to the ENE. Two possible huts lie 150 m to the ENE (NO 0568 6905), and there is an enclosure 150 m to the SSW.

·9 NO 061 692   NO 06 NE 83
A group of five huts, two small enclosures and a large enclosure is situated high up on the SE flank of Sron Charnach. The large enclosure and two of the huts (one stone-built, the other turfed over and occupying a low mound) are situated on a low rise. The two small enclosures lie in the shallow gully to the WNW, and the other three huts are on the slope above them.

·10 NO 0658 6941   NO 06 NE 81–2
A two-compartment building (10·8 m by 4·5 m overall) lies 400 m E of (·9) and 100 m NW of the Allt a' Choire Charnaich. The E compartment is the better preserved and may be a free-standing stone-built hut re-using an earlier site. A second hut lies on the SE bank of the burn 100 m to the SE (NO 0669 6935).

·11 NO 068 690   NO 06 NE 80
Two huts and an enclosure are situated on the SW flank of Sron na Lairige 150 m W of the march fence between Gleann Fearnach and Dirnanean. One is stone-built (6·6 m by 4 m over walls 0·6 m high) with an outshot at the NW end; the other, which lies 60 m to the NW, has three compartments (16 m by 3·8 m overall) and has been built across an earlier mound.

·12 NO 0630 6866   NO 06 NE 78
Two huts and two enclosures are situated on a low spur between the Allt a' Choire Charnaich and the Allt an Leth-choire. The more northerly of the huts is stone-built with two compartments (10·5 m by 4·5 m overall), and there is a small enclosure immediately to the WSW; the more southerly has three compartments (12 m by 5 m overall) and an outshot, and it has been built across an earlier mound about 1 m high. Another small enclosure lies to the WSW.

·13 NO 0603 6876   NO 06 NE 79
About 300 m WNW of (·12), at the foot of the S spur of Sron Charnach, there are at least three huts. The largest (9 m by 3·8 m overall) is stone-built and overlies an earlier hut with a funnel-shaped entrance. The second hut (5·5 m by 4·5 m overall) lies 10 m to the NW, and there is what may be a third 17 m to the SSW.

·14 NO 057 675   NO 06 NE 90
Up to six huts and an enclosure can be identified in the vicinity of the hut-circles in the wood on the E shore of Loch Crannach (see no. 142·6). The largest is crossed by the deer fence on the N side of the wood and measures 12·5 m by 4·4 m overall.

·15 NO 0591 6728   NO 06 NE 87
Three shieling-huts are situated 30 m NW of the NE corner of the wood to the SE of Loch Crannach. Two stand on a narrow ledge at the foot of a steep scarp; one of them has three compartments (16 m by 4·2 m overall), but the central compartment is probably a free-standing structure built into an earlier two- or three-compartment building. The third hut lies at the top of the scarp about 30 m to the N.

·16 NO 059 671   NO 06 NE 73
The largest of the groups of shieling-huts around Loch Crannach extends up the slope to the E of the wood on the SE shore. It consists of at least thirteen huts and five enclosures. Most of the huts are between 7 m and 10 m in length, their walls reduced to low stony banks. Two overlie earlier mounds, one of which measures 16 m by

12 m and 0·6 m in height, and there is a stone-built hut (7 m by 3·5 m over walls up to 0·5 m high) overlying a circular enclosure with an overall diameter of about 11 m.

·17 NO 056 670   NO 06 NE 71–2

'A two-compartment hut is situated on a low rise 25 m SW of the SW corner of the wood on the SE shore of Loch Crannach. A further three huts (the largest 11 m by 4 m overall) and an enclosure lie on gently sloping ground 100 m to the S.

·18 NO 0575 6683   NO 06 NE 70

There are traces of two huts on a slight shoulder 200 m SSE of (·17).

·19 NO 0555 6664   NO 06 NE 69

At least three huts are situated on a low ridge immediately E of the forestry plantation on the E side of the burn that flows out of Loch Crannach. Two of the huts are built into low mounds; another hut and an enclosure lie in the gully to the SE.

274 Gleann Taitneach, farmsteads, buildings and shielings

At Dalmunzie the valley of the Shee divides into its head-waters. The Shee Water is joined on the N by the Allt Ghlinn Thaitneich and on the WNW by the Glen Lochsie Burn. Gleann Taitneach is a long and deeply incised upland glen which bears the evident traces of glaciation. From its confluence with the Shee Water to the Allt Coire Shith (about 1·4 km) the valley floor is relatively broad, and disposed on both sides there are a number of farmsteads, a few shielings and, on the E, a well-preserved group of broad strip-fields as well as a series of lynchets. At the Allt Coire Shith, however, both the character of the landscape and the pattern of settlement change markedly. Scree slopes and valley moraines predominate and are interspersed with a few areas of rough grazing. The latter provide the most favoured locations for the shielings; other sites include glacial knolls, terraces high up on the valley sides and saddles in the lee of moraine deposits.

·1 NO 0916 7169   NO 07 SE 17, 18

Due N of Sheanval (no. 278·10) and occupying a narrow shelf there are the remains of what was probably a two-compartment building (10·6 m by 4·5 m over stone walls up to 0·7 m thick and 0·7 m high in five courses) with a drainage-trench on the E and an entrance towards the N end of its W wall. About 230 m to the N (NO 0917 7191) there are the remains of a second building (11·8 m by 4·1 m overall) which is similarly located; it has an entrance towards the S end of its W wall. To the E of the modern track ascending the glen, and in proximity to the above buildings, there is a series of lynchets and extensive traces of broad-rig cultivation.

·2 NO 0903 7245   NO 07 SE 19

Some 550 m N of (·1) in broken ground beside the Allt Coire Shith, there are the remains of a farmstead which comprises at least seven buildings and an enclosure. With one exception, the buildings are reduced either to the lowest courses of their stone walls, or to their wall-footings. They range from 6 m by 2·6 m to 12 m by 5·2 m overall (the smallest let into the slope and probably a potato store). The best preserved building (still roofed in 1808) stands immediately to the ENE of the modern track. It is substantial (9·5 m by 5·2 m over walls 0·8 m thick and up to 1·3 m high) and well constructed, with walls of rubble masonry built to a course. The interior is divided into two compartments by an inserted cross-wall

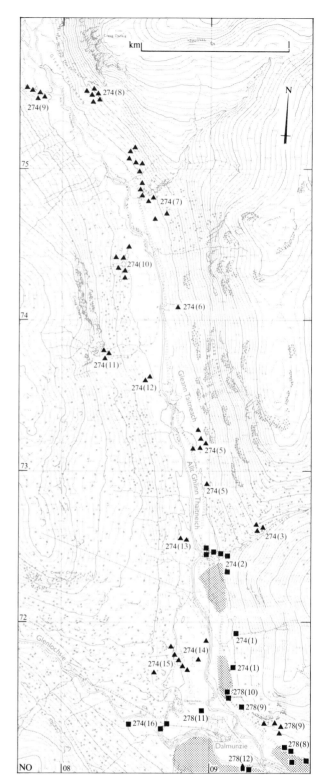

274 Gleann Taitneach, 1:25 000

with independent access to each compartment. Of note, however, are the wasted remains of a still larger building which occupies a stance within the present sheep-pens to the N of the Allt Coire Shith. At right angles to it, and overlain by the modern field-wall, there is a two-compartment building with a pen at its NE angle. The buildings correspond to an unnamed farmstead which is depicted by Stobie (1783); Brown (1808) provides the name of 'Sheal of Ault Corrhee'. To the S there is a series of broad strip-fields (about 3·3 ha in extent) within which can be seen a number of lynchets and traces of rig-and-furrow. At the head of the fields (NO 0911 7232) there are the remains of another building (12·6m by 4·2m over stone walls 0·8m thick and up to 1·3m high in eight courses), which has been levelled into the slope; the S end-wall appears to have been unusually thick. The building was still roofed in 1808.

·3   NO 0934 7261   NO 07 SE 43
About 300m ENE of (·2) on the S flank of Creag Lamhaich (490m OD), there are the remains of two buildings at right angles to each other, which measure respectively 8·6m by 4m and 6·2m by 3·2m over turf-covered stone wall-footings. To the NNW (NO 0932 7263) there are the remains of what may be a small hut (4·1m by 2·5m overall).

·4   NO 0985 7286 to 0979 7303   NO 07 SE 42,
                                    NO 17 SW 103
Some 560m ENE of (·3), between Gleann Taitneach and Coire Shith (outside the area shown on the map) there are the remains of a shieling. Beside the path at the foot of the S-facing slope there are the remains of a hut (4·9m by 3·9m overall), which overlies an earlier building measuring 8·3m by 4·3m overall. To the SE there is an enclosure. Upslope (575m OD), on a terrace, there are the well-preserved remains of a hut (3·9m by 3·5m over stone walls 0·6m thick and up to 0·6m high in five courses); the jamb-wall at the entrance in the S wall stands 1·5m high. The hut overlies an earlier building (12·5m by 5m over turf- and heather-covered stone wall-footings 1m thick), which has a drainage-trench on its NNW side and a small pen on the NE. On a higher terrace (600m OD) there are the remains of a two-compartment building (5·9m by 3m over rubble walls which originally stood at least 0·7m high); its ENE end has been modified to form a pen, and on the S there is an enclosure. Some 750m to the E (NO 1055 7317) there are the well-preserved remains of a subrectangular building (4·4m by 3m over stone walls 0·5m thick and up to 1·3m high), possibly a shooting-bothy, which overlies an earlier building (6·8m by 4·2m over boulder-walls of orthostatic construction up to 0·5m high). The abandoned shieling of 'Rie-na-hiskin' which went with the grazings of Gleann Taitneach and Cuthels, is depicted by Brown (1808).

·5   NO 0897 7291 to 0892 7325   NO 07 SE 21
About 450m N of (·2) and disposed over broken, heather-covered ground at the foot of Creag Lamhaich, there is a shieling which comprises at least three huts, a building, an enclosure and a pen. The huts are all reduced to their turf-covered stone wall-footings and range from 3m by 2·3m to 8m by 3·8m overall. The building, which stands beside a conspicuous valley-moraine, is of two compartments and measures 9·3m by 3·3m over stone walls 0·6m in thickness and up to 0·8m in height in five courses; it has an entrance central to its W wall and, on the N, a pen.

·6   NO 0876 7407   NO 07 SE 22, 38
Some 830m N of (·5), on a knoll, there are the remains of a shieling which consists of at least two buildings and an enclosure. The first building is round-angled and measures 9·8m by 4·7m over turf-covered stone wall-footings up to 1·2m in thickness; its masonry has been re-used to form a grouse-butt. The neighbouring building, which is also round-angled, measures 6·6m by 4·1m overall. An enclosure lies in a hollow immediately to the E, and adjoining its N side there are the remains of what may be a hut (5·8m by 2·2m overall) with a lintelled creep on the E. To the NNW (NO 0871 7412), at the foot of the knoll and beside an unnamed burn, there is another enclosure.

·7   NO 0846 7512 to 0861 7465   NO 07 SE 11
Disposed across the lower slopes crossed by the Allt Aulich, some 500m N of (·6), there are at least twelve shieling-huts, an enclosure and a pen. The huts are reduced to either the lowest courses of their stone walls or to their wall-footings and range from 4·6m by 2·8m to 8·3m by 3·3m overall; three have attached pens, one has an outshot, and several have drains emitting from their side-walls.

·8   NO 0821 7544 to 0815 7551   NO 07 NE 1-2, 5
In broken ground, on and peripheral to the saddle at the rear of a knoll (490m OD), about 410m NNW of (·7), there are the remains of a shieling comprising at least seven huts, an enclosure and a pen. The huts are reduced to the lowest courses of their stone walls, or to their wall-footings, and range from 3·3m by 2·5m to 8·9m by 6·4m overall (the largest of two compartments). One hut possesses an outshot, and at least two may overlie earlier buildings (NO 0819 7545 and NO 0815 7551 respectively). To the SW, beside the track (NO 0809 7538), there are the remains of what may be another hut (5·5m by 3·6m overall), while about 400m to the NNW, at the foot of Creag Dallaig (NO 0793 7574), there is an enclosure. This enclosure, formed within a boulder scree, marks the limit of shieling activity on the E side of the valley.

·9   NO 0779 7550   NO 07 NE 3-4
On the W side of the glen there is an extensive area of rough grazing flanking the lower slopes beneath Glas Choire Mhor, and towards the rear of the river terrace there are a number of well-preserved shielings. On the N bank of the Allt Glas a' Choire Mhoir (470m OD), there are the remains of four buildings and a 19th-century fank. The first building (NO 0778 7550) measures 5·4m by 3·2m over stone walls 0·9m in thickness and 0·3m in height, and overlies what is probably an earlier building on its S side (5·3m by 4·3m overall). Immediately to the S, there are the remains of a two-compartment building (8·9m by 3·8m over walls 0·9m thick and 0·3m high). Around the two buildings the ground has largely been cleared of boulders and is divided into a series of strips, presumably for cultivation. At the head of the cleared ground (NO 0774 7552) there is a rather unusual building which has been levelled into the slope. It measures 11·3m by up to 3·9m over heather-covered stone walls up to 0·8m in height internally. The end-walls are round-angled and that on the SE, which encloses a small mural chamber or annexe, is battered. The entrance is at the NW end of the SW wall and is fitted with an internal baffle-wall. Another building is set end-on to the burn (NO 0784 7550). It measures 7·6m by up to 2m within walls up to 1·1m in thickness, and has been partially constructed by digging-away the centre of a natural mound to achieve some internal depth for the structure (the inner wall-face on the N is up to 0·4m high in five courses). There are traces of a partition-wall at the narrower N end, and the entrance is central to the W wall which is slightly out-turned. To the S of the burn (NO 0787 7546) there are the remains of two more buildings ranged with a yard; both buildings are reduced to turf-covered wall-footings, and the larger of the two measures 6·2m by 3·5m overall. The shieling of 'Glass Chorry' is shown as abandoned on Brown's 1808 survey.

·10 NO 0844 7446 to 0839 7426   NO 07 SE 10
Disposed over the lower slopes of Creag Dhearg, to the SSE of (·9), there are the remains of a shieling comprising five buildings, three enclosures and two pens. The buildings are either subrectangular or rectangular on plan and range from 5·8m by 3·8m to 15·8m by 3·2m over

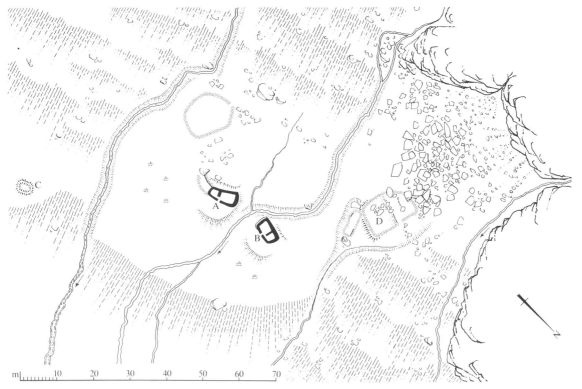

274·11 Gleann Taitneach, shieling, 1:1000

stone walls up to 1·5 m high (the largest is a two-
compartment building). The best preserved building (NO
0844 7446) is of one compartment but has an outshot on
the E, and in the interior there are a number of possible
cruck-slots.

·11 NO 0829 7375   NO 07 SE 24
To the SSW of (·10) and occupying a commanding
position, high up on the W side of Gleann Taitneach
(480 m OD), there are the remains of a shieling
comprising two stone-built huts (A, B), a turf-built hut
(C), two enclosures, and a pen. The terrace on which the
huts are located is drained by a number of streams. Huts
A and B are similar in design and both are reduced to the
lowest courses of their stone walls. Each is round-angled
with battered end-walls and divided into two
compartments by an upstanding cross-wall (probably an
original roof support); that of A stands 1·2 m high in eight
courses. Both huts are furnished with drainage-banks,
and A has a pen at its SSE end. A structure, which may
be a building, adjoins the subdivided enclosure at the foot
of a boulder scree (D).

·12 NO 0858 7361   NO 07 SE 23
To the ESE of (·11), at the foot of the slope, there are the
turf-covered stone wall-footings of at least two
rectangular buildings, the larger of the two measuring 9 m
by 3·6 m overall.

·13 NO 0882 7255   NO 07 SE 20
About 1 km S of (·12), at the rear of a natural hollow,
there are the remains of a shieling which consists of two
stone-built huts and an enclosure. The larger of the two
huts is subrectangular and measures 9·9 m by 3·9 m over
stone walls 0·8 m in thickness and 0·5 m in height. It has an
entrance central to its E wall and a corbelled pen has been
constructed towards the S end of the interior.

·14 NO 0897 7187   NO 07 SE 16, 26
At right angles to the Allt Ghlinn Thaitneich there are the
remains of an open-ended building (6·2 m by 4·9 m over

stone wall-footings); about 130 m to the SSW (NO 0891
7175) there are the remains of another building (9·5 m by
4·8 m overall).

·15 NO 0870 7189 to 0882 7169   NO 07 SE 14–15
Upslope of ·14 and partly within a modern plantation,
there are the remains of at least six buildings, two
enclosures and a pen. The buildings range from 7·2 m by
4·4 m to 9·9 m by 4·6 m overall; one is of two
compartments and another (NO 0873 7181) overlies an
earlier building. Upslope (NO 0861 7165), on a ridge of
higher ground, there are the remains of a further
building. This has an entrance central to its S wall and
measures 6·7 m by 3·7 m over stone walls reduced to their
lowest courses (0·8 m in thickness and up to 0·5 m in
height).

·16 NO 0867 7131   NO 07 SE 3, 25
About 100 m SSW of Glenlochsie farmsteading there are
the remains of a building and, 30 m to the NE, a kiln-and-
chamber. The building measures 10·4 m by 3·8 m over
turf-covered stone wall-footings; the entrance is central to
the S wall and what may be a byre-drain issues from the E
end-wall. Some 240 m to the W, at the edge of the river
terrace of the Glen Lochsie Burn, there are the remains
of a two-compartment building (16·5 m by 4·1 m over turf-
covered stone wall-footings).

·17 NO 0767 7189   NO 07 SE 27
About 1 km NW of (·16), beside the track on the S side of
Glen Lochsie Burn, there are the remains of two
buildings, an enclosure and a pen. Both buildings are
reduced to turf-covered stone wall-footings and measure
respectively 5·7 m by 3·8 m and 9·3 m by 3·4 m overall; the
latter forms the SW side of the adjoining enclosure.

275 Glendams, building
    NO 1976 4868   NO 14 NE 15
About 70 m N of Glendams Reservoir there are the
remains of a possible building and three enclosures

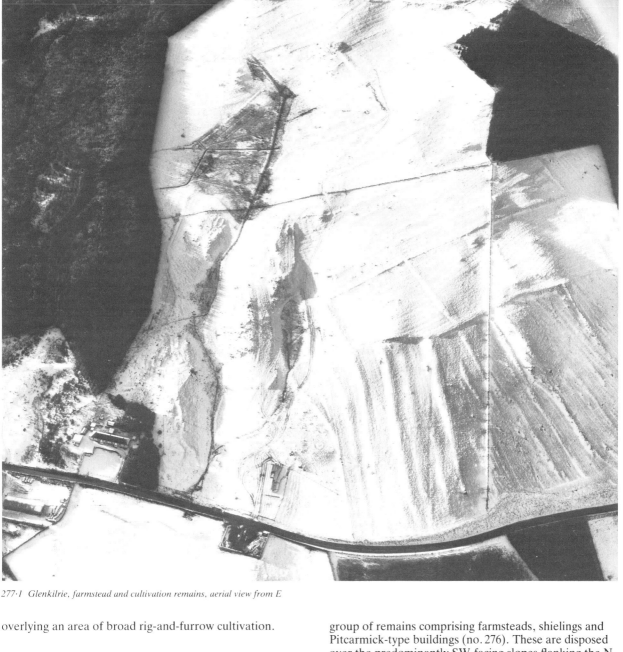

277·1 Glenkilrie, farmstead and cultivation remains, aerial view from E

overlying an area of broad rig-and-furrow cultivation.

276 Glenkilrie, Pitcarmick-type buildings

·1   NO 1327 6120   NO 16 SW 102

This Pitcarmick-type building lies on gently sloping
ground. It measures 25·2 m by up to 7·1 m overall and,
overlying its slightly sunken ESE end, there are the
remains of what was probably a hut (10·1 m by 6·2 m
overall). Around the building there is a scatter of small
cairns, field-banks and a hut-circle (no. 128·2, ·4).

·2   NO 1318 6134   NO 16 SW 101

About 160 m NNW of (·1) there are the remains of a
probable Pitcarmick-type building. It measures 12·2 m in
overall length, ranges from 5·5 m to 7·2 m in width, and
has a partially sunken floor.

277 Glenkilrie, farmsteads, buildings and shielings

To the N of Glenkilrie House (19th century), there is a
group of remains comprising farmsteads, shielings and
Pitcarmick-type buildings (no. 276). These are disposed
over the predominantly SW-facing slopes flanking the N
bank of the Ennoch Burn. To the NW there is a second
building cluster and this is bounded on the WNW and
ENE respectively by the Ashintully/Glenkilrie march
dyke and the Allt a' Choire Liathaich. Further farmsteads
and shielings extend up the valley to the NW of the march
dyke. There are no visible remains of the mansion of
Glenkilrie which is depicted by Stobie (1783). Its policies
are probably those shown on Roy's map (1747–55, sheet
18/4) and this suggests that the house stood to the SSE of
Glenkilrie steading (NO *c.* 145 600). In 1746 it was the
property of Andrew Spalding, a cadet of the Spaldings of
Ashintully (Spalding 1914, 210).

·1   NO 1405 6085   NO 16 SW 132–3

On an E-facing slope and occupying a slight rise, there
are the remains of a farmstead. It consists of five
buildings, each reduced to turf-covered stone wall-
footings, and these range from 12 m by 5 m to 18 m by

131

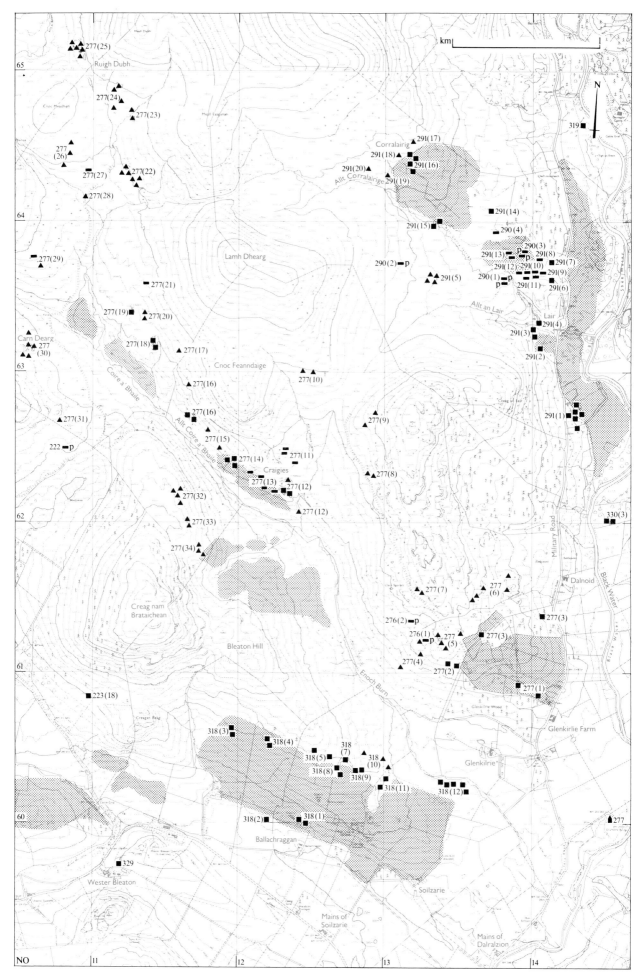

277(25)
Ruigh Dubh

277(24)
277(23)

277
(26)
277(27)   277(22)
277(28)

Meall Dubh

Cnoc Meadhon

Meall Easganan

291(17)
Corralairig
291(18)   291(16)
291(20)   291(19)
Allt Corralairige

319
N

291(14)
290(4)
290(3)
p   290(3)
291(13) p   291(8)   291(7)
291(12) 291(10)
290(1) p   291(9)
290(2) p   291(11) 291(6)

277(29)

Carn Dearg
277
(30)

277(21)

Lamh Dhearg

290(2) p
291(5)

Allt an Lair

Lair
291(4)

291(3)

277(19)   277(20)

277(18)

277(17)

Cnoc Feanndaige

277(16)

277(10)

291(2)

291(1)

Coire a' Bhaile

277(31)

222 p

Allt Coire a' Bhaile

277(16)

277(15)

277(14)   277(11)
Craigies
277(13)   277(12)

277(9)

277(8)

330(3)

277(32)

277(33)

277(34)

Creag nam
Brataichean

277(12)

277(12)

277
(6)

277(7)

Dalnoid

Black Water

276(2) p

Bleaton Hill

Enoch Burn

276(1)
p   277
(5)

277(4)

277(3)

277(2)

277(3)

277(1)

223(18)

Creagan Bead

Military Road

Glenkirlie Wood

Glenkirlie Farm

318(3)

318(4)

318(5)

318
(7)
318(8)

318
(10)
318(9)

318(11)

318(12)

Glenkirlie

318(2)   318(1)

Ballachraggan

277

329

Wester Bleaton

Soilzarie

Mains of
Soilzarie

Mains of
Dalralzion

NO   11   12   13   14

65
64
63
62
61
60

km

277 Glenkilrie, 1:25 000

4·8m overall (the last is a two-compartment building). This may be the farmstead of Mid Ennoch which is depicted by Roy (1747–55, sheet 18/4) and named by Stobie (1783) and Ainslie (1794). Some 150m to the WNW of the farmstead (NO 1391 6092) there are the remains of a two-compartment building (12m by 6·2m over turf-covered stone banks up to 1·8m thick and 0·3m high). A series of turf-banked fields and cultivation terraces are visible to the N.

·2 NO 1349 6104 NO 16 SW 137–8
On a terrace at the NNW angle of Glenkilrie Wood, there is a farmstead. This consists of two buildings and an enclosure; both buildings are reduced to turf-covered stone wall-footings and the larger measures 19m by up to 4m overall. Close by there are two hut-circles (no. 128·1). Another farmstead lies immediately to the WNW and it too consists of two buildings and an enclosure; the larger of the two buildings measures 12m by 4·5m overall. Either or both of these farmsteads may be identified with that depicted by Roy (1747–55, sheet 18/4) and named 'Wester Ennoch' by both Stobie (1783) and Ainslie (1794). 'The lands and town of Wester Enoch in the barony of Balmacrewchie' are on record in 1664 (Spalding 1914, 207).

·3 NO 1366 6125 NO 16 SW 136, 160
Some 270m NE of (·2) there are the remains of a farmstead comprising two buildings and a kiln; the larger of the two buildings measures 13·6m by 4·8m over turf-covered stone wall-footings up to 1·2m in thickness. The farmstead lies within a well-defined field-system delineated by a series of turf-covered, earth-and-stone banks. About 400m to the ENE and now obscured by trees, there are the remains of another farmstead (NO c.140 613). Either or both of these may be that depicted by Roy (1747–55, sheet 18/4) and named 'Easter Ennoch' by Stobie (1783) and Ainslie (1794). 'Easter Enoch, in the barony of Balmacrewchie' is on record in 1664 (Spalding 1914, 208).

·4 NO 1311 6103 NO 16 SW 103, 151
On a terrace and overlying an enclosed pair of hut-circles (no. 128·3), there are the heather-covered remains of two subrectangular huts. These measure 7m by 4·8m and 9·8m by 5·3m overall (the latter has an outshot on the E). Adjacent to the N wall of the E hut-circle there is what may be either a pen or a hut (5·7m by 3·7m overall), while on its SW side there is an enclosure. On a ridge immediately to the WSW there are the wasted remains of a further two huts (11·7m by 7·8m and 10·4m by 5·3m overall respectively), and a third (8·5m by 5·5m over wall-footings 1·3m thick) lies to the ENE (NO 1325 6112).

·5 NO 1337 6125 NO 16 SW 104–6
In a sheltered hollow there are the heather-covered remains of a hut (7·2m by 3·7m overall). To the SSE (NO 1340 6119 and 1342 6116) there are two more huts (9m by 4m and 10·9m by 5·5m overall respectively) and, to the SE of a probable burial cairn (no. 21), there is another (7m by 5m overall). In the vicinity there is a scatter of small cairns (no. 128·4).

·6 NO 1361 6148, 1362 6150 NO 16 SW 107–9
Some 250m NNE of the last hut described in (·5) there are two huts (6·5m by 4·2m and 8m by 4·9m overall respectively). On a knoll immediately to the NE (NO 1368 6155) there are the heather-covered stone wall-footings of a two-compartment building (16·4m by 6·2m overall), while to the E and ENE respectively (NO 1383 6155, 1384 6164) there are two more buildings, one of two compartments (14·9m by 5m over stone wall-footings

0·9m thick), the other of one compartment (10·8m by 5·7m overall). On a terrace to the W there are two hut-circles and a scatter of small cairns (no. 128·5).

·7 NO 1323 6154, 1325 6152 NO 16 SW 110
Set at the rear of a natural hollow beside the track which ascends Glenkilrie, there are the remains of a two-compartment building (8·7m by 4·5m over heather-covered stone walls 1·1m thick and up to 0·4m high) with an outshot on the NW and an enclosure on its NE side. On a slight rise immediately to the SE there are the remains of a hut (7m by 3·8m overall). Close by there are a number of small cairns (no. 128·4).

·8 NO 1291 6229, 1289 6230 NO 16 SW 111
About 800m NNW of (·7) and to the NE of the track there are two two-compartment buildings. The first (10·6m by 3·2m over stone wall-footings 1m thick) has an outshot on the SE and an enclosure to the NE; the second (11·2m by 3·7m overall) has a pen adjacent to its NE wall. On the W side of the track 100m to the S there are five hut-circles, one of which is overlain by a third two-compartment building (no. 127·1).

·9 NO 1286 6263, 1292 6271 NO 16 SW 88
Some 330m N of (·8) there is a shieling-hut. It lies at the rear of a terrace and, though severely wasted, measures 4·7m by 7m overall; at its ESE end there is an enclosure. A second hut (8·6m by 5·1m overall) lies about 100m to the NE.

·10 NO 1251 6298, 1243 6299 NO 16 SW 81
On the SE flank of Lamh Dhearg and about 500m NW of (·9) there are two subrectangular huts. The first measures 8·7m by 6·3m over a low bank 1·8m in thickness and the second 9·5m by 6·4m over a wall 0·5m thick. In the vicinity there is a scatter of small cairns (no. 127·3).

·11 NO 1232 6247, 1239 6237 NO 16 SW 123–4
On the SE flank of Cnoc Feanndaige there are the remains of two buildings set roughly parallel to each other. The principal building measures 26·2m by up to 5·9m overall and is slightly sunken at the NW end. The

277·11A

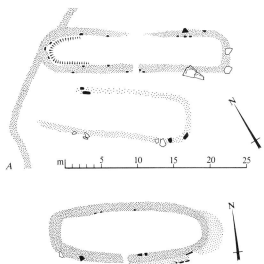

227·11A, B Glenkilrie, buildings, 1:500

second building is severely wasted and is probably earlier than the first. A stretch of field-bank abuts and possibly overlies the NE end of the principal building.

On an E-facing slope 100m to the SE, immediately
277·11B below two hut-circles (no. 127·4), there are the remains of a large bow-sided building (22m by up to 8m over walls about 1m thick and up to 0·3m high) which is set at right angles to the contour; on the E the building overlies a small cairn. The entrance is central to the S wall; the function of the thickening of the wall to the E of the entrance is unknown. To the S of this building and to the NW of the first there are a number of small cairns.

·12 NO 1232 6219 NO 16 SW 3, 125
This farmstead is the first of three situated in the narrow valley to the S of Cnoc Feanndaige. It occupies a terrace on the SSE flank of the hill and comprises at least two buildings. The first, on the NW, which has been levelled into the slope, has three compartments (23·8m by 4·7m over stone walls 0·9m thick and up to 1·4m high in nine courses) to which a fourth has been added on the SW (6·6m by 4·7m overall); access to each was obtained by an entrance in the SE wall. There are traces of an original cruck-slot in the main compartment, which has been re-used as a pen, and in the cross-wall there are two aumbries. An enclosure lies to the rear of the building. The second building lies immediately to the ESE and is set across the slope at an angle to the first. It has four compartments (19·4m by 4·9m over battered stone walls 0·8m thick and up to 1·5m high in seven courses) with access to each provided by an entrance in the SSW wall. Internal to the WNW compartment there is a blocked doorway and beside the main entrance there is a collapsed window-opening. On a low ridge immediately to the SW there are the wasted remains of a pen (9·6m by 3·1m overall), in front of which there is a terrace. To the ESE a stone-setting, which is revetted on its downslope side, may be an oven. On the slope below the second building there is an enclosure and on its SSW side what is either a pen or a building (7·3m by 3·6m overall) with an outshot at its NW end. Some 18m to the SSW there is a probable burial cairn (no. 15), and about 120m to the SSE (NO 1240 6205) there are the remains of what may be a shieling-hut (4·7m by 3·9m overall). In the lee of a boulder 26m to the NNE of the farmstead, there is an enclosure and to the N (NO 1235 6226) there are the remains of a building (6·4m by 4·1m over walls 1m thick and up to 1·3m high) which overlies another (at least 5·9m by 3·8m over walls 0·7m thick); the earlier building has an enclosure on its SW side. Another enclosure lies to the NW of the farmstead (NO 1228 6221). All three farmsteads are depicted with the name Craigies on both Stobie (1783) and Ainslie (1794) (see ·14 and ·16 below).

·13 NO 1226 6223 NO 16 SW 117–21
In an area of partially cleared ground to the NW of (·12), there is an oval enclosure. Extending along the slope from the enclosure, and earlier than (·12), there are a series of stony banks, terraces and field-plots. Some 40m to the S, and enclosed by a low bank, there are the remains of a building (10·3m by 4·8m over turf-covered stone wall-footings 0·8m thick). This stands at the head of a series of broad strip-fields which descend the slope and extend for about 300m to the WNW; where the terrain is steeper the field-divisions take the form of lynchets. Terraced into the slope, some 70m to the WNW (NO 1218 6221), there are the remains of a building measuring 19·5m in length and ranging from 6·4m in breadth on the SE to 7·1m on the NW over turf-covered stone wall-footings 0·9m thick; the entrance is central to its SW wall. Two further buildings lie to the N (NO 1215 6228) and WNW (NO 1208 6231). The first is levelled into the slope and measures 15·1m by 6·2m over turf-covered stone wall-footings 1·1m thick; the second measures 9·4m by 5·7m overall. Downslope the lynchets are overlain by field-banks.

·14 NO 1197 6240 NO 16 SW 116
Some 380m WNW of (·12) there are the well-preserved remains of the second farmstead. The principal building, which lies across the contour, consists of a range of seven compartments and measures 38·5m by 5·1m over stone walls 0·8m in thickness and up to 1·2m in height in nine courses; each compartment has an independent entrance in the SW wall. To the SSE, and set with an enclosure, there is a kiln-barn (12·6m by 4·7m over stone walls 0·9m thick and up to 1·5m high) with opposed lateral entrances; the bowl measures 2·1m in diameter and 1·1m in depth and the lintelled flue survives intact. On the W (NO 1194 6240) there is a third building (9·1m by 4·2m over stone walls 0·7m thick and 0·8m high) which lies within an enclosure. Extending downslope from the farmstead to the NW, there is a well-preserved group of lynchets (up to 2m high and 4m broad) which is bounded by a head-dyke.

·15 NO 1187 6247 NO 16 SW 114–15
In a saddle to the NW of (·14) a spread of rubble may conceal the levelled remains of a building; a pen has been constructed on the SSE. To the NNW (NO 1179 6260) and close to a hut-circle group (no. 127·5), there is another building (7·3m by 4·1m over stone walls 1m thick and up to 0·9m high).

·16 NO 1165 6270 NO 16 SW 112–13
Some 400m NW of (·14) there is the third farmstead. On the WSW there are two buildings set at right angles to each other with an adjoining enclosure on the NE. Both buildings are reduced to the lowest courses of their stone walls and measure respectively 7·3m by 4·9m and 7·8m by 4·6m overall. Upslope (NO 1169 6270) there is a building and an enclosure (the building measures 6·7m by 4·5m overall) and to the SE a two-compartment building (14·6m by 5·3m overall) and an enclosure; the building has been levelled into the slope and has a drainage-trench to the rear. Due N of the farmstead (NO 1166 6290) there is another building (13·2m by 4·2m overall), the SE end of which has been partially rebuilt as a pen.

·17 NO 1160 6314 NO 16 SW 21
Immediately NW of the march dyke there is a possible building measuring 10·2m by 6·2m over a low bank.

·18 NO 1140 6319 NO 16 SW 22
Situated on an elongated knoll 200m NW of the march
dyke there is a farmstead. At least three buildings can be 277·18
identified (A, B and C), all reduced to their stone wall-footings. Building A, upon which a pen has later been built, is of two compartments, with either a third compartment or the remains of an earlier building on the ENE, whilst what is probably a shieling-hut has been built upon the NNW end of (B). Further buildings may be represented by (D and E), though (E) would be unusually broad as such.

·19 NO 1126 6339 NO 16 SW 24
Some 200m NNW of (·18) there is a farmstead comprising
at least three buildings and two adjoined enclosures. The 277·19
buildings have been reduced to their stone wall-footings, and a small pen has been built in A. B may be a fourth building.

·20 NO 1136 6339 NO 16 SW 23
At the foot of a steep slope 85m E of (·19) there are two shieling-huts set at opposite corners of a small yard. They measure 7·2m by 4·7m and 5·5m by 3·5m respectively over walls reduced to little more than their stone footings.

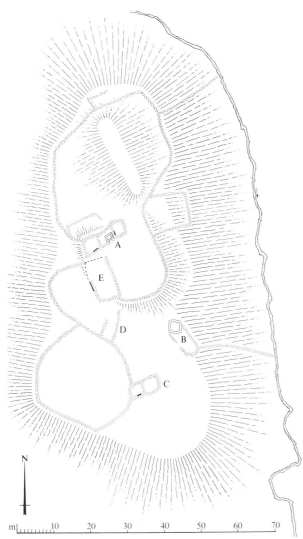

277·18 Glenkilrie, farmstead, 1:1000

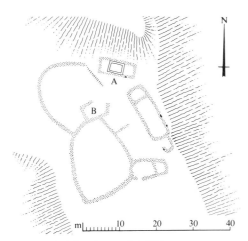

277·19 Glenkilrie, farmstead, 1:1000

·21 NO 1137 6353   NO 16 SW 149
On a low rise 170 m NNE of (·19) there is a building measuring 15·6 m by 6 m overall, its outline defined primarily by differential heather growth.

·22 NO 1122 6434   NO 16 SW 67
Immediately adjacent to and to the SSE of a small, square, stone-walled enclosure there are at least seven shieling-huts. Of the three turf-built huts with funnel entrances, two have been cut into by later stone huts.

·23 NO 1127 6468   NO 16 SW 68
On either side of an unnamed burn there are single shieling-huts. That on the S measures 5·8 m by 3·8 m overall, and the other which measures 5 m by 3·8 m overall, has an enclosure on its NNE side.

·24 NO 1117 6489   NO 16 SW 69–70
About 170 m NNW of (·23) there is a shieling group comprising two buildings and two rectangular enclosures, one adjoined by the remains of what may be a hut; the larger building is of two compartments and measures 12·7 m by 3·9 m over stone wall-footings. Situated 60 m to the SSE (NO 1119 6480) there are a further two huts, measuring 6 m by 4·3 m and 5·5 m by 4 m respectively over turf-covered wall-footings, and 100 m to the S (NO 1115 6475) a fourth hut, measuring 6·1 m by 4·5 m over heather-covered wall-footings, lies within a small enclosure. A small pen lies 100 m to the WNW.

·25 NO 1097 6516   NO 16 NW 77
To the W of a stone-walled enclosure there are at least ten shieling-huts, some of turf and some of stone construction. Four of the turf-built huts have funnel entrances and are cut into or overlain by stone huts. On the first edition of the OS 6-inch map (Perthshire, 1867, sheet 23) the enclosure is named 'Ruidh Dubh' and described as ruinous, though on the modern map the name has been moved to the SSE.

·26 NO 1084 6444   NO 16 SW 29
Immediately adjacent to a hut-circle (no. 105·7) there are the remains of a shieling-hut, measuring 9 m by 5·5 m over stone wall-footings, and a small oval enclosure. Some 70 m to the S (NO 1081 6436) there is a second hut, measuring 8·5 m by 4·8 m over stone wall-footings, and what may be a third lies 70 m to the N (NO 1085 6451).

·27 NO 1098 6432   NO 16 SW 65
Immediately SE of the lower of two hut-circles (no. 105·7) there is a building defined by low banks and visible as little more than a differential growth in the heather. It measures 17·3 m in overall length by 6·2 m at its mid point, narrowing to 5 m at the NW end and 3·5 m at the SE end. What may be a second building, measuring 8 m by 4 m overall, lies 38 m WNW of the hut-circle.

·28 NO 1095 6416   NO 16 SW 97
A single shieling-hut measuring 6·3 m by 5·2 m over a low bank lies 6 m SSE of a modern hut.

·29 NO 1065 6369   NO 16 SW 64
Some 12 m NW of a hut-circle (no. 105·6) there are the remains of what may be two adjoined shieling-huts or a hut and an enclosure, whilst 90 m to the NW (NO 1060 6375) there is a building measuring 17·2 m by 7·3 m over a low bank, its better-preserved NW end being clearly rounded.

·30 NO 1059 6316   NO 16 SW 17
Immediately N of the ruinous 19th-century cottage of Carn Dearg there are two shieling-huts measuring 9·3 m by 4·3 m and 7·6 m by 4·5 m respectively over stone wall-footings, the smaller occupying a mound 1 m high and 12 m across. About 70 m to the N (NO 1056 6324) a rectangular mound measuring 10·8 m by 6·4 m and 0·4 m high is probably the remains of a third hut, and 50 m to the SSW (NO 1055 6310) there is a hut measuring 4·8 m by 4 m over stone wall-footings, together with what may be another hut or a small enclosure.

·31 NO 1078 6266   NO 16 SW 15
Situated 500 m SSE of Carn Dearg and 20 m NE of a
modern dyke there are a single shieling-hut and an
enclosure.

·32 NO 1157 6218   NO 16 SW 155
On a terrace on the NNE flank of Creag nam Brataichean
there are the remains of up to five shieling-huts and an
enclosure. Two of the huts are turf-built with funnel
entrances, one of which has been cut into by a later stone
hut.

·33 NO 1165 6202   NO 16 SW 154
About 100 m SSE of (·32) and some 20 m apart there are
two shieling-huts.

·34 NO 1173 6185   NO 16 SW 153
About 130 m SSE of (·33) there is a group of four shieling-
huts.
With the exception of the 19th-century cottage of Carn
Dearg (NO 1058 6314) documented settlement stops at
the Glenkilrie/Ashintully march dyke. Only two
farmsteads are to be found beyond the dyke (·18–·19),
and these, with their more irregular and rounded
buildings, appear to be of a different character to those at
Craigies (·12, ·14 and ·16) and are probably earlier in
date. Amongst the Craigies farmsteads, however, there is
also a series of what are probably earlier buildings (13).
The long buildings (·21, ·27 and ·29) also stand out
amongst the shieling remains which predominate at the
upper end of the valley, though their date and purpose is
unknown.

278 Glen Shee, fermtoun, farmsteads, buildings, mills and shielings

A remarkably intact pre-Improvement landscape extends
on both sides of the valley of the Shee Water from the
church at Spittal of Glenshee (no. 197) to Dalmunzie, a
distance of 2·4 km from SE to NW. At Dalmunzie the
valley divides into its headwaters: Gleann Taitneach to
the N and Glen Lochsie to the WNW. The principal
visible remains comprise a fermtoun, a series of
farmsteads, and extensive traces of former cultivation;
these, for the most part, are strung out across the break of
slope at the junction of the improved ground and the
rough hill-grazing, a line which is clearly defined by the
turf-and-stone head-dyke that provides a continuum on
both sides of the valley. In addition, there are two
prehistoric monuments: a standing stone (no. 82) adjacent
to the church, and a cairn (no. 39) 415 m to the NW. In the
following description the S-facing slopes are described
first (from SE to NW) and the N-facing second (from NW
to SE). The former are the property of the Invercauld
Estate and were recorded in detail on Brown's 1808
survey; on this, with the notable exception of the Spittal
fermtoun, all the larger farmsteads are depicted.

·1 NO 107 704   NO 17 SW 6, 43
This fermtoun is disposed across the slope at the foot of
the plantation 200 m NNW of Spittal Church. It comprises
the wasted remains of at least sixteen buildings, the
majority of them set around yards. Apart from one three-
compartment building, they range from 6·5 m by 3·3 m to
14·1 m by 5·4 m overall. The three-compartment building
measures 22·4 m by 5·4 m overall, but it may be the result
of more than one period of construction. Indeed, there is
evidence at two places that the layout of the fermtoun has
changed in the course of its history. At the first (A) the W
angle of a two-compartment building appears to overlie
the wall of the yard to the NW; at the second (B) the yard

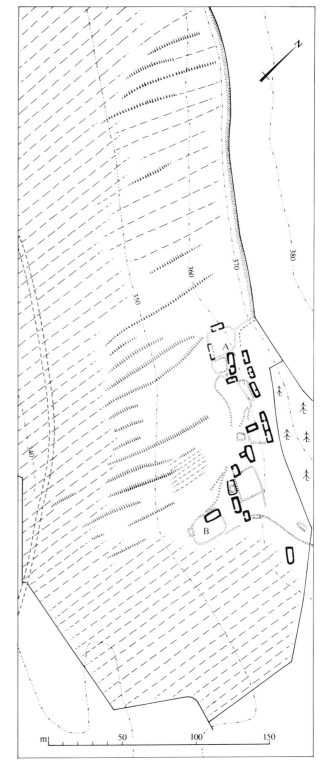

278·1A Glen Shee, fermtoun, 1:2500

has impinged on earlier cultivation ridges. About 100 m to
the NE of the fermtoun there is a building which is
overlain by the modern head-dyke (NO 1092 7047).
    The old head-dyke, which extends virtually unbroken
along the side of the glen, drops down to join the
fermtoun on both the NW and E. On the slopes below
there are extensive remains of rig-and-furrow cultivation
and a series of substantial lynchets, but much of the
evidence has recently been obscured by ploughing.
Overlying the lynchets and their associated rigs, but on a
slightly different alignment, there are traces of a system of

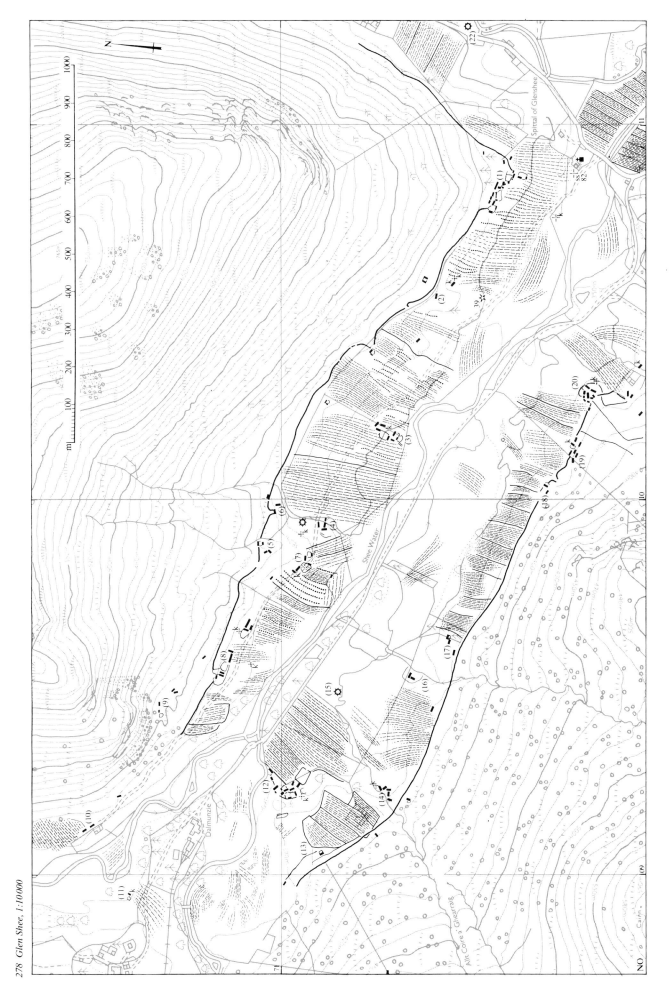

278 Glen Shee, 1:10000

278·1B Glen Shee, cultivation terraces and fermtoun from SW

straight rigs. The haughland also bears traces of
cultivation and at NO 1075 7025 there are the remains of
a kiln.

The lands of 'Spittale of Glensche' are on record in
1542 and the 'Chapel-crofts' in 1615, but it is unclear to
what the latter refers. Brown (1808) annotates the
settlement 'Old House Lets', and thus distinguishes it
from Wester Spittal (·2), which is shown as ruinous.

·2   NO 1054 7053   NO 17 SW 37–41
The farmstead of Wester Spittal (in ruins by 1808) stands
on the neck of a spur some 250m WNW of (·1). It consists
of a two-compartment building (23m by 4·2m over turf-
covered stone wall-footings) with traces of what may be a
second on its NE side. On the uphill side of the head-dyke
and terraced end-on into the slope (NO 1058 7060), there
are two buildings set on opposite sides of a yard. Both are
similar in size (about 8m by 4m overall) and have
entrances central to their side-walls opening to the yard.
In the lee of a hollow on the SSE side of the spur (NO
1056 7053) there are the remains of two kilns, one with a
chamber. To the WNW of the farmstead, at the edge of
an area recently re-seeded, there are the remains of what
is probably a two-compartment, round-angled building
(10·7m by 4·1m overall). Some 130m to the NNW, close
to what may be an original break in the old head-dyke,
there are the wasted remains of another building (9·1m by
4·0m overall) with an enclosure on its S side (8·9m by
12·3m internally). This building is shown by Brown (1808)
but there is also what may be a second building (12·6m by

4·1m overall), which lies at right angles to the first along
the W side of the enclosure. In the vicinity there are a
number of lynchets together with traces of rig-and-
furrow.

·3   NO 1017 7071   NO 17 SW 9, 42
The remains of the farmstead of 'Cuhacherach' (Roy
1747–55, sheet 18/4), later 'Easter Cuthel' (Stobie 1783;
Brown 1808), lie to either side of a modern field-wall on a
tract of gently sloping ground 320m WNW of Wester
Spittal. It comprises at least six buildings and a kiln,
disposed variously round three yards. The buildings range
in size from 6·7m by 4·2m to 16·6m by 6·3m over turf-
covered stone wall-footings spread up to 2·1m thick; the
kiln has an ingle-chamber on its SSW side. The farmstead
is surrounded by rig-and-furrow and there are
fragmentary traces of a number of earlier lynchets. At the
head of the field to the NNE (NO 1026 7087), there are
the remains of buildings on two sides of a yard; the larger
of these (10m by 3·9m overall), on the NNE, is depicted
by Brown (1808), together with another on the SSW, of
which there are now no visible remains.

·4   NO 0993 7087   NO 07 SE 30
About 270m to the NW of (·3), close to where the track
from Easter Cuthel fords an unnamed tributary of the
Shee Water, there are the remains of the farmstead of
Mid Cuthel, which is depicted by Stobie (1783) and
named by Brown (1808). It comprises four buildings, two
of them set on opposite sides of a yard. The largest of the

buildings measures 16 m by 6·2 m overall and lies immediately to the W of the yard. To the N (NO 0994 7092) there are the remains of what may be a mill (9·3 m by 5·2 m over stone wall-footings). This is set end-on to the burn in low-lying ground; traces of another possible building (9·5 m by 4·7 m) lie immediately to the W. Upstream a tributary has been diverted to increase the head of water; the burn has been canalised and, in part, dammed. To the W of the mill (NO 0991 7094) there is a kiln with a baffle-wall to its rear.

·5   NO 0987 7105   NO 07 SE 32, 41
At the rear of a hollow beside a burn, and interrupting the head-dyke, there are the well-preserved remains of a small farmstead comprising buildings on two sides of a yard. That on the N is round-angled on the W and has

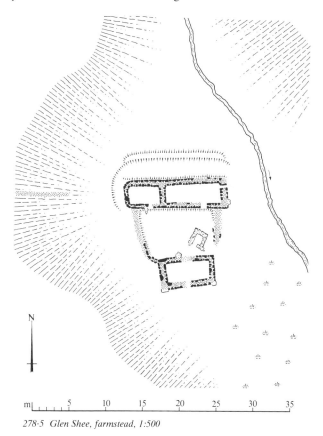

278·5 Glen Shee, farmstead, 1:500

two compartments (14·3 m by 4·2 m over stone wall-footings 1·3 m thick); its E wall incorporates a byre-drain and a drainage-bank extends the length of the rear wall. The neighbouring building measures 7·8 m by 4·2 m overall. The yard has been terraced into the hillside and a stone plinth is set into the SE corner. Some 20 m to the SW there are the wasted remains of a hut (5 m by 4 m overall) and on the N, at right angles to it, the remains of a rectangular building (12·5 m by 4·1 m overall) with an enclosure on its WSW side (7 m by 13·5 m internally).

·6   NO 0998 7100   NO 07 SE 29
About 75 m to the ESE of (·5) the head-dyke turns abruptly downslope to form a yard on the N side of a probable building (9 m long overall); a second building (11·2 m by 4·3 m overall), set end-on to the slope, lies to the E, while 28 m to the NE, adjoining the uphill side of the head-dyke, there is a third (6·6 m by 3·8 m overall). The yard opens N to allow direct access to the hill pastures.

·7   NO 0981 7094   NO 07 SE 31, 39
Some 70 m to the WNW of (·4), there are the remains of a farmstead, which is depicted both by Stobie (1783) and Brown (1808), but is unnamed. It comprises at least six buildings, a yard and an enclosure, all reduced to turf-covered stone wall-footings. At the SE end of the farmstead a two-compartment building (9 m by 3·8 m overall), with a drainage-bank to the rear, stands beside the track. On the SE there is a yard adjoined by a second building (8·1 m by 4·8 m overall). The enclosure, whose interior has been cultivated, lies to the W and is adjoined on the E by one building (10·6 m by 5 m overall) and on the N by another. The latter is a substantial, two-compartment building (19·3 m by 3·9 m overall); immediately to the NW of it, set at right angles, there are the remains of a further building (7·4 m by 3 m overall). This building has been terraced into the slope and is open-ended. Some 50 m to the NNW there is a building (12·8 m by 4·1 m overall) possibly overlying the remains of an earlier one. To the S and E of the farmstead, extending obliquely downslope, there is a series of well-preserved lynchets, some with risers up to 2 m high; these are partially overlain by later rig-and-furrow. At the break of slope (NO 0978 7085), now almost entirely covered by field clearance, there is an outbuilding (5·5 m by 4 m overall) with an entrance central to its W wall.

·8   NO 0965 7109   NO 07 SE 33, 34
Some 120 m to the NW of (·7), there are the remains of Wester Cuthel (Brown 1808). The buildings and enclosures, which are all reduced to either their lowest courses or wall-footings, fall into two groups. The ESE group consists of two buildings set at right angles to each other, an enclosure and a kiln, and there are also traces of what may be an earlier building on the S. The buildings are substantial; that on the NW (possibly a threshing-barn) is of two compartments (15·9 m by 5·2 m over walls 0·8 m thick and 0·4 m high in three courses), with opposed lateral entrances 1·7 m wide. Its neighbour on the E is also of two compartments (24·8 m by 5·3 m overall) but has an outshot on the SE (2·7 m by 4·4 m overall); central to each compartment there is a byre-drain. Latterly the building has been remodelled with the insertion of a partition wall at its NW end; the end-wall is masked by a considerable rubble spread. A drainage-bank extends the length of the rear-wall, and to the front there is a stone-revetted terrace, on the SSE side of which there are two rick-bases. An enclosure adjoins the NW side of the first building, and upslope from it there are the remains of a kiln.

The second group of buildings associated with the farmstead of Wester Cuthel are disposed over a terrace immediately to the NW (NO 0954 7116). These buildings, together with their associated enclosures, can be divided into two phases. The earlier (that on the NW) comprises three buildings and an enclosure; the buildings are all reduced to their stone wall-footings and range in size from 5·8 m by 3·6 m to 11·2 m by 4·1 m overall. The enclosure within which they stand measures 57·2 m by 28·7 m internally. On the NNW the enclosure is joined by the head-dyke, while on the ESE it is overlain by two other enclosures (measuring respectively 19·8 m by 13·1 m and 25·3 m by 14·9 m internally). The latter are associated with the two buildings of the later phase. The principal of these, which lies immediately to the SE, is substantial, round angled and of two compartments (13·2 m by 5·6 m over stone walls 0·8 m thick and 0·5 m high); a further two units have been added on the ESE (12·5 m by 4·6 m overall). Each compartment is entered independently from doorways in the SSW wall, and two of the four

274

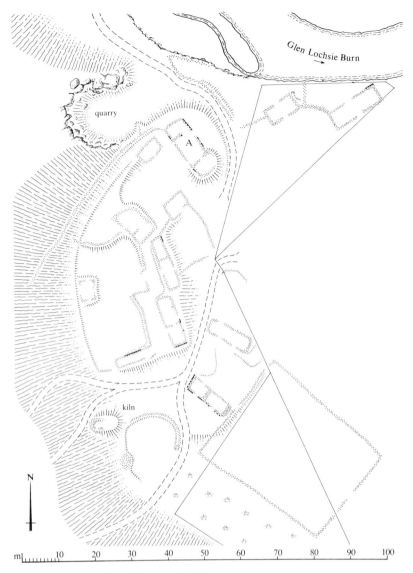

278·12 Glen Shee, Dalmunzie, fermtoun, 1:1000

compartments possess byre-drains that emit from these doorways. A drainage-bank extends the length of the building to the rear, and there are traces of a stone-revetted terrace to the front; to the E there are the remains of a building of slighter construction (8·4m by 3·2m overall). The slopes below the farmstead are covered in rig-and-furrow and let into the slope 55m to the S there is a kiln. Some 60m to the NNW, and occupying a tract of higher ground, there are the remains of a further building, possibly a shieling-hut (8·2m by 4·2m over stone walls 0·8m thick and up to 0·5m high in five courses). The first-phase buildings and enclosure may be identified as the farmstead of 'Chial', which is depicted by Roy (1747–55, sheet 18/4).

·9 NO 0948 7129 to 0945 7133   NO 07 SE 35–6

To the NW of (·8), at the foot of the scree on the SW flank of Ben Gulabin, there are the remains of at least four shieling-huts and an enclosure. The huts range from 5·1m by 3m to 9m by 4·4m over stone walls up to 0·9m thick and 0·3m high: the best preserved (and the largest) is round-angled with a lateral entrance. A similar building lies in broken ground beside the track some 250m to the WNW (NO 0922 7143).

·10 NO 0913 7150   NO 07 SE 120

All that remains visible of the farmstead of Sheanval some 100m to the NW of (·9) are two rectangular buildings adjacent to the roofless ruin of a 19th-century cottage. The larger of the two (11·7m by 4·6m over turf-covered stone wall-footings) has an entrance in its SW wall and a drainage-bank on the NE. Immediately to the SE there are traces of a small cultivated plot. The second building (10·6m by 5·6m overall) is aligned with the first and is of similar form; to the N, and on the haughland to the SW, there are extensive traces of rig-and-furrow. The lands of 'Seanbhail' are on record in 1686 (Atholl Muniments, 23, xvii, 9–10); a farmstead is depicted by Roy (1747–55, sheet 18/4–5) and Stobie (1783), but is shown as ruinous by Brown (1808).

·11 NO 0892 7140   NO 07 SE 13

On a low spur about 200m WSW of Sheanval but on the opposite side of the Allt Ghlinn Thaitneich, there are the wasted remains of what may be a kiln with a chamber on its SSW side, while in a hollow immediately to the N there is an enclosure. On the SSW there are traces of rig-and-furrow.

·12 NO 0923 7098   NO 07 SE 8

Some 500m to the SE of (·11) and on the S side of the Glen Lochsie Burn, there are the remains of the Dalmunzie fermtoun. It comprises at least eleven buildings (some with yards), two enclosures and a kiln.

274

140

The buildings and enclosures are all reduced to their turf-covered stone wall-footings, and, with one exception, range from 6·1 m by 3·7 m to 13·7 m by 3·2 m overall. The largest building (A), possibly the remains of a laird's or tackman's house which occupies a slightly more prominent position, is a substantial structure measuring 16·5 m by 5·4 m over wall-footings up to 1·3 m in thickness; it probably has three compartments and there is a yard to the SW with outbuildings to either side. The haughland to the ESE of the fermtoun has been extensively cultivated and fragmented traces of rig-and-furrow are also evident in the more broken ground to the WNW (in what is now the Dalmunzie Golf Course).

The lands of Dalmunzie are on record in 1510 (*Reg. Mag. Sig.*, ii, no. 3450) and were the property of Robert McIntosh by 1686 (Atholl Muniments, 23, xvii, 1 and 10). Dalmunzie is depicted as ruinous by Stobie (1783), and Miller (1929, 15) notes that 'the foundation lines of the old castle of Dalmunzie' were still to be seen on the S side of the Lochsie Burn. These are probably to be equated with (A). For a datestone which may have come from Dalmunzie see (·21).

·13 NO 0898 7097   NO 07 SE 7, 9, 28
About 215 m to the W of (·12) there are the footings of a two-compartment building (11·8 m by 3 m overall); a second 9·5 m by 3·7 m overall), with a yard on its NE side, lies 115 m to the SSE (NO 0905 7089). Upslope, 350 m to the SW (NO 0873 7070), partially overlain by the modern field-wall, there are the wasted remains of a rectangular building (7·6 m by 4·7 m over turf-covered stone wall-footings 1·2 m thick) with what may be a pen on its SW side.

·14 NO 0921 7070   NO 07 SE 6
This farmstead is situated on the S side of an unnamed tributary of the Shee Water. It is separated from (·13) by a series of broad strip-fields enclosing rig-and-furrow and comprises at least seven buildings and what may be a kiln; with the exception of the kiln, all are reduced to their turf-covered stone wall-footings and the buildings range in size from 5·9 m by 3·7 m to 9·2 m by 4·4 m overall. Above the head-dyke there are two buildings, one (6·7 m by 4·3 m overall) with an enclosure on its W side lying 50 m to the SSW, the other (7·7 m by 4·2 m overall) 100 m to the WNW (NO 0920 7066 and 0911 7074 respectively). The site is depicted by Stobie (1783) but is unnamed.

·15 NO c.094 708   NO 07 SE 37
There are now no visible remains of the mill depicted by Stobie (1783), which stood on the same tributary as (·14), on the haughland of the Shee Water, about 250 m ESE of the Dalmunzie fermtoun.

·16 NO 0950 7059   NO 07 SE 5
To the SSE of (·14) and adjacent to an unnamed tributary of the Shee Water, there are the remains of two buildings set within an enclosure, as well as the site of what may be a flax mill; the burn has been masonry-faced on both sides from the rear of the terrace to the edge of the haughland. The buildings, which are reduced to turf-covered stone wall-footings, measure 14·8 m by 4·8 m and 10·2 m by 5·1 m overall respectively. On both sides of the burn the ground has been terraced; this, together with a number of dry water channels suggests, that the original purpose was to provide a number of retting pools. A third building lies 100 m to the SW. It is round-angled with battered end-walls and has an outshot on the E; the entrance appears to have been at the SE angle. Stobie (1783) depicts the site as 'Balneton'.

·17 NO 0960 7052   NO 07 SE 4
To the ESE of (·16), disposed across a N-facing slope to the N of the head-dyke, there are the remains of three buildings, one of which lies just within a conifer plantation. They range from 13·7 m by 3·4 m to 14·4 m by 4·5 m over turf-covered stone wall-footings up to 1·1 m in thickness; one is of three compartments and another (on the ENE) has a small enclosure to one side.

·18 NO 1002 7028   NO 17 SW 36
The ground between (·17) and (·18) is taken up by a series of ridged fields, but has recently been improved. These extend downslope from the head-dyke and are each defined by a narrow, unploughed strip or baulk, which has often been enhanced by field-clearance. To the ESE, interrupting the course of the head-dyke, there are the remains of at least two buildings, a probable yard and an enclosure. The buildings are reduced to turf-covered stone wall-footings and measure respectively 10·5 m by 4 m and 11·4 m by 4·7 m overall; that on the E, set end-on to the slope, has what may be a yard on its SSE side. Adjacent to the yard there is an original break in the head-dyke, the terminals of which are out-turned to provide a funnelled exit to the rough grazing beyond.

·19 NO 1013 7019   NO 17 SW 35
The farmstead of 'Lenoch-beg', which is depicted by Roy (1747–55, sheet 18/4) and named by Stobie (1783), is disposed across a tract of uncleared ground between the old head-dyke and the modern field-wall. It comprises at least six buildings, a kiln-and-chamber and at least one enclosure. The westernmost building (14·6 m by 5·9 m overall) is overlain by the modern wall and is linked to the head-dyke by what is probably an enclosure on its NNE side. To the ESE of this building, there are two more, both of two compartments (13·3 m by 4·4 m and 14·3 m by 4·3 m overall respectively), while further to the ESE there are the wasted remains of a fourth (8·3 m by 3·8 m overall). Adjoining the head-dyke there are at least two more buildings (5·4 m by 3·4 m and 11·9 m by 5·6 m overall respectively). They are set to either side of an enclosure (11·5 m by 10·8 m), which is incorporated in the head-dyke and has the kiln-and-chamber on its E side. Lynchets and rig-and-furrow extend across the slopes to the NNW and E of the farmstead.

·20 NO 1028 7015   NO 17 SW 34
The farmstead of 'Lenoch-more', which is depicted by Roy (1747–55, sheet 18/4) and named by Stobie (1783), occupies a terrace at the foot of a boulder-strewn slope some 80 m to the ESE of (·19). The head-dyke deviates in its course to take in the farmstead. Although reduced to the wasted remains of its wall-footings, the farmstead is characterised by the use of large boulders in its construction. It comprises at least nine buildings (A–J) and a kiln. The principal buildings (A, B) are set parallel to each other on two sides of a small yard; with the exception of C and D, the remaining buildings form a tight group around A and B, and are set back into a natural depression at the rear of the terrace. Building C blocks what may have been the original approach to the site; the terrace itself is enclosed by a low bank, which extends from the NW corner of B. A kiln is let into the slope on the ESE; its flue was on the E, probably enclosed by a small chamber. The slopes below the head-dyke and around the terrace have traces of rig-and-furrow cultivation and there are a number of lynchets. Upslope, on uncleared ground, a number of possible field-boundaries composed of rows of boulders are visible. About 12 m to the W of G there is another building on the

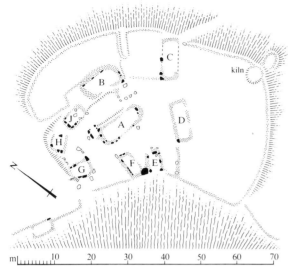

278·20 *Glenshee, Lennoch-more, farmstead, 1:1000*

line of the head-dyke; about 100 m to the S there are at least three more buildings (NO 1028 7004, 1027 7003 and 1022 7001), while 150 m to the ESE (NO 1036 7000) there are the remains of a kiln-and-chamber. The buildings, which are all reduced to turf-covered stone wall-footings, range from 8·7 m by 4·7 m to 10·6 m by 4·1 m overall.

·21 NO 1037 6992   NO 16 NW 78
An inscribed lintel is incorporated in re-use over the SW door of the cottage at Leanoch Mhor. It bears the inscription '[T]HE LORD DEFEND THIS HOUS'

278·21 *Glen Shee, inscribed lintel*

together with the monogram initials 'PMT' and 'IR', and the date 1658. It is possible, that the stone came from the laird's house at Dalmunzie (·12).

·22 NO 1125 7049   NO 17 SW 92
The remains of the Mill of Spittal, which is depicted by Stobie (1783) and by Brown (1808), but which is shown abandoned on the first edition of the OS 6-inch map (Perthshire, 1867, sheet 23), occupy a meander in the Allt a' Ghlinne Bhig about 120 m NE of the farmhouse at Old Spittal. The site of the mill-building is represented by a terrace (9·7 m by 5·3 m). A lade has been taken off the river about 30 m to the ENE, where there are traces of a weir, and it feeds into a pond, which is cut on the SE by a second more recent lade that runs parallel with the first.

The lands of 'Spittale of Glensche' are on record in 1542, and those of Cuthil and Dalmunzie in 1510 and 1543 (*Reg. Mag. Sig.*, ii, no. 3450; Atholl Muniments, 23, xvii, 1). Evidence for settlement at this period is sparse but it is possible that the Spittal fermtounn (·1) is of this date or earlier. Habitation at Dalmunzie and Cuthel (Cuthley) about 1600 is confirmed by Pont, although he reverses their positions and displaces the name 'Dalmunoy' to the S; the 'Spittel' is shown, as is the chapel site and the name 'Chapel of Glenshy' (see no. 197). In addition 'scheeles' are indicated at the head of both Gleann Taitneach and

Glen Lochsie (no. 274); the two merklands of 'Seanbhail' are on record in 1686 (Atholl Muniments, 23, xvii, 9). By the time of Roy's Military Survey (1747–55, sheets 18/3 and 4) the Spittal fermtoun appears to have been abandoned; the main population centre appears to have regrouped NE of the chapel beside the Military Road and close to the Mill of Spittal (·21). Three farmsteads are represented on the N side of the Shee Water: 'Shanwall' (·10); 'Chial' (·8); and 'Cuhacherach' (·3). Three others appear to the S; these are Dalmunzie (·12) and two others, which, though unnamed, may be identified as 'Lenoch-beg' and 'Lenoch-more' (·19 and ·20). By the late 18th century the population had undergone a rapid expansion (*cf.* Stobie 1783). Seven farmsteads are present on the N side of the valley, amounting to the division of the Cuthell holdings into Wester and Easter Cuthell (the latter supplanting the farmsteads at Cuhacherach) with satellite farmsteads between. Similarly there are a corresponding number of holdings on the S side of the valley mill at NO *c*.094 708. Dalmunzie, formerly probably the seat of the McIntosh laird, was in ruins; to the NW and NNW two new farmsteads had emerged: Sochach and Strounaloyn, of which there are now no visible remains, while to the SE lay the farmstead of Balneton (·16). By the turn of the 19th century the picture had altered dramatically. None of the farmsteads on the S side of the valley are shown by Brown (1808), and of those on the N Wester Spittal (·2) and Sheanval (·10) are shown as ruinous; it may be assumed that the remaining farmsteads were abandoned shortly after. At the time the first edition of the OS 6-inch map was prepared (1862–6) only Sochach remained; the farmstead of Sheanval had been replaced by the existing cottage.

On face value the map evidence accounts for most of the archaeology. The significance of the Spittal fermtoun, apparently lost to living memory by 1808 when the site is described simply as 'Old house lets', has already been alluded to. However, of the remaining structures that fall outside the scope of the map evidence some could be earlier. The relationship of the remaining farmsteads to the head-dyke, probably one of the oldest features in the pre-Improvement landscape, is not without interest. Ties between the two can be suggested at the Spittal fermtoun (·1), Chial (·8), Lenoch-beg (·19) and Lenoch-more (·20), sites which all display some chronological depth and whose origins may long pre-date the map evidence. It is noteworthy too, that it is with these farmsteads that the principal groups of lynchets also occur. The head-dyke, though serving to define the extent of the cultivable ground, may in itself reflect an earlier land-division whose origins lie in the medieval period. Upslope of Chial (later Wester Cuthell) there are a number of shieling-huts (·9), which do not appear on any map. These could be broadly contemporary with the farmsteads, but they may also be earlier. Following the pattern attested by the documentary evidence for Gleann Beag (no. 265) it is possible that the farmsteads brought under cultivation a number of former shieling-grounds, thereby displacing the shielings, in this instance, to the higher glens to the N and WNW (see no. 274·4–17).

279 Glen Shee, Old Spittal, buildings
NO 1127 7080   NO 17 SW 63–4
At the NW corner of the sheep pens at Old Spittal there
are the wasted remains of a two-compartment building
(14m by 4·9m overall) which is set end-on to an
enclosure. On a terrace, some 50m to the NNW, there are
the turf-covered remains of three buildings. These range
from 7·6m by 3·2m to 10·5m by 4·5m overall, and one,
possibly slightly earlier in date, is of two compartments.

280 Heatheryhaugh, buildings
·1 NO 1888 5102   NO 15 SE 40
This building lies in pasture 1·2km SE of Heatheryhaugh
farmhouse; it measures 21m from NW to SE and ranges
in breadth from 5·7m at the SE end to 7·3m midway
along its length over walls reduced to banks no more than

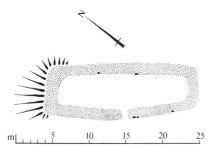

280·1 Heatheryhaugh, building, 1:500

1·6m thick and 0·3m high. An entrance-gap is situated
midway along the SW side. At the NW end the building
overlies a possible burnt mound (no. 171).

·2 NO 1862 5090   NO 15 SE 41
Situated adjacent to a disused trackway on a gentle S-
facing slope 1·2km SE of Heatheryhaugh farmhouse,
there are the footings of a two-compartment building
measuring 12·3m by 5m over walls reduced to banks up to
1·8m in thickness and 0·3m in height. Immediately to the
SW there are the poorly-preserved remains of what may
be a second building.

281 Hill of Alyth, Pitcarmick-type building
NO 2285 5020   NO 25 SW 20
The remains of this building are situated on a terrace on
the SW flank of the Hill of Alyth immediately S of a hut-
circle group (no. 129·1) and some 330m NE of Whiteside
steading. It measures 26m in length and ranges in width
from 7·8m at the W end to 6·4m on the E over walls
reduced to a turf-covered bank up to 2·8m in maximum
thickness and 0·2m in height.

282 Hill of Ashmore, Pitcarmick-type building
NO 1493 5335   NO 15 SW 36
Immediately N of a plantation on the SW flank of the Hill
of Ashmore there are the remains of what is probably a
Pitcarmick-type building adjoined on the W by an
enclosure. The building, which has been reduced to turf-
covered stone wall-footings, measures 15·7m in overall
length and varies in width from 6·6m at the NW end to
4·8m at the SE end.

283 Hill of Cally, buildings
·1 NO 1308 5169   NO 15 SW 28
The remains of two rectangular buildings survive on a
wooded terrace at the foot of the Hill of Cally, 370m E of
Steps of Cally. They measure 14m by 4·5m and 8·7m by

5·6m overall respectively, and the larger, the more
westerly, has an outshot at its WNW end. Both buildings
have entrances on their S sides.

·2 NO 1216 5280   NO 15 SW 21, 31
On a terrace on the SW flank of the Hill of Cally, there
are the remains of three subrectangular buildings (the
largest 10·8m by 5·7m overall). To the NE there is a field
of rig-and-furrow.

284 Hill of Kingseat, fermtoun and shieling
·1 NO 1523 5477   NO 15 SE 30
On the SW flank of the Hill of Kingseat there is a small
fermtoun comprising two groups of buildings about 80m
apart. In the westerly group there are four buildings (their
walls generally reduced to their lower courses and
standing to a maximum height of 1m), a kiln-and-
chamber, and an enclosure. Three of the buildings,
including the largest, which measures 18·7m by 5·5m
overall, are set parallel to the contour; the smallest, which
measures 10·6m by 5·2m overall, is set at right angles to
the contour.

The buildings of the easterly group (NO 1537 5474), of
which there are three, together with two further
structures which may be either small buildings or pens,
are more loosely spaced, and all are set parallel to the
contour. The largest, which has been incorporated into a
later stone dyke and partially reconstructed for use as a
pen, is of three compartments and measures 15·2m by
4·7m over walls up to 1m high.

·2 NO 1543 5536   NO 15 NE 35
Three oval shieling-huts are situated within the group of
cairns no. 134·3 on the NW flank of Hill of Kingseat,
some 600m N of the fermtoun; the largest measures 9·7m
by 6·6m over low banks 1·3m in thickness by 0·3m in
height. The huts probably overlie the broad cultivation
ridges that are visible amongst the small cairns.

285 Invereddrie, fermtoun
NO 1363 6895 to 1353 6781   NO 16 NW
11–14, 29
The extensive and well-preserved remains of this
fermtoun lie to the N and SW of Invereddrie farmhouse.
It comprises at least sixty-four buildings, together with   *285A*
their enclosures, yards and pens; in addition there are
three kilns and at least two mill-sites. The fermtoun can
be subdivided into a number of discrete building-clusters,
several undoubtedly farmsteads in their own right. Some
chronological depth is apparent both in the form of the
buildings and in their relationships to one another. Many
of the buildings are either connected by or closely
associated with the head-dyke, whose course, although
irregular in places, can be traced through the length of the
fermtoun.

A particularly well-preserved group of buildings,
probably an early improvement farmstead (1 on plan), are   *285B*
drawn out in detail (A–D). The buildings are disposed in
the lee of a knoll and are associated with three
enclosures. The principal building (A) which is
remarkable for its size, has a drainage-trench to the rear
and a stone-revetted terrace in front; this served to set the
building apart from the midden which is represented by a
pronounced, scooped depression immediately to the SW.
These features also recur at building B. Building D,
perhaps a store, has been let into the slope, and in the
interior there are traces of a scarcement. Immediately to
the N, two slightly divergent wall-lines may be the
remains of a stack-stand. Building E, which forms part of
a second building-cluster to the SE of the above

farmstead, is noteworthy for its porch.

Of particular interest is a group of five single-compartment huts and a pen (2 on plan), which are randomly disposed over the boulder-strewn slopes to the ENE of (1). These huts are distinguished by their marked similarity in size and design. Four are illustrated, and of these F is of particular note as its W end-wall incorporates a large earthfast boulder; exceptionally, it also has an outshot. A lade, which brought water from a source upslope of the huts, fed into what is now a morass, but was possibly a retting-pool. To the W of (1) there are extensive traces of rig-and-furrow; to the S a number of baulks have been left between rigs.

Representative of the fermtoun's smaller and more nucleated building-groups is (3). It consists of two buildings set at right angles to one another and ranged with a yard. Both buildings are reduced to the lowest courses of their stone walls; that on the ESE is of two compartments and measures 12·8 m by 4 m overall, while its neighbour to the NNE measures 9 m by 4 m overall. A stance within the yard may be for a peat-stack.

The largest group of buildings (4) clusters round a knoll to the E of the modern steading. Here, at least fifteen buildings are variously disposed; some are set along and across the slope close to an enclosure which occupies the summit of the knoll, while others are grouped round the base of the knoll and are associated with a series of interrelated enclosures. Let into the slope on the W side of the knoll, there are the remains of a kiln. The buildings vary in their state of preservation, but some have evidently been substantial; at least one has opposed lateral entrances. They range from 5·3 m by 3·9 m to 14·3 m by 4·6 m overall; the largest is a two-compartment building with stone walls up to 0·9 m thick and 0·5 m high.

To the SE of the present steading there is a series of mill lades which drew water from the Allt Mor. A possible horizontal mill (6) is represented by a mill-race and the wasted remains of a rectangular building; the position of another (5), which stood close to the ruinous building shown on plan, can only be surmised in relation to a lade of impressive proportions, which traverses the edge of a ridge of higher ground to the ESE of the 19th-century farmhouse and grain-mill. The latter, which formerly incorporated a kiln, remains intact and has its overshot wheel still in place.

To the SSW of the steading in proximity to two hut-circles (no. 136), there are the remains of a farmstead (7), together with a number of ancillary buildings and two enclosures. The farmstead is exceptional in that it has an L-plan range; the two blocks measure respectively 14·2 m by 5 m and 14·6 m by 4·5 m over turf-covered stone wall-footings up to 1·2 m in thickness.

Pont (c.1600) provides the names 'Alt Edery' and 'Inner Edery'. The lands and mill of 'Innereddre', in the barony of Dunie, are on record in 1510 and 1629 (*Reg. Mag. Sig.*, ii, no. 3450; *Retours*, Perth, No. 367; Spalding 1914, 206). Roy (1747–55, sheet 18/4) depicts a building-cluster, which is probably to be identified with the buildings grouped round the knoll to the ESE of the present steading, and annotates it 'Innerederg'. To the N he depicts a second group of buildings and gives the name as 'Runnavey' but this is probably erroneous as the name properly applies to another building-cluster immediately to the NW (no. 313·9). Stobie (1783) depicts a fermtoun of three building-clusters and a mill, and provides the names (from N to S) 'Kerrow, Tombey and Inveridry', names which also appear on Ainslie's map (1794) along with the name of the landowner, 'Kinloch Esq'.

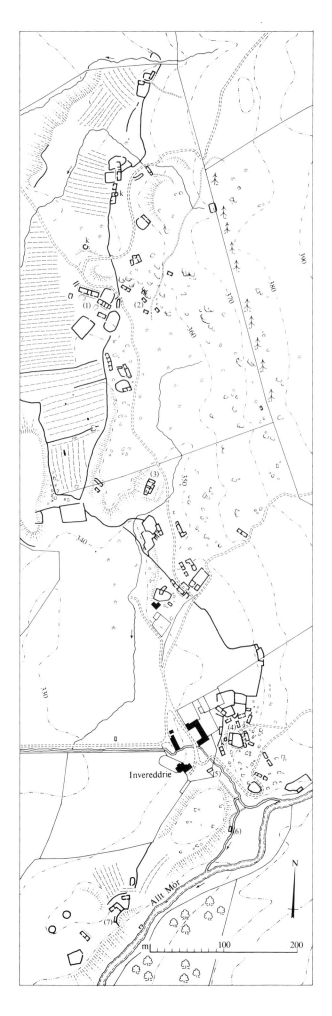

285A Invereddrie, fermtoun, 1:5000

285B Invereddrie, fermtoun, showing (1) and (2) on figure 285A, aerial view from NW

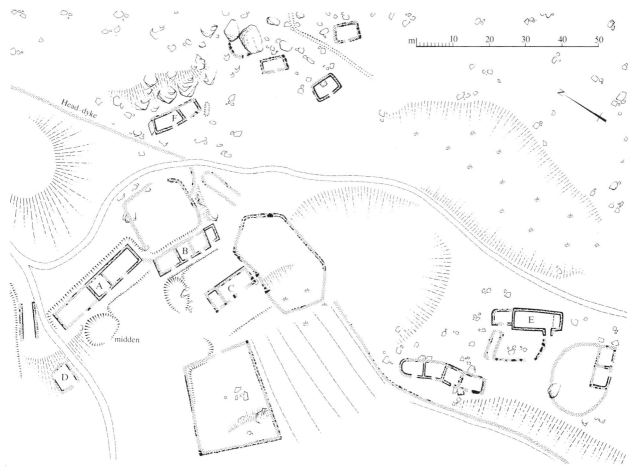

285C Invereddrie, fermtoun (detail), 1:1000, (1) on 285A

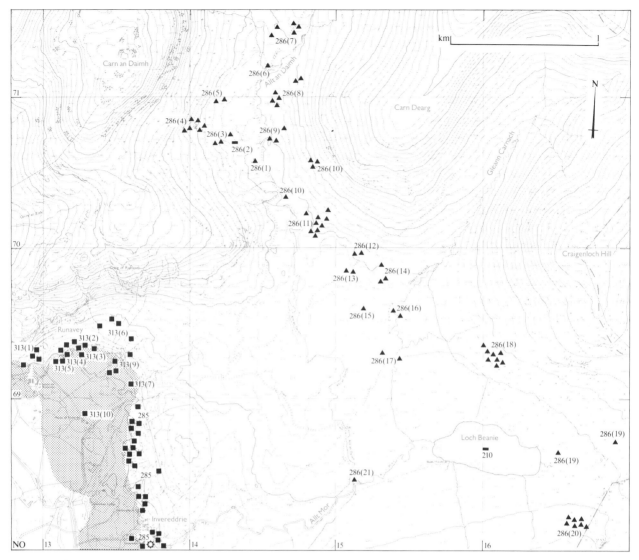

286 Invereddrie, 1:25 000

286 Invereddrie, shielings and still

To the E of Invereddrie the hills that hem in Glenshee
open out to form a large basin. The bottom of the basin
(400 m to 430 m OD) undulates gently in a series of knolls,
low ridges and peat bogs, but to the N, E and S the hills
rise to heights of over 700 m OD. Two glens, the Green
Glen (drained by the Allt an Daimh) and Gleann Carnach
(drained by the Allt Carnach) lead off to the N and NE
respectively, while to the E the basin narrows around
Loch Beanie before rising gradually to a saddle on the
Angus border. See also no. 137.

·1 NO 1444 7058   NO 17 SW 85

This hut is on a low rise 50 m W of the track and 300 m N
of a prominent glacial moraine that juts out from the W
side of the Green Glen. It measures about 3·8 m by 2·5 m
overall, and the wall is composed of little more than a line
of boulders.

·2 NO 1431 7069   NO 17 SW 83

In broken ground to the SE of Carn an Daimh, in the lee
of a prominent pyramid-shaped boulder, there are the
remains of what may be a still and one other building, the
latter severely wasted. The still has been let into the NW
side of a knoll and, but for its WNW end-wall and NW
angle, would have been entirely below ground level. It is
constructed of rubble-masonry and is divided into three
bays divided by opposed cruck-slots (the walls stand 1·6 m

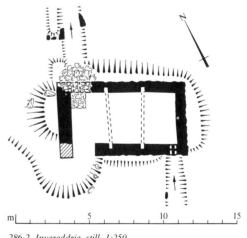

286·2 Invereddrie, still, 1:250

high internally). The doorway is at the W end of the SSW
wall, and the W jamb has been remodelled. Water was
tapped from a burn some 70 m to the WSW by means of a
lade, and entered the building through a lintelled-opening
at the SE end of the SSW wall. Diametrically opposite,
there is a plinth and an outflow-channel, but the extant
side-wall has evidently collapsed outwards and
subsequently been rebuilt, thus obscuring the channel.

146

·3   NO 1421 7070   NO 17 SW 77–8
The remains of what is probably a two-compartment
building with an outshot at its NW end lies on a low spur
90 m W of the still (·2). It measures 11·8 m by 3·8 m
overall, and there are traces of an earlier building
extending for a further 8·5 m from its SE end. To the W
there is a stone-walled enclosure and a small pen, and at
the foot of a boulder 80 m to the NE a probable hut.

·4   NO 140 708   NO 17 SW 76
A group of at least thirteen huts and associated small pens
are scattered around a triangular stone-walled enclosure
built amongst the screes to the WNW of the still (·2).
Some of the huts are little more than cleared spaces in the
scree, but the better-formed are rectangular, ranging
from 4·8 m to 8·9 m in overall length by 3·8 m to 5 m in
breadth. One, a two-compartment structure at the foot of
the scree, overlies a low mound.

·5   NO 1424 7098   NO 17 SW 75
A two-compartment hut is situated on a low spur at the
foot of the slope about 250 m NE of (·4). The building
measures 8·5 m by 4·5 m overall and has an enclosure
attached to its N side. A second hut lies at the foot of an
outcrop 55 m to the W.

·6   NO 1453 7120   NO 17 SW 72
Two huts are situated in a hollow on the NW side of the
track at the S extremity of the low spur which drops down
from the SE flank of Carn Aig Mhala. Overall they
measure 4·8 m by 4·2 m and 4·4 m by 3 m respectively.

·7   NO 1460 7145   NO 17 SW 71, 84
A hut and a mound are situated on a terrace on the W
flank of the spur dropping from Carn Aig Mhala. The hut
appears to have three compartments, but the central one
is probably a separate structure built over an earlier two-
compartment hut; the earlier hut measures 10·8 m by
4·1 m overall. The mound lies immediately to the NW and
measures 10·8 m in diameter by 0·3 m in height. Another
hut (7·4 m by 3·8 m overall) lies on a lower terrace 60 m to
the SW, and there are also traces of another turf-built
structure 70 m to the ENE. Three possible cairns lie
beside the track due E of the hut and mound, and another
lies a further 160 m to the N (NO 1473 7162).

·8   NO 1459 7099   NO 17 SW 73–4
On the E side of the glen, at the foot of Carn Dearg,
there is a cluster of five huts set around a stone-walled
enclosure. The best preserved is rectangular, measuring
7·5 m by 4 m over walls up to 0·7 m high, and lies in a
shallow saddle to the W of the enclosure. The walls of the
rest have been reduced to stony banks no more than 0.3 m
high. Two small cairns are situated about 100 m to the E,
and there are two further huts beside a shallow gully
180 m to the NE. These two huts measure 8·8 m by 4·3 m
and 4·8 m by 3·6 m overall.

·9   NO 1457 7071   NO 17 SW 86–7
The remains of two buildings are visible on the E bank of
the Allt an Daimh due E of the still (·2). Both are
reduced to boulder footings, the more westerly measuring
10·7 m by 4·7 m overall and the other 5 m by 4·4 m. The
latter, however, probably overlies an earlier building,
which extends eastwards for a further 3·9 m to a
rectangular structure measuring 6·4 m by 3·8 m overall.
The remains of another hut are visible 100 m to the NNE;
it has been reduced to a roughly circular mound (9 m in
diameter and 0·6 m in height) with a rectangular
depression at its centre.

·10   NO 148 705   NO 17 SW 89–90
On a terrace high up on the E side of the glen, there are
three huts and a stone-walled enclosure. The largest of
the huts measures about 8 m by 4·8 m overall and has been
set into a turf-covered mound. At the foot of the slope
200 m to the SSW, immediately S of a prominent glacial
moraine, there is a hut measuring 4·5 m by 3·7 m overall.

·11   NO 1488 7009 to 1500 7021   NO 17 SW 91
Disposed on either side of the fence on the S flank of
Carn Dearg, there are five buildings, at least one hut, a
pen, and an enclosure (see also no. 137·5). The buildings
are all reduced either to the lowest course of their walls,
or to their wall-footings, and range from 6·9 m by 4 m to
11 m by 6·7 m overall. Towards the foot of the slope (NO
1486 7010) there is a hut (9·8 m by 4·1 m overall) with a
pen at its NW end. Upslope (NO 1486 7011) there is a
building, which has been set into a mound with a funnel-
entrance on its WSW side. Beside a large boulder (NO
1487 7012) there are the remains of a pen. On a shelf of
higher ground (NO 1489 7014) there is a two-
compartment, round-angled building with outshots at
both ends and a drainage-hood on the NE. Immediately
to NNW there is another round-angled, two-compartment
building, and to the NNE (NO 1488 7018) what may be
either a pen or a small hut. Nearby (NO 1494 7019) there
are the well-preserved remains of a round-angled building
with an entrance central to its SW wall. A low turf-
covered mound (5·1 m in diameter) with a slight central
depression, lying immediately to the SSW, is of uncertain
origin. Upslope (NO 1495 7025), there is another building
which has been let into a mound; this too has a funnelled
entrance-passage (7·7 m long), but on its SW side. At the
foot of the neighbouring scree there is a stone-walled
enclosure.

·12   NO 1517 6997   NO 16 NE 13
On the NE side of a knoll, which is occupied by a hut-
circle (no. 137·6), there are the heather-covered remains
of two adjoining shieling-huts measuring respectively
7·8 m by 4 m and 5·8 m by 4·5 m overall.

·13   NO 1510 6983 and 1509 6983   NO 16 NE 21
Beside the track there are the well-preserved remains of
two shieling-huts. The first (8 m by 5·7 m over a low turf-
covered stony bank 1·7 m thick), is set end-on to the slope
and overlies what is probably an earlier building (5·8 m by
4 m overall). The second hut (7·4 m by 5 m overall), has an
outshot at its SE end (3·8 m by 2·1 m overall).

·14   NO 1531 6988 and 1533 6979   NO 16 NE 19
On a grassy knoll there is a shieling-hut (7·3 m by 4·4 m
overall) with an enclosure on its NE side and a pen to the
ENE. A second hut lies to the NE (9·8 m by 4·4 m overall)
and beside it there is an enclosure. Disposed over the
neighbouring slope to the E, there are several field-banks
and at least eight small cairns. To the WSW of the first
hut there is a hut-circle (no. 137·7).

·15   NO 1519 6959   NO 16 NE 16
The remains of what is probably a turf-built shieling-hut
(8·2 m by 3·9 m overall) occupy a low knoll, overlooking
the raised bog, between the Allt Carnach and the modern
track.

·16   NO 1539 6958   NO 16 NE 18
In a loop of the Allt Carnach, on relatively level ground,
there are the remains of two buildings. The larger of the
two, which is reduced to turf-covered stone wall-footings,
measures 10·6 m by 4·4 m overall, and has an outshot on

the ESE (3·3 m by 2·3 m overall); the entrance is towards the ESE end of the SSW wall and there is a drainage-bank on the NNE.

·17 NO 1532 6930   NO 16 NE 15, 17
On a low ridge flanking the S side of the raised bog, there are the turf-covered stone wall-footings of a hut (5·2 m by 3·2 m overall), while beside the Allt Carnach (NO 1544 9266), some 120 m to the ESE, there are the remains of a building (5 m by 4·4 m overall).

·18 NO 1599 6935 to 1611 6930   NO 16 NE 20
A shieling on the SW flank of Craigenloch Hill comprises at least ten huts, two enclosures and a pen. The huts are all reduced to turf-covered stone wall-footings and range from 4·3 m by 3·7 m to 8·7 m by 4·6 m overall. Of particular note is a series of huts set into three mounds. The first of these mounds, which adjoins the larger enclosure, occupies a low knoll (NO 1602 6931) and is up to 9·5 m in diameter; the hut has a funnelled entrance-passage 5·8 m long on its WSW side and a pen on the NW. There are two huts in the second mound (NO 1604 6926), and yet another in the third (NO 1609 6923). The last mentioned is particularly well preserved with a funnelled entrance-passage 5·8 m long at the E end of its SW wall; the WNW portion of the interior has been adapted as a grouse-butt.

·19 NO 1649 6864   NO 16 NE 11, 12
On a knoll to the ENE of Loch Beanie there are the remains of two shieling-huts measuring respectively 6·5 m by 3·5 m and 8·7 m by 5 m overall; the latter has an outshot on the ESE. Some 400 m to the E (NO 1688 6871) there are three more huts (the largest measuring 10 m by 5·5 m overall) and two enclosures.

·20 NO 1656 6818 to 1670 6812   NO 16 NE 14
Situated on the NE flank of Duchray Hill, there are at least two buildings, six huts, two enclosures, and three ancillary turf-built structures which could all be pens. Both buildings are reduced to turf-covered stone wall-footings and measure respectively 8·6 m by 4·9 m and 10 m by 4·8 m overall; the last has two compartments. The huts range from 3·7 m by 3·2 m to 8·1 m by 4 m overall; one (NO 1658 6821) may overlie an earlier structure (5 m by 3·2 m overall).

·21 NO 1512 6846   NO 16 NE 10
On an area of raised ground in an ox-bow of the Allt an Daimh, there are five probable huts, a building and an enclosure. The huts are set side-by-side in two rows. All are reduced to their turf-covered stone wall-footings, and they range from 4·1 m in diameter to 5·1 m by 4·7 m overall. The building (6·9 m by 2·9 m overall) is set at right angles and to the E of the huts, and the enclosure lies to the N.

287   Kerrow, farmstead and buildings
A farmstead and two buildings lie to the SE and NE respectively of the abandoned 19th-century steading of Kerrow.

·1 NO 1240 6953   NO 16 NW 26
This farmstead occupies a saddle towards the edge of a low ridge about 150 m to the SE of Kerrow. It comprises buildings ranged on two sides of a yard, an adjoining enclosure and, incorporated in the enclosure-wall, a kiln. The buildings are reduced to turf-covered stone wall-footings and measure respectively 9·1 m by 5·4 m and 18 m by 5·2 m overall; the latter has an outshot at both ends and an entrance-doorway central to its SW side-wall which is provided with a short baffle-wall. Immediately to

the NW what may be the site of a third building is suggested by a terrace (10·8 m by 5·2 m). The lands of 'Keranich' in the barony of Dunie are on record in 1510 and 1629 ('Kerrow' 1681); the name also appears on Roy (1747–55, sheet 18/4). Stobie (1783) depicts the farmstead and names it 'Conra', as does Ainslie (1794).
— *Reg. Mag. Sig.*, ii, no. 3450; *Retours*, Perth, Nos. 367, 782; Atholl Muniments, 23, xvi.

·2 NO 1236 6980   NO 16 NW 24, 25
Some 150 m NE of Kerrow, adjacent to the old head-dyke, there are the remains of a two-compartment building (14·5 m by 3·3 m overall) with an entrance and what may be an outshot (3·6 m by 3·1 m overall) on its WSW side. To the NNW (NO 1233 6986), and levelled into the hillslope, there are the remains of what may be another building (5·6 m by 4·1 m overall).

288   Knockali, Pitcarmick-type buildings
The remains of at least five Pitcarmick-type buildings are situated in heather moorland at the head of the valley of the Drumturn Burn; four lie on the lower slopes of Knockali, whilst the fifth is situated on the opposite side of the valley (for prehistoric settlement in this area see no. 124).

·1 NO 1531 5811   NO 15 NE 25
This building is the southernmost of those on the W side of the valley; it measures about 17 m in length overall and ranges in width from 6·8 m at the SW end, to 8·4 m at the centre, and 8·3 m on the NE; and there is a possible internal partition about 3·2 m from the SW end.

·2 NO 1516 5856   NO 15 NE 39
The remains of this building (A on plan) are situated within an enclosure in a saddle on the SE flank of Knockali. It measures 18·3 m in length overall and ranges

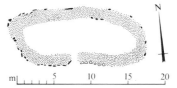

288·2 Knockali, Pitcarmick-type building, 1:500

in width from 7·6 m at the W end to 6 m on the E. The wall (1·5 m thick) survives as a low earthen bank with an outer face of boulders and slabs set on edge; only on the N are there traces of an inner face. It is not known whether the surrounding enclosure is contemporary with the building or simply part of the earlier field-system on this flank of the hill (no. 124·5).

·3 NO 1531 5859   NO 15 NE 40
Situated about 140 m E of (·2), there are the remains of a building (B on plan) which measures about 19 m in length and ranges in width from 7 m on the W to 4·9 m on the E over a wall about 2 m thick and 0·3 m high. The entrance,

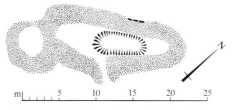

288·3 Knockali, Pitcarmick-type building, 1:500

which lies on the S, has a small porch, and part of the interior has been excavated into the slope; there is a small annexe on the SW. About 4m to the NE there is an irregularly-shaped hollow (measuring 10m in length by up to 3·6m in width and 0·7m in depth), which may be the remains of another Pitcarmick-type building (not shown on plan).

·4   NO 1551 5874   NO 15 NE 33
This Pitcarmick-type building is situated at the foot of a gentle S-facing slope. The building itself measures 21m in overall length by between 8m and 5·5m in breadth, but on the E it has been extended by at least one, and possibly two, additional compartments. The interior of the main building has been excavated into the slope and the entrance is midway along its S side. At the SW angle there is a possible entrance into a small annexe, which, in turn, has an entrance opening on to a roughly paved terrace. On the W there is also an attached enclosure, with possibly a second lying immediately to the NW.

·5   NO 1678 5841   NO 15 NE 44
Two buildings, one of them of Pitcarmick type, and an enclosure are situated on a terrace low down on the W flank of Burnt Cairns. The Pitcarmick-type building measures 24m in length overall and ranges in width from 4·5m on the NNE to 8m on the SSW. The wall is 1·5m thick and up to 0·5m high, and there is a drainage gully

on the E. The second building, which measures 12m by 6·6m overall, has a probable entrance midway along its N side.

289   Knockali, shielings
      NO 1575 5897, 1518 5884   NO 15 NE 32, 45
Within the prehistoric field-system on Knockali (no. 124·5) there are two shieling-huts. Both are reduced to their wall-footings and measure 6m by 4m and 3·6m by 2·8m overall respectively; the latter has a pen attached to its NW side.

290   Lair, Pitcarmick-type buildings
An important group of Pitcarmick-type buildings has been identified amongst the farmsteads and buildings in the valley of the Allt Corra-lairige.

·1   NO 1381 6360   NO 16 SW 35
On a low knoll on the SW side of the Allt Corra-lairige, 400m NW of Wester Lair cottage there are the remains of three buildings defined by little more than low banks and depressions up to 0·4m deep. Two of the buildings are set end-on to each other, that on the SE measuring 20·9m by 7·2m overall, that on the NW 16·8m by 6·3m. The third building lies to the S and appears only as a depression 10·3m long.

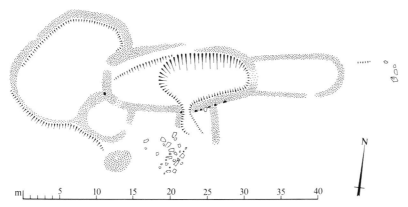

288·4 Knockali, Pitcarmick-type building, 1:500

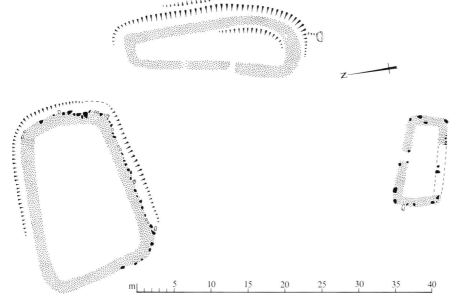

288·5 Knockali, Pitcarmick-type building, 1:500

149

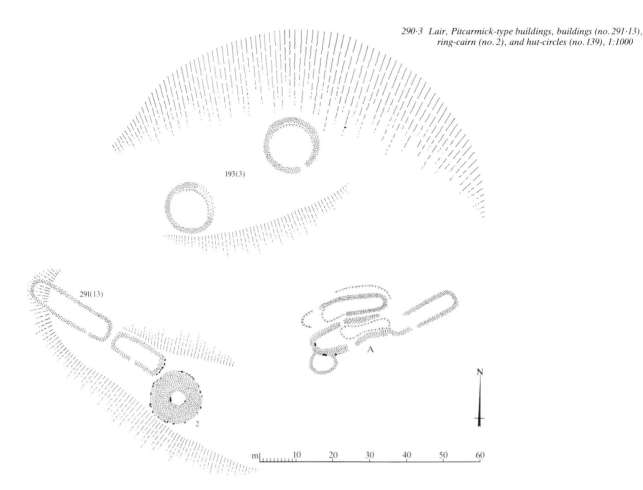

193(3)

291(13)

2

A

N

m | 10 20 30 40 50 60

·2   NO 1311 6372   NO 16 SW 135
On a terrace on the E flank of Lamh Dhearg, 700 m W of
(·1), there are the remains of what is probably a
Pitcarmick-type building. It measures 19 m in overall
length and narrows from 7 m at its WSW end to 5·3 m at its
ENE end which is slightly sunken. Close by there are at
least seven small cairns.

·3   NO 1392 6376   NO 16 SW 127
Some 30 m E of the ring-cairn on the S flank of Torr
Lochaidh (no. 2) there is a complex of three Pitcarmick-
type buildings defined by low, stony banks. The best
preserved (A) is 22·5 m in overall length and varies in
width from 7·7 m at the W end to 5 m at the E end which is
slightly scooped; it has what may be opposed entrances,
and attached to its SW corner there is a small D-shaped
enclosure. It appears to overlie the second building,
which lies immediately to the N and measures about 19 m
by 6 m overall. The third building, which measures about
18·8 m by 6·8 m overall, is set end-on to the first, the
relationship between the two is unclear.

·4   NO 1375 6392   NO 16 SW 51
Situated 200 m NW of (·3), on a slight terrace overlooking
badly-drained ground to the S, there is a probable
Pitcarmick-type building. Round-ended, it measures 17 m
in length over low banks and varies in width from 5·5 m on
the SSE, where the interior is sunken, to 7 m on the
NNW.

291   Lair, fermtouns, farmsteads, buildings and shielings
The modern farm of Lair and the cottage of Wester Lair
stand together on the W side of Glenshee immediately W
of the A93 public road and E of the confluence of the Allt
Corra-lairige and the Allt an Lair (NO 1415 6333). The
sites described here extend from the fermtoun of Easter

Lair, 570 m S of Lair farmhouse, to the farmstead of
Corra-lairig some 1·8 km to the NW.

·1   NO 1432 6275   NO 16 SW 126
The remains of the fermtoun of Easter Lair lie to the E of
the A93 public road and comprise at least seventeen
buildings, reduced to turf-covered wall-footings, together
with their associated enclosures, pens and two kilns. The
buildings are disposed on either side of a canalised burn,
the major concentration being to the E of the burn, in
close proximity to a fank and a ruinous 19th-century
cottage in which two pairs of infilled cruck-slots are
visible. The cottage is shown unroofed on the first edition
of the OS 6-inch map (Perthshire, 1865–7, sheet 33).
  Amongst the buildings close to the cottage there
appear to be two principal units with their buildings
ranged around yards; each has a large three-compartment
building on its NE side, and these measure 16·7 m by 4·8 m
and 21·7 m by 5·2 m overall respectively. On the W side of
the burn, where the ground rises steeply to the A93, the
buildings are more dispersed, although again it may be
possible to identify two units, the axes of their buildings
lying across the contour. One comprises two buildings set
parallel to each other and measuring 7·6 m by 4·3 m and
9 m by 5·5 m overall, the other, to the S of a stone wall,
comprises three buildings measuring 14·3 m by 3·4 m,
12·2 m by 5·5 m and 8·3 m by 4·5 m overall.

·2   NO 1406 6314   NO 16 SW 33
At the foot of a steep slope 180 m SSW of Wester Lair
cottage there is a farmstead comprising three buildings.
Two of the buildings are set parallel to each other. The
larger, on the ENE, is probably of three compartments
and measures 22·3 m by 5·3 m over turf-covered wall-
footings; the smaller, on the WSW, appears as little more
than a rectangular platform (6·4 m by 2·2 m) with a
possible outshot. The third building is set at right angles

277

to the first at its NNW end but has been heavily robbed, and its size and the relationship between the two buildings are undetermined.

·3 NO 1400 6321   NO 16 SW 46
Situated 100 m WSW of Wester Lair cottage, on the edge of a scarp which falls steeply to the Allt an Lair on the N, there is a farmstead comprising up to three buildings and a kiln. Two of the buildings are set at right angles to each other; the larger, which may be of three compartments, measures 24·3 m by 6 m over stone wall-footings, whilst the smaller, which is defined largely by robber-trenches, is of two compartments and measures 8·2 m by 6·1 m overall. What may be a third building or a pen, measuring 10·8 m by 3·2 m over a low bank, lies to the S.

The remains are probably those of the farmstead of 'Knock' depicted on the maps of Stobie (1783) and Ainslie (1794).

·4 NO 1403 6333   NO 16 SW 50
On a narrow terrace on the N bank of the Allt an Lair, 100 m W of Wester Lair cottage, there is a farmstead comprising two buildings set at right angles to each other, along the sides of what is probably a small yard. Both buildings have been reduced to turf-covered wall-footings; the larger is of two compartments, measures 14·6 m by 4·6 m overall and has an outshot at its E end, whilst the smaller measures 7 m by 4·6 m overall.

·5 NO 1334 6363   NO 16 SW 134
Disposed over a series of low knolls at the foot of Lamh Dhearg, there are six shieling-huts and a scatter of small cairns. The huts, which have been reduced to their wall-footings, range in size from 5 m by 4·4 m to 10·5 m by 7·2 m overall, and one of them (NO 1338 6367) is associated with an enclosure.

·6 NO 1413 6360   NO 16 SW 141
On a terrace 260 m N of Lair and 60 m W of the Military Road, there are the remains of a two-compartment building and a hut, both reduced to turf-covered wall-footings. The building measures 15·8 m by 5·8 m overall, the hut 5·8 m by 4 m overall.

·7 NO 1412 6372   NO 16 SW 41
Situated 110 m N of (·6), about 80 m W of the A93 public road, there is a building adjoined by a roughly rectangular enclosure. The building measures 14·5 m by 4·4 m over stone wall-footings.

·8 NO 1403 6374   NO 16 SW 42
Some 80 m W of (·7) there are the remains of a building comprising a slight rectangular depression defined on the

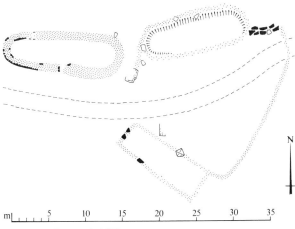

291·9 *Lair, farmstead, 1:500*

E by a low bank and on the W by a scarp 0·1 m high. It measures 16·9 m by 6·9 m overall.

·9 NO 1401 6365   NO 16 SW 38, 40
About 150 m W of the A93 the modern track crosses the remains of a farmstead comprising three buildings, reduced to their stone wall-footings, and an irregularly shaped enclosure. The best-preserved building, which superficially resembles a Pitcarmick-type building, lies outside the enclosure, immediately to the W; it has rounded ends, measures 16·4 m in overall length and varies in width from 3·6 m at the W end to 5·4 m at the E end. The second building is also external to the enclosure, but adjoins its SSW side, whilst the third building lies within the enclosure, adjoining its N side. There is a further building to the E (not shown on plan).

·10 NO 1396 6365   NO 16 SW 37
Single building lies about 30 m W of (·9) and is also crossed by the track. Appearing as a rectangular depression flanked by banks up to 0·2 m high, it measures 23·8 m by 6 m overall.

·11 NO 1396 6362   NO 16 SW 140
Alongside a field-bank to the SW of (·10) there are what may be the remains of a building measuring 11·5 m by 5·8 m overall.

·12 NO 1390 6365   NO 16 SW 36
A building adjoined on the S by an enclosure lies 100 m W of (·10). It measures 8·8 m by 4·7 m over stone wall-footings; its W end is rounded and at its E end there are traces of what may be an outshot or an earlier building.

·13 NO 1386 6376   NO 16 SW 48
Immediately NW of the large ring-cairn (no. 2), there are the remains of what are probably two buildings set end-on to each other. With the exception of the SE end of the SE building, which is formed of kerb-stones removed from the cairn, the buildings are ill-defined but measure about 15 m by 7·2 m and 25 m by 7 m respectively overall. *290·3*

·14 NO 1372 6406   NO 16 SW 43
A single building measuring 8 m by 5·5 m over low banks lies amongst a group of small cairns on the NW flank of Torr Lochaidh.

·15 NO 1135 6399   NO 16 SW 30
Situated on the NE bank of the Allt Corra Lairige there is a farmstead comprising three buildings ranged around a yard. The buildings measure 8·3 m by 4·6 m, 8·2 m by 4 m and 9·9 m by 4·5 m respectively over walls reduced to little more than stone footings; what may be a fourth building, measuring 8 m by 5·3 m over stone wall-footings, lies on the opposite bank of the burn. The farmstead is depicted as 'Balriadi' on Stobie's map (1783).

·16 NO 1317 6438   NO 16 SW 5
Some 350 m NNW of (·15) there are the remains of a small fermtoun. The buildings, their walls generally reduced to the lowest courses but elsewhere up to a maximum height of 1 m, appear to be disposed in three units. On the S there is a cluster of five buildings, ranging in size from 5·8 m by 4·5 m to 17·2 m by 4·2 m overall, and a possible kiln. To the N there are two buildings set at right angles to each other (9·5 m by 5·2 m and 12·8 m by 4·8 m overall respectively) and to the NE of these two more buildings (6·4 m by 4·6 m and 10·7 m by 4·6 m) which are also set at right angles to each other. The largest building, which measures 18·4 m by 5·2 m overall, stands alone on the N edge of the settlement, and a second possible kiln lies further to the N.

L

Depicted as 'Corra-lairig' on the first edition of the OS 6-inch map (Perthshire, 1865–7, sheet 33), it is shown as 'Conglarich' on Stobie's map (1783), whilst 'the toun and lands of Conglerg' are on record in 1700 (Spalding 1914, 214).

·17 NO 1325 6453   NO 16 SW 45
Situated 130 m NNE of Corra-lairig there is a shieling-hut measuring 10·5 m by 4·7 m overall. What may be the remains of another hut and an enclosure lie about 50 m to W.

·18 NO 1308 6445   NO 16 SW 142
About 80 m WNW of Corra-lairig, beside the modern track, there is a shieling-hut measuring 9·4 m by 5·2 m overall. A second hut lies 40 m to the SSW.

·19 NO 1301 6430   NO 16 SW 143
On a promontory 140 m WSW of Corra-lairig there is a shieling-hut measuring 9·4 m by 5·2 m overall.

·20 NO 1288 6435   NO 16 SW 32
The remains of a building are situated at the head of a slope dropping to the Allt Corra-lairig, 130 m WNW of (·23). It measures 9·3 m by 3·6 m over walls standing up to 0·8 m in height and has a D-shaped outshot at its WSW end.

Lair is depicted on Pont's map (c.1600) and is mentioned in 1674, when it formed part of the barony of Balmachreuchie granted to the Spaldings of Ashintully (Spalding 1914, 75). In 1730 both Easter and Wester Lair are recorded (Spalding 1914, 240), and Roy's map (1747–55, sheet 18/4) shows Lair in approximately the position occupied by the existing farm, whilst an unnamed settlement, probably Easter Lair (·1) lies on the E side of the road to the S. Both Easter and Wester Lair appear on the maps of Stobie (1783) and Ainslie (1794), though a settlement named 'Burnside' occupies what seems to be the present site of Wester Lair, with Wester Lair then possibly straddling the Military Road a little to the N. Only Easter Lair is shown on Thomson's map (1825). Apart from the buildings of the 18th-century farmsteads, there is a series of earlier buildings in this valley. These include eight buildings of Pitcarmick-type (no. 290) and the slight remains of four others (·8, ·10, ·13).

292   Leduckie, farmstead
NO 0705 4667   NO 04 NE 29
This farmstead is situated 200 m ENE of Leduckie and comprises a building, measuring 18 m by 4·4 m over stone wall-footings, adjoined by an enclosure. Some 18 m to the E there are traces of what may be a second building forming the chord of a D-shaped enclosure.

293   Loch Charles, shielings,
·1 NO 0845 5400   NO 05 SE 16
Situated 110 m S of Loch Charles, there is a group of three rectangular shieling-huts. Two of the huts are set at right angles to each other and measure 4·6 m by 3·9 m and 5 m by 3·5 m respectively over stone wall-footings; the third measures 6·7 m by 4 m over stone wall-footings and is adjoined on the NE by a small oval structure which has been sunk into a mound. Some 50 m to the W (NO 0840 5398) there are a further two rectangular huts and a small enclosure; the huts measure 7·9 m by 3·5 m and 8·3 m by 4·5 m respectively over stone walls standing to a maximum height of 0·5 m. Both the larger hut and the enclosure overlie the remains of what may be earlier huts.

·2 NO 0866 5400   NO 05 SE 63
What are probably the remains of two rectangular huts lie 160 m SE of Loch Charles; the smaller, which is 6 m in overall length, overlies one end of the larger, which measures 9·5 m by 5·2 m overall. Two more probable huts, set side by side, are situated 100 m to the SE.

·3 NO 0836 5453   NO 05 SE 66
A single rectangular hut (5·5 m by 3 m overall) is situated in the gully that marks the edge of the group of small cairns surrounding the hut-circles no. 141·1. Other possible huts are visible overlying hut-circles C and E.

·4 NO 085 549   NO 05 SE 65
Three huts are situated on the N side of a shallow gully 230 m NW of the triangular plantation to the NNE of Loch Charles. They are all subrectangular and the largest measures 5·5 m by 3·7 m overall.

294   Lornty Burn, buildings
NO 110 480   NO 14 NW 76–8
On the banks of the Lornty Burn some 650 m SE of Bog Mill (no. 310·5), there are the remains of three buildings, one on the N bank and two on the S. That on the N (NO 1103 4825) is situated on a low rise and measures 7·1 m by 3·7 m over stone wall-footings. One of those on the S (NO 1085 4811) is of at least two compartments and measures 14·8 m by 5·4 m over turf-covered wall-footings; the other (NO 1116 4796), which lies immediately N of a small rectangular enclosure, measures 7·4 m by 5·3 m over clay-bonded walls up to 0·9 m high and has an outshot at each end.

295   Macmaridge, buildings
·1 NO 0600 4733   NO 04 NE 43
About 370 m N of Macmaridge steading there are the remains of a building and enclosure. The building measures 8·2 m by 5·2 m over turf-covered stone wall-footings and has an entrance on its SW side.

·2 NO 0546 4756   NO 04 NE 44
On the SE flank of Conlan Hill and set roughly 40 m apart there are a further three buildings. All are reduced to their wall-footings and range from 7·2 m by 5·2 m to 8·6 m by 4·7 m overall.

·3 NO 0564 4666   NO 04 NE 40
The remains of two buildings are situated 400 m SW of Macmaridge and 130 m E of the ruins of Over Cardney. Both are reduced to their wall-footings, the larger measuring 15 m by 5·6 m overall, and the smaller, which is round-ended and has an entrance on the S, 8·8 m by 5·6 m. The farmstead of 'Cairnie' is depicted by Stobie (1783).

296   Mill of Drumturn, mill
NO 1540 5700   NO 15 NE 26
The Mill of Drumturn is situated on the E bank of the Drumturn Burn 950 m WNW of Corb. The remains are difficult to interpret, A and possibly B may be mill-buildings, and C a kiln. The well-preserved lade can be traced northwards for a distance of about 80 m. The steading, which lies to the E, comprises two buildings (D and E) ranged on the SW side of an enclosure. Both have been reduced to their stone wall-footings and measure 19 m by 6 m and 33 m by 5 m respectively overall.

Stobie's map (1783) records what is probably the steading, but omits to show a mill symbol, while a mill

141·1

310

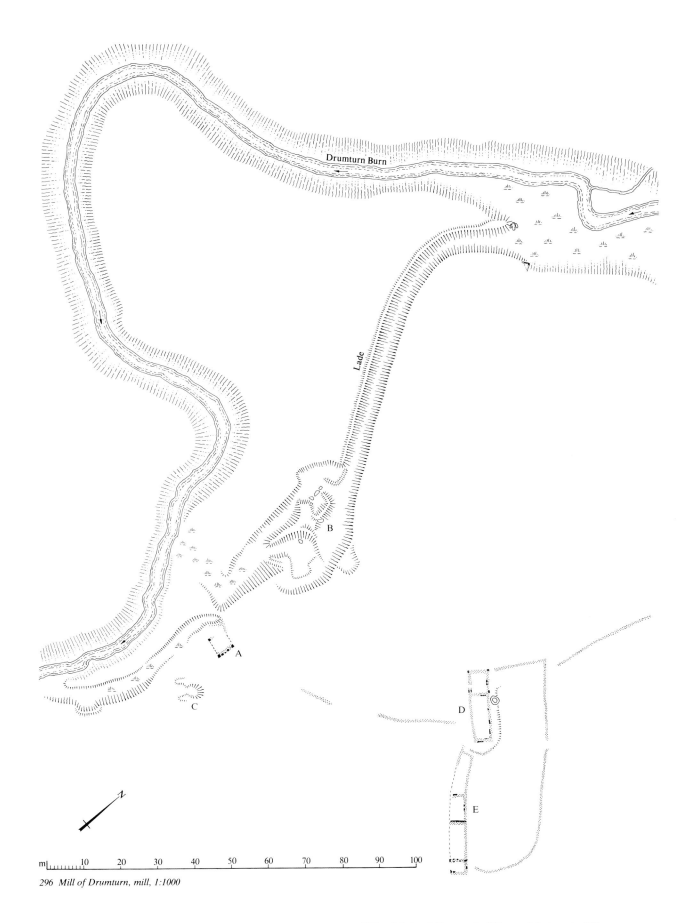

296 Mill of Drumturn, mill, 1:1000

appears as ruinous on the first edition of the OS 6-inch map (Perthshire, 1867, sheet 42).

297   Muir of Gormack, Pitcarmick-type building
NO 1320 4689   NO 14 NW 84
The remains of this Pitcarmick-type building are situated 100 m E of the the ruined 19th-century farmstead of

Marleehill, within an area of ridge-and-furrow cultivation on a gentle S-facing slope. It measures 15·5 m by a maximum of 6·1 m over low, turf-covered banks and is widest at its rounded E end; the W half of the interior is lower than the E half, and there is an entrance midway along the S side. Situated about 50 m to the SE there are the poorly-preserved remains of a building measuring about 15·8 m by 6·1 m overall.

298 Old Milton of Drimmie, mill
NO 1599 5123   NO 15 SE 87
A well-preserved mill-building is let into the foot of the slope 110 m to the SE of Old Milton of Drimmie. It is rectangular on plan (12·7 m by 6·5 m over stone walls 0·7 m thick and up to 1·3 m high in eight courses) with an entrance central to its E wall, and on the N it incorporates a kiln (now choked with debris); access to the kiln-floor was by a forestair. Central to the S wall there are a

lintelled axle-opening and traces of a scarcement for the stone-floor. The position of the wheel-pit can still be seen and the lade (up to 2·4 m wide and 1·6 m deep) may be traced for a distance of over 280 m to the WNW. There is what may be another structure (6 m by 4·2 m overall) 11 m to the WSW. A series of tracks descends the slope from Old Milton of Drimmie to the mill-site. The mill is depicted by Stobie (1783) and is shown as unroofed by Brown (1808).

299 Olies Burn, buildings
NO 1817 5269   NO 15 SE 59, 62
On the S side of the Olies Burn 730 m SW of Smyrna cottage there are the remains of two buildings measuring 7 m by 5·4 m and 20·5 m by 4·4 m overall; the larger is of two compartments. Immediately to the E, traces of a possible third building are visible, while 170 m to the SE (NO 1833 5262) the remains of a further two (each about 9 m by 6 m overall) can be seen amongst a group of small cairns (no. 150·3).

300 Parkhill, inscribed lintel
NO 1891 4649   NO 14 NE 83
A lintel wrought with a chamfered arris and the date 1642, and the initials 'DDCS', is incorporated in the fabric of the NNW wall of Parkhill House, a 19th-century mansion. The policies of the house are depicted by Roy (1747–55, sheet 18/3) and the mansion of Parkhill is named and depicted by Stobie (1783).

301 Persie, farmsteads and buildings
Several farmsteads and buildings are visible to the E, N and W of Persie (see also no. 130·1).

·1   NO 1384 5501   NO 15 NW 41
Situated on a NE-facing terrace 230 m ENE of Persie House, there is a farmstead comprising two buildings and three enclosures. The largest of the buildings has four compartments and measures 20·5 m by 4·8 m over walls 0·8 m thick and 0·3 m high; at the SW corner there is a small kiln which appears to be integral with the building. The enclosures lie immediately to the N, W and E respectively of this building. The second building, which measures 14·4 m by 4 m over walls 0·8 m thick and 0·4 m high, is situated immediately E of the E enclosure.

·2   NO 1352 5527   NO 15 NW 33
The wasted remains of a bow-sided building are situated amongst a group of small cairns (no. 135·3) 400 m NNE of Mains of Persie steading. The building measures 16·9 m by

up to 6·2 m over turf-covered stone wall-footings, and there is an enclosure at its N end. About 35 m to the NW there are traces of another enclosure.

·3   NO 1242 5508   NO 15 NW 43
Some 970 m WNW of Mains of Persie steading there are the remains of a farmstead comprising four buildings and a kiln-and-chamber. The buildings range from 9 m by 5·8 m to 18 m by 4 m overall; the last has an outshot on the E. Both Stobie (1783) and Ainslie (1794) depict a farmstead, and the former names it 'Craigiegowan'.

302 Pitcarmick (West), Pitcarmick-type buildings
NO 05 56/06 56   NO 05 NE 22, 73
Situated amongst the hut-circles and field-systems (no. 151·8) to the N of Pitcarmick Loch there are eight Pitcarmick-type buildings.

·1   NO 0546 5688   NO 05 NE 22·5–·6
This Pitcarmick-type building (H on fig.) is situated at the rear of a natural terrace; it measures 19·3 m in length by 7·7 m in width at the W end and 5·6 m in width at the E end over a stony wall up to 2 m thick and 0·4 m high. The

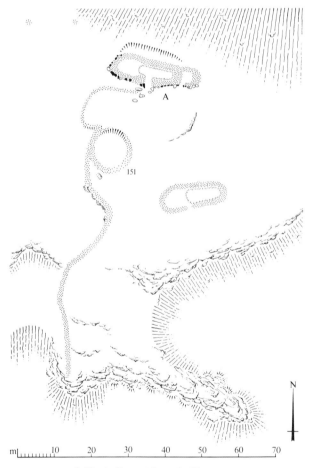

302·1 Pitcarmick (West), Pitcarmick-type buildings, 1:1000

wall has a prominent outer boulder face, but no inner face is visible, and on the N the wall is predominantly of earth. The E half of the interior has been hollowed out, and on the E there is an outshot which may be later than the main body of the structure, as it is not covered by the drainage gulley that runs parallel to the N wall. A stony bank, which extends from a point close to the entrance, runs over the W edge of a hut-circle (no. 151) and terminates on the edge of a steep rock-face.

A second Pitcarmick-type building is situated on level

ground 27 m closer to the front of the terrace; it measures 18·5 m in length by 7·5 m in width at the W end and 5·5 m at the E end over a low bank (1·5 m thick and 0·3 m high), and the E half of the interior has been hollowed out.

·2   NO 0507 5674   NO 05 NE 22·1
Situated on the S edge of a terrace overlooking the W end of Pitcarmick Loch, there is an irregularly-shaped Pitcarmick-type building (J on fig.) which measures 30 m in overall length by up to 7·8 m in width at the W end and

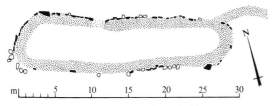

302·2 Pitcarmick (West), Pitcarmick-type building, 1:500

6 m at the E end. The wall comprises an outer face of slabs set on edge and backed by a peat-covered, largely earthen, bank 1·3 m thick and up to 0·3 m high. There may be an original entrance on the N side. A short length of bank, which abuts the E end of the building, extends, for a short distance to the E before being lost in an area of boggy ground.

·3   NO 0518 5666   NO 05 NE 22·2
The heather-covered remains of this Pitcarmick-type building (K on fig.) are situated on a gentle, S-facing slope some 110 m SE of (·2). It measures about 18·6 m in overall length by about 10·3 m in width on the W and 7·1 m on the E. The E half of the interior has been hollowed out.

·4   NO 0531 5658   NO 05 NE 22·3
Situated about 180 m SE of (·3) and on a gentle S-facing slope, there are the remains of a Pitcarmick-type building (L on fig.) which measures 23·3 m in length by 6·9 m in

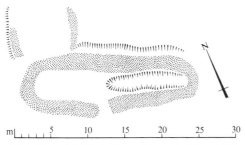

302·4 Pitcarmick (West), Pitcarmick-type building, 1:500

width at the W end, 8·5 m at the centre and 5·9 m at the E end. The E part of the building has been hollowed out and its N side, at the W end of which there are traces of a possible enclosure, is protected by a drainage gully.

·5   NO 0535 5670   NO 05 NE 22·4
The slight remains of this Pitcarmick-type building (M on fig.) are situated on the S edge of a narrow terrace about 110 m NNE of (·4). It measures 18·8 m in length and ranges in width from 6·6 m on the W to 5·4 m on the E over a low peat-covered wall up to 1·7 m thick and 0·1 m high. The E half of the interior has been hollowed out and, although the position of the entrance is not clear, there are two opposed breaks in the wall at about the mid-point.

·6   NO 0554 5669   NO 05 NE 22·7
Situated on the same terrace as (·5), but lying 160 m to the E, there is a complex sequence of buildings and enclosures (N on fig.). What is probably the earliest building (A) is subrectangular on plan and measures about 14·7 m by up to 7·4 m over a turf-covered stony wall. The S side of this building is partly overlain by an enclosure bank, which runs round to the entrance of a Pitcarmick-type building (B) measuring 20 m in overall length and ranging in width from 7·7 m on the W to 5·2 m

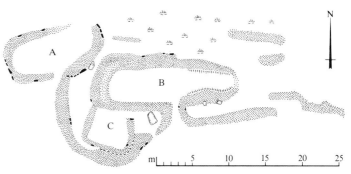

302·6 Pitcarmick (West), Pitcarmick-type building, 1:500

on the E; the E third of the interior of the second building has been hollowed out. A small square enclosure (C), which abuts the SW side of the building, overlies the earlier enclosure bank.

·7   NO 0570 5664   NO 05 NE 22·8
Situated about 145 m E of (·6) and situated on the same narrow terrace, there are the remains of a Pitcarmick-type building (P on fig.). It measures 18·2 m in overall length and ranges in width from about 8 m at the W end to 6·7 m at the E end; the E part of the interior has been hollowed out.

·8   NO 0627 5614   NO 05 NE 73
Situated in moorland about 890 m ESE of Pitcarmick Loch, there are the remains of two superimposed

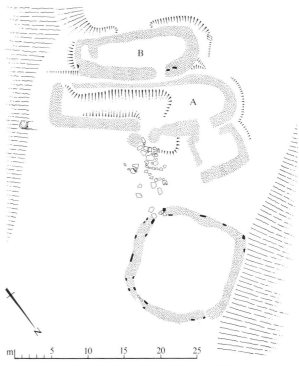

302·8 Pitcarmick (West), Pitcarmick-type buildings, 1:500

Pitcarmick-type buildings and two enclosures. The earlier building (A) measures about 25·1 m in length overall and ranges in width from 7·5 at the NW end to 6 m on the SE; the SE end of the interior has been hollowed out, and immediately outside the entrance there is a low platform with a path leading to an adjacent enclosure. At the N corner of the earlier building there is a small enclosure or annexe defined by a footing built of small slabs set on edge. The later building (B), which lies over the SW wall of the earlier, measures 16·8 m in overall length by about 6·5 m in width at the NW end and 5 m at the SE end, and there are external drainage gullies on the NW and SW.

303 Pitcarmick (North), Pitcarmick-type buildings

153   The remains of up to three Pitcarmick-type buildings are situated within heather moorland some 1·9 km W of Cultalonie steading; on the date of visit all were masked by deep heather.

·1 NO 0610 5810   NO 05 NE 84

154·4A   Situated about 30 m SW of a hut-circle (no. 154·4), there are the remains of a building (C on fig.) which has been levelled into the gentle S-facing slope. It measures some 25·4 m in length overall and ranges in width from 5·3 at the E end to 6·3 m at the W. The N wall has been reduced to little more than a scarp, and on the S there is a poorly-defined rubble bank. The entrance lies on the S, and the E half of the interior has been hollowed out. Abutting the W end there are the remains of a possible enclosure, and the building is crossed from N to S by a substantial earth-and-stone bank.

To the NE there are the probable remains of a second Pitcarmick-type building. It lies parallel to the slope and measures at least 14·5 m in length by a maximum of 3·4 m in breadth over its hollowed interior.

·2 NO 0598 5812   NO 05 NE 136

The remains of this building (D on fig.) are situated on a gentle, NE-facing slope about 110 m W of (·1); it

154·4A   measures about 28·5 m in length overall and ranges in width from 8·5 m at the W end to 6·5 m on the E. The E two-thirds of the interior have been hollowed out. There are two enclosures attached to the N wall of the building, and a third to the S. Situated a short distance to the NE, there are the footings of a subrectangular building, which measures about 10 m by up to 7 m overall and has a small outshot at its NE end.

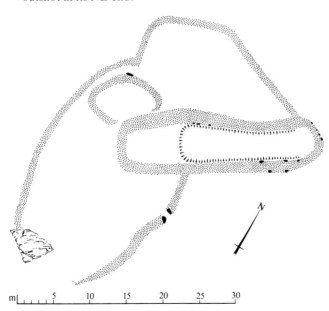

m |_____| 5   10   15   20   25   30

303·2 Pitcarmick (North), Pitcarmick-type building, 1:500

304 Pitcarmick, fermtoun and buildings
NO 0836 5661   NO 05 NE 46–7

Beside a burn some 200 m to the NNW of Pitcarmick steading there are the remains of a small fermtoun comprising twelve buildings and a kiln-and-chamber; nine of the buildings are grouped to the SE of a 19th-century sheepfold, the remainder lie immediately to the S on the opposite side of a burn. The buildings are reduced to the lowest courses of their stone walls or to turf-covered wall-footings; four are of two compartments and two of three, and they range from 5·5 m by 4·4 m to 24·5 m by 5·6 m overall. Scattered over a distance of 100 m to the SW, there are five buildings which range in size from 5·8 m by 4 m to 17·5 m by 4·7 m overall; one (NO 0823 5650) has an enclosure on its S side. A sixth is situated below the track on the N bank of the Pitcarmick Burn, a further 70 m to the SW (NO 0818 5642). To the N of the sheepfold (NO 0833 5671), there is a two-compartment building (9·4 m by 4·3 m overall) and on its SW side a possible stance.

The principal building-cluster is probably to be identified as 'Wester Pitcarmick' which is depicted by both Roy (1747–55, sheet 17/2) and Stobie (1783). The lands and touns of Easter and Wester Pitcarmick, and a corn mill, are on record in 1674 (Spalding 1914, 75).

305 Pitcarmick (East), buildings

On the E edge of the high moorland between the Pitcarmick Burn and the Allt Cul na Coille about 1 km WNW of Pitcarmick steading, there is a series of individual buildings and groups of buildings here described from S to N. Another building lies on the flank of Creag Mholach to the N of the Allt Cul na Coillie.

·1 NO 0734 5662   NO 05 NE 115

The remains of a subrectangular building (not shown on plan) measuring 5·2 m by 4·5 m over stone wall-footings are situated on a heather-covered knoll. A small enclosure lies immediately to the NW.

·2 NO 0743 5671   NO 05 NE 119

A subrectangular building (A), measuring 5 m by 4 m overall, lies 130 m NE of (·1).

·3 NO 074 567   NO 05 NE 117

In a natural depression to the S of the track to Pitcarmick Loch and 40 m WNW of three tangential hut-circles (no. 153·7) there is an enclosure (B) (63 m by up to 37 m within a low stony bank), in which there are the remains of four buildings. The westernmost, which is bow-sided, measures 10·2 m by up to 4·9 m overall, whilst the other three range in overall size from 7·7 m by 4·6 m to 9·2 m by 4·7 m. A fifth building, on the N, is overlain by the bank of the enclosure.

·4 NO 074 568   NO 05 NE 116

To the N of the track there are ten buildings and, with the exception of C, all are either round-ended, round-angled or bow-sided. Of particular note are the two largest buildings (D and E), both defined by boulder-faced banks. The best preserved building is D, which measures 17 m by up to 7 m overall, whilst E, which is only well preserved on the W, measures 26·5 m by 7·8 m overall.

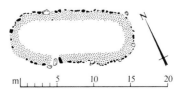

m |_____| 5   10   15   20

305·4 Pitcarmick (East), building (D), 1:500

156

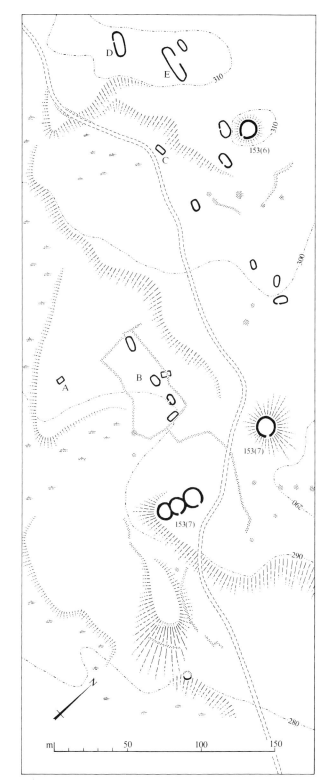

305 Pitcarmick (East), buildings, and hut-circles, 1:2500

The remaining buildings range in overall size from 6·5 m by 3·7 m to 12·8 m by 7 m.

·5   NO 075 569   NO 05 NE 121
Disposed amongst a group of hut-circles (no. 153·6), 100 m NE of (·4), there are the remains of five buildings ranging in overall size from 5 m by 3·1 m to 9 m by 5·5 m. About 60 m to the N (NO 0752 5704), immediately ESE of a hut-circle, there is a round-ended building measuring 17 m by 7 m overall, whilst 130 m to the NNW (NO 0743 5708) there is a building measuring 9 m by 5 m overall.

·6   NO 0771 5767   NO 05 NE 91
On a terrace to the E of Creag Mholach and 70 m NW of a pair of hut-circles (no. 153·1) there is a building measuring 10·8 m by 6·2 m over stone wall-footings.

306   Pitcarmick (North), buildings
A series of buildings and cultivation remains is disposed over the W side of a ridge which extends in a series of rocky shelves for over 3 km between the Allt Cul na Coille and Glen Derby; these are described from E to W (see also no. 303).

·1   NO 0653 5825   NO 05 NE 93
The remains of two buildings are situated at the SE corner of a terrace which is swathed in rig-and-furrow. Both buildings are reduced to their heather-covered wall-footings and measure respectively 14·7 m by 4·4 m and 7 m by 4 m overall. The first is of three compartments (one overlain by a pen) and has an enclosure on the E; another enclosure lies to the SE of the second building.

·2   NO 0640 5834   NO 05 NE 85
Beside a track about 150 m NW of (·1), there are the remains of what may be a building. It measures at least 14·7 m by 6·6 m over a heather-covered bank 1·5 m in thickness and 0·3 m in height; at its NW end there is a compartment with a circular interior measuring roughly 4·7 m in diameter.

·3   NO 0630 5805   NO 05 NE 80
Some 300 m SSW of (·2) and disposed over a low rise which bears extensive traces of rig-and-furrow, there are the remains of at least nine buildings and a possible enclosure. The buildings are all reduced to turf-covered wall-footings and range from 5·4 m by 4·3 m to 11·5 m by 3·7 m overall; two are of two compartments, three are associated with pens, and one (NO 0635 5798) is overlain by a bank which encloses the cultivated area.

·4   NO 0594 5804   NO 05 NE 83
To the W of (·3) there are the remains of ten buildings and at least one enclosure. The buildings are all reduced to turf-covered stone wall-footings and range from 5·3 m by 3·5 m to 14·2 m by 5·8 m overall; two have more than one compartment and one has an attached pen. Close by there are the remains of a Pitcarmick-type building (no. 303·2).

·5   NO 0557 5812   NO 05 NE 82, 94, 138
Some 300 m W of (·4) there are the remains of a subrectangular building (8·2 m by 4·2 m overall); another building (11 m by 3·9 m overall) lies about 290 m to the WNW (NO 0528 5813) and about 500 m N of this (NO 0532 5866), there are the remains of a third (5·5 m by 3·5 m overall).

307   Pitcarmick (West), shielings
Disposed over the slopes between the Allt Cul na Coille and the Pitcarmick Burn to the E of Creag na h-Iolaire, there are a series of shielings comprising both buildings and huts (see also no. 151·4). These are described from E to W.

·1   NO 0672 5652   NO 05 NE 69
On a S-facing terrace overlooking the Pitcarmick Burn there are the turf-covered wall-footings of four huts ranging from 5 m by 3·5 m to 7·2 m by 3·7 m overall. Each has an outshot and an entrance central to its S wall. The remains of a building (8·3 m by 4·9 m overall) occupy a terrace to the E (NO 0667 5654).

·2 NO 0609 5677   NO 05 NE 113, 120
On the SE shoulder of Creag na h-Iolaire some 650 m
WNW of (·1), there are the boulder wall-footings of two
buildings measuring respectively 7·2 m by 3·5 m and 8·2 m
by 4·9 m overall. A further two buildings and a pen are
located on a terrace to the WNW (NO 0602 5688, 0604
5691); the larger of the two buildings measures 8 m by
4·5 m overall.

·3 NO 0601 5703 to 0605 5715   NO 05 NE 111
Five huts, two buildings and three pens are set at the rear
of a terrace about 120 m to the N of (·2). All are reduced
to turf-covered stone wall-footings; the huts range from
4·2 m by 4 m to 7·4 m by 4·1 m overall and the buildings
measure 9·4 m by 3·6 m and 11 m by 4 m overall
respectively. The larger of the two buildings (NO 0603
5710), which is possibly of three compartments, has been
sunk into a shieling-mound (14·7 m in diameter) and has a
funnel-entrance on its SE side.

·4 NO 0626 5717   NO 05 NE 108–10
About 200 m E of (·2) there is a building and pen. The
building measures 7·3 m by 5·7 m over turf- and heather-
covered wall-footings spread up to 1·2 m in thickness. A
hut (6·2 m by 4·3 m overall) occupies a knoll about 200 m
to the ENE (NO 0644 5731) and on slightly higher ground
to the NNW (NO 0627 5753), there are the turf-covered
wall-footings of another building (8 m by 4·5 m overall)
and pen.

·5 NO 0609 5753 to 0604 5749   NO 05 NE 106
Three buildings and a hut are disposed over a low ridge to
the W of (·4). All are reduced to their wall-footings and
range from 5·2 m by 3·3 m to 9·6 m by 4·4 m overall.

·6 NO 0548 5749, 0549 5748   NO 05 NE 68, 103
To the W of (·5) and partially overlying a hut-circle
(no. 154·6), there are the remains of a subrectangular
building (8·5 m by 4·8 m overall); another building 8·2 m
by 4·3 m overall) lies immediately to the SSE. About
380 m to the SW (NO 0529 5715), there are the remains of
what may be a hut (3·4 m by 3·3 m overall).

·7 NO 055 569, 056 569, 055 568   NO 05 NE 71
Grouped in three clusters amongst the small cairns
151·8 (no. 151·8) scattered in a saddle to the SE of Creag na h-
Iolaire, there are at least fourteen huts, two enclosures
and two pens. The huts are reduced to turf-covered stone
wall-footings (some are severely wasted) and range from
5 m by 3·6 m to 8·1 m by 5·3 m overall. Some chronological
depth is apparent; one of the huts (NO 0558 5694)
overlies an enclosure, and another (NO 0553 5688) seems
to impinge on its neighbour. Beside the second enclosure
(NO 0558 5690), there are traces of cultivation.

·8 NO 0562 5667   NO 05 NE 67, 70
The remains of a building are situated on a terrace some
151·8 250 m S of (·7). It measures 13·5 m by 6·7 m over turf-
covered stone wall-footings 1 m in thickness and has an
entrance central to its W wall; on the S it may overlie the
remains of a cairn. Close by, and overlying a hut-circle
(no. 151·8), there are the remains of a hut (6·2 m by 5·3 m
overall). Another building (12·3 m by 6·6 m overall) lies
about 230 m to the SSE (NO 0572 5646).

308 Pitcarmick (South), shielings
Disposed amongst the groups of cairns and hut-circles
(no. 151·9–·26) on the slopes to the SE and E of
Pitcarmick Loch, there is a series of shielings comprising
both buildings and huts. These are described from E to
W.

·1 NO 0680 5587   NO 05 NE 77, 89
On a terrace beside a stream gully, there are the remains
of a three-compartment building, an enclosure and a pen.
The building measures 15·5 m by 5 m over stone wall-
footings 1 m in thickness and 0·5 m in height. On the N
side of the gully and impinging upon a hut-circle group
and field-system (no. 151·26), there are at least eight huts.
The huts are reduced to turf-covered wall-footings and
range from 5·6 m by 4·3 m to 7·6 m by 5 m overall; three
overlie earlier hut-circles and one (NO 0672 5536), which
is of two compartments, is provided with a pen. Another
is associated with the low walls that enclose the scatter of
small cairns around the hut-circles. Some 250 m to the
NW (NO 0643 5615), close to a hut-circle and a scatter of
small cairns (no. 151·21), there is another hut (4·6 m by
3 m overall).

·2 NO 0634 5645, 0629 5647   NO 05 NE 50, 88
At the edge of a group of small cairns (no. 151·22) on the
S side of the Pitcarmick Burn, there are the stone wall-
footings of two huts; the largest measures 5·2 m by 3·1 m
overall. To the WSW (NO 0613 5641), there are the
remains of an open-ended building (about 8 m by 4·5 m
overall).

·3 NO 0603 5591   NO 05 NE 74–6
Disposed amongst an extensive group of cairns
(no. 151·20) on the undulating ground S of (·2), there are
the turf-covered wall-footings of at least eighteen huts;
two are roughly circular on plan, the rest subrectangular,
and as a group they range from 4 m by 3·3 m to 8 m by 4 m
overall. Five of the huts have an adjoining pen or
enclosure, one is of two compartments and another (NO
0603 5591), is distinguished by the provision of aumbries.
On the SE side of the burn there are a further seven huts
and buildings. Four of them are clustered around a hut-
circle (one occupying its interior) (NO 0623 5608); the
fifth lies beyond two Pitcarmick-type buildings 100 m to
the NE (no. 302·8) and the remaining two are set 90 m
apart some 230 m to the SSW.

·4 NO 0616 5564   NO 05 NE 57
On a knoll to the S of (·3), there are the turf-covered
wall-footings of a hut within a scatter of small cairns
(no. 151·24). The hut measures 6·5 m by 5·2 m overall.

·5 NO 058 558   NO 05 NE 78, 87, 90
At the SW extremity of the group of small cairns
no.151·20 (see ·3), there are three huts ranging from 4 m
by 3 m to 7·8 m by 4·1 m overall (NO 0593 5586). About
100 m to the W there are the remains of a three-
compartment building and enclosure (NO 0584 5588).
The building (11·5 m by 4·2 m over stone wall-footings
0·8 m thick and 0·7 m high) is furnished with aumbries and
its walls are partially embanked. Immediately N and NE
respectively, there are two huts, the larger of which is
oval on plan and measures 9·3 m by 4·3 m overall. A
further 60 m to the SSW (NO 0581 5582), there are the
remains of a hut with an enclosure on its SE side; the hut
measures 4 m by 2·9 m overall.

·6 NO 0564 5592   NO 05 NE 86, 137
About 200 m to the NW of (·5) there are the remains of a
hut with an enclosure on its S side; the hut measures 4·4 m
by 3·1 m overall. Some 280 m to the NW (NO 0541 5608),
there are the remains of another hut (6·8 m by 5·3 m
overall) with a pen on its S side.

309 Ranageig, Pitcarmick-type building
    NO 1025 4947   NO 14 NW 54
About 200 m NW of Ranageig there is a Pitcarmick-type

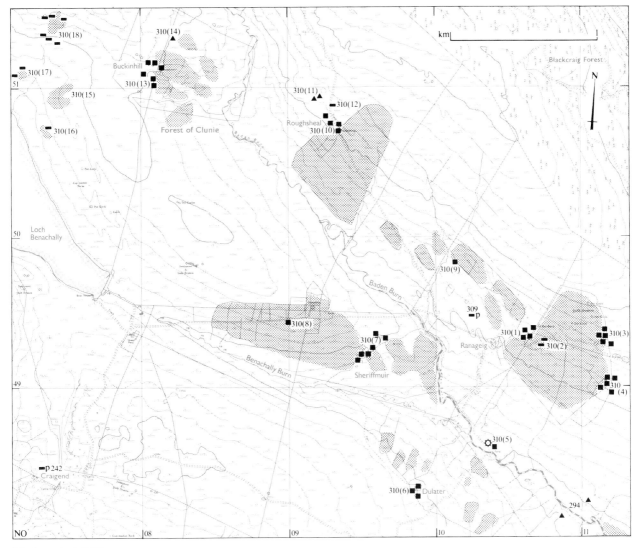

310 Ranageig, 1:25 000

310·3–·4

310 building overlying the W arc of a hut-circle (no. 155·4). Defined by a low bank, it measures at least 23·3 m in overall length, varies in width from 6 m at the SSE end to 8·3 m at the NNW end, and most of the interior is scooped. The position of the entrance is unclear, but it probably lies on the W, between two short lengths of bank that abut the side of the building.

310   Ranageig, fermtoun, farmsteads, buildings and mill
Some 2·7 km SE of Loch Benachally the Benachally Burn and the Baden Burn come together to form the Lornty Burn which flows ESE through the Buzzart Dikes (no. 216) and Middleton Muir to join the River Ericht. In the valley to the NW of the Buzzart Dikes, in an area centred on the steading of Ranageig (NO 1037 4929), but extending beyond the N end of Loch Benachally, there are a number of farmsteads and buildings.

·1   NO 1062 4931   NO 14 NW 56
About 200 m E of Ranageig there are two single-compartment buildings (12·3 m by 4·8 m and 11·3 m by 4·4 m respectively over stone wall-footings) adjoined on the NW by an enclosure. Some 30 m to the N a single-compartment building and outshot (14·7 m by 5·4 m over stone wall-footings) overlies an earlier building (20·3 m by 4·7 m over stone wall-footings), whilst 64 m to the NNE there is a further single-compartment building (6 m by 4·3 m over stone wall-footings), immediately to the NE of

which there are the remains of what may be an earlier building or an enclosure.

·2   NO 1072 4927   NO 14 NW 79
On the S side of the track 340 m E of Ranageig there is a building measuring at least 19 m by 6·2 m over boulder footings. The SE end of the building is rounded, but the NW end has been obscured by the construction of the track. At right angles to the building, on the opposite side of the track, there are traces of what may be either a second building or an enclosure.

·3   NO 1115 4930   NO 14 NW 37
The farmstead of Over Bog comprises at least six buildings and two kilns; the buildings range in size from 16 m by 4·4 m to 22·5 m by 5 m over walls standing to a maximum height of 1·7 m.

·4   NO 1118 4903   NO 14 NW 38
The farmstead of Little Bog lies on the S side of the track 240 m S of (·3) and is partly overlain by a sheepfold. It comprises at least five buildings and two kilns, the buildings range in size from 11·4 m by 4·8 m to 27 m by 5 m overall.

·5   NO 1035 4859   NO 14 NW 52
Bog Mill is situated on the NE bank of the Lornty Burn 130 m SE of the confluence of the Baden and Benachally Burns. The mill-building measures 8·7 m by 5·4 m over

159

*310·3–·4 Ranageig, farmsteads, aerial view from NW. In the foreground is
the farmstead of Over Bog (no.310·3), whilst Little Bog
(no.310·4) lies beneath the rectangular sheepfold*

walls up to 1·2 m high and has a wheel-pit at its SSW end;
immediately adjacent to it there is a kiln with an external
ramp to the drying floor on the NW and a chamber
enclosing the flue on the SE. A further four buildings
range in size from one of a single compartment,
measuring 9·5 m by 5·1 m over walls up to 1·1 m high, to
one of four compartments and an outshot, measuring
46·5 m by 5 m over walls up to 1·2 m high. Some 150 m to
the NW (NO 1024 4872) there are the remains of what
was probably a sluice controlling water entering a lade
from the Baden Burn.

·6   NO 0985 4832   NO 04 NE 22
Overlooking the valley from the shoulder of the hill to the
SW, 580 m SW of (·5), is the farmstead of Dulater. Most
of the buildings are ranged around four sides of a yard,
but two stand apart. The proportions of A (13·6 m by at
least 7·5 m over stone wall-footings) suggest that it may be
a laird's or a tackman's house comparable to that at
Craigsheal (no. 245).

·7   NO 0950 4921   NO 04 NE 12–13
On the spur of ground formed at the confluence of the
310·7A Baden Burn and the Benachally Burn there is the
fermtoun of Sheriffmuir. The buildings and enclosures, all
reduced to little more than their stone wall-footings, fall
310·7B into two groups, that on the SW (NO 0950 4921) being

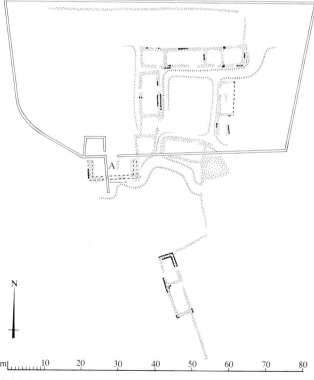

310·6 Ranageig, Dulater, farmstead, 1:1000

160

Z

Baden Burn

Benachally Burn

310(7)

270

280

290

300

310

320

330

340

38

k

k

k

m 100 200

310·7A Ranageig, Sheriffmuir, fermtouns, 1:5000

161

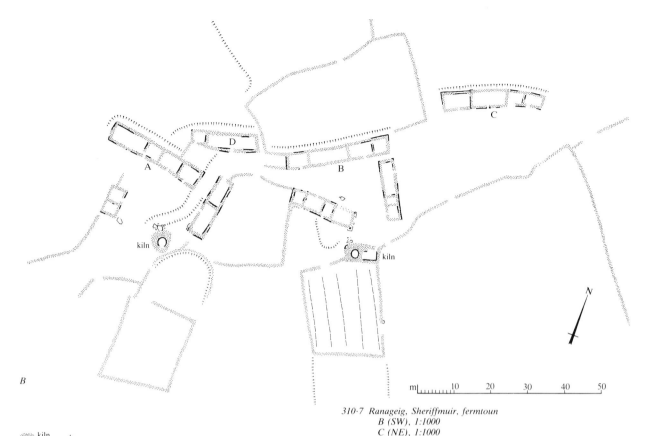

310·7 *C*

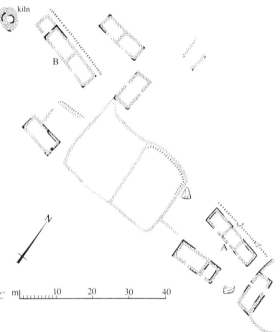

310·7C

310·7 Ranageig, Sheriffmuir, fermtoun
        B (SW), 1:1000
        C (NE), 1:1000

they vary in width from about 7 m to 11 m and in height
from 0·5 m to 1 m, but where best preserved, immediately
overlooking the Baden Burn, they reach a maximum
height of 2·3 m. There are traces of plough furrows on
many of the terraces and stones have been cleared on to
the risers.

·8   NO 0899 4944   NO 04 NE 45
Immediately S of the modern track 500 m NW of (·7),
there is a single building measuring 10·5 m by 4·8 m over a
low bank. It is probably all that remains of the farmstead
of 'Whistlebair', which appears on an estate plan
prepared by Stobie (c.1780) and on Stobie's map (1783).
Other remains may have been obliterated by the
construction of later sheepfolds and the track.

·9   NO 1013 4981   NO 14 NW 53
Some 550 m NNW of Ranageig there is a farmstead
comprising a four-compartment building (33 m by 5·4 m
over stone wall-footings) and a rectangular enclosure. A
drainage gully has been dug on the uphill side of the
building.

·10 NO 0931 5072   NO 05 SE 24
The farmstead of Roughsheal is situated 1·7 km NW of
Ranageig, on the W side of a modern track, and
comprises six buildings and a kiln. Their walls are
generally reduced to the footings or lowest courses, but
still stand in places to a height of 1·3 m. Four of the
buildings are ranged on three sides of an enclosure. The
two largest form the NE side of the enclosure and
measure 21·6 m by 5 m and 18·4 m by 5·3 m overall
respectively; the latter, which is the best-preserved
building, has an outshot on the SSE and the footings of
what may be an earlier building protrude at either end.
The fifth building lies immediately to the NW. The sixth
building, which together with three adjoining enclosures
lies adjacent to a sheepfold about 50 m to the NW, may
also represent an earlier period of occupation on the site.

the larger and comprising eight buildings and two kilns.
Clusters are formed around two of the large buildings (A,
27·3 m by 4·4 m overall, and B, 28·5 m by 4·6 m overall),
although a third (C, 27·3 m by 4·6 m overall) stands alone;
each of the buildings A, B, C and D has a drainage-gully
on its uphill side, whilst one of the kilns has a chamber
enclosing the flue. The buildings of the NE group (NO
0961 4933) also fall into two clusters, and each of the two
larger buildings (A, 17·1 m by 4·3 m overall, and B, 21 m
by 4·7 m overall) has a drainage gully on its uphill side.

The fermtoun lies at the focal point of an extensive and
well-preserved system of cultivation remains comprising
both cultivation ridges and terraces. The terraces lie
principally to the E of the fermtoun; for the most part

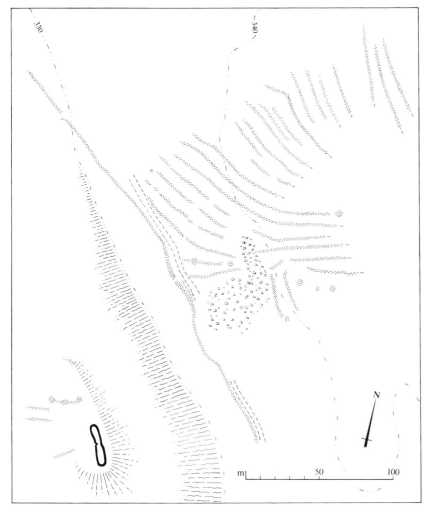

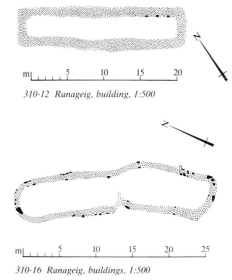

310·12 Ranageig, building, 1:500

310·16 Ranageig, buildings, 1:500

310·15–·16 Ranageig, buildings and strip-fields, 1:2500

Its remains are largely turf- and heather-covered, and it measures 28·8 m by 5·2 m overall with a possible outshot at the SSE end.

·11 NO 0921 5091   NO 05 SE 52
Situated 190 m NNW of (·10) there are two buildings set about 30 m apart. They measure 7·5 m by 3·9 m and 8·3 m by 4·2 m respectively over heather-covered stone wall-footings.

310·12

·12 NO 0931 5086   NO 05 SE 53
A building is situated 100 m N of (·10); it measures 23 m by 5·2 m over heather-covered stone wall-footings.

·13 NO 0813 5112   NO 05 SE 22
The farmstead of Buckinhill is situated 1·2 km WNW of Roughsheal. The principal buildings are ranged on three sides of a yard and measure 11·3 m by 5 m, 25·4 m by 5·1 m and 15·3 m by 5·8 m respectively over walls standing to a maximum height of 1·6 m; the N range forms the chord of a D-shaped enclosure. A further two buildings lie to the W and measure 14·6 m by 4·6 m and 16·8 m by 4·4 m respectively over walls up to 1·2 m high, whilst between them there are footings of a building measuring 11 m by 4 m overall. The yard opens to the S where there are two adjoining enclosures, that on the E having a kiln at its SE corner. About 100 m to the WSW there is a two-compartment building measuring 11·8 m by 3·8 m over walls up to 0·6 m high, whilst 100 m to the S there are at least two buildings and a group of small enclosures, two of which are overlain by a dyke associated with the farmstead.

·14 NO 0821 5131   NO 05 SE 27
About 200 m NNE of (·13) there are the remains of a building measuring 8·6 m by 4 m over a low bank.

·15 NO 074 509   NO 05 SE 51
Some 500 m WSW of (·13), disposed across the slope from NE to S over a distance of about 200 m, there are at least twenty-eight stony banks forming strip-fields set across the contour and measuring up to 110 m in length and up to 9 m in width. A hollow trackway which runs along the foot of the fields on the W, on the uphill side of a bank, may be later in date.

310·15–·16

·16 NO 0739 5078   NO 05 SE 20
On the summit of a knoll 220 m upslope from Loch Benachally there are the ruins of what appear to be two buildings adjoined end-on and with a combined length of 28 m by 6·2 m transversely over a low bank. On the slopes to the W there are traces of at least nine stony banks forming strip-fields about 9 m broad set across the contour (not shown on plan), and others may be concealed by heather.

310·16

·17 NO 0718 5113   NO 05 SE 21
Situated on a knoll about 300 m WNW of (·15) and 230 m upslope from the shore of Loch Benachally, there are the remains of two buildings. That on the SE flank of the knoll is of two compartments, though these are on slightly different alignments, and measures 19·7 m by 6·5 m over a low stony bank. On the slopes to the SW of the building there are traces of at least ten stony banks forming strip-fields set across the contour. The second building, which

163

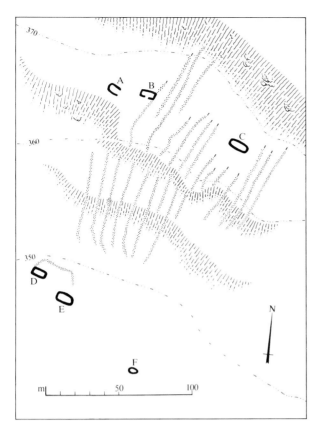

310·18 Ranageig, buildings and strip-fields, 1:2500

appears to be round-angled, lies 90 m to the SW (NO 0711 5108) and measures 16 m by 5·8 m over boulder footings.

·18 NO 074 514   NO 05 SE 38
Extending over three terraces, 550 m upslope from Loch Benachally, there are six buildings, all reduced to their wall footings, and what is probably a contemporary field-system. There are three buildings on the upper terrace: A, which has a rounded W end but is open on the E, measures 9 m by 6·1 m overall; B measures 11 m by 5·4 m overall; and C, which is bow-sided, measures 16 m by 6 m overall. On the lower terrace building D measures 11·8 m by 5·8 m, E 13·5 m by 6·5 m, and F 7·5 m by 5·5 m overall. The field-system comprises sixteen strip-fields between 5 m and 8 m broad, set across the contour and separated by stony banks up to 2 m thick and 0·2 m high.

The earliest map of the area is a sketch by Timothy Pont (c.1600), which depicts only Dulater and Bog Mill, placing them upon the opposite sides of the river to those upon which they now stand. In 1635, however, the lands of Buckinhill, Roughsheal, Sheriffmuir, Dulater and Bog, together with Bog Mill, are all on record (*Retours*, Perth, No. 451). Documented settlement is depicted at its peak in the late 18th century on Stobie's map (1783), which shows Buckinhill, Roughsheal, Whistlebair, Sheriffmuir, Dulater, Bog Mill, 'Bogs' and Ranageig, although an undated but broadly contemporary estate plan, also the work of Stobie (1780), omits both Dulater and one of the clusters at Sheriffmuir.
   Whilst much that is visible at the named sites is likely to be of relatively late date, some chronological depth is apparent amongst the remains. However, it is amongst the completely undocumented sites that the earliest remains are likely to be found, principally the Pitcarmick-type building (no. 309), the buildings and strip-fields which overlook the N end of Loch Benachally (·15–·20), and the single building to the N of Roughsheal (·12).

311   **Rannagulzion, farmsteads and buildings**
Disposed over the S flank of Drumderg, to either side of the public road between Smyrna and Rannagulzion farm, there is a series of farmsteads and shielings.

·1   NO 1815 5360   NO 15 SE 47
On the S side of the road some 620 m NW of Smyrna cottage there are the remains of a farmstead comprising five buildings ranged to the N of two enclosures and a kiln. The largest building measures 19 m by 4 m over stone wall-footings 1 m in thickness. The farmstead of 'Cowstyle', which is on record in 1682 (Meikle 1925, 74), is depicted by Stobie (1783), Ainslie (1794) and Thomson (1825).

·2   NO 1777 5389   NO 15 SE 46
Some 400 m NW of (·1) and to either side of the road, there are the remains of a farmstead comprising eight buildings, three enclosures and a kiln. The two principal buildings measure 26·5 m by 3·5 m and 46 m by 5·5 m overall respectively; one is of five compartments, the other six. The farmstead of 'Stripiereid' is on record in 1681 (Meikle, 1925, 159–60), and is depicted by Stobie (1783), Ainslie (1794) and Thomson (1825).

·3   NO 1751 5403   NO 15 SE 65, 67
About 260 m WNW of (·2) there are the remains of two buildings; one is severely wasted, the other measures 12·5 m by 4·3 m over turf-covered stone wall-footings 1 m in thickness. To the W (NO 1736 5404) there is a three-compartment building and enclosure. The building measures 18 m by 5·4 m overall and has a drainage-trench to the rear; immediately to the E there are traces of what may be another building.

·4   NO 1770 5429   NO 15 SE 64, 72
Some 300 m NE of (·3) there are the remains of a building and enclosure; the building (7·9 m by 3·9 m overall) has been modified by the addition of a pen. About 400 m to the SE (NO 1795 5400), there are the remains of another building (10·4 m by 5 m overall) occupying the NW corner of an enclosure.

·5   NO 1815 5397   NO 15 SE 63, 68, 84
To the E of (·4) there are the stone wall-footings of a three-compartment building (15·2 m by 4·5 m overall) with an enclosure on its S side, and 110 m to the ENE of this (NO 1826 5402) there are the remains of another building (8·1 m by 4·6 m overall). To the N (NO 1831 5421), adjacent to two hut-circles (no. 122·5), there are a further two buildings (4·2 m by 3·1 m and 3·6 m by 2·9 m overall respectively).

·6   NO 1852 5367   NO 15 SE 48
To the ENE of (·1) and bounded by a modern field-wall, there are the remains of a farmstead comprising two buildings, an enclosure and a kiln. Both buildings are reduced to the lowest courses of their stone walls and measure respectively 12·8 m by 4·2 m and 34·7 m by 4·3 m overall; the first, which is of two compartments, has an outshot on the W. The farmstead of Broomhill is on record in 1674 (Meikle, 1925, 63) and is depicted by Stobie (1783), Ainslie (1794) and Thomson (1825).

312   **Riemore, farmsteads**
Two farmsteads are situated to the E of the track leading up to the back of Riemore Lodge.

·1   NO 0530 4890   NO 04 NE 28
The first is the farmstead of Easter Riemore, which is situated at the S end of a low rocky ridge beside the track

some 500 m SSE of the kennels. The two principal buildings are set end-on to each other to form a range at least 57 m long on the S side of an enclosure. A kiln-and-chamber lies on the W bank of the burn to the E, whilst to the N and NW there are the footings of four other buildings. Easter Riemore is on record in 1663 (*Retours*, Perth, no. 714) and is depicted on Stobie's map (1783).

·2   NO 0520 4950   NO 04 NE 27
The second farmstead is situated on gently sloping pasture 90 m NE of the kennels. It comprises a building (12·2 m by 5·7 m over walls 1 m thick and 0·6 m high) fronted on the S by an enclosure in which there is a small pen. An outshot at the SE end of the building measures 3·6 m by 4·7 m internally, and attached to its SE side there is a slighter structure measuring 7·8 m by 4·8 m overall.

313   Runavey, fermtoun and farmstead
The remains of an extensive fermtoun, are disposed in a broad arc to the ENE of Westerton of Runavey farmsteading. While an additional farmstead is situated to the N of Mains of Runavey some 360 m to ESE, the fermtoun can be divided into a series of building-clusters, each probably a farmstead in its own right, and these are described from W to E.

·1   NO 1300 6925   NO 16 NW 3·1
Grouped round a knoll in rough ground to the N of the steading there are three buildings; all are reduced to turf-covered stone wall-footings. The first (10 m by 4·5 m overall) is overlain on the S by an enclosure, to the E of which there is a pen. On the W flank of the knoll there is a round-ended, two-compartment building (13 m by 3·7 m overall), while lower down the slope there is a round-angled building (8·7 m by 3·9 m overall). On slightly higher ground (NO 1294 6930) there are two buildings set parallel to each other. These measure respectively 6 m by 3·7 m and 8·4 m by 4·4 m overall. On a terrace overlooking the steading (NO 1285 6922) there is another building (6·5 m by 3·5 m overall).

·2   NO 1312 6932   NO 16 NW 3·2
This building-cluster lies on both sides of the modern field-wall to the ENE of the steading. On a low ridge beside the track that leads to the steading there is a three-compartment building (19 m by 3·9 m overall), beside which there is an enclosure; to the WSW there are the remains of what may be either a hut or a pen (4·6 m by 3·3 m overall). On an adjacent knoll there are the remains of a round-angled two-compartment building (10·3 m by 3·8 m overall) with an enclosure to the N. Beside the track there is another building (7·2 m by 4·3 m overall) and this has an enclosure on its S side. To the ESE beside the field-wall, there is a building (9 m by 4 m overall) with an outshot on the W. On the S side of the field-wall there are three buildings ranged with a sunken yard together with a larger enclosure (27 m by 16 m internally). The buildings range from 6 m by 4·8 m to 11·7 m by 5·2 m overall. One is of two compartments and has a kiln on its SSE side. A second kiln has been let into a low knoll (NO 1334 6931).

·3   NO 1325 6929   NO 16 NW 3·3
Another farmstead occupies an uncultivated knoll to the S of (·2). It comprises buildings on three sides of a yard and an enclosure. The buildings are all reduced to turf-covered stone wall-footings and range from 6·8 m by 5 m to 18 m by 5·1 m overall (the largest is of two compartments); one is markedly oval on plan.

·4   NO 1315 6927   NO 16 NW 3·4
This farmstead lies to the W of (·3) and consists of four buildings, a kiln and an enclosure. The buildings are all reduced to turf-covered stone wall-footings and range from 7·4 m by 4·3 m to 10·4 m by 4·2 m overall; the largest has two compartments.

·5   NO 1311 6925   NO 16 NW 3·5
Immediately to the WSW of (·4) there is a farmstead comprising three buildings and an enclosure. The principal building (12·5 m by 4·6 m over turf-covered stone walls is round-ended and has a drainage-gully on the N. The other two are reduced to turf-covered stone wall-footings and measure respectively 6·1 m by 4·1 m and 6·6 m by 4·7 m overall (the latter has an outshot on the N); within the adjoining enclosure (26 m by 20 m internally) there is a series of lazy beds.

·6   NO 1338 6947   NO 16 NW 3·6
Disposed over broken ground there are at least five buildings, together with a number of clearance cairns and field-banks which are probably prehistoric (no. 137·2). The first building (5 m by 3·6 m overall) occupies a low knoll, to the NNE of which there is a pen. About 80 m to ENE there is an open-ended building (10·6 m by 5·6 m over boulder-footings 1·2 m thick), and to the SE (NO 1350 6948) there are the wasted remains of another (7·3 m by 5 m overall). On a low knoll at the edge of the scatter of small cairns there is a substantial rectangular building (8·6 m by 4·4 m overall). Beside a modern sheep-pen, on the line of a deer fence, there are the remains of a two-compartment building (12 m by 4 m overall) which has a yard on its W side and an enclosure to the S.

·7   NO 1359 6909   NO 16 NW 3·7
On a spur to the SW of (·6) there are the remains of another farmstead. The principal building (20·9 m by 4·8 m overall) has three compartments and a drainage-bank. A second building, set at right angles to the first, measures 9·6 m by 3·9 m overall and has a trapezoidal-shaped enclosure on its SE side; the enclosure has been internally subdivided. The first building adjoins the old head-dyke, which traces an irregular course to the N and W. To the NNW there are at least five small cairns and a hut-circle (no. 137·3).

·8   NO 1348 6918   NO 16 NW 3·8
On a spur beside a burn about 100 m NW of (·7), there are the remains of a farmstead comprising buildings on three sides of a yard and an enclosure. The buildings are all reduced to turf-covered stone wall-footings and range from 7·2 m by 4 m to 13·4 m by 4·5 m overall; the largest is a two-compartment building with an outshot on the SSE (4 m by 3·6 m overall). Towards the corner of the modern field (NO 1348 6924) there are the remains of what may be an outbuilding. It is of two compartments and measures 10·3 m by 4·3 m overall.

·9   NO 1328 6890   NO 16 NW 27
The farmstead to the N of the roofless ruin of Mains of Runavey farmhouse (1760) lies towards the edge of a terrace which has been partially disturbed by quarrying; it comprises at least six buildings, a yard and a kiln. The buildings are either reduced to their turf-covered stone wall-footings, or are severely wasted, and range from 6·8 m by 4·1 m to 18 m by 6·2 m overall. Central to the group are buildings on two sides of a yard and each is of two compartments. Quarrying immediately to the SE has largely removed what was probably a third building. To the N there are the turf-covered remains of an attached stone-walled enclosure, which is skirted by two hollow trackways, while on the NE (NO 1333 6891), and let into the slope, there is bowl-kiln. Terraced into the slope (NO 1332 6893), and cut by the most recent of the two

trackways, there are the remains of another building, and between this and the ruined farmhouse there are traces of what may be a further two. The farmstead is depicted by Roy (1747–55, sheet 18/4) and the 18th-century farmhouse is denoted as a mansion by Stobie (1783).

The lands of 'Randeveyois', in the barony of Dunie are on record in 1510 (*Reg. Mag. Sig.*, ii, no. 3450) and in 1642 were the property of William Spalding (Spalding 1914, 206); the town and shieling of 'Runabervie' are on record in 1680 (Atholl Muniments, 23, xvi, 8) and the toun may also have possessed shielings in Gleann Beag (Alt-Ruy-na Vey on Pont *c*.1600). For the fermtoun Pont supplied the name 'Ruy na Vey'. It appears as 'Westerntown' on Roy (1747–55, sheet 18/4), who distinguishes it from 'Runnavey', probably the farmstead noted in (·9) above, and 'Invererderg' to the S (no. 285), and is named 'Uppertown' by both Stobie (1783) and Ainslie (1794). The name 'Pool' also appears on the maps of Stobie and Ainslie, and may correspond to the buildings described in (·6) above.

314   St Fink, house
NO 2138 4722   NO 24 NW 64

There are no visible remains of the house which is depicted by Stobie (1783) at St Fink. However, incorporated in re-use in a first-floor window on the S side of the steading at St Fink, there is a lintel which bears the date 1734 and the initials DA BM. In the 19th century the property belonged to the Andersons (Name Book, Perth, No. 9, p. 7).

315   Seefar, buildings
NO 0927 4691   NO 04 NE 31–2

On a S-facing slope to the SW of Seefar there are the remains of two buildings; two more lie immediately to the SSE (NO 0932 4684, 0930 4682). All are reduced to the lowest courses of their stone walls or to their wall-footings, and they have entrances in their S walls. The largest measures 15·6 m by 5·3 m overall and the NNW pair, which are set end-on to one another, are round-ended. To the NNW there is a group of small cairns (no. 114·8).

316   Shieldrum, building
NO 1462 5535   NO 15 NW 60

The building is situated 420 m SSW of Shieldrum farmhouse on the W side of the stone wall which separates improved pasture to the E from rough ground to the W. It measures 10·5 m by 5·8 m over walls 0·7 m thick and up to 1·6 m high and there is a slightly-built outshot at its N end.
— OS 6-inch map, Perthshire, 1st ed. (1867), sheet 42.

317   Slochnacraig, farmstead and buildings
Two clusters of buildings are situated at the foot of Craig Bhinnein 150 m NNW and 150 m S of Slochnacraig respectively.

·1   NO 1251 6879   NO 16 NW 17

The first is a farmstead, which lies immediately SW of the A93 public road on a terrace traversed by the Military Road. It comprises two buildings ranged with a yard, and, to the WNW a kiln-and-chamber. The buildings are reduced to turf-covered stone wall-footings and measure respectively 13·8 m by 5·3 m and 16·2 m by 5·5 m overall; the latter has two-compartments. Extending over the adjacent ground there are traces of rig-and-furrow. The remains may be those of the farmstead of 'Laganacraig', which is depicted by Stobie (1783), Ainslie (1794) and

Blackadder (1825). It appears as 'Easter Binzean' on Brown's 1808 survey.

·2   NO 1257 6851 to 1261 6846   NO 16 NW 18

Disposed over broken ground close to the Military Road, there are the remains of three rectangular buildings and a circular stance. The first building is severely wasted and measures 11 m by 4·6 m overall; the second is round-angled and measures 10 m by 4·3 m over turf-covered stone wall-footings spread up to 1·1 m in thickness. The third lies in a depression (NO 1261 6846) and measures 7 m by 4 m overall. The circular stance adjoins the NE side of the Military Road and is a conspicuous feature, but its function is not known. To the SSW, on the S flank of Creag Bhinnein, Brown depicts two huts (each annotated 'Old Sheal'), of which there are now no visible remains.

318   Soilzarie, fermtoun, farmsteads, buildings and shieling
The farm of Soilzarie is dominated by the bulk of Bleaton Hill, a spur which projects south-eastwards from Creag nam Brataichean, falling from its highest point (444 m OD) to the Ennoch Burn on the NE and to a break of slope at about 280 m OD on the SW.

·1   NO 1243 6002   NO 16 SW 156

At the foot of the hill, 170 m N of Ballochraggan, there is a farmstead comprising eight buildings, what is probably a narrow pen, and a kiln. The buildings have been reduced to little more than their stone wall-footings, although the walls of the best-preserved building, which was still roofed in the 1860s (OS 6-inch map, Perthshire, 1st ed., 1865–7, sheet 33), stand to a maximum height of 1·9 m; this building (13·9 m by 5·6 m overall) has two compartments and an outshot. At right angles to it at its ESE end, apparently overlain by the outshot, there is a second building, measuring 7·2 m by 5·3 m overall. About 10 m to the ESE a building measuring 12·6 m by 4·2 m overall stands on the N side of a yard, at the NE, SW and SE corners of which there are respectively the kiln, the probable pen (10·4 m long) and a building measuring 8 m by 4·6 m overall. To the S of the yard there is a building measuring 7·1 m by 5·2 m overall, and to the NW of the best-preserved building there are a further two buildings, the larger measuring 11·2 m by 5·3 m overall, the smaller 6·4 m by 4·2 m overall; what may be a building platform 11 m long lies to the WNW. Situated in the NW corner of an enclosure, to the SW of the farmstead, there are the remains of a small building partly overlain by debris from an adjacent quarry.

·2   NO 1219 6003   NO 16 SW 157

At the foot of the hill, 230 m W of (·1), there is a farmstead comprising two buildings and two enclosures. The larger building is of four compartments, though those at either end may be only outshots, and it measures 29·5 m by 5·2 m over walls standing up to 1·1 m in height. Set at roughly right angles immediately S of its ESE end, the second building measures 10 m by 4·8 m over walls reduced to little more than their footings; the enclosures adjoin each side of this building.

·3   NO 1197 6062   NO 16 SW 93

About 400 m upslope from the remains of the old farm of Wester Bleaton (the modern farm lies 900 m to the SW, NO 1110 5966) there is a farmstead comprising three buildings, forming a tight cluster on the SW side of a roughly triangular enclosure, at the apex of which there is a kiln. The largest building, which is L-shaped in plan, its principal range (17 m by 5 m overall), combining with the smallest building, (8 m by 5·3 m overall), to define the

277

NNE and WNW sides of a yard; the third building lies immediately to the WNW and measures 15·8m by 4·7m overall. A fourth building, measuring 5·9m by 3·8m over stone wall-footings, lies 36m to the E.

·4 NO 1220 6053   NO 16 SW 94
Situated some 240m ESE of (·3) there is a farmstead comprising four buildings, all reduced to little more than their stone wall-footings, a kiln-and-chamber, and what are probably two pens. The largest building is of at least four compartments and measures 36·5m by 4·8m overall. A single-compartment building is set approximately at right angles to it at the SE end and measures 11·4m by 4·8m overall; it is adjoined on the E and SSW by two enclosures, whilst to the SW there is a third enclosure. The kiln and the remaining two buildings lie to the ENE and NE respectively. The buildings, which are set parallel to each other on the same alignment as the largest building, are of two compartments and measure 11·7m by 3·8m and 13·1m by 3·9m overall.

·5 NO 1252 6048   NO 16 SW 53
Immediately N of the head-dyke, 320m E of (·4), there is a two-compartment building measuring 15·8m by 3·5m over stone wall-footings. A further 100m to the ESE (NO 1262 6045), also to the N of the head-dyke, there is a four-compartment building measuring 22·6m by up to 4·1m over stone wall-footings.

·6 NO 1269 6049   NO 16 SW 58
On the broad crest of the spur of the hill, some 20m apart, there are two retting-pools. The better-preserved is rectangular and measures 6m by 4·5m; the other is square and measures 4·5m across. They are fed by a lade from a spring 50m to the NW.

·7 NO 1272 6042   NO 16 SW 95
A possible farmstead, comprising what may be a building, two small rectangular enclosures and a pen, lies within the more north-westerly of two adjoining enclosures. The remains of the building, 33·7m in overall length, are overlain by a stone dyke.

·8 NO 1268 6037   NO 16 SW 59
The remains of a farmstead comprising an irregular cluster of five buildings and a kiln are situated on a rocky knoll. The buildings range in size from 8·4m by 3·4m to 10·9m by 5·5m over stone wall-footings.

·9 NO 1280 6035   NO 16 SW 54
Some 100m SE of (·7) and about 30m apart there are the remains of two buildings.

·10 NO 1286 6048   NO 16 SW 55–6
On the E slope of the hill, where there are two hut-circles and a well-preserved field-system (no. 112), two shieling-huts are situated 130m apart. That on the WNW (NO 1286 6048) measures 8·8m by 4m over stone wall-footings, that on the ESE (NO 1299 6044) measures 8·7m by 4·4m over stone wall-footings. The wasted remains of what is probably a third hut lie a further 70m to the SSE (NO 1303 6037).

·11 NO 1301 6029   NO 16 SW 96
A building adjoined by a small rectangular enclosure lies on the inner edge of an old plantation and measures 8·4m by 4·1m over stone wall-footings. A second building, measuring 9m by 4·4m over stone wall-footings and adjoined by a possible rectangular enclosure, lies on the inner edge of the plantation 70m to the SW (NO 1296 6023).

·12 NO 1345 6025   NO 16 SW 92
This small fermtoun is situated on a terrace on the SW bank of the Ennoch Burn and comprises at least seven buildings (reduced to their stone wall-footings) and a kiln. The buildings have an almost linear disposition, all but two being aligned from WNW to ESE, and fall into two groups about 70m apart and to either side of a fence. The two largest buildings lie in the westerly group; one is of three compartments and measures 21·8m by 4·4m overall, whilst the other is of two compartments and measures 21·3m by 5·5m overall. The remaining buildings are all of a single compartment and range in size from 6·4m by 4·7m to 10·9m by 6·8m overall, though one is overlain by a stone wall and cannot be accurately measured.

The site would appear to be that depicted on the maps of Stobie (1783) and Ainslie (1794) as a single unnamed rectangle, suggesting that by the 1780s it was largely abandoned. It may have been a predecessor to what was probably the late 18th-century farmstead of Tomnamoan, the ruins of which lie 120m to the SW.

Soilzarie itself appears on Pont's map (c.1600), and in 1615, together with other farms on or around Bleaton Hill, namely Ballachraggan, 'Tomphin' and 'Over and Nether Tomenamowen', it formed part of the newly erected barony of Ashintully (Spalding 1914, 45–6); all were subsequently mentioned in 1641 (*Retours*, Perth, No. 498) and 1661 (*Retours*, Perth, No. 684). Roy's map (1747–55, sheet 18/4) names 'Soilery', 'Ballachlagan', 'Wr Bletown', 'Braeside' and 'Tomnoan'or 'Tonmoan', whilst later in the 18th century, when recorded settlement appears to have reached its peak, the maps of Stobie (1783) and Ainslie (1794) depict 'Soilarzie', 'Ballochraggan', 'Tynluig', 'W. Bleaton', 'Brae', 'Tomfun', 'Auld Soilarzie' and 'Tomnamean'. By the 1860s, however, Tynluig, Brae or Braeside, Tomfun and Auld Soilzarie (OS 6-inch map, Perthshire, 1st ed., 1865–7, sheet 33) had been abandoned and the surviving farms were Mains of Soilzarie (NO 1259 5927), Soilzarie (NO 1320 5958), West Craig of Soilzarie (NO 1279 5997), which presumably came into being after 1783 or 1794, Ballachraggan (NO 1243 5984), Wester Bleaton (NO 1186 6020) and Tomnamoan (NO 1335 6014). West Craig of Soilzarie, Wester Bleaton and Tomnamoan were abandoned after 1865.

Settlement was situated primarily on the SW side of the hill, and it is probable that farmsteads (·1) and (·2) are to be identified with Ballachraggan and Tynluig respectively, and that the remains of Brae or Braeside, Tomfun and Auld Soilzarie are to be found amongst farmsteads (·3), (·4), (·7) and (·8).

319 Tigh an Eileen, building
     NO 1437 6462   NO 16 SW 74
On the W side of a low ridge 160m N of the ruins of Tigh an Eileen, there are the remains of a building and enclosure. The building measures 13·6m by 4·6m over turf-covered stone wall-footings and has an outshot on the S.

320 Tom an t-Suidhe, farmsteads and buildings
Two farmsteads and a scatter of buildings lie to the W of the A93 public road at Tom an t-Suidhe.

·1 NO 1287 6771 to 1277 6778   NO 16 NW 19, 54
This farmstead occupies an area of broken ground and comprises at least six buildings, two kilns, a yard and what may be a store. The buildings are principally grouped round a natural depression. All are reduced to

112

M

turf-covered stone wall-footings and they range from 5·3 m by 4·3 m to 13·2 m by 5 m overall; the largest is a two-compartment building with a yard on its NE side. Let into the slope to the N of the yard there is what may be a kiln and a second kiln is levelled into the slope to the SE of the farmstead (NO 1287 6771); a stone-revetted hollow (NO 1277 6778) could be a potato store. Stobie (1783) depicts the farmstead of 'Craigvey' ('Craig bey', Ainslie 1794), but it is unclear whether the name relates to this farmstead or to (·2).

·2 NO 1291 6770   NO 16 NW 51
Some 90 m to the ESE of (·1), in rough ground beside the A93, there are the remains of another farmstead. This consists of buildings on four sides of a yard with an attached enclosure on its SE side. The buildings are all reduced to turf-covered stone wall-footings and range from at least 9·2 m by 4·4 m to 14·4 m by 5·4 m overall; the largest is a two-compartment kiln-barn with the bowl at its SSW end.

·3 NO 129 676   NO 16 NW 52–3
To the S of (·2) there are the remains of at least a further three buildings. The first (NO 1291 6764) measures 14·6 m by 4·7 m overall and has a yard on its W side. Close by (NO 1290 6759) there are the remains of the second, a two-compartment building (13·8 m by 3·9 m over stone walls 0·8 m thick and 0·7 m high) with a drainage-trench on the E and a small pen on the SE, while the third (NO 1290 6756) is both well-proportioned and of two compartments (10·9 m by 6·5 m overall), and has a drainage-trench on the N.

321 Tomb, laird's house, fermtoun and farmstead
·1 NO 1213 7005   NO 17 SW 51–3, 65–70
This fermtoun and farmstead are set at the foot of Coire Bad an Loin. Around the 19th-century steading at Tomb there are the remains of a fermtoun comprising at least twelve buildings, what may be a tower or laird's house, a mill-site and a kiln. The principal building (NO 1213 7005), which may be the remains of a tower or laird's house, lies to the ENE of the farmhouse; it has been solidly built and incorporates a number of substantial boulder footings; the interior measures at least 7·5 m by 3·7 m and the ESE end-wall is up to 2·8 m in thickness and 0·5 m in height. A stub of wall extends from the S angle parallel to an earth-and-stone bank; the latter defines the edge of a garden terrace which extends to the edge of the Allt Bad an Loin. Nine roll-moulded rybats, which are incorporated in re-use in the entrance to the 19th-century farmhouse, are probably of 17th century date and may have been removed from this earlier building. Smith (1899, 23) notes that the farmhouse at Tomb 'bears traces of having been erected out of the remains of a superior building', and that a lintel above one of the windows bore the date 1668 and the initials DMK/EM. Duncan M'Kenzie, a cadet of the M'Kenzies of Finegand, inherited Tomb in 1665.

The remaining buildings are all reduced to turf-covered wall-footings and range from 5·6 m by 3 m to 14·3 m by 5·5 m overall. Immediately to the NW of the laird's house there are the remains of what may be a building, while upslope, adjacent to the enclosure at the rear of the steading, there are two more (NO 1210 7014 and NO 1209 7013 respectively). To the N of the steading (NO 1214 7006) there is a mill dam, which was fed by a stone-lined lade that drew water from the burn draining Coire Bad an Loin. In the 19th century the pond was used in conjunction with the steading, and there are now no visible remains of an original mill. Let into a low knoll on the W side of the dam there is a kiln. Some 55 m to the

SSW the stone wall-footings of an open-ended structure may be the remains of a stance or pen. On the E bank of the burn (NO 1221 7009), there are the remains of a building which abuts the stone wall-footings of an earlier building on its NW side. To the ESE (NO 1224 7006), beside a burn draining Coire an Eich, there are the remains of a two-compartment rectangular building with a drainage-hood on its uphill side. Downslope (NO 1221 7005), the site of another building, set end-on to the slope, is indicated by a terrace (9·4 m by 4·3 m overall). To the WSW (NO 1219 7002), on an area of relatively level ground between the modern stone wall and the Allt Bad an Loin, there is a cluster of buildings which is named by Brown (1808) 'The Ellen'. Three of the buildings are ranged with a yard; one, on the N, is of two compartments and is provided with a drainage-hood, and another, on the W, overlies the wasted remains of an earlier building. A fourth building (also of two compartments) is set within a hollow immediately to the SE. Stretching downslope there are extensive traces of rig-and-furrow.

The 'lands of Thom' are on record in 1550 and the 'Town and Lands of Thom' in 1599. It is 'Touym' on the maps of Pont (c.1600) and Gordon (1636/48), and the fermtoun is depicted by Roy (1747–55, sheet 18/4), Stobie (1783), Ainslie (1794) and Brown (1808).
— OS 6-inch map, Perthshire, 1st ed. (1865–7), sheet 24; Michie 1901, 218–20.

·2 NO 1189 7015   NO 17 SW 50
This farmstead occupies a ridge of ground between Cambs and Tomb. It comprises at least nine buildings, a yard and a kiln. The buildings are reduced either to the lowest courses of their stone walls, or to their wall-footings, and range from 6·6 m by 3 m to 15·9 m by 5·2 m overall. On the WNW side of the yard there is a substantial building with opposed lateral entrances (possibly a threshing-barn), while to the N there are the well-preserved remains of a two-compartment building which has an unusually thickened end-wall, the entrance is towards the E end of its S Wall. Set slightly back but on the same alignment, there is a two-compartment building, also with a thickened end-wall. The remaining buildings are disposed to the E and on marginally higher ground to the NNW; the kiln adjoins the SE corner of the yard and beside it there is a large stone-filled depression. In Coire Bad an Loin to the ENE, there are field banks and a number of clearance cairns. The farmstead is depicted by Brown (1808) but is unnamed.

322 Tullochcurran, farmsteads and buildings
In the area of Tullochcurran Cottage (NO 0708 6059), between Balnakilly on the S and the major forestry plantation of Kindrogan Wood on the N, there is a series of farmsteads and buildings. Across the same area Stobie's map (1783) depicts an unbroken line of ten named settlements, and the majority of the remains, described below from S to N, are probably to be associated with these, though it is not possible to ascribe specific identities to individual sets of remains with any certainty. The mansion of Tullochcurran, also shown on Stobie's map, may have stood to the ENE of the present house, which appears to be of 19th-century date. An additional building has been recorded adjacent to a hut-circle (no. 158·9) in the valley of the Tullochcurran Burn, some 1·5 km WNW of (·3).

·1 NO 0713 6007   NO 06 SE 95
Situated 160 m W of Balnakilly Cottage, there are the wasted remains of a farmstead, its E side clipped by a modern track. It comprises a building, measuring 10·6 m

324·3 Tullymurdoch, cultivation terraces from SE

by 7 m overall, with a slightly sunken yard on the S. In the SW corner of the yard there is a kiln, whilst at the SE corner an ill-defined platform may indicate the site of another building.

·2   NO 0693 6046   NO 06 SE 94
In a plantation 200 m SW of Tullochcurran Cottage there is a three-compartment building, measuring 25·2 m by 4·8 m overall, with an outshot at its E end. To the S of the building there are the remains of what were probably enclosures.

·3   NO 0664 6079   NO 06 SE 62
Levelled into a steep SE-facing slope there is a building measuring 11·8 m by 5·8 m overall. To the SE there is a small enclosure, named 'Cnoc Dubh' on the first edition OS 6-inch map (Perthshire, 1867, sheet 32), and to the SSE, on the left bank of the Tullochcurran Burn, there is a probable retting-pool.

·4   NO 0688 6094   NO 06 SE 133
Immediately E of two adjoining enclosures there is a two-compartment building measuring 16·4 m by 4·8 m overall, whilst 15 m to the W there is a kiln. The northernmost enclosure is probably contemporary with the building and the kiln, but that on the S is probably of later date.

·5   NO 0684 6100   NO 06 SE 98
About 60 m NW of (·4), adjoining the W side of the old head-dyke, there is a building and enclosure. The building, which lies on the N side of the enclosure, measures 7 m by 3·4 m over stone wall-footings, whilst what may be a second building, measuring 7·8 m by 4·3 m overall and open-ended, lies on the S. Some 30 m to the SSE there is a third building, measuring 7·8 m by 3·2 m overall, and 25 m to the SW there is a kiln.

·6   NO 0726 6116   NO 06 SE 99
A farmstead is situated on the edge of the river terrace 370 m E of Loch Cottage. It comprises a building of two compartments and an outshot (23 m by 4·4 m overall), with a kiln-and-chamber on the NW, as well as the remains of an enclosure and what may be a second building on the SW and SE respectively.

·7   NO 0705 6124   NO 06 SE 97
Some 200 m WNW of (·6) there is a building measuring 5·7 m by 4·6 m over low banks.

·8   NO 0705 6134   NO 06 SE 96
Some 250 m NW of (·6) there are the remains of a two-compartment building measuring 14·3 m by 3·9 m overall.

·9   NO 0690 6151   NO 06 SE 100
On the W bank of the River Ardle, 80 m SSE of Kindrogan Wood, there is a farmstead comprising two buildings, adjoined on the SW by an enclosure, and a kiln. The buildings have been reduced to their wall-footings, the larger measuring 15·7 m by 4·8 m overall, the smaller, which is set at right angles to its NW end, measuring 7 m by 4·5 m overall. A third building, measuring 11 m by 4·2 m, lies 45 m to the W.

323   Tullymurdoch, Pitcarmick-type building
NO 2034 5334   NO 25 SW 27
The remains of this building lie at the SE end of a field-system containing hut-circles and later buildings (see nos. 103·4 and 324). It measures 13·7 m in length by 7 m in width at the W end and 4·7 m at the rounded E end. The walls have been reduced to little more than turf-covered banks (1·1 m thick and 0·3 m high), but an external boulder face is visible at the E end, and there is an entrance gap midway along the SW side.

324   Tullymurdoch, farmsteads, buildings and mills
Three farmsteads and a number of buildings survive in the fields around Tullymurdoch. Two mills on the Alyth Burn are also described, along with a well-preserved group of cultivation terraces. The present house at Tullymurdoch (NO 1983 5248) incorporates an inscribed lintel over the back door. The lintel bears a series of extravagant letters and symbols and, although effaced, may incorporate the monogram 'INRI'; it was probably removed from the earlier farmhouse which stood immediately to the W. Stobie (1783) depicts a mansion and Pont (c.1600) gives the name 'Tillumurdoch'.

·1   NO c.204 517   NO 25 SW 32
The first of the mills was situated on the E bank of the Alyth Burn to the N of its confluence with the Olies Burn, but it was obscured by dense vegetation at the date of visit. It is named 'Tillimurdoch' on Stobie's map (1783).

·2   NO 2042 5229   NO 25 SW 32
The second mill, which is also depicted by Stobie (1783), lies 80 m NNE of the road bridge across the Alyth Burn. It stands in trees at the foot of a steep scarp and consists of a building (9·8 m by 5·9 m over stone walls reduced to their lowest courses 0·7 m thick and up to 1·3 m high) which has been levelled with the slope; the entrance was probably at

the NNW end of its SW wall. The lade is indistinct, but the tail-race is well defined and where best preserved is up to 4·8 m wide and 1·8 m deep.

·3   NO 2016 5241   NO 25 SW 2
About 200 m to the SW of (·2), on both sides of the public road, there is a remarkably well-preserved series of cultivation terraces, which have developed from broad curving rigs. The farmstead of 'Blacklands' is depicted in this area by Stobie (1783) and Ainslie (1794).
— Graham 1939, 301, pl. 89·2.

·4   NO 2010 5269   NO 25 SW 30
About 280 m to the NNW of (·3), in the corner of a field, there are the remains of a building (7·2 m by 4·6 m overall).

·5   NO 201 534   NO 25 SW 6
At least five huts and two buildings are scattered amongst the hut-circles on a terrace above the NE bank of the Alyth Burn (no. 103·4). Both buildings (H and J on plan) have adjoining enclosures.

·6   NO 1982 5281   NO 15 SE 88
Some 270 m N of Tullymurdoch steading, at the edge of a plantation, there are the remains of three buildings and an enclosure. The largest building, which is of three compartments, measures 13·3 m by 4·8 m overall. In 1974, when visited by the OS, a further six buildings were visible; these probably now lie within the plantation.

·7   NO 1928 5227   NO 15 SE 90
In rough grass some 580 m to the SW of Tullymurdoch farmhouse, there are the remains of a five-compartment building (29·5 m by 3·6 m over turf-covered stone wall-footings) with an enclosure on its S side. Both within the enclosure and over the adjoining slopes, there are traces of rig-and-furrow. The farmstead of 'Whitefold' is named and depicted by Stobie (1783) and Ainslie (1794).

·8   NO 1960 5218   NO 15 SE 89
A substantial kiln and enclosure at the edge of the field some 320 m to the ESE of (·7) are all that remain of the farmstead of 'Netherton' (Stobie 1783).

·9   NO 1905 5184   NO 15 SE 36
This farmstead lies on the E end of a ridge to the S of the Olies Burn, some 500 m SSW of (·7). It comprises a two-compartment building (11·5 m by 4·8 m over walls 1·3 m thick and 0·3 m high) with an outshot at its E end and an enclosure on the S.

325   Watersheal, buildings
NO 2059 5532, 2059 5523   NO 25 NW 23
About 500 m NW of the ruins of the 19th-century steading of Watersheal there are the remains of two buildings. These measure respectively 11·4 m by 5·1 m and 15·9 m by 4·5 m overall; the first has an entrance in its S wall, and at the SE angle there is a possible byre-drain.

326   Welton of Creuchies, Pitcarmick-type buildings
NO 1981 4957   NO 14 NE 75
Situated in improved pasture 1·4 km WSW of Welton of Creuchies, there are at least three Pitcarmick-type buildings defined by low banks. The largest (A) is 28·4 m in overall length and varies in width from 6·6 m at the E end to 8·2 m at the W end; its interior is scooped and its entrance opens on to a small area of turf-covered paving. At its SW corner there is what may be a building or an enclosure, and on the N it overlies another Pitcarmick-type building (17 m in overall length) with an annexe at its WNW end. The third Pitcarmick-type building (B) is also 17 m in overall length, and varies in width from 6 m at the E end, where the interior is scooped, to 7 m at the W end. The entrance is flanked by a porch and opens on to a small area of turf-covered paving; a slight depression adjoining the W end may indicate the position of an enclosure. The remains of three other buildings are visible, 50 m ENE (NO 1987 4958), 90 m NE (NO 1988 4963) and 150 m WNW (NO 1967 4959) respectively, the last adjacent to a hut-circle; they range from 8·8 m by 4·9 m to 18·5 m by 6·7 m overall.

327   Welton of Creuchies, farmstead
NO 1999 5042   NO 15 SE 38
The farmstead of Myde is situated on the E face of a rounded hill overlooking Welton of Creuchies steading. It comprises two rectangular buildings, which lie to the W and NW of a stone-walled enclosure. The larger building measures 30·5 m by 4·9 m over walls reduced to footings 0·8 m thick and 0·5 m high.
— OS 6-inch map, Perthshire, 1st ed. (1867), sheet 52.

328   Wester Binzian, fermtoun
NO 1161 6928 to 1188 6916   NO 16 NW 15, 61
The remains of this fermtoun are disposed over the slopes and broken ground to the W and SSE of Wester Binzian and comprise at least eleven buildings and an enclosure. All are reduced to turf-covered stone wall-footings and they range from 8·2 m by 3·4 m to 20·9 m by 5·8 m overall. The largest, a substantial structure (NO 1169 6927), is especially noteworthy; it is divided into two compartments by an inserted cross-wall, and at its SE end has an outshot (6·2 m by 5·5 m over walls 1·2 m thick). Nearby (NO 1167 6928) there is a well-preserved building with a slab-ingo for a fireplace in the centre of its NNW wall. Another building (NO 1165 6927), the second largest (16·5 m by 4·7 m over boulder-footings 1·1 m thick), has a shallow depression at its SE end (possibly a byre area) and a stone plinth towards its NW end (perhaps a hearth); a small mural recess is visible at the NE end of its

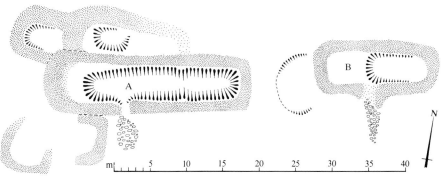

326 Welton of Creuchies, Pitcarmick-type buildings, 1:500

N wall and there are two possible cruck-slots. To the SE of the modern house of Wester Binzian, beside the burn, there are the remains of at least three more buildings (all roofed in 1865–7), as well as traces of a series of probable retting-pools (NO 1181 6918) and a kiln incorporated in the line of the old head-dyke (NO 1188 6916).

The lands of Binzean Mor (later Meikle Binzean), in the barony of 'Middle Dourney', are on record in 1510 and in 1565 and went with 'the shieling in Glen Beag'. By 1738 they were the property of a cadet of the family of Farquharson, and in 1788 'Binzeanmore' was in the hands of a tenant, Donald Robertson of Stronymuick, and his subtenants. The fermtoun of 'Bingan' is depicted by Roy (1747–55, sheet 18/4); it appears as 'Little Bingun' on Stobie (1783), Ainslie (1794) and Blackadder (1825), but 'Mains of Binzean' on Brown's survey (1808).
— *Reg. Mag. Sig.*, ii, no. 3450; *Retours*, Perth, no. 367; OS 6-inch map, Perthshire, 1st ed. (1865–7), sheet 24; Michie 1901; 213–14; Atholl Muniments, 23, xiii, 1.

329 Wester Bleaton, farmstead
NO 1118 5972   NO 15 NW 70

277   On a S-facing slope to the NNW of the cottage at Wester Bleaton, there are the remains of a farmstead comprising two buildings and a kiln. Both buildings are reduced to turf-covered stone wall-footings and they measure respectively 11·9 m by 4·8 m and 7·4 m by 4·5 m overall. On a knoll immediately to the S there is a pen. The remains may be those of the farmstead of 'Dareyday' which is depicted by Stobie (1783); the name is given as 'Dunidea' on the first edition of the OS 6-inch map (Perthshire, 1867, sheet 33).

330 Westertown, farmsteads and buildings
There are several groups of buildings and enclosures in the fields around Westertown. The farmstead of Westertown is named and depicted by Roy (1747–55, sheet 18/4), Ainslie (1793) and Thomson (1825).

·1   NO 1491 6168   NO 16 SW 144–6
In the field to the N of Westertown steading, there are the remains of a farmstead, a building and a hut, all reduced to their footings. The farmstead consists of a two-compartment building (10·5 m by 3·9 m overall) and outshot (2·4 m by 3·9 m overall), on the SE side of which stances for a further two buildings have been terraced into the slope. One of the latter occupies the N side of a roughly oval enclosure; this is paired with another enclosure, which has been internally divided. To the NNW (NO 1489 6173) there are the remains of a two-compartment building (13·5 m by 4·5 m overall) and an enclosure with a pen on its NNW side. To the N (NO 1489 6179) there are the wasted remains of what may be a hut (8 m by 5 m overall); a fragment of masonry towards the edge of the field is associated with a spring. An enclosure lies on the E side of the public road 100 m N of the hut (NO 1496 6155).

·2   NO 1496 6155   NO 16 SW 147–8
On the E side of the public road, opposite Westertown steading, there are the remains of a two-compartment building (9·1 m by 5·4 m overall) and an enclosure, and at the edge of the same field (NO 1494 6157), but cut by the road, there are the turf-covered wall-footings of what may be another building (at least 9 m by 4·7 m overall). To the SE (NO 1498 6153) there is an enclosure, and in the neighbouring field (NO 1499 6150) there are the wasted remains of what may be a building (8·3 m by 4 m overall) with an enclosure on its SW side; some 20 m further S there is another enclosure. Still further S, in the angle

between the public road and an unnamed burn (NO 1497 6140), there are the remains of three buildings which have been set end-on to one another. All are reduced to turf-covered stone wall-footings (the middle structure is severely wasted) and range from 6 m by 4·4 m to 7·5 m by 4·4 m overall; that on the S is set at right angles to the burn and may be a mill. On the NE there is an enclosure.

·3   NO 1453 6200   NO 16 SW 128
On a low ridge projecting from the floor of Glenshee 550 m NW of Westertown, there is a farmstead comprising two buildings (reduced to turf-covered wall-footings) and an enclosure overlain by a sheepfold. The buildings are set parallel to each other; that on the E is of a single compartment and measures 9·2 m by 4 m overall, while that on the W is of two compartments, measures 11·8 m by 3·4 m overall and is adjoined on the S by the enclosure. On the first edition of the OS 6-inch map (Perthshire, 1865–7, sheet 33) the remains are depicted as an old sheepfold.

331 Whin Craigie, shieling
NO 1971 5573   NO 15 NE 24
To the E of the summit of Whin Craigie and set against a rock outcrop, there are the remains of a hut measuring 2·6 m by 2 m overall.

332 Whitehouse, Pitcarmick-type building
NO 1561 5994   NO 15 NE 41
Situated immediately SW of a hut-circle within a field-system (see no. 161·1), there are the remains of a building which measures 13 m in length over a wall reduced to a turf-covered bank 1·3 m thick and 0·3 m high. The W end is rectangular while the E is rounded, and the building is widest (6·2 m) at the centre. The entrance lies on the S and is protected by short wing-walls forming a porch.

333 Whitehouse, building
NO 1553 6014   NO 16 SE 35
The remains of a rectangular building, measuring 11 m by 5 m overall, are situated within a young conifer plantation some 370 m SSW of Whitehouse steading.

MISCELLANEOUS

334 Ardle's Grave, Enochdhu, stone
NO 0631 6279   NO 06 SE 2
This stone stands at the NW end of a low mound in the garden of the lodge cottage of Dirnanean. The stone measures 0·4 m by 0·15 m in section by 1·7 m in height, and there is a shallow rectangular rebate cut into its SE face. The mound measures 5·8 m in length by 1·8 m in breadth and 0·4 m in height; at its SE end there is a rounded boulder about 0·5 m high. Although none of these features appears to be of any great antiquity 'many human bones' are supposed to have been dug up around them (Dixon 1925, 104).
— Coles 1908, 99–100.

335 Bamff, mound
NO 2205 5139   NO 25 SW 34
Situated 100 m SW of the tower-house of Bamff (no. 201) there is an elongated natural mound 3 m high. Its level summit measures 10·8 m from E to W by 5·4 m transversely and on its S edge there is a line of stone footings 7·5 m long; there are also traces of a slight scarp

on the W and N edges. The date and purpose of these
remains are unknown.

336 Hill of Alyth, mounds
On the S side of the Hill of Alyth there are four mounds,
their date and purpose unknown.

·1   NO 2363 5004   NO 25 SW 18
The northernmost is a low rectangular mound measuring
12·7 m by 5 m. Immediately to the W side there is a
shallow rectangular depression from which the mound

material appears to have been derived. The second
mound overlies a cultivation ridge 50 m to the SE (NO
2367 5002); it is circular, measuring 8 m in diameter and
1·2 m in height.

·2   NO 2374 4993   NO 24 NW 53
The third mound lies 110 m to the SW. It is oval and
measures 13·5 m by 8·8 m and 0·7 m in height. The final
mound is situated 50 m to the E (NO 2379 4993),
immediately beyond a modern fence, though an earlier
field-bank lies upon its W side. It measures 15·8 m by
5·8 m and 1 m in height.

ABBREVIATIONS AND BIBLIOGRAPHY

Abercromby, J 1912
—*A Study of the Bronze Age Pottery of Great Britain & Ireland, and its associated grave goods*
Oxford

Acts Parl Scot
—*The Acts of the Parliaments of Scotland*
T Thomson and C Innes (eds)
Edinburgh, 1814–75

Adams, I H 1978
—*The Making of Urban Scotland*
London

Ainslie, J 1794
—Map of the County of Forfar or Shire of Angus

Allen, J R 1881
—Notice of Three Cup-marked Stones, and the Discovery of an Urn, in Perthshire
Proc Soc Antiq Scot
15 (1880–81), 82–92

Allen, J R 1882
—Notes on some Undescribed Stones with Cup-Markings in Scotland
Proc Soc Antiq Scot
16 (1881–2), 79–156

Allen, J R and Anderson, J 1903
—*The Early Christian Monuments of Scotland*
Edinburgh

Archer, I 1749
—A survey of the road made by the detachment of General Guise's Regiment in Brae Marr; beginning where General Blakeney's left off and continued to the Spittle of Glen-Shee
MS map in NLS

Atholl Muniments
—Muniments of His Grace the Duke of Atholl, Blair Castle, Perthshire

Brown, T 1808
—Survey of the Invercauld Estate
SRO, RHP 3896

Burl, H A W 1971
—Two 'Scottish' stone circles in Northumberland
Archaeol Aeliana
49 (1971), 37–52

Burl, H A W 1973
—Stone Circles and Ring-cairns
Scot Archaeol Forum
4 (1972), 31–47

Burl, H A W 1976
—*The Stone Circles of the British Isles*
London

Burl, H A W 1988
—*Four-Posters*
Brit Archaeol Rep, Brit Ser, 195
Oxford

Caird, J B (n.d.)
—Introduction
in Gibson (n.d.), 5–8

Callander, J G 1925
—Long Cairns and other Prehistoric Monuments in Aberdeenshire and Banffshire, and a Short Cist at Bruceton, Alyth, Perthshire
Proc Soc Antiq Scot
59 (1924–5), 21–8

Caseldine, C 1979
—Early Land Clearance in South-east Perthshire
Scot Archaeol Forum
9 (1977), 1–15

Childe, V G and Graham, A 1943
—Some notable prehistoric and medieval monuments recently examined by the Royal Commission on Ancient and Historical Monuments of Scotland
Proc Soc Antiq Scot
77 (1942–3), 31–49

Christison, D 1900
—The Forts, 'Camps', and other Field-works of Perth, Forfar and Kincardine
Proc Soc Antiq Scot
34 (1899–1900), 43–120

Coles, F R 1908
—Report on Stone Circles surveyed in Perthshire – North-eastern Section; with measured plans and drawings
Proc Soc Antiq Scot
42 (1907–8), 95–162

Coles, F R 1909
—Report on Stone Circles surveyed in Perthshire (South-east District), with measured Plans and Drawings; obtained under the Gunning Fellowship
Proc Soc Antiq Scot
43 (1908–9), 93–130

Coles, J M and Simpson, D D A 1965
—The excavation of a Neolithic Round Barrow at Pitnacree, Perthshire
Proc Prehist Soc
31 (1965), 34–56

Coutts, H 1970
—*Ancient Monuments of Tayside*
Dundee Museum and Art Gallery

Cowan, I B 1967
—*The Parishes of Medieval Scotland*
Scottish Record Society, 93
Edinburgh

Cowan, I B and Easson, D E 1976
—*Medieval Religious Houses: Scotland*
2nd ed., London

Cowie, T G 1978
—*Bronze Age Food Vessel Urns*
British Archaeol Rep, Brit Ser, 55
Oxford

Crawford, O G S 1949
—*Topography of Roman Scotland North of the Antonine Wall*
Cambridge

DES (Date)
—*Discovery and Excavation in Scotland*
Annual Publication of Scottish Group, Council for British Archaeology

Dixon, J H 1921
—The Balvarran Cupped Stone, the 'Bloody' Stone of Dunfallandy, and a Cup-marked Stone in Glen Brerachan
Proc Soc Antiq Scot
55 (1920–1), 95–9

Dixon, J H 1925
—*Pitlochry Past and Present*
Pitlochry

Dodgshon, R A 1981
—*Land and Society in Early Scotland*
Oxford

Douglas, J 1826
—Map of Lower Glenfernate
Atholl Muniments

Douglas, R 1798
—*The Baronage of Scotland*
Edinburgh

Dunbar, J G 1966
—*The Historic Architecture of Scotland*
London

Easson, D E (ed.) 1947
—*Charters of the Abbey of Coupar Angus*
Edinburgh

Easson, D E 1957
—*Medieval Religious Houses Scotland, With an Appendix on the Houses in the Isle of Man*
London

Feachem, R W 1965
—*The North Britons*
London

Feachem, R W 1973
—Ancient Agriculture in the Highland Zone of Britain
Proc Prehist Soc
39 (1973), 332–53

Franklin, T B 1952
—*A History of Scottish Farming*

Gibson, C (n.d.)
—*Bonnie Glenshee*
Coupar Angus

Gilbert, J M 1979
—*Hunting and Hunting Reserves in Medieval Scotland*
Edinburgh

Gordon, R 1636/48
—'Glen Yla, Glen Ardle, Glen Shye, out of Mr. T. Pont's papers yey ar very imperfyt'
Manuscript map in NLS

Graham, A 1939
—Cultivation terraces in south-eastern Scotland
Proc Soc Antiq Scot
73 (1938–9), 289–315

Graham, A 1966
—The Military Road from Braemar to the Spittal of Glen Shee
Proc Soc Antiq Scot
97 (1963–4), 226–36

Grainger, T 1818
—Map of the Lands of Fonn and Glenfernate, property of William Spottiswood Esq
Atholl Muniments

Harris, J 1985
—A Preliminary Survey of Hut Circles and Field Systems in SE Perth
Proc Soc Antiq Scot
114 (1984), 199–216

Hart, C R 1981
—*The North Derbyshire Archaeological Survey to A.D.1500*
The North Derbyshire Archaeological Trust
Chesterfield

Hill, P H 1982
—Settlement and Chronology
Later Prehistoric Settlement in South-East Scotland (ed. D Harding)
Edinburgh

Hogg, J 1829
—Anecdotes of Highlanders
The Edinburgh Literary Journal
2 (June 1829–December 1829), 293–5

Jervise, A 1853
—*The History and Traditions of the Land of the Lindsays in Angus and Mearns, with Notices of Alyth and Meigle*
Edinburgh

Kinnes, I A and Longworth, I H 1985
—*Catalogue of the Excavated Prehistoric and Romano-British Material in the Greenwell Collection*
London

MacDonald, J A R 1899
—*The History of Blairgowrie (Town, Parish and District), Being an Account of the Origin and Progress of the Burgh from the Earliest Period*
Blairgowrie

Macfarlane, W 1906
—*Geographical Collections Relating to Scotland*, 1
Mitchell, A (ed.)
Edinburgh

Macfarlane, W 1908
—*Geographical Collections Relating to Scotland*, 3
Mitchell, A (ed.)
Edinburgh

MacGibbon, D and Ross, T 1887
—*The Castellated and Domestic Architecture of Scotland from the Twelfth to the Eighteenth Century*, 2
Edinburgh

MacGibbon, D and Ross, T 1889
—*The Castellated and Domestic Architecture of Scotland from the Twelfth to the Eighteenth Century*, 3
Edinburgh

MacGibbon, D and Ross, T 1892a
—*The Castellated and Domestic Architecture of Scotland from the Twelfth to the Eighteenth Century*, 4
Edinburgh

MacGibbon, D and Ross, T 1892b
—*The Castellated and Domestic Architecture of Scotland from the Twelfth to the Eighteenth Century*, 5
Edinburgh

Mackenzie, G 1831
—Description of Barry Hill, near Alyth
Archaeologia Scotica
4, pt 1, 184–6

MacKie, E W 1969
—Radiocarbon Dates and the Scottish Iron Age
Antiquity
43 (1969), 15–26

Mackinlay, J M 1914
—*Ancient Church Dedications in Scotland; Non-scriptural Dedications*
Edinburgh

Maclagan, C 1875
—*The Hill Forts, Stone Circles and other Structural Remains of Ancient Scotland*
Edinburgh

McLean, N 1810
—Lands of Fonn and Glenfernate, property of William Spottiswood
Atholl Muniments

MacMillan, H 1884
—Notice of Cup-Marked Stones near Aberfeldy
Proc Soc Antiq Scot
18 (1883–4), 94–102

McPherson, J G 1885
—*Strathmore: Past and Present*
Perth

Marshall, W 1881
—*Historic Scenes in Perthshire*
Edinburgh

Meikle, J 1925
—*Place Names around Alyth*

Meikle, J 1933
—*The History of Alyth Parish Church*
Edinburgh

Michie, J G (ed.) 1901
—*The Records of Invercauld 1547–1827*
New Spalding Club, Aberdeen

Miles, H and McGhie, J 1930
—*Fair Perthshire*
London

Millar, A H 1890
—*The Historical Castles and Mansions of Scotland, Perthshire and Forfarshire*
Paisley and London

Miller, T D 1929
—*Tales of a Highland Parish (Glenshee) on the Royal Route*
Perth

Name Book (County)
—Original Name Books of the Ordnance Survey

Neish, J 1873
—Notes of Stone Celts Found in Glenshee, Forfarshire 1870
Proc Soc Antiq Scot
9 (1870–2), 174–5

NLS
—National Library Scotland
Map Library, 33 Salisbury Place, Edinburgh

NMAS 1892
—*Catalogue of the National Museum of Antiquities of Scotland*
Edinburgh

NMRS
—National Monuments Record of Scotland
6–7 Coates Place, Edinburgh

NSA
—*The New Statistical Account of Scotland*
1845, Edinburgh

O'Drisceoil, D A 1988
—Burnt Mounds: cooking or bathing?
Antiquity
62 (1988), 671–80

Ogston, A 1931
—*The Prehistoric Antiquities of the Howe of Cromar*
Aberdeen

OS
—Ordnance Survey
Romsey Road, Maybush, Southampton

Panton, W 1772–3
—Estate map of Inverqueech, Shanzie, Cult, and Blackridges, with the contour of Upper Balloch

Parry, M L 1978
—*Climatic Change, Agriculture and Settlement*
Folkestone

Paul, J B (ed.) 1906
—*The Scots Peerage Founded on Wood's Edition of Sir Robert Douglas's Peerage of Scotland Containing an Historical and Genealogical Account of the Nobility of that Kingdom*, 3
Edinburgh

Paul, J B (ed.) 1907
—*The Scots Peerage Founded on Wood's Edition of Sir Robert Douglas's Peerage of Scotland Containing an Historical and Genealogical Account of the Nobility of that Kingdom*, 4
Edinburgh

Pennant, T 1776
—*A Tour of Scotland, 1772*, Pt 2
London

Pont, T c.1600
—Strathardle and Glenshey
Manuscript map in NLS

Pryde, G S 1965
—*The Burghs of Scotland: a Critical List*
Oxford

Reg. Mag. Sig.
—*Registrum Magni Sigilli Regum Scotorum*
J M Thomson and others (eds.)
Edinburgh, 1882–1914

Reid, A G 1986
—*Strathardle, its History and its People*
Blairgowrie

Retours 1811–16
—*Retours Inquisitionum ad Capellam Domini Regis Retornatarium quae in Publicis Archivis Scotiae adhuc servantur, Abbreviatio*

Rideout, J S forthcoming
—An Excavation at Craighead Settlement, Alyth, Perthshire

Robertson, J 1794
—*General View of the Agriculture in the County of Perth: with Observations on the Means of its Improvement*

Rogers, C (ed.) 1880
—*Rental Book of the Cistercian Abbey of Cupar-Angus with the Breviary of the Register*, 2
London

Roy, W 1747–55
—Military Survey of Scotland
Photocopy in NMRS

RCAHMS
—Royal Commission on the Ancient and Historical Monuments of Scotland

RCAHMS 1967
—*Peeblesshire: an inventory of the ancient monuments*
Edinburgh

RCAHMS 1983
—*Central Angus*
The Archaeological Sites and Monuments Series, 18
Edinburgh

RCAHMS 1988
—*Argyll: an inventory of the monuments*, 6
Mid Argyll and Cowal, Prehistoric and Early Historic Monuments
Edinburgh

RMS
—Royal Museum of Scotland
1 Queen Street, Edinburgh

Scott, H *et al.* (eds.) 1923
—*Fasti Ecclesiae Scoticanae: The Succession of Ministers in the Church of Scotland from the Reformation*, 4
Edinburgh

Scott, H *et al.* (eds.) 1925
—*Fasti Ecclesiae Scoticanae: The Succession of Ministers in the Church of Scotland from the Reformation*, 5
Edinburgh

Scott, H *et al.* (eds.) 1950
—*Fasti Ecclesiae Scoticanae: The Succession of Ministers in the Church of Scotland from the Reformation*, 8
Edinburgh

SRO
—The Scottish Record Office
HM General Register House
Edinburgh

Simpson, W D 1923
—The Royal Castle of Kindrochit in Mar
Proc Soc Antiq Scot
57 (1922–3), 75–97

Simpson, W D 1949
—*The Earldom of Mar*
Aberdeen

Small, J W 1900
—*Scottish Market Crosses*
Stirling

Smith, J S 1987
—Deserted farms and shealings in the Braemar area of Deeside, Grampian Region
Proc Soc Antiq Scot
116 (1986), 447–53

Smith, M S 1889
—*Some Account of the M'Kenzies of Finegand in Glenshee, from their origin to the present time*
Blairgowrie

Smith, W M 1895
—Recent Antiquarian Research in Glenshee
Proc Soc Antiq Scot
29 (1894–5), 96–9

Spalding, F J and M 1914
—*Notes and Traditions Concerning the Family of Spalding*
Liverpool

Stat. Acct.
—*Statistical Account of Scotland*
 1791–9, Edinburgh

Stevenson, J B 1975
—Survival and destruction
 The Effect of Man on the Landscape: The Highland Zone
 CBA Research Report, 11

Stewart, M E C 1961
—Strath Tay in the Second Millennium B.C. – a Field Survey
 Proc Soc Antiq Scot
 92 (1958–9), 71–84

Stewart, M E C 1964
—The Excavation of two Circular Enclosures at Dalnaglar, Perthshire
 Proc Soc Antiq Scot
 95 (1961–2), 134–58

Stewart, M E C 1967
—The Excavation of a Setting of Standing Stones at Lundin Farm near
 Aberfeldy, Perthshire
 Proc Soc Antiq Scot
 98 (1964–6), 126–49

Stobie, J 1780
—Plan of the Forest of Cluny Belonging to His Grace John Duke of
 Atholl
 Atholl Muniments B11; SRO, RHP 44004

Stobie, J 1783
—*The Counties of Perth and Clackmannan*
 Surveyed and Published by James Stobie
 Engraved by Thomas Conder
 London

Stuart, J 1856
—*Sculptured Stones of Scotland*, 1
 Aberdeen

Stuart, J 1868
—Account of Excavations in Groups of Cairns, Stone Circles, and Hut-
 circles on Balnabroch, Parish of Kirkmichael, Perthshire, and at West
 Persie, in that Neighbourhood
 Proc Soc Antiq Scot
 6 (1864–6), 402–10

Talbot, E 1974
—Early Scottish Castles of Earth and Timber – Recent Fieldwork and
 Excavation
 Scot Archaeol Forum
 6 (1974), 48–57

Third Stat. Acct.
—*The Third Statistical Account of Scotland*
 1951–85, Glasgow

Thompson, J 1825
—(1) Northern Part of Angusshire
 Map in NLS

Thoms, L M 1979
—The excavation of a circular enclosure at Tulloch Field, Strathardle: an
 interim statement
 Scottish Field Studies Association
 1979, 15–16

Thorneycroft, W 1933
—Observations on Hut-circles near the Eastern Border of Perthshire,
 North of Blairgowrie
 Proc Soc Antiq Scot
 67 (1932–3), 187–208

Thorneycroft, W 1948
—Further Observations on Hut-circles
 Proc Soc Antiq Scot
 80 (1945–6), 131–5

Wainwright, F T 1952
—*Archaeological News Letter*
 vol. 4, no. 8 (May 1952), 123

Wainwright, F T 1963
—*The Souterrains of Southern Pictland*
 London

Walker, F 1961
—*Tayside Geology*
 Dundee

Warden, A J 1885
—*Angus or Forfarshire, the Land and People, Descriptive and Historical*
 Dundee

Webster, B (ed.) 1982
—The Acts of David II, King of Scots 1329–1371
 Edinburgh

Willsher, B 1987
—Scottish Gravestones, Perthshire
 Unpublished manuscript in NMRS

Wise, T A 1859
—Notice of the Outfort on Barry Hill, Forfarshire, recently Removed
 Proc Soc Antiq Scot
 2 (1854–7), 70–1

Location Maps

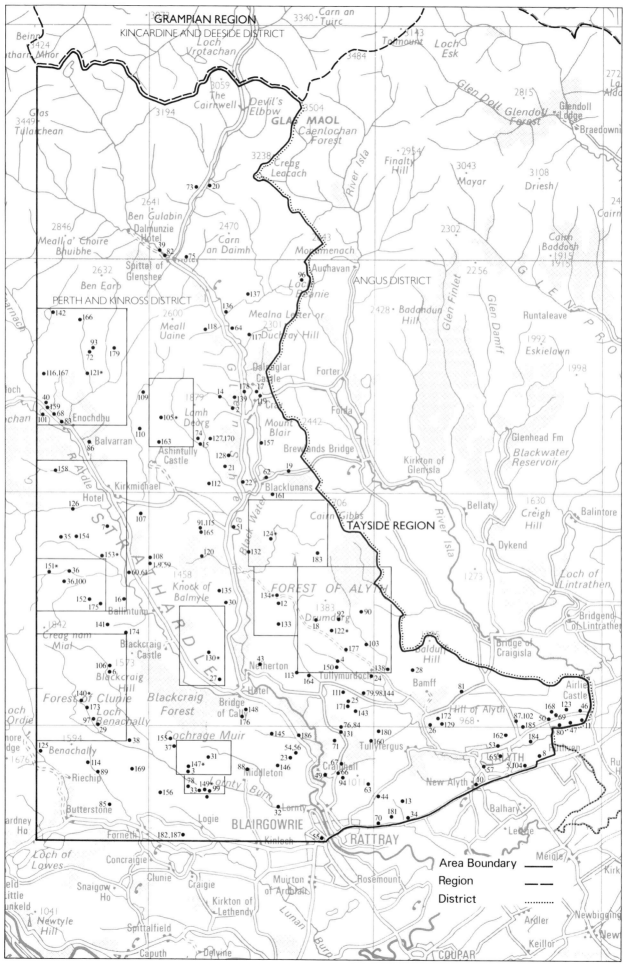

Prehistoric monuments with their article numbers (see article number for more detailed maps)*

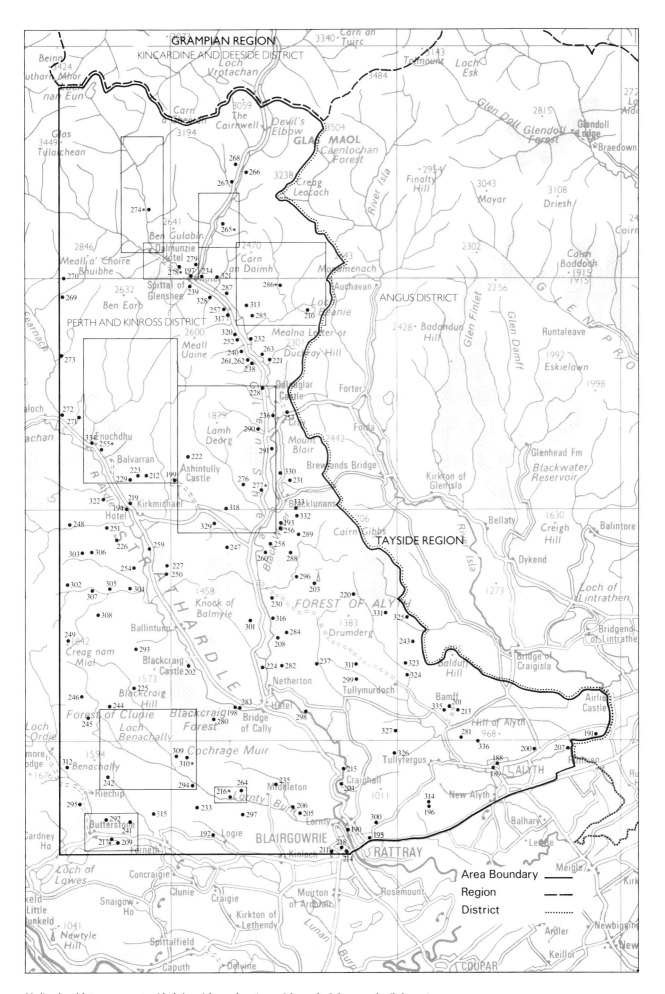

Medieval and later monuments with their article numbers (see article number* for more detailed maps)